Lecture Notes
in Business Information Processing   **210**

More information about this series at http://www.springer.com/series/7911

João M. Fernandes · Ricardo J. Machado
Krzysztof Wnuk (Eds.)

Software Business

6th International Conference, ICSOB 2015
Braga, Portugal, June 10–12, 2015
Proceedings

 Springer

Editors
João M. Fernandes
University of Minho
Braga
Portugal

Ricardo J. Machado
University of Minho
Guimarães
Portugal

Krzysztof Wnuk
Blekinge Institute of Technology
Karlskrona
Sweden

ISSN 1865-1348   ISSN 1865-1356   (electronic)
Lecture Notes in Business Information Processing
ISBN 978-3-319-19592-6   ISBN 978-3-319-19593-3   (eBook)
DOI 10.1007/978-3-319-19593-3

Library of Congress Control Number: 2015940442

Springer Cham Heidelberg New York Dordrecht London

Printed on acid-free paper

Springer International Publishing AG Switzerland is part of Springer Science+Business Media
(www.springer.com)

Preface

Welcome to the proceedings of the 6th International Conference on Software Business!

Universidade do Minho (UMinho) hosted the 6th International Conference on Software Business (ICSOB 2015) held during June 10–12, 2015, in Braga, Portugal. Founded in 1973, UMinho is currently among the most prestigious institutions of higher education in Portugal, and it has also gradually come to assert itself on the international scene. The recent Times Higher Education Ranking 2013 included only two Portuguese universities, listing UMinho as one of the top 400 universities in the world. The Times Higher Education 100 under 50 years University Ranking 2015 ranked UMinho in 64th position worldwide. UMinho is also the best Portuguese university in the CWTS Leiden Ranking 2014.

Minho is a former province of Portugal with its capital in the city of Braga and 23 municipalities. The area included the districts of Braga and Viana do Castelo. Minho has substantial Celtic influences and shares many cultural traits with the neighboring Galicia in Spain. The region was a part of the Roman Province and early medieval Kingdom of Gallaecia. Historical remains of Celtic Minho include Briteiros Iron Age Hillfort, the largest Gallaecian native stronghold in the Entre Douro e Minho region, in north Portugal.

Braga is considered the oldest Christian archdiocese in the country and one of the oldest in the world. Under the Roman Empire, known as Bracara Augusta, the settlement was the center of the province of Gallaecia. Guimarães, located in the district of Braga, is one of the country's most important historical cities and is often referred to as the "birthplace of the Portuguese nationality" or "the cradle city." Its historical center is a UNESCO World Heritage Site, making it one of the largest tourist centers in the region.

ICSOB was first launched in 2010 to address contemporary issues emerging in the intersection of software and business domains and to bring together researchers interested in the software industry, with a specific focus on the business of software. Since then, ICSOB has been established as a series of annual conferences. Previous conferences were held in Boston (USA), Brussels (Belgium), Jyvaskyla (Finland), Paphos (Cyprus), and Potsdam (Germany).

This year, we selected as the conference theme "Enterprising Cities" to focus on a noticeable spillover of software within other industries (e.g., manufacturing, entertainment industry) enabling new business models: Companies bundle their physical products and software services into solutions (e.g., using subscription models or in-app purchases) and start to sell independent software products in addition to physical products.

Software business carries many inherent features with other international knowledge-intensive businesses making it a challenging domain for research. In particular, software companies have to depend on one another to deliver a unique value proposition to their customers or a unique experience to their users. This year, the conference attracted researchers and practitioners who are concerned with software business in different ways as well as the start-up community, which is increasingly focusing on mobile and social software. The main theme of 2015 focused on addressing the challenges that modern cities face regarding the innovative software products and services.

This year's two exciting keynotes spanned both the reach and the new developments in the software business economy:

- "One Size Does NOT Fit All – Software Product Management for Speedboats vs. Cruise Ships," by Hans-Bernd Kittlaus, InnoTivum Consulting, Germany
- "Trends and Lookout of the Automotive Software Industries," by Christoph Gaertner, Bosch Car Multimedia Portugal

The conference received 42 submissions. Each submission was reviewed by at least two, typically three, Program Committee members. The committee decided to accept 16 full, five short, and three doctoral symposium papers. For full papers, this gives an acceptance rate of 38%. The accepted papers follow various methodologies, and represent the diversity in research in our community.

The papers span a wide range of issues related to contemporary software business-from strategic aspects that include external reuse, ecosystem participation, and acquisitions to operational challenges associated with running software business, e.g., the effects of workaround, communication in global software development, or business modeling and experimentation. The strong presence of software ecosystem papers confirms its importance and influence on software business. At the same time, we observed interesting emerging topics, e.g., open innovation as a form of leveraging external innovation sources, continuous customer validation, and the usage of customer feedback data. Finally, (Lean) start-up and innovation also appeared among the topics for this year's program. We arranged the program into eight sessions that together provided a good insight into current software business research. The industry papers are included at the end of the proceedings.

We acknowledge the following institutions for the support, sponsoring, and cooperation they kindly established with ICSOB 2015: Universidade do Minho, Blekinge Institute of Technology, InvestBraga, Startup Braga, ISPMA, and Young Minho Enterprise. Last, but not the least, we also want to show appreciation for the work of those who created and maintain the EasyChair conference system. It has definitely eased our work.

We would like to extend our warm thank you to the members of the Program Committee, who did a fantastic job in reviewing the papers, ensuring the quality of the conference, as well to the local organization team, whose engagement was essential in making this event a special experience. Furthermore, we extend our heartfelt thanks to Anna-Lena Lamprecht from the University of Potsdam and Tobias Tauterat from the University of Stuttgart for managing the ICSOB 2015 Doctoral Consortium.

We sincerely trust that your participation in the ICSOB 2015 conference was a rewarding experience.

April 2015

João M. Fernandes
Krzysztof Wnuk
Ricardo J. Machado

Organization

General Chair

João M. Fernandes — University of Minho, Portugal

Program Chairs

Ricardo J. Machado — University of Minho, Portugal
Krzysztof Wnuk — Blekinge Institute of Technology, Sweden

Program Committee

Sergey Avdoshin — Higher School of Economics, Russia
Richard Berntsson Svenson — Chalmers University of Technology and University of Gothenburg, Sweden
Jan Bosch — Chalmers University of Technology, Sweden
Sjaak Brinkkemper — Utrecht University, The Netherlands
David Callele — University of Saskatchewan, Canada
Michael Cusumano — MIT, USA
Torgeir Dingsøyr — SINTEF, Norway
Samuel Fricker — Blekinge Institute of Technology, Sweden
Georg Herzwurm — University of Stuttgart, Germany
Thomas Hess — LMU Munich, Germany
Slinger Jansen — Utrecht University, The Netherlands
Thomas Kude — University of Mannheim, Germany
Olli Kuivalainen — Lappeenranta University of Technology, Finland
Stig Larsson — SICS, Sweden
Casper Lassenius — Aalto University, Finland
Ulrike Lechner — Universität der Bundeswehr München, Germany
Andrey Maglyas — Lappeenranta University of Technology, Finland
Konstantinos Manikas — University of Copenhagen, Denmark
Tiziana Margaria — University of Limerick and Lero, Ireland
John McGregor — Clemson University, USA
Rory O'Connor — Dublin City University, Ireland
Samuli Pekkola — Tampere University of Technology, Finland
Wolfram Pietsch — FH Aachen, Germany
Maryam Razavian — VU Amsterdam, The Netherlands

Björn Regnell	Lund University, Sweden
Dirk Riehle	Friedrich-Alexander University, Germany
Matti Rossi	Aalto University, Finland
Gunter Ruhe	University of Calgary, Canada
Kari Smolander	Lappeenranta University of Technology, Finland
Pasi Tyrväinen	University of Jyväskylä, Finland
Krzysztof Wnuk	Blekinge Institute of Technology, Sweden
Donald Wynn	University of Dayton, USA

Steering Committee

Jan Bosch	Chalmers University of Technology, Sweden
Sjaak Brinkkemper	Utrecht University, The Netherlands
João M. Fernandes	University of Minho, Portugal
Georg Herzwurm	University of Stuttgart, Germany
Slinger Jansen	Utrecht University, The Netherlands (Chair)
Casper Lassenius	Aalto University, Finland
Eetu Luoma	Jyväskylä University, Finland (Chair)
Ricardo J. Machado	University of Minho, Portugal
Tiziana Margaria	University of Limerick and Lero, Ireland
Björn Regnell	Lund University, Sweden
Kari Smolander	Lappeenranta University of Technology, Finland
Pasi Tyrväinen	Jyväskylä University, Finland
Krzysztof Wnuk	Blekinge Institute of Technology, Sweden

Additional Reviewers

Saskia Bick
Jens Förderer
Johan Linåker
Paula Monteiro
Maleknaz Nayebi
Maike Winkler

Keynotes

Trends and Lookout of the Automotive Software Industries

Christoph Gaertner

Software Development Department for Bosch in Braga, Portugal

Abstract. Modern low-end cars have embedded more than 30 to 50 so-called Electronic Control Units (ECUs), featuring around 50 million lines of code (LOC). At commercial rate, it represents $1,500 Mio (1.5 billion/milliard). However, a modern high-end car features around 100 million LOC, and this number is planned to grow to 200–300 millions in the near future. As a comparison, a F-22 fighter jet features less than 2 million LOC and a Boeing 787 around 14 million LOC. This presentation focuses on the Automotive Software Development market, the value chain in this market, and how to be part of it. Upcoming new trends as autonomous driving and the car as part of the Internet of Things lead the future automotive software development. Software engineers play an important role in the automotive industry to build up more sophisticated and added-value technology. I will talk about the balance act between being predictable by using processes conform to ASPICE and the need to be cost efficient and agile in the fast changing environment pushed by the influence of Consumer Electronic and Internet Services. I will be discussing the AUTOSAR approach as the upcoming industry standard in this business area, mentioning safety requirements and the ISO 26262. This talk will be interesting to professionals and students who intend to understand and know more about Automotive Software, and to clarify concepts of the car industries.

Christoph Gaertner is responsible for building up a Software Development Department for Bosch in Braga. He is working for Bosch since 2008 and before coming to Portugal he was a section head at Bosch Car Multimedia in Leonberg developing augmented reality solutions for the car driver. He was leading Software Projects for developing display based Instrument Cluster for a German premium car brand. He was an Software Developer and Architect for Head-Unit System at Harman Becker.

He started his career in a consultancy company during the new economy hype end of the 90ies where he already researched and developed smart appliances for the connected home. He has a Diploma in software engineering from the University of applied sciences Esslingen, Germany.

One Size Does Not Fit All: Software Product Management For Speedboats vs. Cruiseships

Hans-Bernd Kittlaus

InnoTivum Consulting
Im Sand 86, 53619 Rheinbreitbach, Germany
hbk@innotivum.com

Abstract. A product manager responsible for an established licensed software product that is used by hundreds or thousands of enterprise customers in regulated industries feels hopelessly old-fashioned when she listens to a Silicon Valley consultant talking about his latest experiences. Multiple releases per day? "Very funny! We are happy if our customers install one release per year." So there is certainly business justification for different scenarios. Which scenarios do we need to consider? Which factors influence the way SPM needs to be implemented and applied so much that they define the scenarios? Which SPM approaches and methods fit which scenario best? The presentation will provide a taxonomy of relevant scenarios with their defining characteristics and suggest appropriate SPM approaches for the scenarios based on practical experience in different customer environments.

Keywords: Software product management · Software product scenarios

Hans-Bernd Kittlaus is the owner and CEO of InnoTivum Consulting (www.innotivum.com) which he founded in 2001. Before he was Director of SIZ GmbH (Computing Center of the German Savings Banks Organization, Germany) and Head of Software Product Management and Development units of IBM. His main focus area is software product management. Hans-Bernd has been working as a trainer, coach and consultant for both corporate IT organizations and companies in the IT industry. He has published numerous books and articles, his latest being "Software Product Management and Pricing" [1]. He is Diplom-Informatiker (corresponds to M.S. in Computer Science) and certified as ISPMA Certified Software Product Manager, Certified Scrum Product Owner (CSPO), and PRINCE2 Practitioner. He is a member of ACM (Association for Computing Machinery, USA), GI (Gesellschaft für Informatik, Germany) and board member of ISPMA (International Software Product Management Association).

Over the last ten years, the software industry has seen an increasing heterogeneity in a large spectrum of aspects, from hardware and software platforms through development methodologies to business models. This makes life more difficult for everybody, be it customers, vendors, researchers or consultants. It does not mean that proven methods and techniques do not work anymore, but we need new approaches for the classification of scenarios and we need to study the applicability of methods and techniques in these scenarios. This talk is focussed on software product management (SPM) and is intended as food for thought by providing some ideas based on extensive consulting and training experience with a large number of different companies.

Software Product Scenarios		Life Cycle Phase	
		New Product Revolution	Existing Product Evolution
Runtime Environment	Vendor-Controlled	Powerboat	Speedboat
	Customer-Controlled	Icebreaker	Cruiseship

Fig. 1. Software Product Scenarios

Fig. 1 suggests a classification by using two types of runtime environments and two life cycle phases. Vendor-controlled means that the software vendor decides which changes are made when in the runtime environment. This is typical for rather unregulated environments like B2C internet platforms and SaaS or B2C license products that offer automated maintenance over the internet. In this scenario continuous agile development has become a de-facto standard, usually at a high frequency of incremental small releases, and often without a traditional project management structure. Trial-and-error approaches, known as customer discovery, are common.

If customers want to be in charge of the runtime environment, often for quality and/or regulatory concerns, we use the term customer-controlled. This is typical for a lot of B2B software license products, and also for software provided by corporate IT organizations. In this scenario, a broad range of development methodologies continue to be in use, from waterfall through iterative to agile, usually combined with a traditional project management structure. Releases tend to be bigger and less frequent.

It also makes a difference whether we consider the initial development of a new product or the evolutionary development of a product that already exists and has customers. With new product development, there is a high level of uncertainty and risk, and the focus is on releasing a minimum viable product as fast as possible. Once the product is rolled out, the focus shifts to extending the product scope and target market while compatibility and migration aspects become relevant. In this paper, we do not consider later phases of the life cycle.

Combining these two classification criteria leads to four scenarios that we can now analyze from a software product management perspective:

Powerboat: SPM is focused on defining the minimum viable product for the first customers. This requires a close link with development, often by assuming the product owner role (in Scrum terminology), and extensive prototyping. In parallel SPM needs to work on positioning and pricing with Marketing. Investments need to be justified based on a more strategic perspective, i.e. business model (one-page canvas), business plan (aggressive), product vision (aggressive), product strategy (very high-level), and roadmap (high-level). Release planning is not applicable, requirements engineering is more experimental than analytical.

Speedboat: SPM is focused on extending the product scope and thereby increasing the target market. This requires ongoing analysis of the actual usage of the product, of the market and competition. Depending on the organization's size, SPM and product owner roles may be separated, but closely linked. Product strategy and roadmapping become more important in combination with life cycle management. Release planning continues not to be applicable, requirements engineering is a mix of analysis and experimentation through customer discovery. If the organization does not implement some governance functions like Architecture things can become messy very quickly. Aspects like governance, compatibility and migration tend to slow the organization down a bit compared to the Powerboat phase.

Icebreaker: SPM is focused on defining the minimum viable product for the first customers. This requires extensive domain analysis as a basis for requirements engineering and planning of the first release with special emphasis on regulatory requirements. If a pilot customer is involved a major SPM task is making sure that requirements are sufficiently generalized so that the first release does not become totally customer-specific. The interface between SPM and Development depends on the chosen development methodology. Product strategy and roadmap already need some focus not only for internal investment decisions, but also since B2B customers want to understand the longer-term perspective before they make their investment decisions.

Cruiseship: SPM is focused on extending the product scope and thereby increasing the target market. Since customers do not want to test and install new releases often, the frequency of releases is rather low, often one or two per year. As a consequence, the new and changed contents of these releases is more significant and requires thorough release planning based on analytical requirements engineering. Product strategy and roadmap continue to be important as is life cycle management.

The increasing heterogeneity of the software industry poses challenging new opportunities for research. Do we need different criteria for defining scenarios? Do we need to differentiate more scenarios?

References

1. Kittlaus, H.-B., Clough, P.: Software Product Management and Pricing – Key Success Factors for Software Organizations. Springer, Heidelberg (2009)

Contents

The Benefits and Consequences of Workarounds in Software Development Projects

Jesse Yli-Huumo$^{(\boxtimes)}$, Andrey Maglyas, and Kari Smolander

School of Business and Management, Innovation and Software,
Lappeenranta University of Technology, Lappeenranta, Finland
{jesse.yli-huumo,andrey.maglyas,kari.smolander}@lut.fi

Abstract. Workarounds have existed in software from the very beginning. Being a formalized collection of knowledge rather than a physical artifact, software allows shortcuts in its development process. The shortcuts serve various purposes, like releasing a product to the market faster or postponing the solution of a problem. In this article, we present the findings of an investigation of workarounds in two software companies. Our analysis reveals that the decisions to take a workaround to resolve a technical issue are often intentional and forced by time-to-market requirements. However, the stakeholders are not always familiar with the negative consequences of taking workarounds, like additional hours, costs, and poor quality. We argue that the decision to take a workaround is often made by business managers who see short-term benefits only while developers have to deal with negative consequences in long-term.

Keywords: Workarounds · Technical debt · Case study · Software development project

1 Introduction

Starting from the release of the first software systems, the "software crisis" has been discussed widely by researchers and practitioners [1]. Many development and process management approaches have been developed to increase the productivity of programmers and to deliver products of higher quality to the market [2,3]. However, software companies are still constantly looking for new competitive advantages that would allow them to release new versions to the market faster than their competitors [4]. In the business of software, this can be achieved sometimes by taking workarounds in the development process. A workaround is a temporary solution that can be implemented in a shorter time than a proper solution, but it can also have a negative impact on the maintainability of the code base.

Workarounds are not specific for software business only, they have also been widely discussed in relation to management and public administration [5]. Although they have been applied in technological fields for a long time, workarounds have recently become known as technical debt. The concept of technical debt was introduced by Cunningham as "every minute spent on not-quite-right code counts as interest on debt. Entire engineering organizations can be brought to a stand-still under

© Springer International Publishing Switzerland 2015
J.M. Fernandes et al. (Eds.): ICSOB 2015, LNBIP 210, pp. 1–16, 2015.
DOI: 10.1007/978-3-319-19593-3_1

the debt load of an unconsolidated implementation, object-oriented or otherwise" [6]. Initially defined as related to coding, technical debt has also been extended to other software development processes and artifacts. Therefore, it is common nowadays to talk about quality debt, testing debt, documentation debt and other debts [7]. To avoid misinterpretation of what technical debt is, we use the term workaround in this article and understand it similarly to [8] as "a plan or method to circumvent a problem without eliminating it."

The aim of this study is to identify the benefits and consequences of taking workarounds, and to discuss the observations of how the decisions to take them are made in practice. The empirical data for the study has been collected from two case organizations. The first case is a middle-sized software development company with two separate product lines. The second case is a large telecommunication company currently conducting a software development project with subcontractors. To gain deeper understanding of the companies' processes, we interviewed managers and technical specialists, which provided us with different perspectives to the studied phenomenon.

2   Background

Alter [9] defines a workaround as a goal-driven adaptation and improvisation aiming at minimizing negative consequences like anomalies or structural changes. Alter also proposes four preconditions for taking a workaround. These preconditions include (1) the existing workflow or work practice, (2) personal or organizational goal for taking a workaround, (3) an issue that requires taking a workaround to resolve or overcome it, and (4) skills to develop the workaround for this particular issue [9]. All these preconditions are not specific for software development processes only, but can be used to describe also structural changes in organizations. In software engineering, a more precise definition of a workaround is given by IBM as "some action that results in alleviating a computing or hardware problem, but which does not solve the problem" [10]. The term workaround has been widely used in information systems research when studying the use and development of various information systems like customer relationship management (CRM) and medical information systems (e.g. [11,12]). In software engineering, the term technical debt is also used to describe workarounds and other pitfalls of software development [7]. Guo and Seaman [13] discuss technical debt from the viewpoint of the portfolio theory, and conclude that up-to-date documentation is critical for the modules in which workarounds have been taken. Without documentation, changes in the module may lead to taking new workarounds. In addition, the authors confirm theoretically that several small workarounds are better to have than a big one, because it reduces the risk of breaking the system through diversification [13].

Since workarounds are often associated with making some changes in the code base, they can be described as "code smells" [14]. The perceived quality of code varies a lot among developers, and their evaluation of the code quality is subjective without uniform criteria [14]. This has a negative effect on code maintainability, as software developers' viewpoints on what tricks are allowed to be used in the code differ.

Tom et al. [7] describe the two primary interrelated reasons for taking workarounds as pragmatism and prioritization. Pragmatism relates to setting goals, like releasing a minimal viable product (MVP) to the market quickly rather than developing it until its quality is high. Prioritization is about implementing the most critical tasks first, even if the overall product quality remains low. In this regard, prioritization involves pragmatism unconsciously in deciding the limitations and constraints of the project. Since prioritization is a collaborative process that involves technical and business people, the priorities of different parties may differ. Nagarjuna and Mamidenna [15] have studied engineering and business students. According to their results, engineering students have a tendency to perfectionism. Although the authors studied students only, this conclusion may also hold with real practitioners. For example, business-minded people, e.g. managers, aim at developing a minimum viable product in a shorter time with an appropriate level of quality, while engineers often aim at developing a cutting-edge solution [16,17].

When releasing a product to the market, a company aims at satisfying customers' needs [18]. Therefore, the perceived product quality is essential for product success. Dzida et al. [19] have identified seven dimensions of perceived quality as (1) self-descriptiveness, (2) user control, (3) ease of learning, (4) problem adequate usability, (5) correspondence with user expectations, (6) flexibility in task handling, and (7) fault tolerance. Out of these seven dimensions, only the last is directly related to the technical problems in the code base that could be raised because of the taken workarounds. The other six dimensions are primarily associated with usability and user experience. The perceived quality of web applications can be measured by four dimensions: technical adequacy, specific content, content quality, and appearance [20]. Only the first dimension of technical adequacy, which includes security, reliability and availability can be affected directly by taking workarounds in the code base. In both models of perceived quality, the quality of the code base itself plays only a partial role in how the user perceives the product. Therefore, technical excellence is only one dimension of how the product is perceived by customers.

Overall, the research on workarounds covers different aspects from organizational workarounds to shortcuts in the source code. In this study we focus on the latter case and contribute to the theory of workarounds, as e.g. Alter [9] states that workarounds are understudied and undertheorized. In this regard, we contribute to the theory of workarounds by providing empirical results of real practice of workarounds in the industry. Alter's theory of workarounds is a model consisting of seven layers: (1) intentions, goals, interest; (2) structure; (3) perceived need for a workaround; (4) identification of possible workarounds; (5) selection of workarounds to pursue, if any; (6) development and execution of the workaround; and (7) consequences [9]. In this study, we focus particularly on the first and last layers in order to understand how the idea of taking a workaround is born and the workaround then taken, and what benefits and consequences workarounds bring to the organization.

3   Research Methodology

Interpretive case study was selected as the research method for the study. We followed the guidelines of Klein and Myers [21] for conducting interpretive case studies, because the selected topic focuses on understanding of social processes and interactions between development and management teams within a company that lead to making the decision about taking a workaround. To make a valuable contribution to theory and practice, interpretive case studies should be carried out and written up carefully, and therefore we adopted the principles for reporting interpretive case studies presented by Walsham [22]. These principles enumerate a minimum information required to be reported such as "details of the research sites chosen, the reasons for this choice, the number of people interviewed, their hierarchical positions, what other sources of data were used, and over what period the study was conducted" [22].

3.1   Case A

Company A is a middle-sized software company that offers SaaS business solutions. It has three product lines that are managed independently. We selected two of the product lines for this study. The first product line provides a financial management solution as a cloud service that has more than 10 000 customers. The second product line is a SaaS-based project management solution for multi-organization projects. The solution is used by around 1000 companies worldwide. Both development teams use agile methodologies and especially practices from Scrum. The development teams of the product lines are rather small and consist of 13 and 18 employees, respectively.

3.2   Case B

Company B is a telecommunications company offering services for communication and entertainment. The company employs around 4200 people and has about 2.3 million customers. We chose one of the projects conducted by Company B for this study. Five subcontractor companies have participated in this project, but the project has been mainly developed by Company C, which is a middle-sized development company. The project started in 2007 and is still running today. It has over one million lines of code and it has been integrated to over 70 background systems. The goal of the project is to create a self-service channel for customers and switch manual work to automated processes inside the system. The organization had used Scrum during the first years of the project, but has currently moved to the use of Kanban.

3.3   Selection of Companies, Data Collection, and Data Analysis

The selection of the companies for this study was primarily dictated by a list of partners (in total 30) in a research project. Out of several potential candidates for the study, the selected companies were chosen on the basis of various reasons. The first reason for the selection of Case A was related to the phase of the lifecycle of the company. Company A has been growing through mergers and acquisitions of several smaller companies. In addition, the company itself is nowadays a part of a larger international enterprise. Due to these mergers and acquisitions, the company combines several product lines. We assumed that studying workarounds in the two product lines of this company should produce insightful details of how two product lines and teams coming from different backgrounds and cultures, but currently sharing the same environment, deal with workarounds. This also allowed us to constantly compare and cross check the information collected by interviews in two product lines. The second reason for the selection of the company was related to the type of products the company develops. Both product lines are SaaS products that share such characteristics as a common set of features for all users and short release cycles. These characteristics, together with the increasing number of SaaS products attracted our attention to their connection to taking workarounds in the development process. The selection of case B was primarily done based on the company size and the interesting nature of the project they were working with. We assumed that the development processes in large organizations are more mature than in smaller organizations, and therefore there should be less workarounds.

In both cases we focused on understanding why workarounds had been taken and what positive and negative effects they had. We conducted semi-structured interviews with 17 representatives related to the cases during February-June 2014. The positions of the interviewees are listed in Table 1. All interviews were sound-recorded and later transcribed. The interviews lasted from 25 to 105 minutes with an average of 50 minutes.

Table 1. Roles of the interviewees

ID	Company	Product line	Role
I1	A	a	Software architect
I2	A	a	Software designer
I3	A	a	Project manager
I4	A	a	Software test engineer
I5	A	a	Production director
I6	A	b	Software architect
I7	A	b	Software developer
I8	A	b	Product line manager
I9	A	b	Software test engineer
I10	A	b	Software architect
I11	A	b	Software developer
I12	A	b	UI designer
I13	B	-	Software architect
I14	B	-	Project owner
I15	B	-	Project owner
I16	C	-	Senior consultant
I17	C	-	Software architect

The data analysis was done by identifying categories related to workarounds. We used an iterative approach of data collection and analysis, and coded the data using a procedure similar to open coding in the grounded theory [23]. The interview transcripts were read and their workaround-related parts categorized into labelled concepts. These initial concepts guided us to an explanation of how and why workarounds are taken in practice.

4   Findings and Results

We identified seven scenarios related to taking a workaround during software development in the studied cases. Below, we explain the context and environment in which the workarounds were taken with the reasons, benefits, and consequences.

4.1   Scenario 1: Upcoming Deadline

In Case B the company decided to develop a new feature to their system. The development task was given to a team that consisted of a few junior coders only. The management asked for a preliminary timetable from the development team in order to create a marketing campaign for the feature. The development team gave an estimate of the development time, and the marketing team started to plan the campaign. However, it was discovered later on that the development team had estimated the release date wrong, and they would not be able to deliver the feature before the deadline. At this point the company did not have the option to postpone the release date anymore, and they decided to implement heavy workarounds to the feature in order to get it released in time.

"A media campaign was designed, radio commercials were starting, and commercials for magazines were ordered. So at that point there were just no more options. There would have been so much business damage to us." – I15.

In this scenario the feature itself was not very important for the company's overall strategy. However, the company decided to use a workaround to reach the given deadline in order to meet the promised release date. With taking the workaround, the company was able to release the feature in time, and therefore damage to the company's reputation by releasing late was prevented. If the company had announced that the feature release will be postponed, it could have had a significant effect on the company's reputation and customer satisfaction.

The workaround for releasing the feature in time had some consequences. The released feature was taken in production unfinished and unstable. The feature itself looked the same in the user interface as it would have looked when done properly. However, the code base was unfinished and consisted of several critical components. This forced the company to fix and refactor the feature right after the release, which required extra working hours and costs for the project, in order to fix critical errors and to be able to develop the product further.

"Well, of course everything was working from the outside, but we knew that there are scary things inside. However, we appointed developers immediately to fix them after the release." – I15.

4.2   Scenario 2: Complex Part of the Code Base

In case A (product line a), the software designer described a scenario that often required a workaround during the development. He explained a situation where fixing a feature demanded a lot of time due to the complexity of the code base. The complexity of the code base meant that some parts of the features were developed with bad solutions and architecture. Therefore, refactoring them was challenging and risky. Since the deadlines were strict, there was not enough time to analyze the whole code base. This was the reason why it was faster just to implement a simple workaround instead of fixing the bigger problem of the feature. Also the risk that the code base might not work anymore due to changes in a complex part of the code base was seen as a reason why it was safer to implement a workaround.

"Yeah, we often have to do some kind of a fix because it is complex and we can't go any further. So we need to release a hotfix pretty soon and we don't have enough time to make it work as it should be because of time." – I2.

The benefit that the company gained from taking a workaround in this scenario was customer satisfaction, because the fix was released earlier. Also sometimes even the development team was happy for getting rid of the problem fast and being able to move on to other tasks.

"In the short term, the customer will be happy because the problem is fixed. Sometimes the development team is also happy because we can start different kind of work and tasks. So sometimes for us it is okay to have shortcuts." – I2.

According to a company survey on user satisfaction, the users were happy with this workaround strategy and were not eager to switch to another solution by a competitor. Therefore, the company's internal policy allowed taking workarounds and fixing them later.

However, these workarounds started to produce negative consequences later on. Sometimes the workarounds created temporary system breakdowns or slowness that needed to be fixed with other fast workarounds. This required many extra working hours for fixing and refactoring that were not planned in the beginning, and in some cases even a completed rewrite of the feature was required.

"For example let's say we do one fix and take a shortcut and then after a while, like after a month or two months, something else comes up and we need to do another hotfix because of this previous fix. When time progresses, that feature needs to be redone because it is getting out of date or other fixes are getting slower or whatever." – I2.

4.3   Scenario 3: Unpleasant Work

Case B has a long history, and the system has been developed for many years. During the project, the code base has grown to be large and complex, and there are features in the code base that have been implemented either properly or with workarounds. When the code base grows and becomes inconsistent, development becomes much harder. This was the situation in case B, and the senior consultant in the project felt that this generated serious effects on the developers' mindset towards the code base.

"The pattern that the developers were talking about was this thing called princess-driven development. In other words, "This code is so ugly, I don't want to do it like this. I will implement something else."" – I16.

In this scenario some of the developers experienced that the old part of the code base that had been developed with complex solutions was not pleasant to work with. Instead of refactoring the entire code base, it was just easier to implement a workaround. The only benefit that this type of workarounds had was the faster release of the solution. The developer could move to other tasks sooner and start to implement features with more interest to him. However, when workarounds were implemented and not fixed afterwards, it turned the code base difficult to understand, especially for new developers.

"This led to a situation where you don't clean up the old code and you implement something else next to it. When a new guy comes after a year and looks at this and sees "ok, well it has been done like this in here, and then this is implemented like this..." and it says nowhere how it should be done, and what our common way of implementing things is." – I16.

This incomprehensible code base increased the lack of interest in developing solutions properly and therefore increased the amount of workarounds taken because it did not require much effort.

4.4   Scenario 4: Significant Economic Benefits

A large number of workarounds were taken at the early stages of case B to create significant internal financial saving for the company. The reason for this was that the company would be able to change their manual work to automated processes within the system. With the change, the company would be able to cut down personnel costs. A software consultant in company C estimated that by creating the feature, company B would save a significant amount of money.

"Roughly estimating, if the levels are correct, when we got a certain order type, like for example closing a subscription to self-service and automation, it started to save 30 000 euros a month to company B." – I16.

When it was noticed that the savings were so significant, it was understood that the features had to be released as soon as possible. This created pressure for the development team to get the features released. The development team was able to release the features really quickly, but it required some workarounds. However, with the workarounds the company started to make significant savings early. One of the product owners considered the decision to take workarounds as a smart one, even if it required extra effort from the company.

"If we had started to build this project really well and with a really fancy architecture, it might be that we might have been cut out of funding before it got to the production and we wouldn't have gotten anything done. It has paid back a multiple amount of money, probably tens of times." – I15.

The decision to take workarounds resulted later in extra working hours and slower development. Another negative consequence of these workarounds was difficulties in further development. Whenever the development team wanted to implement something to a certain part of the code base, it broke down something else.

4.5   Scenario 5: Unnecessary Work

In case A (product line a) we found that the company did not document the workarounds, as they were considered as temporary solutions. When a developer decided to take a workaround in a certain task, it was not documented. The developers relied on the information of workarounds as they remembered it and paid no attention to documentation. This way the developers could work faster, and large amount of documentation work would not slow them down.

The consequences of not documenting workarounds were especially well observed when new developers joined the team. When a new developer started to work with the code base that included workarounds, it was challenging because the code base was not self-documenting and actually no documentation existed.

"At least it affects situations when someone new comes to work for us. There has to be a place where people can get answers without asking, if they will have to work alone someday." – I10.

The lack of documentation affected the future development a lot. When the developers had no documentation available about workarounds, they could just copy/paste the old code because it worked. In the situation where the old code was done with workarounds, the workaround code started to accumulate and show in the overall quality of the code base.

"They should be listed somewhere and we should be fixing them all the time, but we would need time for it. The reason is that every bad solution we implement intentionally, will be used also as copy/paste code and that is really bad for the future. I think that bad solutions will multiply in time and spread to other parts." – I10.

4.6   Scenario 6: Outdated Version of Components

In case A (product line b), the workarounds had effects on compatibility with other systems. A software designer mentioned compatibility problems in integration with different versions of the database. The current version of the database server used in the company was from 2012, but due to the workarounds taken previously, the database server worked in the compatibility mode with the 2008 version and in some cases even with the 2005 version.

"Well, when you think about it, there are compatibility problems between different versions. Now we have the 2012 version of the Microsoft SQL server, but it is up and running in compatibility mode with the version of 2005. So we can't use new commands because of this."- I2.

Due to this workaround, new commands were not available and the developers had to implement low-level features already implemented in the newer version of the database server. For example, some commands could be run in the default server mode but not in the compatibility mode, and the team had to implement the database features already available in the newer version by themselves. If this had been done properly from the beginning and kept up to date continuously, these problems could have been avoided. Now the team had to put additional efforts into implementing the middleware between the product and the database.

4.7   Scenario 7: Low Priority Features

In case A (product line b), the development team intentionally did not implement some of the features properly, as they were requested by a couple of customers only. The company put only minimal effort to this type of features because it was not planned to scale the feature to all customers.

"There might be some cases where there is a certain need coming from a customer that is really valuable to that customer, but it is not a scalable feature, so it is not valuable to any other customer. So in that kind of cases we can only put minimum effort to that feature, because it is not a scalable feature. Customers are happy if they just get what they want." – I3.

A project manager in company A explained that the company evaluates the value of every feature and then decides what the planned effort for them is. If the business value of the feature is low for the company, it just simply gets done as easily as possible, with workarounds.

"Well, everything is based on the value of the feature. If the value of the feature is low from the business point of view, you always have to weigh the time used by the coder. Let's say that implementing a feature takes one week, and we know that we can go with that solution like one or two years forward, it could be a good decision now, because we don't have those two or three weeks to implement that." – I3.

However, the company also faced situations where some of these low value features were so successful that the decision to release them to all customers was made later. Because these features were developed with a minimum effort, this led to a situation where the features had to be refactored and developed more as scalable when the number of users started to grow.

4.8   Summary of Scenarios

In Table 2 we summarize the scenarios observed in the studied cases with identified categories of reasons for workarounds, their benefits and consequences. The main reason for taking a workaround was related to the challenge of meeting a deadline (category: *time pressure,* Scenarios 1-5). The release planning of features defined by business managers was so important that the developers had to take workarounds in order to reach deadlines. *Time pressure* from business managers also affected architectural decisions because developers had *no time to change the selected software components* (Scenario 6) even if it would be beneficial for the development. The other reason was the *complicated code base,* which increased the number of workarounds to be taken, as the workarounds were easier to implement than refactoring the complex code. In Scenario 7 *prioritization of the features based on their business values* led to workarounds in implementing low priority features.

Table 2. Summary of scenarios

Scenario #	Case	Reason for workaround	Benefits of workaround	Consequences of workaround
1	B	Time pressure.	Time-to-market, Company reputation, Increased customer satisfaction.	Decreased code maintainability, Extra working hours, Extra costs.
2	A (a)	Time pressure, Complicated code base.	Time-to-market, Increased customer satisfaction.	Decreased code maintainability, Extra working hours, Major refactoring.
3	B	Time pressure, Complicated code base.	Time-to-market.	Decreased code maintainability, Lack of motivation to work with the code base.
4	B	Time pressure.	Time-to-market, Significant financial savings due to early release.	Decreased code maintainability, Extra working hours.
5	A (a)	Time pressure.	Time-to-market, Increased speed of development.	Decreased code maintainability, Increased time for newcomers to start.
6	A (b)	No time for changing the selected software components.	Time-to-market.	Outdated software components, Lack of new features available in newer versions of components, Decreased code maintainability
7	A (b)	Prioritization of features based on their business value.	Increased speed of developing high priority features.	Decreased code maintainability when scaling the feature.

The primary benefit of workarounds observed in the scenarios was *time-to-market* (Scenario 1-6). Taking workarounds was helpful for companies to deliver the needed features in time, which resulted in *increasing customer satisfaction* and *saving company reputation*. In Scenario 4 implementing the feature was critically important for the company because its implementation instantly allowed getting *significant financial savings* by using the feature in production. Workarounds in processes like documentation in Scenario 5 allow allocating more time for other processes, e.g. *increased speed of development* due to lack of documentation. Similarly, Scenario 7 is an example of *increased speed of developing high priority features* due to workarounds made in lower priority features.

However, when the workarounds gave the companies the ability to deliver the features in time and development seemed faster, they also had negative consequences. In all scenarios the workarounds resulted in *decreased code maintainability* and consequently *extra working hours* and *extra costs*. In Scenario 2 this required *major refactoring* of the code base. It seems that other scenarios will end up with major refactoring too because workarounds lead to *lack of motivation to work with the code base* (Scenario 3). In Scenario 5, *increased speed of development* led to *increased time for newcomers to start* working on the project due to lack of documentation. Being under pressure of *time-to-market* developers had to use *outdated software components* and introduce new workarounds due to *lack of new features available in newer versions of components*. The lack of time for architectural changes prevented the company from reducing the effects of accumulated workarounds and *decreased code maintainability* (Scenario 6). Focusing on high priority features (Scenario 7) led to the situation when workarounds in lower priority features were implemented on top of each other without any documentation. Finally it led to *decreased code maintainability when scaling the feature,* when the feature was so valued by customers that its priority had to be increased.

5   Discussion

The results of the study of the two cases show that taking workarounds is a daily practice in software development. This does not necessarily lead to business disruption, but it has negative consequences that a company should be aware of. Lim et al. [24] report that developers always try to make the best decisions based on the information, knowledge, and experience they have, but these decisions can lead to workarounds quickly and unintentionally. In the two companies in our study the decision to take a workaround was often intentional. This decision was often made by business managers who understood the negative consequences, but could underestimate their long-term impact. Regardless of their awareness of the consequences, they made the decision intentionally to benefit from releasing a product to the market faster. This was particularly done to satisfy customers, save company reputation, and gain an edge over competitors.

Kekre et al. [25] have developed a model of seven drivers of customer satisfaction for software products. The authors conclude that capability and usability are the main drivers for customer satisfaction. Capability presents the product functionality in terms of its key features. Usability is a multidimensional driver itself, but it is not related to the product code base where workarounds have been taken. In this study, we identified decreased code maintainability as a major consequence of taking workarounds that has limited direct impact to seven drivers of customer satisfaction but has impact to the company ability to maintain releasing new versions of the product with increasing time and costs to maintain the code base in long term.

The negative consequences of workarounds have been already identified separately. For example, Li and Shatnawi [26] have studied the relationships between workarounds associated with "code smells" and class error probability. They revealed that refactoring a bad code is difficult after release, and associated with introducing new errors to the code. In addition, the authors argue that "code smells" should be constantly identified to find problematic pieces of code and refactored. In the studied companies, only one scenario went through major refactoring and we expect to other scenarios will also end up in refactoring the code base. Other consequences like a lack of documentation were already identified back in 1979 [27], but this problem still remains like in Scenario 5. In this regard, we do not consider the identified negative consequences of workarounds as a significantly new contribution. The value of this list is in the consideration of the impact of workarounds to the maintainability of the code base. Developers are aware of these consequences, and therefore our primary aim is to attract the attention of decision makers who see the immediate benefits of workarounds, but do not fully understand their drawbacks. It is important to release a product quickly to the market, but it is also important to understand the accumulation of workarounds and the related waste of time and resources in the future.

Alter [9] provides an integrative view on workarounds and states that the theory of workarounds will evolve over time. The study contributes to the theory by providing an explanation for the intentions of taking workarounds and their consequences. Alter believes that the theory of workarounds could be used in making "more realistic assumptions for systems analysis and design" [9]. Although the theory can be used this way, we see the underlying problem of workarounds is in misunderstanding and underestimation of their impact by decision makers. By pointing out that workarounds have consequences and these consequences impact on how further releases should be planned, we bridge the gap and provide a communication tool for developers and managers to find a balance between maintaining the code base and releasing a product to the market.

With this study we contribute to the theory of workarounds [9] in the context of software development organizations that take shortcuts in the code base. According to Gregor's taxonomy of theories in information systems research [28], Alter's theory of workarounds can be considered as an explanation theory that defines the phenomenon, describes and explains it, but does not make attempts to specify hypotheses for prediction. The present study contributes to the theory by providing an empirical investigation of the phenomenon in a real environment, and extends the scope of validity of the theory [29]. Rather than making a prediction on the long-term impact of workarounds to the business success, we explain the reasons behind taking workarounds and the ability of workarounds to accumulate over time.

The study has also limitations. The selection of the case organizations was partially limited to project partners. However, out of several organizations, the selected organizations could meet all our criteria. In addition, as we had two unrelated cases to study, we were not limited to one team only and could interview and compare the results from two cases to avoid the bias of interviewing only one team with its own experiences and culture. Both companies develop customer SaaS kind of software, therefore the transferability of the results is primary related to similar companies while it requires additional study to investigate workarounds in other types of products like embedded systems.

6   Conclusion

In this study, we explored how the decisions of taking workarounds are made in the organization, and used the qualitative case study approach as recommended by Klein and Myers [21]. The use of the interpretive case study allowed us to investigate social processes in the organizations in an attempt to understand how business and technical professionals communicate with each other regarding taking workarounds, and how they consider their benefits and consequences. We found that business people often deal with the benefit of time-to-market only and therefore can underestimate the negative consequences of workarounds, like decreased maintainability of the code base. In contrast, engineering people have to deal with all consequences and therefore they hesitate to take workarounds. However, they are often under the pressure from the business and have little power to make the final decision. We observed that the decisions to take workarounds are often made intentionally but the consequences of these decisions can be underestimated by the business people due to the lack of technical knowledge.

Acknowledgements. We would like to thank the companies for being a valuable source of information and all interviewees who found time to share their experiences. This research has been carried out in Digile Need for Speed program, and funded by Tekes (the Finnish Funding Agency for Technology and Innovation).

References

1. Brooks, F.: The Mythical Man-Month: Essays on Software Engineering, Anniversary Edition. Addison-Wesley Professional (1995)
2. Boehm, B.: A spiral model of software development and enhancement. Computer 21(5), 61–72 (1988)
3. McConnell, S.: Rapid Development: Taming Wild Software Schedules. Microsoft Pr. (1996)
4. Fan, M., Kumar, S., Whinston, A.: Short-term and long-term competition between providers of shrink-wrap software and software as a service. European Journal of Operational Research 196(2), 661–671 (2009)

5. Azad, B., King, N.: Enacting computer workaround practices within a medication dispensing system. European Journal of Information Systems 17(3), 264–278 (2008)
6. Cunningham, W.: The WyCash Portfolio Management System. In: OOPSLA Addendum to the Proceedings, pp. 29–30 (1992)
7. Tom, E., Aurum, A., Vidgen, R.: An exploration of technical debt. Journal of Systems and Software 86(6), 1498–1516 (2013)
8. Halbesleben, J., Wakefield, D., Wakefield, B.: Workarounds in health care settings: Literature review and research agenda. Health Care Management Review 33(1), 2–12 (2008)
9. Alter, S.: Theory of Workarounds. Communications of the Association for Information Systems 34, Article 55 (2014)
10. IBM, Customer Care Handbook (2004)
11. Koppel, R., Wetterneck, T., Telles, J.L., Karsh, B.-T.: Workarounds to Barcode Medication Administration Systems: Their Occurrences, Causes, and Threats to Patient Safety. Journal of American Medical Information Association 15(4), 408–423 (2008)
12. Russell, B.: You gotta lie to it: software applications and the management of technological change in a call centre. New Technology, Work and Employment 22(2), 132–145 (2007)
13. Guo, Y., Seaman, S.: A Portfolio Approach to Technical Debt Management. In: 2nd Workshop on Managing Technical Debt, New York, NY, USA, pp. 31–34 (2011)
14. Mäntylä, M., Lassenius, C.: Subjective evaluation of software evolvability using code smells: An empirical study. Empirical Software Engineering 11(3), 395–431 (2006)
15. Nagarjuna, V., Mamidenna, S.: Personality Characteristics of Commerce and Engineering Graduates – A Comparative Study. Journal of the Indian Academy of Applied Psychology 34(2), 303–308 (2008)
16. Perrow, C.: The Analysis of Goals in Complex Organizations. American Sociological Review 26(6), 854–866 (1961)
17. Ritti, R.: Work Goals of Scientists and Engineers. Industrial Relations: A Journal of Economy and Society 7(2), 118–131 (1968)
18. Dver, A.: Software Product Management Essentials, 2nd edn. Anclote Press (2008)
19. Dzida, W., Herda, S., Itzfeldt, W.D.: User-perceived Quality of Interactive Systems. In: Proceedings of the 3rd International Conference on Software Engineering, Piscataway, NJ, USA, pp. 188–195 (1978)
20. Aladwani, A., Palvia, P.: Developing and validating an instrument for measuring user-perceived web quality. Information & Management 39(6), 467–476 (2002)
21. Klein, H., Myers, M.: A Set of Principles for Conducting and Evaluating Interpretive Field Studies in Information Systems. MIS Quarterly 23(1), 67–93 (1999)
22. Walsham, G.: Interpretive case studies in IS research: nature and method. European Journal of Information Systems 4(2), 74–81 (1995)
23. Corbin, J., Strauss, A.: Basics of Qualitative Research: Techniques and Procedures for Developing Grounded Theory, 3rd edn. SAGE Publications, Los Angeles (2007)
24. Lim, E., Taksande, N., Seaman, C.: A Balancing Act: What Software Practitioners Have to Say about Technical Debt. IEEE Software 29(6), 22–27 (2012)
25. Kekre, S., Krishnan, M., Srinivasan, K.: Drivers of Customer Satisfaction for Software Products: Implications for Design and Service Support. Management Science 41(9), 1456–1470 (1995)

26. Li, W., Shatnawi, R.: An empirical study of the bad smells and class error probability in the post-release object-oriented system evolution. Journal of Systems and Software 80(7), 1120–1128 (2007)
27. Boehm, B.: Software Engineering-as It is. In: 4th International Conference on Software Engineering, Piscataway, NJ, USA, pp. 11–21 (1979)
28. Gregor, S.: The Nature of Theory in Information Systems. MIS Quarterly 30(3), 611–642 (2006)
29. Sjøberg, D., Dybå, T., Anda, B., Hannay, J.: Building Theories in Software Engineering. In: Shull, F., Singer, J., Sjøberg, D. (eds.) Guide to Advanced Empirical Software Engineering, pp. 312–336. Springer, London (2008)

The Relationship Between Business Model Experimentation and Technical Debt

Jesse Yli-Huumo[✉], Tommi Rissanen, Andrey Maglyas, Kari Smolander, and Liisa-Maija Sainio

Lappeenranta University of Technology, Lappeenranta, Finland
{jesse.yli-huumo,tommi.rissanen,andrey.maglyas,kari.smolander,
liisa-maija.sainio}@lut.fi

Abstract. The use of lean software development methodology and business model experimentation has become popular in software companies in recent years. Business model experimentation is used to validate assumptions made on a product from real customers before the actual product is created. A minimum viable product is used to test the business model by gathering and measuring customer feedback. However, in many cases creating a minimum viable product requires the development team to take shortcuts and workarounds in the product. This phenomenon in software development is called 'technical debt', where companies trade long-term software quality to short-term gain in time-to-market. We investigated four software companies and conducted nine interviews to understand the relationship between business model experimentation and technical debt. The goal was to study how business model experimentation is affecting to technical debt. The results showed that business model experimentation has a clear relationship to technical debt.

Keywords: Business model experimentation · Technical debt · Case study · Startup company · Large company · Software development lifecycle · Minimum viable product

1 Introduction

Startups and increasingly also larger companies use business model experimentation as a way to accelerate their product development cycles. The well-known process of business model experimentation is the lean startup framework introduced by Ries [1]. The lean startup framework considers learning to be the essence of the product development process and everything else is waste, following the lean manufacturing thinking. A lean startup creates a minimum viable product (MVP) that is a simple prototype of the product attached with a business model. The product team measures different elements of the product functionality and the business model, learns from the customer feedback and builds a better product with an adjusted business model to start the cycle again.

When a company accelerates its product development cycle to create a minimum viable product instead of releasing a ready and complete product, the development

© Springer International Publishing Switzerland 2015
J.M. Fernandes et al. (Eds.): ICSOB 2015, LNBIP 210, pp. 17–29, 2015.
DOI: 10.1007/978-3-319-19593-3_2

team has to make shortcuts in the implementation of the product. In the software development lifecycle this is called 'technical debt' [2]. The term technical debt refers to a situation in the software development lifecycle, where long-term quality is traded for short-term gains. Taking shortcuts and workarounds in the development can give a company an advantage to release faster and to acquire customer feedback earlier, but if this 'debt' is not paid back later, it can affect to the quality and further development of the product.

When a new product is launched, it rarely has the optimal business model. The business model has so many elements and variables that it is impossible to predict how all components of the business model pan out when it is in the market. The lean startup process allows the tweaking of the business model efficiently.

The objective of this paper is to study the relationship between business model experimentation and technical debt. We explore if conducting business model experimentation has any effect to the amount of technical debt occurring during the software development lifecycle. We study four case companies and interview their key persons related to business models and technical debt and analyze the interviews for theoretical results.

The rest of the paper is organized as follows. Chapter 2 provides the background and the terminology related to this research. Chapter 3 describes the research process and methodology used in this study. Chapter 4 introduces the results analyzed from the gathered data. In Chapter 5 we discuss about the results and Chapter 6 concludes the paper.

2   Background

2.1   Business Model Experimentation

Every business enterprise either explicitly or implicitly employs a particular business model [3]. There are multiple interpretations of the concept, however. The business model can be defined as a system of interdependent activities that enables the firm to create value and also to appropriate a share of that value [4]. It can also be defined as the logic of the firm, the way it operates and how it creates value for its stakeholders [5] or the basic unit of business and process or operational advantages [6]. Business models generate feedback loops or virtuous cycles that strengthen components of the business model through iteration [5]. There are many other slightly different interpretations of the concept. In this study the business model is defined as the way a firm creates value and appropriates a share of that value following the definition by Zott & Amit [4]. The difference between a strategy and a business model is not always clear. Casadesus-Masanell & Ricart [5] see the business model as a reflection of the firm's realized strategy.

Many business model studies take the dynamic nature of the business model into consideration. The current dynamic business environment with a multitude of simultaneous changes shortens the lifecycles of business models and requires companies to be constantly able and ready to adapt their business models. McGrath [6] points out that business models can rarely be anticipated in advance but rather learned over time based on experiences and learning. Doz & Kosonen [7] also emphasize the need for companies to transform their business models more rapidly, more frequently and more far-reachingly now at the era of global competition, discontinuities and disruptions. Business model innovation is the term often used to refer the development of new business models. Business model innovation has been described as "a type of organizational innovation in which firms identify and adopt novel opportunity portfolios" [8] , "the discovery of a fundamentally different business model in an existing business" [9] and "the search for new logics of the firm and new ways to create and capture value for its stakeholders: it focuses primarily on finding new ways to generate revenues and define value propositions for customers, suppliers and partners" [10]. Following the chosen business model definition, the business model innovation definition of Casadesus-Masanell & Zhu [10] is best suited for this study.

Minzberg & Waters [11] separated deliberate and emergent strategies and defined entrepreneurial strategy to be relatively emergent but able to emerge depending on the entrepreneur. Emergent strategy formation is therefore closely linked to business model experimentation, which is one distinct way of doing business model innovation. McGrath [6] sees experimentation as a way to discover which are the most effective models of allocating resources in the market, considering the constraints that are set by the competitive environment. Dunford et al. [12] see experimentation as one of the four processes in business model replication of an internationalizing multinational company. Companies conduct business model experimentation in most cases only after external innovations have disrupted their existing business model, because there are several barriers especially in large companies for creating experiments [13]. Many startup companies have utilized business model experimentation using the specific lean startup method, which originates from Steve Blank's Customer development methodology [14] and was made popular by Eric Ries with his book The Lean Startup [1]. The lean startup methodology is based on validated learning where every action a startup does that does not increase learning how its products can serve customers better is considered waste. In addition to startups, also larger companies have started using the lean startup method for boosting their internal startup activities.

2.2   Technical Debt

The concept of technical debt was introduced by Cunningham as a metaphor to financial debt: "every minute spent on not-quite-right code counts as interest on debt. Entire engineering organizations can be brought to a stand-still under the debt load of an unconsolidated implementation, object-oriented or otherwise" [2]. Technical debt has recently become widely used for describing all shortcuts and workarounds in software development processes and artifacts though it was initially used for coding only [15]. As a result, there is a number of corresponding terms to describe shortcuts and workarounds related to other than coding processes and artifacts like quality debt, testing debt, documentation debt [15]. These types of technical debt are considered as subtypes of technical debt but their distinctive characteristics has not been established [16]. Therefore, this article uses the term technical debt to refer to any type of debt taken in the process of developing a minimal viable product.

In general, technical debt is an action or plan to circumvent a problem without developing a proper solution to solve it [17]. This is often done through developing a quick fix that is supposed to be replaced with a proper solution later but it is never done in practice. The temporary solutions that can be implemented in a shorter time in comparison with proper solutions provide companies with a competitive advantage to release new products to the market faster than their competitors. In a longer perspective, temporary solutions accumulate over time having a negative impact to the codebase maintainability [15].

The development of a minimal viable product done in startup companies or special internal startup departments of large companies through corporate venturing and experimentation requires the generation and testing of numerous ideas [18]. However, only a few ideas can potentially generate significant revenue to the company. The selection of the ideas for implementation is often done through experimentation by developing a product that is not fully functional but has primary features partially implemented for testing the product in the market [19]. The trade-off between releasing the product faster and having features properly implemented requires a company to take technical debt. By accepting that time-to-market is more critical than code quality, the company incurs intentional technical debt according to the McConnell's taxonomy [20]. In addition to intentional technical debt, any company is prone to unintentional technical debt. The sources of unintentional technical debt are out of control and the company can be even unaware of them. For example, it can be the result of significant changes in the product architecture that were not planned in advance but suddenly became essential for the product success in the market.

Overall, intentional and unintentional technical debt contribute to uncertainty of the environment in which the company operates [21] by setting limitations on features that can be implement and time required for their implementation. Finding the right balance between time-to-market and amount of technical debt accumulated in the product can be seen a success factor of experimenting with various ideas and delivering these ideas to the market in forms of products that provide value to the customer.

3   Research Methodology

The study began with a literature review on business model experimentation and technical debt. Based on the literature, we argue that the current knowledge about the relationship between technical debt and business model is not well-studied and requires more examination. Therefore, this study is exploratory in nature and the goal is to find the linkages between the constructs and understand the relationship. We decided to use case study as the research methodology. We conducted multiple inductive case-studies with semi-structured interviews to gather data from the companies' representatives. Semi-structured interviews can provide rich and detailed data for a specific research question. Interviews bring forth the respondents' own perspective and provide insight to particular experiences they have had with the topic [22].

The cases selected for this study were three large companies in different fields of business and one small startup. From one of the large companies multiple informants were interviewed to ensure the understanding of the whole phenomena of conducting business model experimentation and the effect on technical debt. In other companies only one informant was interviewed in a company. These interviews were used to confirm the findings in the first company with multiple interviewees.

The data collection was initiated with the large company that had multiple informants. They are studying technical debt in their own processes quite closely and the idea of investigating the relationship between technical debt and business model experimentation came up in discussions with this first case company. The research questions were drawn from those discussions and more informants were selected to increase the understanding in this company. In order to validate the findings, other companies were needed to be interviewed. The initial large case company is in the software development industry. The three other companies were chosen to represent other industries and company sizes; one large media company, one medium-sized software consultancy and one startup in software services business. Interviews with representatives from these companies enforced and proved the findings made in interviews with the first large case company.

The fact that there are six informants in one case company and one from each of the remaining three companies is a limitation in this paper. A wider selection of informants from the other three companies would have validated the findings more soundly.

The informants were experts in the particular area in companies. The interviews were semi-structured and conducted in November-December 2014. The duration of the interviews varied from 28 minutes to 52 minutes. In total there were nine interviews. The roles of the interviewees are shown in Table 1.

We analyzed the interview data with Atlas.ti software by making a thematic analysis, concentrating on the aspects related to technical debt and business model experimentation and identifying elements that played a role in their relationship. In the analysis, the following elements emerged: intentional and unintentional technical debt, the amount of focus on business model experimentation, emphasis on product quality and competence of the development team. As this was not a cross-case analysis trying to identify and examine the possible company-specific differences in the relationships between technical debt and business model experimentation, we present our findings by discussing the results on the level of the phenomenon itself.

Table 1. The roles of the interviewees

ID	Company	Role
A1	A	Test manager / project manager
A2	A	Project owner
A3	A	Technical coordinator
A4	A	Software developer
A5	A	Software developer
A6	A	Lead developer
B1	B	Development manager
C1	C	Managing partner
D1	D	Chief executive officer

4   Results

4.1   Finding 1: Business Model Experimentation Creates and Requires Intentional Technical Debt

We were able to identify a clear relationship between business model experimentation and technical debt. The studied companies used often a lean methodology and experimentation to build new idea, feature or service in iterative cycle with a minimal effort to product quality to receive faster feedback from the customer. The companies' goal was to test the assumptions of the current business model by experimenting the idea first at the customer before the actual development. To have minimal effort to the quality and fast feedback cycle, the development team had to take shortcuts and workarounds to produce a simple demo or prototype for the customers to use. This demo or prototype consisted only the most minimal amount of source code necessary and sometimes they were just graphical presentations done on the paper to demonstrate the possible functionality in the real version.

"We have done this product in few iterative steps and always tried to produce the minimal amount to validate the next steps and hypotheses. This has worked for us really well and we have gone always one step forward, but on the other hand we have accumulated technical debt there during that." – B1.

When companies got an idea to improve the current business model by creating a new feature or a service, the assumption that it would improve the current business model needed to be validated with an experimentation before the actual development phase could start. The companies did not want to waste time and money to first build something and realize afterwards that the assumption of beneficial feature or service was not correct. The reason was that it would have resulted to a significant loss in the development time, because the feature or service would not have been valuable to the customer and therefore to companies' new business models. This was the reason why the case companies first created a demo or a prototype from the idea and experimented it at the customer to receive a fast feedback that would help the company to make the decision for further development.

"Every thought, idea, or a single feature in the product that you have in mind must be validated somehow before you start to implement it. Otherwise you could use valuable time to build something that does not necessarily have value." – B1.

The demo or prototype created by the companies were usually developed as fast as possible with minimal amount of source code. At this stage companies made a decision to intentionally take technical debt to the product, as the quality of the feature was really low compared to what it should have to be in the future if the experimentation turned out to be successful. This resulted to situations where a company gave the customer a demo or a prototype of the feature that had a lot of usability issues and bugs, but that would still somehow demonstrate the main functionality that the company assumed would make customers interested.

"The goal is not to code everything when you have an idea. For example we had a lot of weird usability issues in the prototypes we had this summer, or actually in the beta version, but we decided not to fix them. It is in the accordance of MVP method that you must be little bit ashamed of your product that is going to customer first time." – B1.

The opinion of most interviewees was that technical debt is bad for the company and product, because it starts to hurt overall quality and it is challenging to manage. However, one informant thought that taking technical debt is not necessarily a bad thing to do in the beginning of the business model experimentation. The reason was that when companies are looking for the correct business model, it does not matter if technical debt keeps accumulating, because the goal is to find the correct business instead of developing something that does not have value to the business model. It would be easy for companies to just throw away the demo or prototype consisting of technical debt, if it would not be good part of the business model.

"I think that in the beginning start-up does not have to be worried about technical debt, because at that point you have not even validated if your idea good and does it grow to actual business. So technical debt at that point... just get features released and it might even be that the whole product will go to trashcan and also the technical debt at the same time. At that point let's just do something else." – D1.

The results indicate that while business model experimentation was clearly creating intentional technical debt, it was also required to be taken. The goal of the business model experimentation was to acquire customer feedback as fast as possible to confirm the assumptions made in the business model. This is the reason why companies had to take technical debt intentionally. It made the customer feedback cycle much faster and hypothetically decreased the possibility of unintentional technical debt as the next software development steps were validated with customer.

4.2 Finding 2: Development without Business Model Experimentation can Create Unintentional Technical Debt

Business model experimentation has also a relationship to unintentional technical debt. The interviewees described situations where the companies did not use business model experimentation as a tool to develop the business model. Instead, when companies got an idea to improve the business model with a new feature or a service, the software development was begun immediately without conducting customer validation first. We were able to see scenarios where the new ideas were successful without experimentation and the companies were able to improve the business model. However, we also saw scenarios where the idea got developed and after the release the company realized that customers had no need for that certain feature or service.

"When you think portfolio companies we have worked with that have not used any iterative development of business model, instead they have just gone after some big idea, they have also made huge mis-steps in their technology." – C1.

The reason for not to use experimentation was that the new idea appeared to be so good that the company decided to begin the development immediately. In addition, experimentation was seen as time consuming and expensive practice to do that could give competitor an edge to be first on the market. Instead, the company could just develop the feature instantly without losing any time while trying to get the feedback from the customers. One of the interviewees also mentioned that reason not to conduct experimentation was that customers were not always willing to take part to the experimentations, since the customer might not be interested in intermediate results.

"Sometimes it happens like that but not all the time customers are actually Interested in the intermediate results, so sometimes they don't want to be involved in that cycle. They just want the feature because they have a business need for it and they think everything is clear and it should be just implemented." – A3.

Sometimes companies go after a big idea and start the development instantly without first conducting customer validation through experimentation. These are examples where companies can incur technical debt to the product unintentionally. Even if the new idea would be developed really well with good scalability for the future ideas, if the idea does not fit to the current business model and the customer does not have any need for it, the unnecessary time used for the development can be seen as technical debt.

"Actually you could say that if we would now put a lot of effort and development to the idea we think is good and would develop it really well, we would not make a lot of technical debt. But actually if the business model would be wrong at that point, we would great a huge amount of technical debt." – A6.

4.3   Finding 3: Both Intentional and Unintentional Technical Debt can be Reduced with Business Model Experimentation

Business model experimentation can cause accumulation of technical debt because the goal of lean startup methodology and business model experimentation is to create a viable product with minimum effort. It requires shortcuts and workarounds in the development that is considered technical debt. However, business model experimentation can reduce both intentional and unintentional technical debt if used properly. We were able to identify situations where the business model experimentation was used to reduce intentional technical debt and to prevent unintentional technical debt.

The reason for the reduction of intentional technical debt was the customer feedback, which was acquired through business model experimentation that gave companies information how to prioritize the developed components in the product. With customer feedback, the companies were able see what was the most important for customers and were able to reduce previously intentionally taken technical debt from those areas.

The benefit of lean startup methodology and business model experimentation was the identification of wrong assumptions in the business model early and avoid wasting developer time on matters that customer's do not need or want. In these cases there is a possibility for a quick adaptation based on customer feedback. If the company learned that some feature did not have any business value, it was easy to just throw that part of the product to the trash without having a huge damage, since the solution was done already with major shortcuts and it would in any case have required refactoring and rewriting.

"I think that if we move forward by doing demos it is a good thing. When we have like weekly sprints, it does not matter if we go to wrong direction, we have only lost that one week by then, and sometimes not even that much." – A4.

"On the other hand we have thrown so much stuff to the trash can that we developed really fast previously and they should have been refactored, but we did not need them anymore because they were not important to customer." – D1.

Business model experimentation was also used to prevent unintentional technical debt. One of the interviewees explained us a situation that happened when a team had a great new business idea. One of the managers in the company assumed that the feature was so brilliant that there was no need for experimentation and customer feedback before development. However, the lean startup team insisted on gathering customer feedback to confirm the assumptions. The result was that the majority of customers thought the feature was useless and there was no need for it.

"So we had this good idea and we had little time to do the experiment design. But one of the managers was like "well I think that this is not necessary because it is so good idea". Anyways a team went to interview 20-30 customers and when they came back they said "Dammit, no one was interested, people thought it sucks." – B1.

In this case, by conducting the experimentation, the company was able to prevent unnecessary work and technical debt from happening. If the company would have skipped the experimentation and started to develop the feature, the amount of technical debt would have been huge, since all the work of the developers would have gone to waste and company would have not needed that feature in the business. However, now the company was able to prove that the assumptions of the current business model were wrong and it got valuable customer feedback to not develop the feature.

4.4   Finding 4: Focusing Too much on Business Model Experimentation and not on Technical Debt Reduction can have Consequences to the Product Quality

Business model experimentation is a great way for companies to receive fast customer feedback and to realize how to improve or change the current business model and the product. However, it can also create some challenging consequences in a long-term. We were able to identify some long-term problems that the case companies were facing when using the business model experimentation. The biggest challenge was the balance between developing new features and improving already existing features. Some of the interviewees felt that the business model experimentation is creating too much pressure to the development team and it is hard to improve features already consisting technical debt, because there is all the time a need for new features and prototypes demanded by customers. It can be argued that this has not been business model experimentation in the same sense that the lean startup method suggests, however.

"That is the problem because you also get a lot of features requested by the product line, and the problem is because they actually set deadlines on them. The thing is that those deadlines are not even related to the release window that we have. Although writing the code is quite easy, getting it in requires this downtime cycle. The downtime cycle is the biggest legacy or technical debt that we have. So architectural decisions have been made based on our customer and those decisions are killing us." – A3.

The consequence of continuing business model experimentation instead of paying technical debt back in already existing product was that the code base started to become too complex and challenging for further development. This resulted to slowness, breakdowns, bugs and scalability problems and the companies had to conduct a lot of refactoring and rewriting to fix the issues.

"Yes it is really complex at the moment and you really do not know what happens if you change some part of the code. Another problem is the scalability issues that is currently really weak. So we have had discussions that should we write this again." – A3.

"For example we talk now a lot about architecture because we just got three new developers and they told us that the product is slow and when you change something you will break something else. The team and product is getting bigger, so we must have some process to get technical debt in control, because otherwise nothing gets developed anymore." – D1.

The balance between business model experimentation and technical debt reduction is something that companies need to improve in the future. However, it is challenging because the competitive business environment forces companies to constantly improve and change their business model to gain advantages over competition. When the majority of company's focus goes into finding new business model possibilities through a series of experimentations, the focus on technical debt decreases and that can have consequences to the product quality.

5   Discussion

When combining the experiences and examples described by the interviewees, we can see that the growth of the business and product quality were connected with business model experimentation, reduction of technical debt and competence of the development team. We were able to see that companies had two ways to test their current business model and its assumptions. The first one was to develop the idea with a good design and scalability and release it to a customer when it was ready. We saw situations where companies developed the idea with a good design and then the release was a success. However, we could also identify cases where the well-designed new features were not that successful. The reason was in most cases wrong assumptions about the actual customer needs. According to McGrath [6] business model cannot be fully anticipated in advance and it should be rather learned through experimentation in discovery and development.

The second way was to test the business model with experimentation. There the companies figured out the minimal way to experiment with the customer if the assumptions were right or wrong before even starting the actual development. When a company had a clear vision about the business model and all the assumptions were confirmed, the company started to improve the feature that was previously developed with shortcuts for experimentation purposes. In these situations the overall development time was often longer and more expensive, since companies had to conduct series of experimentations before starting the development. Chesbrough [23] claims that some companies do not use business model experimentation, because it is time-consuming to create, conduct, obtain, interpret and understand the experimentations. This is why some companies prefer to just grow the current business model [23]. However, the experimentations conducted in studied cases helped a company to find the correct business model instead of using the wrong one. Most of the interviewees thought that even though using experimentations might take a longer time to create and release the features to the customer, it is still a better way to grow the business and create a good-quality product.

Another factor for a business to grow and create a quality product is the competence of the development team [24]. The use of a lean methodology and business model experimentation required a lot of competence to experiment and develop features in fast iterative cycles with a product in minimum viable state. When the development team had to work with the code base that had incurred already technical debt during the experimentation, it required a lot of experience and knowledge to be able to create solutions that have high quality and scalability, when the business model is evolving in the future.

Having a growing business and quality product can also depend on the reduction of technical debt. The companies in this case study were eager to make experimentations and try out demos and prototypes in fast phase to find out possible new business ideas and areas to great more successful business. However, when companies had a high focus on creating new businesses and features to answer to the demand of customer, the focus on improving existing features and reducing technical debt was low. The improvement and refactoring of existing code is important part of product overall quality [25,26]. We were able to identify situations where technical debt started to affect to the success of business and product quality. Sometimes there were situations where too much technical debt started to show as slowness and bug errors in the product. The quality of the product has a strong relationship with the customer satisfaction [27]. The problems in the product could transfer to negative customer satisfaction that can have consequences to the business of the company. At this stage companies had to start massive operation to refactor and rewrite parts of the product, which led to significant economic costs.

6   Conclusion

This paper has explored the relationship of business model experimentation and technical debt in the context of software development. Our analysis reveals that technical debt should be divided into intentional and unintentional in this context, and that product quality and the competence of the development team are elements that need to be considered. The overall result is that with business model experimentation, the amount of technical debt can be reduced. However, there may be an inverted U-shaped curve concerning the benefits of business model experimentation – it is a balancing act to do enough experimentation but not too extensively, and simultaneously pay careful attention on the amount of accumulating technical debt. The targets of experiments must be well-chosen and the competence of the development team sets pragmatic limitations on the amount of experiments that can be executed with a reasonable time-to-market goal. Further research could compare and measure both the amounts of technical debt and business model experimentation in specific projects and compare the levels to the success of the products and business model launch to learn more about the interrelationships of these constructs. As a limitation, this research mainly used informants from R & D. To get a more complete picture of this phenomenon, also marketing and product managers' viewpoints could be incorporated in the analysis more strongly.

Acknowledgement. We would like to thank the companies for being a valuable source of information and all interviewees who found time to share their experiences. This research has been carried out in Digile Need for Speed program, and funded by Tekes (the Finnish Funding Agency for Technology and Innovation).

References

1. Ries, E.: The Lean Startup: How Today's Entrepreneurs Use Continuous Innovation to Create Radically Successful Businesses, 1st edn. Crown Business, New York (2011)
2. Cunningham, W.: The WyCash Portfolio Management System, Experience Report (1992)
3. Teece, D.J.: Business Models, Business Strategy and Innovation. Long Range Planning 43(2-3), 172–194 (2010)
4. Zott, C., Amit, R.: Business Model Design: An Activity System Perspective. Long Range Planning 43(2-3), 216–226 (2010)
5. Casadesus-Masanell, R., Ricart, J.E.: From Strategy to Business Models and onto Tactics. Long Range Planning 43(2-3), 195–215 (2010)
6. McGrath, R.G.: Business Models: A Discovery Driven Approach. Long Range Planning 43(2-3), 247–261 (2010)
7. Doz, Y.L., Kosonen, M.: Embedding Strategic Agility: A Leadership Agenda for Accelerating Business Model Renewal. Long Range Planning 43(2-3), 370–382 (2010)
8. Bock, A.J., Opsahl, T., George, G., Gann, D.M.: The Effects of Culture and Structure on Strategic Flexibility during Business Model Innovation. Journal of Management Studies 49(2), 279–305 (2012)
9. Markides, C.: Disruptive Innovation: In Need of Better Theory*. Journal of Product Innovation Management 23(1), 19–25 (2006)

10. Casadesus-Masanell, R., Zhu, F.: Business model innovation and competitive imitation: The case of sponsor-based business models. Strat. Mgmt. J. 34(4), 464–482 (2013)
11. Mintzberg, H., Waters, J.A.: Of strategies, deliberate and emergent. Strat. Mgmt. J. 6(3), 257–272 (1985)
12. Dunford, R., Palmer, I., Benveniste, J.: Business Model Replication for Early and Rapid Internationalisation: The ING Direct Experience. Long Range Planning 43(5-6), 655–674 (2010)
13. Chesbrough, H.: Business Model Innovation: Opportunities and Barriers. Long Range Planning 43(2-3), 354–363 (2010)
14. Blank, S.: The Four Steps to the Epiphany, 2nd edn. K&S Ranch (2013)
15. Yli-Huumo, J., Maglyas, A., Smolander, K.: The Sources and Approaches to Management of Technical Debt: A Case Study of Two Product Lines in a Middle-Size Finnish Software Company. In: Jedlitschka, A., Kuvaja, P., Kuhrmann, M., Männistö, T., Münch, J., Raatikainen, M. (eds.) Product-Focused Software Process Improvement, pp. 93–107. Springer International Publishing (2014)
16. Tom, E., Aurum, A., Vidgen, R.: An exploration of technical debt. Journal of Systems and Software 86(6), 1498–1516 (2013)
17. Halbesleben, J.R.B., Wakefield, D.S., Wakefield, B.J.: Work-arounds in health care settings: Literature review and research agenda. Health Care Manage. Rev. 33(1), 2–12 (2008)
18. Corbett, A., Covin, J.G., O'Connor, G.C., Tucci, C.L.: Corporate Entrepreneurship: State-of-the-Art Research and a Future Research Agenda. J. Prod. Innov. Manag. 30(5), 812–820 (2013)
19. C. ©. M. I. of Technology and 1977-2015 All rights reserved, "Why Companies Should Have Open Business Models. MIT Sloan Management Review
20. McConnell, S.: Technical Debt-10x Software Development | Construx (November 1, 2007), http://www.construx.com/10x_Software_Development/Technical_Deb t/ (accessed: December 02, 2014)
21. Bourgeois III., L.J.: Strategic Goals, Perceived Uncertainty, and Economic Performance in Volatile Environments. The Academy of Management Journal 28(3), 548–573 (1985)
22. Hannabuss, S.: Research interviews. New Library World 97(5), 22–30 (1996)
23. Chesbrough, H.: Business model innovation: it's not just about technology anymore. Strategy & Leadership 35(6), 12–17 (2007)
24. Chow, T., Cao, D.-B.: A survey study of critical success factors in agile software projects. Journal of Systems and Software 81(6), 961–971 (2008)
25. Mens, T., Tourwé, T.: A Survey of Software Refactoring. IEEE Trans. Softw. Eng. 30(2), 126–139 (2004)
26. Middleton, P., Joyce, D.: Lean Software Management: BBC Worldwide Case Study. IEEE Transactions on Engineering Management 59(1), 20–32 (2012)
27. Jun, M., Yang, Z., Kim, D.: Customers' perceptions of online retailing service quality and their satisfaction. Int. J. Qual. & Reliability Mgmt. 21(8), 817–840 (2004)

Network Analysis of Platform Ecosystems: The Case of Internet of Things Ecosystem

Teemu Toivanen, Oleksiy Mazhelis[✉], and Eetu Luoma

Department of Computer Science and Information Systems,
University of Jyväskylä, Jyväskylä, Finland
{oleksiy.mazhelis,eetu.luoma}@jyu.fi

Abstract. Software platform providers are often seen as the cornerstone of their business ecosystem, where the other ecosystem players utilize the platform's standardized components together with complementary components for making applications. These platforms are also becoming a cornerstone of the emerging Internet of Things (IoT) business ecosystem comprised of the companies who provide Internet-enabled devices, applications, connectivity solutions, and the platforms for the IoT usage. While a number of enabling technologies for IoT is available, the question remains what kind of ecosystem emerges around IoT platform providers and whether this ecosystem is evolving in line with the theoretical models describing business ecosystem development. In order to address this question, we constructed a network model for the IoT ecosystem and considered how it had changed over the period of a year and a half. Our findings indicate that the ecosystem is still in early evolutionary phase, although some signs of consolidation are starting to appear. A mainstream solution is still missing and many vendors are trying to make their platform a dominating one.

Keywords: Internet of things · Software platform · Business ecosystem · Network analysis

1 Introduction

A platform can be defined as a cluster of technically standardized components that are used together with complementary components for making applications [1]. Platforms are known to be a critical element of successful businesses [2,3]; often they also serve as a core element of the business ecosystem to be built around it by the platform vendor, along with the producers of complementary elements and end users, among other players [4,5].

Recently, the importance of platforms was emphasized in the domain of the Internet of Things (IoT) that envisions a future worldwide intelligent network, where smart devices and people are all connected and can communicate with each other over standard Internet technologies [6,7,8]. Some parts of the IoT vision already exist in small scale: the smart devices connect to software platforms and applications use the data sent by the devices. Platforms are a critical element of IoT as they mediating heterogeneous smart devices and the applications and are enabling them to interoperate, and they can thus be seen as

© Springer International Publishing Switzerland 2015
J.M. Fernandes et al. (Eds.): ICSOB 2015, LNBIP 210, pp. 30–44, 2015.
DOI: 10.1007/978-3-319-19593-3_3

an integral part of IoT [9]. For the purposes of this study, we define an IoT platform as performing the following three functions: (i) managing and controlling devices connected to it, (ii) gathering and storing data from those devices, and (iii) offering tools to develop, publish and use applications benefiting from the gathered data. At the moment, the market of IoT platforms is fragmented, and there are dozens of different platforms that compete with each other [10].

There is a business ecosystem forming around the companies that provide devices, applications, connectivity and platforms for IoT usage [7]. In such an ecosystem, every participant has its own role and purpose [11]. The roles of the members and leader positions can change as the time passes, but all participants strive for the common goal and vision of developing the IoT domain further. Platform providers are often forming the core of the ecosystem and they supply the crucial building blocks for the other businesses [4,9]. Therefore, studying the partnerships of the platform providers is important for understanding the ecosystem development.

While the IoT enabling technologies – such as sensing and actuating devices, communication protocols, and cloud computing platforms – have been available for several years, the widespread diffusion of the IoT is still awaited. Numerous predictions exist in trade literature on the scale and the timing of such diffusion, though little transparency is usually provided on the background for these estimates. This paper is aimed at systematically assessing the diffusion of the IoT technologies, by comparing the developments in the IoT ecosystem against technology diffusion models described in the next section. Since platforms are the core and the building blocks of the IoT business, the platform providers and their partnerships were chosen for a closer look. The research question addressed in the paper can be formulated as follows: *Is the IoT platform ecosystem, as reflected in the structure and relationships between the platform vendors and the other players, evolving in line with known theoretical models?*

In this paper, we model the IoT platform ecosystem as a network of business partnerships formed around platform providers. By doing this for two distinct points in time (January 2013 and September 2014), we determine if and how the ecosystem had changed – for instance, if there have been changes in companies roles, or if the central players had changed. The model is then analyzed by using social network analysis tools and metrics.

The paper is organized as follows. In the next section, related research works are briefly overviewed. Section 3 describes the data gathering and analysis method used in this study. In section 4, the results of the analysis, i.e. the ecosystem model and its metrics, are presented. Section 5 considers how the results answer the stated research question, and discuss their implications. Finally, section 6 provides conclusions to the paper.

2   Related Work

By offering a set of components that are reusable across a spectrum of applications, platforms often form a core of a business ecosystem, where the platform vendor, the producers of the complementing services and the end users, among other players, co-exist and co-evolve [3,4]. Previous research on software platforms clearly indicates their importance for the business of individual players and for the prosperity of the ecosystem as a whole. In particular, Basole [9] had studied mobile ecosystems and came to the conclusion that platform providers have a central role in the ecosystem. Similarly, the key role of the platform vendors was found in other ecosystems, such as credit card ecosystem and game console ecosystem [12], as well as in the software ecosystem in general [13]. Likewise, in the context of IoT ecosystem, Schlautmann [14] states that the service enabler (i.e., platform provider) will likely occupy the most important and critical position in the IoT value chain, appropriating 30-40% share of total value.

The recent introduction of IoT platforms can be also seen as the phenomenon of technology diffusion, where a new technology is introduced to the market and is eventually adopted in the population of end users. Gort and Klepper [15] have studied the diffusion of product innovations and market entry for new products. They suggest that the markets for new products pass through five distinguishable stages in the course of their evolution. The stages include the commercial introduction of a new product and the first competing products (stage 1), the phase of rapid increase in the entry of competing products (stage 2) the period when the net entry of firms is largely equal to the net exit (stage 3), the period when structural changes in the industry result in a rapid decline in the net entry of new firms (stage 4), and the eventual product obsolescence or displacement with a new technology (stage 5).

The evolution of the IoT domain can be also seen as the vertical software industry evolution. According to Tyrväinen's model [16], a vertical software industry develops through the five phases of innovation, productization and standardization, adoption and transition, service and variation, and finally renewal phase. In the innovation phase, the software to support key business processes is developed mostly in-house by firms in the vertical industry. In the following phases, firms start to imitate each other's best practices in their solutions, which erode the difference between them. Some of these solutions are becoming a basis for spin-offs and, consequently, independent software vendors start developing competing offerings. In the adoption and transition phase, the competition among the solutions intensifies, eventually resulting in one-two leaders whose solutions shape the dominant design for the emerged class of solutions in the service and variation phase.

Several researchers have claimed that device heterogeneity and the lack of standardization is keeping IoT from further development. The rise of cheap sensors, new wireless communication technologies, sensor and actuator networks, and cloud computing has resulted in the application of these technologies to several vertical markets, creating heterogeneity [17]. Therefore, as emphasized by Delicato [18], the need emerges for IoT solutions to scale with millions of devices, as well as for the ability to deal with software and hardware heterogeneity, uncertainty detection and conflict resolution. In a similar manner, Biswas et al. [19] claims that in order to realize IoT vision targeting future markets, several requirements have to be taken into account, including ubiquitous accessibility and connectivity, as well as commonly agreed APIs and standards. To address the heterogeneity and standardization issue, for instance, ETSI and OneM2M alliances are attempting to unify standardization between IoT devices [10]. Nevertheless, due to these and other challenges, is has been noted in Gartner's IT Hype Cycle and forecast that it will take 5 to 10 years for any mature market for Internet of Things to emerge [20].

3   Modeling the Evolution of IoT Platform Ecosystem

The present study aims at building a view of the structure of IoT platform ecosystem and relationships between the firms in the ecosystem. This view can be employed to discuss the current phase and the evolution of the ecosystem. In this section we describe our approach towards modeling the IoT platform ecosystem as a network of inter-firm partnerships. Specifically, the section provides the details of the data gathering and introduces the employed network metrics.

3.1   Research Data

To build a view of the IoT ecosystem, data was collected and classified regarding the IoT firms and their relationships. The initial set of IoT firms to be included in the study was assembled by merging the lists of companies contributing to or following IoT standardization activities. In particular, this was accomplished by merging the member lists of ZigBee, ETSI M2M, and oneM2M alliances that are focusing on standardization of IoT-related communication technologies. In order to categorize the companies, we utilized a subset of five roles from the list of IoT ecosystem roles defined in [7]. The definitions of these roles are provided in Table 1, along with the number of firms found to play this role.

Table 1. IoT ecosystem roles that were included in the study

Role	Definition	Number of firms
Device manufacturer	Makes components and physical devices for IoT use	414
Gateway	Connects IoT-enabled devices to Internet through single access point	20
Network operator	Provides Internet connection to users	47
Platform	Gathers and stores data from IoT-devices and allows applications to use the data	32
Application developer	Creates and deploys software applications on the platform for end users	176

Each company's website was studied and the company was labeled with one or several roles. The total number of companies across these alliances was 1412 (in 2013). Many companies had only the roles irrelevant to this study, such as consultancy or research companies; those were excluded from further consideration.

The connections between platform providers were primarily identified by studying the companies' websites and searching for the list of partners or for other clues indicating partnerships. As a secondary information source, the trade outlets such as M2M Magazine and M2M World News were used to search for the news articles reporting or analyzing partnerships involving platform providers. The data was originally gathered and stored in January 2013, and then verified and expanded in September 2014.

3.2   Data Analysis

A set of network analysis techniques was employed to create a view of the IoT platform ecosystem as a network of inter-firm partnerships. Visualizing the research data helps to distinguish various network elements and they relevance in complex systems [9]. In cases when an exploratory visual representation of the actors and their connectivity is required, a node-link diagram is frequently preferred [21]. This diagram includes only two elements in the network: the nodes (firms) and the links (partnerships). The links can be directed or non-directed. In this study, we created a diagram with non-directed links, for the partnerships implies both firms to be interacting with each other.

In addition, a number of metrics have been calculated and analyzed in order to assess the development of IoT platform ecosystem. Some metrics analyze only a single node, e.g., degree, closeness and betweenness centralities, while the other metrics analyze the whole network [22]. The metrics that were used in this study are summarized in Table 2. The network analysis was executed using Pajek [23], which both produces visual presentations of the network and calculates the relevant metrics.

Table 2. Metrics utilized in the study

Name	Affects	Description
Degree centrality	Single node	Number of links a node has
Closeness centrality	Single node	How close a node is to all other nodes
Betweenness centrality	Single node	Number of shortest paths passing trough a node
Eigenvector centrality	Single node	How connected a node is to other highly connected nodes
Network density	Whole network	Relations between nodes/All possible relations
Network degree centralization	Whole network	How central the most central node is to all other nodes
Network clustering coefficient (Transitivity)	Whole network	How close nodes are clustered
Watts-Strogatz clustering coefficient	Whole network	How easy it is for nodes to reach each other
Number of unreachable pairs	Whole network	Nodes which can't connect with each other
Average distance among reachable pairs	Whole network	Number of nodes on average path length
The most distance between vertices	Whole network	Longest path in the network between two nodes

4   Results

Fig. 1 shows the node-link diagrams of the IoT platform ecosystem for 2013 and 2014, where the large black hubs represent platforms, and the nodes around them represent their partners. Nodes in the middle are partners who have links to at least two platforms, and on the outer edge of the network are partners with one link only.

The network for 2013 has 32 platforms, 399 partners and 555 connecting links, while the network for 2014 has 34 platforms, 548 partners and 870 connecting links. Thus, in 2014, there are significantly more links between platform vendors and their partners compared to a year and a half earlier, i.e. the companies became more interconnected. Still, no clear "platform leader" can be identified in the figure.

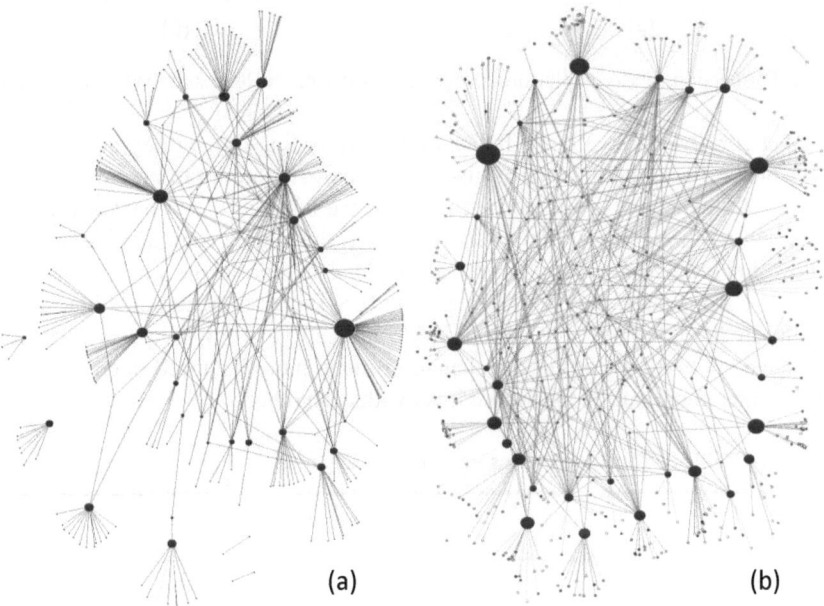

(a)   (b)

Fig. 1. Ecosystem of IoT platform providers and their partners in (a) January 2013 and (b) September 2014 (Fruchterman-Reingold algorithm)

The partnerships between platform providers are shown in Fig. 2. The graph on the left side portraying the situation in January 2013 indicates that there are some platforms that have little or no interaction with other platforms. These companies have vertically integrated their own product built on top of their platforms, and they are selling these products directly to their customers.

The graph on the right side depicts the situation in September 2014. We notice a change in the structure; there are only four platforms, which are not connected with the other platforms in the ecosystem. Also, the platforms have much more connections with each other. We also observed some changes in ownerships. For instance, iDigi has been integrated into Etherios, Sensorlogic was acquired by Gemalto, and SmartThings was acquired by Samsung.

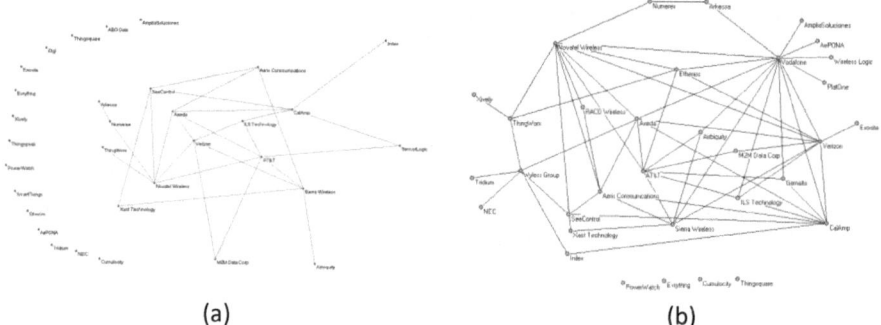

(a)   (b)

Fig. 2. Partnerships between platform providers in (a) January 2013 and (b) September 2014

Degree centrality. Table 3 ranks IoT platforms according to their degree centrality in 2014, which reflects the number of links a node has. According to Freeman [22], high degree centrality nodes are important in the sense that they can control information flow going to other nodes trough them. However, the degree centrality itself does not tell how important nodes' links are. Table 3 also reports the changes in degree centrality. For instance, Novatel Wireless and ILS Technology had the highest degree centrality in 2013, but over the period of one and half year only two new partnerships were added. Overall, we observe a change of much more balanced degree centrality, after the other companies added more links with each other.

Table 3. Top 15 IoT firms ranked according to their degree centrality

Rank	Name	Links in 2014	% of whole network	New links in 2014	Change in %
1	Axeda	94	5,40 %	37	0,26 %
2	Novatel Wireless	93	5,34 %	2	-2,86 %
3	ThingWorx	61	3,51 %	42	1,80 %
4	ILS Technology	60	3,45 %	2	-1,78 %
5	SeeControl	55	3,16 %	22	0,19 %
6	Vodafone	42	2,41 %	35	1,78 %
7	Cumulocity	36	2,07 %	11	-0,18 %
8	Sierra Wireless	35	2,01 %	14	0,12 %
9	Wyless Group	35	2,01 %	30	1,56 %
10	Gemalto	34	1,95 %	10	-0,21 %
11	Airbiquity	30	1,72 %	2	-0,80 %
12	Arkessa	30	1,72 %	19	0,73 %
13	CalAmp	28	1,61 %	4	-0,55 %
14	Aeris Communications	24	1,38 %	7	-0,15 %
15	Verizon	24	1,38 %	13	0,39 %

Closeness centrality. Closeness centrality, reported in Table 4, indicate how close a node is to all other nodes. A high closeness for a node means that it is related to all others through a small number of paths [25,22]. The closer the node is to other nodes, the easier it is for the node to receive information in the network [23]. As can be seen from the table, the closeness centrality has increased for the companies between the two data points from the year 2013 and the year 2014. This can be attributed to the increase in number of nodes and links in the network. Similarly to the degree centrality, the scores between the companies on closeness centrality have become more leveled.

Access to the information can be seen as a success factor in becoming a central player in IoT ecosystem. According to [26], companies benefit also from indirect links, which closeness centrality reflects. They can get information through indirect links without the need to use resources to maintain the relationships. Because IoT ecosystem is not yet fully established, the access to information is critical. Companies with many indirect links gain more information and can use that to get competitive advantage.

Table 4. Top 15 IoT firms ranked according to their closeness centrality

Rank	Name	Closeness centrality in 2014	Closeness centrality in 2013	Change
1	Vodafone	0,4265	0,3540	20,49 %
2	Axeda	0,4154	0,3694	12,44 %
3	Novatel Wireless	0,4136	0,3701	11,75 %
4	Kore Telematics	0,3974	0,3318	19,76 %
5	Verizon	0,3896	0,3363	15,84 %
6	Oracle	0,3862	0,3094	24,83 %
7	Wyless Group	0,3816	0,2814	35,62 %
8	CalAmp	0,3766	0,3121	20,68 %
9	SeeControl	0,3740	0,3375	10,83 %
10	Aeris Communications	0,3740	0,3158	18,44 %
11	Sprint	0,3701	0,3433	7,81 %
12	AT&T	0,3687	0,3442	7,12 %
13	ILS Technology	0,3634	0,3386	7,32 %
14	ThingWorx	0,3634	0,2887	25,86 %
15	Tech Mahindra	0,3620	0,2822	28,29 %

Betweenness centrality. Betweenness centrality is the number of shortest paths that pass through a given node. It tells how central position the node has in the network based on the amount of traffic that goes trough it [23]. If high betweenness node is removed, a number of links may get disconnected. These nodes are valued in the network and their existence helps the network to grow and function [22].

The betweenness centrality of the IoT firms in the study and the change of the scores are reported in Table 5. Again, we notice some companies – i.e. Novatel and ILS – with decreasing scores balancing the overall differences between company scores. Some companies like Wyless Group (ranked 9th) and Tech Mahindra (ranked 18th) have risen in the rankings, which suggests that these firms are becoming more important in interconnecting other IoT companies.

Table 5. Top 15 IoT firms ranked according to their betweenness centrality

Rank	Name	Betweenness centrality in 2014	Betweenness centrality in 2013	Change
1	Novatel Wireless	0,2643	0,3512	-24,74 %
2	Axeda	0,222	0,2641	-15,94 %
3	Vodafone	0,213	0,0993	114,47 %
4	ThingWorx	0,1624	0,0471	244,79 %
5	ILS Technology	0,1275	0,2062	-38,17 %
6	SeeControl	0,1166	0,1111	4,95 %
7	Cumulocity	0,1002	0,0891	12,46 %
8	Arkessa	0,0804	0,0396	102,96 %
9	Wyless Group	0,0748	0,0128	484,34 %
10	CalAmp	0,0712	0,0930	-23,44 %
11	Gemalto	0,0674	0,0695	-3,09 %
12	AmpliaSoluciones	0,0647	0,0890	-27,30 %
13	Verizon	0,0618	0,0488	26,70 %
14	Airbiquity	0,0603	0,0959	-37,12 %
15	Sierra Wireless	0,0548	0,1161	-52,80 %
(18	Tech Mahindra	0,0417	0,0032	1191,98 %)

Eigenvector centrality. Eigenvector centrality is calculated by assessing how well a node is connected to the parts of the network with the greatest connectivity. This is similar to Google's page rankings, where links from highly linked-to pages are more valued [27]. High eigenvector centrality nodes can be leaders of the network, e.g., public figures with many connections to other high-profile individuals [28].

Table 6. Top 15 IoT firms ranked according to their eigenvector centrality

Rank	Name	Eigenvector centrality in 2014	Eigenvector centrality in 2013	Change
1	Axeda	0,4159	0,3517	18,23 %
2	Novatel Wireless	0,3386	0,5211	-35,01 %
3	Vodafone	0,2183	0,1138	91,77 %
4	SeeControl	0,2023	0,2190	-7,61 %
5	ILS Technology	0,1774	0,2291	-22,58 %
6	Aeris Communications	0,1630	0,1036	57,29 %
7	Wyless Group	0,1627	0,0563	188,85 %
8	ThingWorx	0,1591	0,0935	70,05 %
9	Verizon	0,1531	0,1682	-9,02 %
10	Kore Telematics	0,1518	0,1310	15,91 %
11	AT&T	0,1474	0,1843	-20,04 %
12	Sprint	0,1405	0,1248	12,54 %
13	Etherios	0,1362	0,0166	721,23 %
14	CalAmp	0,1349	0,1311	2,93 %
15	Sierra Wireless	0,1260	0,1043	20,82 %
(16	Oracle	0,1109	0,0851	30,41 %)

As Table 6 indicates, in this study the overall eigenvector centrality is increasing over the period of one and half year. This is associated with the increased number of connections between the platforms. We notice some major changes in the companies' scores. For instance, eigenvector centrality for Novatel and ILS has decreased significantly. However, this is again related to the increase in the number of connections of the other platforms vendors, whereas for these two vendors the number of partnerships has largely remained intact.

Network-wide metrics are summarized in Table 7. Network density is the number of actual relations between nodes divided by the number of possible relations. In inter-firm relation networks, higher density indicates a greater degree of interaction among the firms [9]. In our case, the density has decreased by approximately 12 percent. This can be explained by the increased number of new nodes in the network (149) and by the fact that most of the new partners have connection to only a single platform. Note that in the ecosystem where platform end users or customers would be partnering with each other at a large scale is highly unlikely, and therefore the density can never be very high (0.005 density means 0.5 percent of all possible links are present).

Table 7. Network-wide metrics values for the IoT ecosystem

Metric	2014	2013	Change
Network density	0,00503	0,00571	-11,94 %
Network degree centralization	0,15384	0,19517	-21,18 %
Network clustering coefficient (Transitivity)	0,02211	0,00776	184,89 %
Watts-Strogatz clustering coefficient	0,20469	0,09502	115,43 %
Number of unreachable pairs	2320	16052	-85,55 %
Average distance among reachable pairs	3,68941	4,09916	-10,00 %
The most distance between vertices	6	10	-40,00 %

Degree centralization reflects how central the most central node is in relation to the centrality of all the other nodes. A network with high degree centralization is likely to have a few nodes with many ties and many nodes with few ties, such as a hub in a pinwheel structure [9]. Degree centralization has also decreased in 2014, indicating that smaller platform vendors have gained more links to balance themselves out with the larger ones. In 2013, Novatel, ILS and Axeda had 18,6 percent of all the links in the network, and in 2014 that ratio has decreased to 14,1 percent.

Network clustering coefficient describes clustering in the whole network. In social network context, this means that the friend of your friend is also likely to be your friend [29]. Clustering has almost tripled from 2013, implying that if two platform providers work with a partner, they became more likely to work with each other, too.

Watts-Strogatz clustering, also referred to as "small world network", measures how easy it is for nodes to reach each other [30]. This is related to the largest distance between nodes. While Watts-Strogratz clustering has doubled, largest distance has lowered almost by half. These metrics seem to correlate with each other, reflecting the consolidation starting to take place in the IoT ecosystem.

The number of unreachable pairs measures how many pairs of nodes in the network cannot connect to each other. Decrease from 16052 to 2320 is quite remarkable, meaning that the network is way more interconnected in 2014. Finally, the average distance among reachable pairs – indicating how many nodes are in the path between two nodes – has decreased as well, but not that significantly.

5   Discussion

In the previous sections, the IoT ecosystem was modeled as a network of partnerships formed around IoT platforms, and the development of the ecosystem has been assessed in terms of various network metrics. Given that the data gathering was centered on the IoT platforms, or more specifically, on the partnerships thereof, it comes at no surprise, that platform providers exhibit the most connectivity in the produced network model: according to the degree centrality, all the top ranked companies are platforms providers. It is therefore interesting to consider the cases when the high connectivity is exhibited by the firms other than platform vendors.

Such well-connected non-platform firms are, e.g., Oracle and Sprint, which are ranked high in terms of closeness and eigenvector centralities. Oracle's top position can be attributed to the fact that its database and cloud solutions are often used along with the IoT platforms. Sprint, on the other hand, is a network operator with numerous M2M-related solutions making its various partners to bring complementing capabilities, albeit Sprint does not offer an open platform itself. Another exemplary firm that comes up in closeness and betweenness centrality is Tech Mahindra, an Indian IT firm that had climbed up to the top betweenness ranks with an 1100 percent increase from 2013. The company offers many M2M-related services and solutions, and is partnered with several big platforms including Axeda, Aeris Communications, PowerWatch, Sierra Wireless, ThingWorx and Vodafone. Due to their central position in the information flows within the IoT ecosystem, these three companies have the higher possibilities to become major players in the ecosystem in future.

According to Schlautmann [14], network operators are expected to expand their business model to encompass other roles in the IoT value chain, besides serving as a network operator, in order to become more valuable in the ecosystem and gain a better position to make revenue. Likewise, Visionmobile's research on telecom operator's role in M2M ecosystem implies that most operators are attempting to move up in the value chain towards vertical solutions, even if it is not their core business [31]. This is also visible in our study: in our list of platforms, there are few network operators, including Novatel Wireless, Vodafone, Verizon, and AT&T; among these, Vodafone is pushing towards the top, while Novatel has barely any increase in new partnerships. Nevertheless, all of these operators have taken interest towards IoT development, expanding their roles beyond network provider.

Let us now consider how these network metrics match the technology diffusion models available in the literature. In Gort and Klepper's lifecycle model, the first stage begins with a new product introduction [15]. In the context of IoT, the first products using key enabling technologies, such as RFID-chips and wireless sensor networks, have emerged years ago, although it is difficult to determine who pioneered their use in products. In the stage two, a rapid growth in the number of producers takes place, with dozens of software platforms, many component manufacturers and application developers emerging. This is apparently where the IoT ecosystem is at the moment, as it is still growing and trying to evolve and adapt. In particular, network-wide metrics show that the ecosystem has increased in size, but also tightened up, since there is more clustering, and since platform providers are making more partnerships with each other and with same third parties. This is in line with suggested second stage in the Gort and Klepper's model. The stage three would occur when the number of entering and exiting firms balances net entry to zero; there is no data in the gathered data set to suggest the IoT ecosystem is entering this stage yet.

Tyrväinen's model of vertical software industry evolution [16] suggests that in the first – innovation phase – the leading vendors are reluctant to share their knowledge with external software companies, and hence tend to keep the innovative software development in-house, thereby creating barriers for new competitors. Also, some other competitors may join forces to provide an alternative solution. However, as the technological development continues, in the second phase – productization and standardization phase – the firms competing in an industry start imitating the emerging best solutions and practices. As a result, the differentiation between the competing offerings eventually dissolves, and the companies start replacing in-house development with purchasing software from the other vendors.

This kind of behavior appears to take place in the IoT ecosystem's development. Specifically, there are two platform vendors in our study – Novatel and ILS – that seem to be decreasing their score in every metric. They might have been early adopters of the technology, becoming strong ecosystem players while the competition was relatively low. Later on, however, other platforms emerged and gained success; as a result, while Novatel's closed platform worked for them in the past, now it seems to be hurting their growth. Overall, though the best practices haven't been fully distilled in the IoT field yet, and the rapid proliferation of the platforms indicates the trend towards acquiring software products from external providers – both are indications of the IoT ecosystem being in the productization and standardization phase. The consolidation in the IoT platform ecosystem, which is reflected in the increasing clustering coefficients and decreasing distance among reachable pairs, suggests that the ecosystem is in the productization and standardization phase, too.

Tyrväinen's model also suggests that industry evolution may halt because the lack of sufficient customer base of commonly accepted technology standards needed for proceeding to the further phases [16]. This reflects straight to the previous observations that IoT standardization needs to be develop further.

Based on the available data, it is challenging, if at all possible, to forecast which platform vendor will become the dominant player in the IoT ecosystem. The ecosystem is evolving, and the best practices and standards are still being distilled. One of the keys to success is creating value to the end users and finding such business model constellations that would allow various ecosystem players to co-exist and successfully co-evolve [32]. Further, whereas connectivity and smart devices are enablers, the real value for the end users is likely created by making sense of the data that those devices generate [33]. Many of upcoming IoT platforms today are focused on solving technical challenges, rather than on empowering developers with the tools for efficiently implementing innovative applications. Finally, due to the multi-sided nature of the platform business, managing successful platforms also means managing various people, including users, developers, individuals and companies. We quote Schuermans & Vakulenko [33]: "You can buy an audience, but you can't buy a community". It appears that Vodafone, ThingWorx and Wyless Group are fastest rising platforms in all metrics in 2014, so they might be approaching their community building correctly.

6   Conclusions

Platforms are known to be a critical element of successful software business, and they are often a core element of the business ecosystem built around them. In this paper, in order to assess how the IoT ecosystem is evolving, the IoT platform ecosystem has been modeled as a network of business partnerships formed around platform providers. Furthermore, the change that had happened in this partnership network over the period of a year and a half has been investigated.

The results of the analysis can be summarized as follows:

- The number of connections (partnerships) among the ecosystem players has increased significantly. Furthermore, the former leaders with closed platforms, such as Novatel Wireless and ILS Technology, are losing their positions, as the network metrics demonstrate.
- Meanwhile, some other roles – specifically, integrators (e.g. Tech Mahindra) and network operators (e.g. Vodafone, Sprint) – gain weight in the ecosystem. In line with Schlautmann's prediction, it has been found that the network operators aim for the role of the platform vendor in the ecosystem.
- As of September 2014, no clear "platform leader" can be identified in the IoT ecosystem. Some consolidation is taking place, as reflected in the increasing clustering coefficients and decreasing distance among reachable pairs, in line with the productization and standardization phase of vertical software industry evolution model. An intensifying competition among platforms, common for the adoption and transition phase, can thus be envisioned in near future, followed by the eventual appearance of a dominant design.

The present study signifies the effectiveness of network analysis in studying software and other IT-based ecosystems. Combined with technology diffusion models, the study provides an analysis and an explanation of the IoT diffusion as the phenomenon of interest. This is to say, the combination of network analysis and diffusion models reveals insights to the current state of the IoT diffusion as well as some future predictions. It seems that the IoT diffusion has been slow due to lack of commonly accepted standards and dominant design in general. Under such conditions, majority of the companies are holding back their investments to this novel technology. We expect increased competition in the IoT domain while companies strive for achieving the dominant design.

It shall be noted that, due to the data gathering approach used, the study suffers from some limitations. In particular, only platform provider's partnerships were studied, therefore leaving the second-tier partners out. Further, since not all platform vendors have been included in the studied sample, and since not all platform vendors kept their partnership list available and up to date, the resulting data set is rather limited, and only provides a subset of the partnerships in the IoT ecosystem. In future work, professional databases such as SDC Platinum or LexisNexis will be used in order to gather a more comprehensive list of relevant players and partnerships.

Acknowledgments. This work was partially supported by TEKES as part of the Internet of Things program of DIGILE (Finnish Strategic Centre for Science, Technology and Innovation in the field of ICT and digital business).

References

1. Greenstein, S.: Industrial economics and strategy: computing platforms. IEEE Micro 18(3), 43–53 (1998)
2. Baldwin, C.Y., Clark, K.B.: Design Rules. The Power of Modularity, vol. 1. MIT Press, Cambridge (2000)
3. Baldwin, C.Y., Woodard, C.J.: The Architecture of Platforms: A Unified View. Platforms, Markets and Innovation, 19–44 (2009)
4. Gawer, A., Cusumano, M.A.: Industry Platforms and Ecosystem Innovation. Journal of Product Innovation Management 31, 417–433 (2014)
5. Woodard, C.J., Clemons, E.K.: The Evolution of Modular Product Architectures and the Emergence of Platform Ecosystems, Research Collection School Of Information Systems (2013), http://ink.library.smu.edu.sg/sis_research/1929
6. Haller, S., Karnouskos, S., Schroth, C.: The internet of things in an enterprise context, pp. 14–28. Springer, Heidelberg (2009)
7. Mazhelis, O., Luoma, E., Warma, H.: Defining an internet-of-things ecosystem. In: Andreev, S., Balandin, S., Koucheryavy, Y. (eds.) NEW2AN/ruSMART 2012. LNCS, vol. 7469, pp. 1–14. Springer, Heidelberg (2012)
8. Kim, J., Lee, J., Kim, J., Yun, J.: M2M Service Platforms: Survey, Issues, and Enabling Technologies. IEEE Communications Surveys & Tutorials 16(1), 61–76 (2014)
9. Basole, R.: Visualization of interfirm relations in a converging mobile ecosystem. Journal of Information Technology 24(2), 144–159 (2009)
10. Balamuralidhara, P., Misra, P., Pal, A.: Software Platforms for Internet of Things and M2M. Journal of the Indian Institute of Science 93(3), 487–498 (2013)
11. Moore, J.F.: The Death of Competition: Leadership & Strategy in the Age of Business Ecosystems. HarperBusiness, New York (1996)
12. Evans, D., Hagiu, A., Schmalensee, R.: Invisible Engines: How Software Platforms Drive Innovation and Transform Industries. MIT Press, Boston (2006)
13. Iyer, B., Lee, C.H., Venkatraman, N.: Managing in a small world ecosystem: Some lessons from the software sector. California Management Review (2006)
14. Schlautmann, A., Levy, D., Keeping, S., Pankert, G.: Wanted: Smart market-makers for the 'Internet of Things' (2011), http://www.adlittle.se/prism_se.html?&view=383

15. Gort, M., Klepper, S.: Time paths in the diffusion of product innovations. The Economic Journal, 630–653 (1982)
16. Tyrvainen, P., Mazhelis, O. (eds.): Vertical Software Industry Evolution. Physica-Verlag HD (2009)
17. Berkers, F., Roelands, M., Bomhof, F., Bachet, T., van Rijn, M., Koers, W.: Constructing a multi-sided business model for a smart horizontal IoT service platform. In: ICIN, pp. 126–132 (October 2013)
18. Delicato, F.C., Pires, P.F., Batista, T., Cavalcante, E., Costa, B., Barros, T.: Towards an IoT ecosystem. In: Proceedings of the First International Workshop on Software Engineering for Systems-of-Systems, pp. 25–28. ACM (July 2013)
19. Biswas, A.R., Giaffreda, R.: IoT and cloud convergence: Opportunities and challenges. In: Internet of Things (WF-IoT), 2014 IEEE World Forum, pp. 375–376 (2014)
20. Gubbi, J., Buyya, R., Marusic, S., Palaniswami, M.: Internet of Things (IoT): A vision, architectural elements, and future directions. Future Generation Computer Systems 29(7), 1645–1660 (2013)
21. Keller, R., Eckert, C.M., Clarkson, P.J.: Matrices or Node-Link Diagrams: Which visual representation is better for visualising connectivity models? Information Visualization 5(1), 62–76 (2006)
22. Freeman, L.: Centrality in social networks conceptual clarification. Social Networks 1(3), 215–239 (1979)
23. de Nooy, W., Mrvar, A., Batagelj, V.: Exploratory Social Network Analysis with Pajek, vol. 27. Cambridge University Press (2005)
24. Iyer, B.: M-Payment Ecosystem. Babson College (2012), http://www.slideshare.net/balaiyer/m-payment-ecosystem-analysis
25. Otte, E., Rousseau, R.: Social network analysis: a powerful strategy, also for the information sciences. Journal of Information Science 28, 441–453 (2002)
26. Ahuja, G.: Collaboration networks, structural holes, and innovation: A longitudinal study. Administrative Science Quarterly 45(3), 425–455 (2000)
27. Cheliotis, G.: Social Network Analysis (SNA) including a tutorial on concepts and methods (2010), http://www.slideshare.net/gcheliotis/social-network-analysis-3273045
28. Active Networks: Who is central to a social network? It depends on your centrality measure (2014), http://www.activatenetworks.net/who-is-central-to-a-social-network-it-depends-on-your-centrality-measure/#
29. Newman, M.E.: The structure and function of complex networks. SIAM Review 45(2), 167–256 (2003)
30. Watts, D.J., Strogatz, S.H.: Collective dynamics of 'small-world'networks. Nature 393(6684), 440–442 (1998)
31. Constantinou, A.: The M2M Ecosystem Recipe. How telcos can win the M2M game by playing by ecosystem rules. VisionMobile, London (2013)
32. Jumira, O., Wolhuter, R.: Value chain scenarios for M2M ecosystem. In: 2011 IEEE GLOBECOM Workshops (GC Wkshps), pp. 410–415. IEEE (2011)
33. Schuermans, S., Vakulenko, M.: IoT Breaking Free of Internet and Things. VisionMobile, London (June 2014)

Exploring Network Modelling and Strategy in the Dutch Software Business Ecosystem

Wesley Crooymans[✉], Priyanka Pradhan, and Slinger Jansen

Utrecht University, Buys Ballot Laboratorium, Princetonplein 5, Utrecht, The Netherlands
{W.A.S.Crooijmans,P.Pradhan}@students.uu.nl
slinger.jansen@uu.nl

Abstract. In today's product software market, the practices of re-use, partnering and 3rd party contracting give rise to complex software ecosystems. Over the duration of a product life-cycle, product software vendors build up relationships with their suppliers and other partners, which range from informal acknowledgements of each other's presence to strategic alliances. There is still a lack of understanding surrounding the roles, connections, relationships, and resulting networks within software ecosystems. Using modelling techniques and statistical analysis, these networks can be used as tools to further that understanding. In this paper a collection of 67 software supply networks will be modelled as a network graph. Using clustering and two extensions of basic software supply network data, we identify several major players and domains in the Dutch software industry. Three business strategy perspectives are then related to the data to provide an example of their potential practical use.

Keywords: Software ecosystems modeling · Network modeling · Product software · Software business strategy

1   Introduction

Problem Statement. A Software Ecosystem (SECO) model can be a powerful aid to describe the position and role of a software business within its environment[1]. With various modelling methods and algorithms available today, there is no shortage on fancy visuals and beautiful graphics to shed a light on your ecosystem. The question to ask is, *How can software ecosystem models be used to analyze strategic interests in a local software ecosystem?* In this paper we will answer that question by presenting a method for modelling, analyzing and interpreting ecosystem data, applied to a study of the Dutch product software industry. To portray some of the ways in which these models may be of use as tools to the business world, the data will be related to existing papers on (SECO) business strategy.

Domain. The work in this paper lies firmly within the domain of SECOs. Throughout this paper the definition of Jansen, Finkelstein, and Brinkkemper (2009) will be used: "We define a SECO as a set of businesses functioning as a unit and interacting with a shared market for software and services, together with the relationships among them.

J.M. Fernandes et al. (Eds.): ICSOB 2015, LNBIP 210, pp. 45–59, 2015.
DOI: 10.1007/978-3-319-19593-3_4

These relationships are frequently underpinned by a common technological platform or market and operate through the exchange of information, resources and artifacts."[2]

In a SECO there are number of strategies an organization can adopt. The kind of strategic decisions that are available depend on the individual organization and their perspective on the ecosystem. Iansiti and Levien stated that there are three roles that influence ecosystem health and evolution. Some known strategies are partnering, membership programs, mergers and acquisition etc. For example Cisco used merger and acquisition strategy to be the keystone player in their ecosystem, which helped them to foster success for the whole ecosystem as well as to generate revenue [3].

Our area of interest is business models in the software industry, and particularly the relationships among the various suppliers, vendors, retailers and customers surrounding software products. Software products in this paper include all software packages and services that are traded as standard products [4], including but not limited to Consumer-Of-The-Shelf (COTS), standard software, shrink-wrapped software, Software as a Service (SaaS), open source software, and any packages or configurations of the former.

One way of modelling these SECO relationships, is the so called Software Supply Network (SSN) model. A software supply network, according to Jansen, Brinkkemper and Finkelstein (2007), is "a series of linked software, hardware, and service organizations cooperating to satisfy market demands"[5]. The accompanying modelling method describes SSNs in two parts; the product context and the supply network. The product context describes which products and services make a complete software product, and a supply network describes all parties involved in the SSN including the flows of goods, services and finances between them [5]. The supply network notation from this modelling method was also used to create the dataset used throughout this paper, which will be described in more detail in the method section. In the broad business model definition of Osterwalder, Pigneur, and Tucci, SSN models would occupy the instance level which consists of representations of real world business models [6].

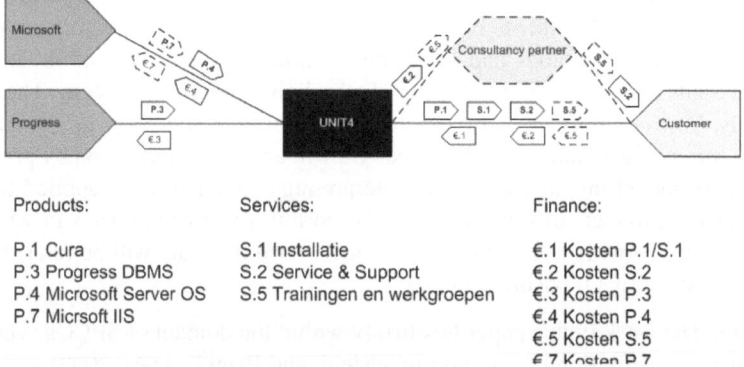

Fig. 1. SSN Supply network example

Suppliers of software, hardware, services or content are drawn as orange rectangles with a pointed right edge. Intermediaries that act as partners, implementers or resellers are drawn as green rectangles with two pointed edges. Customers are represented as yellow rectangles with a pointed left edge. Finally, the vendors of a product are the central focus object of an SSN, and these are drawn as blue rectangles. Flows between elements in an SSN are represented as simple lines, annotated with the contents of the flow in pointed rectangles. See figure 1 above for an example.

Outline. Section 2 covers the clean-up and preparing of data for the rest of the paper, as well as the methods used for analysis. In section 3 the dataset will be described in more detail. This section will also cover the process of modelling the data in Gephi and the methods used to visualize the data. The additions made for the 2013 extended case and Microsoft case are also be described. Section 4 will present the results of community detection and preliminary findings from the extended 2013 case and Microsoft case. In section 5 these findings will be related to SECO strategy literature in academia. The paper concludes with a discussion in section 6 and a conclusion in section 7.

2   Method

In this section, we elaborate on the methods used in this paper, like the collection of data, the process of conducting statistical analysis and the application of analytical methods. Many of the concepts explored in this section are closely related to the research area of Social Network Analysis (SNA), where subjects like node centrality and clustering have long since been explored [7].

Data. The data source for this research was obtained from several SSN modelling case studies performed in the product software market in the Netherlands. These case studies were conducted by Utrecht University undergraduate students as part of a product software course. Our data set consists of supply network models created over three years (2010, '11 and '13).

As a part of the undergrad course, students were asked to perform interviews at a company selling software products. The only criterion on company choices was ownership in the Netherlands. The purpose of these interviews was to investigate how companies built and sold their products, to the point that SSNs could be created by the students. Not all students performed their assignments up to the same standards of quality. To assure that only high quality data was available for this project, several criteria were used to exclude certain low quality cases:

1. **Unnamed Partners.** In cases where a lot of suppliers and/or intermediaries were not given a proper company name (e.g. 'hardware vendor', 'consultant'), the data was considered unusable and the case was removed.
2. **Illogical Flows.** In some cases students failed to accurately model the flow of products, services and finances between parties in the SSN (e.g. finances flowing

from A to B for no product or service from B to A). Singular illogical flows were removed from the cases. Large numbers of illogical flows led to case removal.
3. **Irrelevant for the Vendor Ecosystem.** In some cases students included suppliers that had no interaction with the product or the vendor providing it (e.g. A supplier selling servers to the customer directly). Suppliers that had no meaningful contribution to the product or relationship with the vendor were removed from their case.

In the 2013 iteration of the course, students were also tasked with registering several attributes about the vendors' relationships with other companies in a central datasheet. Four of these attributes were of particular interest to us: The relationship type with a party, the perceived balance of power in that relationship, the perceived importance of that relationship to the vendor's business model, and the frequency of contact with the other party.

The basic data for exploring the Microsoft ecosystem were obtained from the same source. The original data were filtered so that only the 101 parties with a connection to Microsoft remained. 50 Organizations were listed in the Microsoft PinPoint search engine. 47 organizations either claimed a relationship on their website, or made no information available. Only, 10 out of these 47 organizations replied to an e-mail with the information needed. Another two organizations were not available for contact and two more were acquired by Microsoft since the SSNs were made.

Visualization. After collecting data, the open source tool Gephi is used for visualization. Gephi has a flexible and multi-task architecture that allows filtering, navigating, manipulating and clustering for complex graphs of network models [8].

The SSN supply networks from the case studies were converted and used as input parameters. Parties and relationships from the models are entered as the nodes and edges of a network. For the example supply network in figure 1, the nodes and edges in the resulting data tables are visualized in table 1 and 2 respectively.

Table 1. Node table structure

Node	ID	Label	Type	SSN
Microsoft	1	Microsoft	Supplier	1
AIP	2	AIP	Vendor	1
AIP_Customer	3	AIP_Customer	Customer	1

Each node in Table 1 is given a name (Node) and a unique ID. The Type attribute denotes the role of a node in the SECO. The SSN number makes it possible to identify which SSN every node in the network originated from.

Table 2. Edge table structure

Source	Target	Type	ID	Weight	Products	Services	Finances	Content	Hardware
1	2	Directed	1	5	5				
2	1	Directed	2	3			3		
2	3	Directed	3	2	1	1			

Edges carry the Source- and Target-IDs of the nodes that they connect. Gephi automatically gives these source-to-target relationships the Type attribute 'Directed'. The total amount of resources exchanged within a single relationship (i.e. products, services, finances, content and hardware) forms the Weight of the relationship.

For the 2013 dataset the edge tables were expanded with the four relationship attributes (partner importance, relationship type, contact, and balance of power), converted to integer values from their original Likert scale rankings. A partner with 'monthly' contact would, for instance, get a score of 4 on the matching attribute.

Table 3. 2013 extended case relationship attribute coding

Partner Importance		Relationship type		Contact		Balance of Power	
Crucial	5	Cooperation agreement	5	Weekly	5	Partner more powerful	5
Very important	4	Partnership program	4	Monthly	4		
Important	3	License agreement	3	Yearly	3	Power is equal	3
Not very important	2	Informal relationship	2	Rarely	2		
Trivial	1	Animosity	1	Never	1	We are more powerful	1

Edge weights were recalculated as the sum of all four relationship attributes. Edge types were set to 'Undirected', as the direction of edges no longer holds any meaning in this case.

Microsoft certainly seems to be the keystone player of the Dutch ecosystem from previous visualizations. Therefore, we expanded the data related to Microsoft to get the inside view of its ecosystem, as outlined in section 2.1. For Microsoft partnership data structure, the format of nodes is depicted in table 4. The 'partner' attribute describes which type of partnership the organizations has with Microsoft. Partner total is the sum of gold and silver certificates the organization has with Microsoft.

Table 4. Node table structure for the Microsoft case

Node	ID	Label	Type	SSN	Partner	Partner Total
HP	3	HP	Supplier	1	Gold	14
AIP	19	AIP	Vendor	2	Silver	1
Centric	33	Centric	Vendor	3	Gold	11

Edge type is once again undirected, the reason being the same as for the 2013 case. The edge tables were extended with attributes for the amount of gold and silver certifications, and the Weight attribute was made the sum of all certifications.

For the sake of exploration three distinctly different structuring algorithms will be used to draw network graphs throughout this paper. The Fruchterman-Reingold-, Force Atlas-, and Force Atlas 2 - algorithms each offer a different degree of user control, but more control always comes at the cost of ease-of-use.

Clustering. For extracting clusters from the data, the Louvain clustering algorithm is used [9]. The Louvain algorithm is proposed by Blondel, Guillaume, Lambiotte and Lefebvre. This algorithm works by calculating and optimizing the modularity (the density of edges) of groups of nodes. On the first pass of the algorithm, each node is placed in its own community. From there the algorithm follows this pattern:

1. Calculate the modularity of all communities in the network.
2. For each community, for each neighbor, calculate the gain in modularity if it were to merge with that neighbor
3. For the highest detected modularity gain, merge the two neighbors
4. Recalculate modularity for all communities that remain.
5. Repeat from step 1 until no modularity gains are possible.

3   Describing the Dataset

After elimination in accordance to the criteria outlined in section 2, a total of seven cases were removed from the dataset for their lacking quality. A total of sixty seven cases remained in the final dataset. After entering the data into Gephi, as outlined in section 2, a network model was created containing 398 nodes connected by 984 edges. Using the Fruchterman-Reingold algorithm for force directed graph drawing[10] resulted in the network shown in figure 2. Fruchterman-Reingold forces nodes to be placed within a predefined circular space, with only minor variations in inter-node distances based on the weight of their connections. This makes the resulting graphs easy to create and control, particularly for large networks. The same algorithm was used by Rahul Basole in his visualizations of the mobile ecosystem [11]

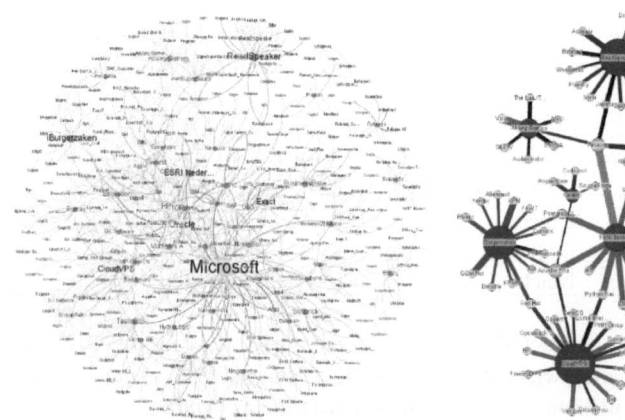
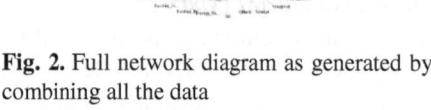
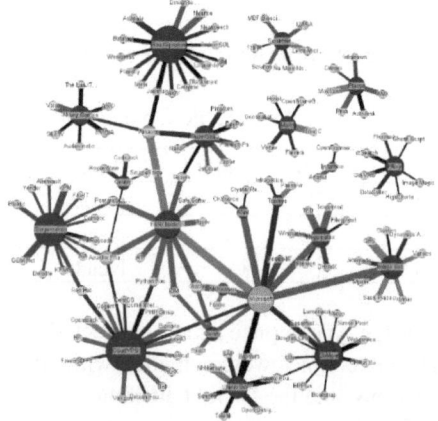

Fig. 2. Full network diagram as generated by combining all the data

Fig. 3. 2013 extended case diagram with edge brightness reflecting contact frequencies

This diagram was created using the following parameters: Node size = degree (amount of incoming and outgoing connections); Edge size = Edge weight

The network has the following composition: 222 suppliers (orange), 52 vendors (blue), 56 intermediaries (green), 60 customers (yellow), 4 supplier/vendor hybrids (purple), and 4 supplier/intermediary hybrids (teal).

A total of 572 products change hands in the network. In addition, 191 services are provided and 6 units of hardware are sold. In return, 40 pieces of content are provided and 521 payments are made. In total the network captures 1329 exchanges being made.

Perhaps unsurprisingly, the best connected node in the entire network is Microsoft, with a total of 79 unique connections. Microsoft is however not the only strongly connected supplier in the dataset. What follows is a top 10 list of the best connected suppliers:

1. Microsoft   6. SAP
2. Oracle   7. IBM
3. Apache Foundation 8. Apple
4. HP   9. AMS IX
5. Google   10. Amazon

The top 3 of the Forbes Global 2000 for software companies in 2013 are all present, namely Microsoft, Oracle and SAP. Also the number one and two hardware providers, (Apple and HP), and the number one and two software service providers, (IBM and Google), made the list[1]. Finding these giants at the centre of ecosystems is not uncommon in ecosystems research [12, 13] Perhaps a good sign of health for the open source software market is the Apache Foundation ranking 3rd. Other open source providers include but are not limited to the Eclipse foundation, The Python foundation, Debian, FreeBSD, Red Hat and the GNU project. The only natively Dutch supplier to make the list is the Amsterdam Internet Exchange (AMS IX).

In the extended 2013 case 152 nodes and 155 edges remained. Using Gephi's own Force Atlas 2 structuring algorithm results in a structure that makes it easier to identify outliers, compared to Fruchterman-Reingold [14]. Force Atlas 2 uses attraction, repulsion and scaling variables to iteratively determine structure. Force Atlas 2 and its predecessor were similarly used by Yu, Yin, Wang and Wang to visualize social groups in the Github ecosystem [15] Default values will often result in groups of connected nodes clustering too tightly and outliers flying off into the void, so some tweaking on part of the user is required. The resulting graph can be seen above in figure 3. This diagram was created using the following parameters: Node size = Degree; Node color = Same as Figure 2 (Valve is yellow); Edge size = Edge weight; Edge color = 5 point gradient for Contact frequency. For this diagram the edges were colored on a 5 point gradient, reflecting the values of the 'contact frequency' attribute. Frequent contact results in a bright purple edge color, whereas no contact whatsoever results in a black edge. Four more diagrams were created with different color schemes for the 'relationship', 'power' and 'importance' and overall 'weight' attributes.

For the Microsoft case, after filtering 55 nodes remained and 54 edges between them. The Force Atlas algorithm was used to structure the data in Gephi [8]. Force

---

[1] http://goo.gl/tir5Tx

Atlas operates on the same principles as Force Atlas 2, but allows users more control. This makes it more flexible for creating visualizations, but also more difficult to use for the inexperienced. The diagram was created using the following parameters: Node size = node weight; Edge size = Edge weight. Nodes for partners with gold and silver partnerships have colors to match. There are also two acquisitions by Microsoft (green) and four partners without certifications (red). There are 48 partners with Gold and/or Silver certificates, 4 partners without certificates and 2 companies are acquired as can be seen in Figure 4.

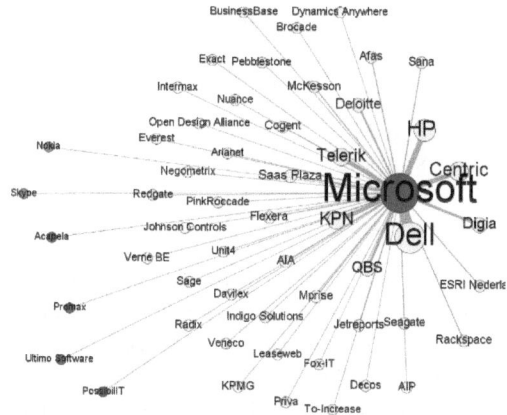

Fig. 4. Full Microsoft network diagram

Microsoft has 33 Gold certified partners in our dataset. The organization with the most certifications is Dell with a total of 25 (21 gold) certificates. There are 15 partners in the network with *only* silver certificates. Comparatively there are more gold certified partners than silver ones. The possible reason for this will be discussed in section 6.3.

4   Preliminary Findings

In this section the preliminary findings of modelling the dataset are discussed. It will discuss the results of clustering, extending the data for 2013, and extending the data for Microsoft respectively.

Clustering. After running the Louvain Algorithm 21 communities were detected within the full dataset. 10 of these are identical to their original SSN diagrams, as described in section 2. Vendors that are only tied to the larger network through single edges can achieve the greatest modularity gain by simply merging into a single node. Five of the detected communities consist of two merged SSNs. This pattern occurs when two central vendors in the SSNs share their strongest connection with a single supplier or intermediary. When this occurs the Louvain detects the highest possible modularity gain in merging those SSNs. This leaves 6 more complex communities:

The Microsoft Community. The largest, is a community centered on Microsoft. Software vendors that do not have ties with any other large suppliers tend to get sucked into this community because it is the only way for the algorithm to improve their modularity.

A Taste of Open Source (fig 5). The second largest community is all about open source. It appears that vendors with ties to one open source supplier tend to get a good taste for more. The central nodes in the community include Red Hat, the Apache Foundation and the Eclipse foundation. Other closed source suppliers also get pulled into this community because of their strong ties with the open-source-using vendors.

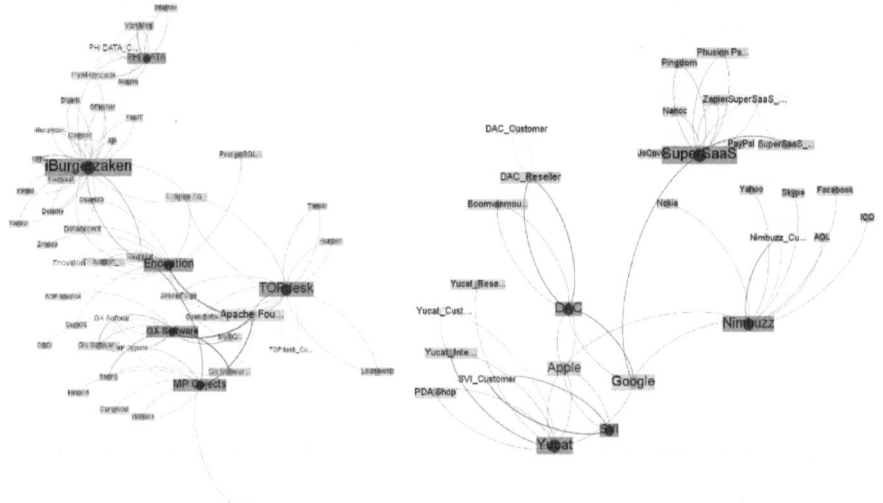

Fig. 5. The open source community   **Fig. 6.** The mobile developers community

The Mobile Developers (fig 6). The third largest community centers on Google and Apple. Digging back into the original SSNs reveals what drives this community. iOS and Android. Those vendors that consider mobile platforms a crucial component of their products are pulled into this community.

The Cloud Providers. The fourth largest community is up in the clouds, whether its hosting services, data centers or specific implementations like video-on-demand. This community centers around CloudVPS, Equinix and the PHP group, providing servers, datacenters and a server-side scripting language respectively.

The Oracle Community (fig 7). The fifth largest community centers on Oracle and includes Autodesk. This may be in part due to a strategic partnership established between the two suppliers in early 2007. Their single shared connection to Centric however, does not provide any conclusive evidence for this assumption. Other vendors that are well connected to Oracle also get sucked in.

The Hardware Community (fig 8). The sixth and last complex community centers on established hardware vendors. Three big names immediately stand out: HP, IBM and Cisco. In an age of increasingly affordable hardware, SaaS and Cloud solutions, some vendors still rely on services of these big name suppliers.

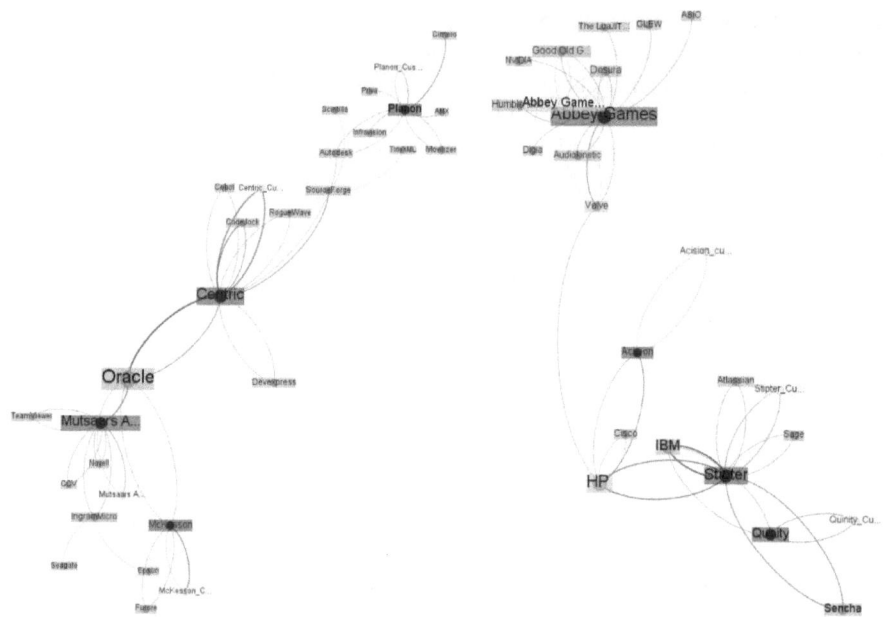

Fig. 7. The Oracle community   **Fig. 8.** The Hardware community

2013 Case. An immediate pattern that arises from the 2013 case models (see figure 3), is the large discrepancy between perceived partner importance for the product and contact frequencies/relationship types with that partner. One marketing software vendor for example, has indicated that Microsoft is absolutely crucial to their product (5/5 rating). When asked on their relationship with Microsoft however, the vendor has indicated that there is none (1/5 rating) and they rarely have contact with Microsoft (2/5 rating). This is in an unexpected contrast, and is repeated on several occasions by others within the network.

On the 1 to 5 rating scale, the differences between importance and relationship ratings (n=155) averaged -.08 (s=1.946). There are 15 outliers (rating difference =>3) for which, despite the high importance of a partner, the relationship with them is informal. The differences between importance and contact frequency ratings (n=155) averaged -.11 (s=1.689). The amount of outliers (rating difference => 3) in this category is exactly the same.

These differences may be indicative of a strategic gap. It is unexpected for software producing companies to have little to no contact and informal relationships with their most important suppliers. There may however, be other factors that can explain these differences. Bigger suppliers may be less available for contact and partnership programs may be expensive to enroll in. Particularly for smaller companies.

Looking back for a moment at the original SSN models, there were no indicators that these differences even existed. In the SSN notation all relationships between eco-system parties are equal. The statistics above show that relationships between parties cannot be assumed to be the same. Whether this indicates a need for change in the SSN notation, or whether this change is outside of the intended scope, is a question for future research. An attempt to include this sort of data in SSN models has been made before by Handoyo, et al. [16].

Microsoft Case. As can be seen in figure 4, the numbers of gold partners are compar-atively higher than silver partners. There may be few reasons for the organizations to become gold certified rather than silver. One of the reasons may be differences in benefits making gold certification more attractive. For instance, Microsoft gives part-ners free licenses for the internal use of some Microsoft products; silver partners can use only up to 25 licenses per product while gold partner can use up to 100 licenses per product. Also, the enrollment procedures for Gold and Silver certificates are not that different. In both cases employees of the prospective partner must take exams and pay license fees (though higher for gold). A minor difference for example: Gold certi-fied organizations must use the customer satisfaction (CSAT) index survey for per-formance measurement, which takes extra work but has its own benefits This may contribute to an attitude that one looking to get certified might as well just 'go for Gold'.

5   Relating the Data to Business Strategy

It is worth noting that even without analysis the dataset and accompanying models already provide interesting information. The model shown in fig. 2 shows SECO structure, basic information on the SECO parties, their roles, and relationships be-tween them. Much of SECO strategy literature in academia already uses this data to identify, classify, create and assess strategies in the business world.

When SECO roles are concerned, most literature will name keystones [17,18] and niche players [19,20] as the two most prominent. Both of which can be easily identi-fied in a network diagram by looking at node centrality and modularity. The role of a company has significant influence on their strategies with regard to their ecosystem.

Ecosystem structure also plays a role in SECO strategy literature. Van den Berk, Jansen and Luinenburg name it as a factor in a SECO strategy assessment model [1], and Iyer, Lee and Venkatraman use structural data as a measure for SECO health [21].

Relationships in ecosystems form the basis for research on partnership programs. For instance Bosch who defines strategic decisions for ecosystem partners to make the most out of their (potential) relationships [22]. Another example is given by Popp, who identifies goals related to partnership programs and communities [23].

Communities. In their 2011 paper on SECO management practices, Viljainen and Kauppinen synthesized four major categories of practices [24]. Three of these categories can play a role in business strategy with model support. Some of those practices are the following:

Technology Scouting. The communities detected in section 4 can be used to support these practices. Having an understanding of one's local community, including its structure and other participants, can provide a basis for choosing targets in technology scouting practices. Particularly targets for joint ventures and acquisitions can be justified by evidence of a shared community.

Orchestration. For keystone players interested in orchestration, the communities can serve as inspiration for identifying closely related parties that they were not previously aware of, potentially extending the boundaries of their perceived SECO. These parties can then be targeted for partnerships and standards adoption.

Technology Asset Management. For those looking to change up their technology asset management practices, communities can help to identify parties with valuable knowledge and similar practices. Vendors in the open source community could for instance find other vendors that use the same open source components. Sharing their requirements and knowledge can help both parties to get the most out of their open source components.

2013 Case. The 2013 extended case provides interesting information on vendor perceived metrics of ecosystems. The data includes partner importance, relationship type, contact frequency, and the balance of power. These metrics could be of particular interest to research in ecosystems health.

Hartigh, Tol and Visscher set out to create formal measures for the concept of SECO health [25]. Their work extended on an earlier paper by Iansiti and Levien, who already defined productivity, robustness and niche creation as the three main categories of SECO health factors [17]. Under the factors "persistence of ecosystem structure" and "predictability" in the ecosystem Robustness category, Hartigh et al. name measures like the amount of connections of each agent and the 'connectedness' of the entire network as measures.

In section 4 large discrepancies between relationship importance and relationship types were detected. This begs the question whether a simple tally of relationships and a number for connectedness are sufficient to measure robustness. The use of such values can certainly be valuable indicators of SECO health, but they do not paint a complete picture. Twenty or more connections are hardly an indicator of network robustness if those connected perceive their relationship as informal. This shortcoming in their measures was also noted by Hartigh et al. Using data and models similar to the 2013 case could help to further improve the measurement of SECO health.

Microsoft Case. For the Microsoft case the partner ecosystem defined by Popp is particularly interesting [23]. In an earlier work Meyer identified the following categories of goals for a software vendor in a partner ecosystem: financial, customer related, product related, network effect related and market related goals [26]. Popp makes these goals explicit for his view of the partner ecosystem. Microsoft already takes its partner ecosystem goals very seriously, as is said on their website: "Microsoft believes that their own advantage shines through the success of their partners" [27]. Microsoft's mission includes partners as a central means to help customers and business throughout the world.

Under product related goals innovation and co-innovation in local and regional markets could be helped by visualizing networks that include geographical data. This does not just show partners on a map, but also makes it easier to identify local and regional keystones and niche players. This can be used to analyze their strongest potential partners for co-innovation in a certain region, and to identify the best partners for reselling Microsoft products in a region.

In the category of financial goals Microsoft gains more from gold certified partners than from silver certified partners. Accurate information about silver certificates in a market as shown in figure 4, could help Microsoft find partners for upgrading to a gold certification in the same competency. These partners could then be contacted or even helped to achieve an upgrade.

6   Discussion

In this paper we discussed a dataset, several modelling approaches, several analysis results and several ways of relating these results to SECO strategy goals and practices from literature. Though there is some research available on SECO modelling and the use of those models, there is as of yet very little to be found on the inter-seco level of ecosystems [2]. On the inter-seco level, ecosystem models provide a view of the connections between multiple vendors, suppliers and intermediaries, rather than taking a single vendor as the Company of Interest as the SSN notation does.

The major validity concern in this paper is the source of data that was used. Three years of bachelor's course results are unlikely to all be of equal quality and reliability. Some filtering was done to exclude particularly bad data, as outlined in section 2, but there may still be faults left. The validity of the data depends on the assumption that all remaining students were honest, objective and diligent in their work.

Regardless, the specific contents of the dataset do not directly threaten the validity of the methods used in sections 4 and 5. Even with a perfect dataset the results would likely still have indicated gaps between relationship importance and contact/strength, community clusters of a similar nature, and similar Microsoft Partnership program results. For future work a systematic data collection method can be used to create a new dataset.

This paper succeeded in showing the potential use of ecosystem models for the business strategy field. There are many other focus areas in the SECO field where models may also contribute to existing practices and goals. A sample of other fields for future research is provided in the conclusion of the paper. The uses of models found can help businesses to create more robust and complete strategies and decisions. There may also be some benefits to be had for other parties. Views of SECOs could for instance help policy makers and market researchers in understanding the product software market as a whole. This is a good subject for future research.

7   Conclusion

The original research question was *'how can software ecosystem models be used to analyze strategic interests in a local software ecosystem?'*. The first step towards answering this question was the creation of models. SSNs gathered from 3 years of bachelor level courses in product software were used to create a view of the Dutch product software ecosystem. This view was then analyzed using a community detection algorithm, and extended using more specific data about relationships and partnerships.

To show that the three created models and the analysis of those models can actually have a benefit for business, the results section tied the data to strategic practices and goals described in scientific literature. The community detection results were related to three categories of SECO management practices, the 2013 case was related to a SECO health measurement framework, and the Microsoft partners case was related to goals for successful SECO partnership models.

In this paper we kept a broad perspective on business strategy. For future research similar work can be done to show the potential uses of models for focus areas within the SECO strategy domain. Some examples of focus areas are ecosystem governance and orchestration, SECO health analysis, partnership management, and software platform development. These subjects were touched upon briefly from the strategy perspective in this paper, but could be further expanded upon in later works. Another option is to move away from software businesses entirely, and to investigate the use of these models for external parties (e.g. governments, market research, or business analytics).

Another opportunity for future research that was identified in this paper is the use of relationship attributes in SSN modelling and SECO health measurement. The potential shortcomings of SSNs without relationship information were discussed in section 4. The lack of relationship data in health measurement was discussed in section 5. Both fields could benefit from the realization that not all relationships are equal when considering the formality and contact frequency of those relationships.

References

1. Van den Berk, I., Jansen, S., Luinenburg, L.: Software Ecosystems: a Software Ecosystem Strategy Assessment Model. In: Proc. of the 4th ECSA, New York, NY, pp. 127–134 (2010)
2. Jansen, S., Finkelstein, A., Brinkkemper, S.: A sense of community: A research agenda for software ecosystems. In: Proc of the 31st ICSE: Companion Volume, pp. 187–190 (2009)
3. Li, Y.: The technological roadmap of Cisco's business ecosystem. Technovation 29, 379–386 (2009)
4. Xu, L., Brinkkemper, S.: Concepts of product software. Eur. J. Inf. Syst. 16, 531–541 (2007)
5. Jansen, S., Brinkkemper, S.: Providing Transparency In The Business Of Software: A Modeling Technique For Software Supply Networks. In: Proc. of the 8th IFIP Working Conference on Virtual Enterprises, pp. 667–686 (2007)

6. Osterwalder, A., Pigneur, Y., Tucci, C.L.: Clarifying business models: Origins, present, and future of the concept. Communications of the association for IS 16(1) (2005)
7. Carrington, P.J., Scott, J., Wasserman, S.: Models and methods in social network analysis, vol. 28. Cambridge University Press (2005)
8. Bastian, M., Heymann, S., Jacomy, M.: Gephi: an open source software for exploring and manipulating networks. In: 3rd AAAI CWSM, pp. 361–362 (2009)
9. Isaksen, A.: Knowledge-based clusters and urban location: the clustering of software consultancy in Oslo. Urban Stud. 41, 1157–1174 (2004)
10. Fruchterman, T.M.J., Reingold, E.M.: Graph drawing by force-directed placement. Softw. Pract. Exp. 21, 1129–1164 (1991)
11. Basole, R.C.: Visualization of interfirm relations in a converging mobile ecosystem. Journal of Information Technology 24(2), 144–159 (2009)
12. Iyer, B., Lee, C.H., Venkatraman, N.: Managing in a small world ecosystem: Some lessons from the software sector. California Management Review 48(3), 28–47 (2006)
13. Iansiti, M., Levien, R.: Keystones and dominators: Framing operating and technology strategy in a business ecosystem. Harvard Business Press (2004)
14. Jacomy, M., Venturini, T., Heymann, S., Bastian, M.: Forceatlas2: A Continuous Graph Layout Algorithm for Handy Network Visualization Designed for the Gephi Software. PLoS One 9(6) (2014)
15. Yu, Y., Yin, G., Wang, H., Wang, T.: Exploring the patterns of social behavior in GitHub. In: Proc of the 1st International CrowdSoft Workshop, pp. 31–36 (2014)
16. Handoyo, E., Jansen, S., Brinkkemper, S.: Software ecosystem modeling: the value chains. In: Proc. of the 5th ICMEDES, pp. 17–24 (2013)
17. Iansiti, M., Levien, R.: The keystone advantage: what the new dynamics of business ecosystems mean for strategy, innovation, and sustainability. Harvard Business Press (2004)
18. Riis, P.H., Schubert, P.: Upgrading to a new version of an erp system: a multilevel analysis of influencing factors in a software ecosystem. In: Proc. of the 45th HICSS, pp. 4709–4718 (2012)
19. Kazman, R., Chen, H.: The metropolis model: a new logic for development of crowdsourced systems. Commun. ACM 52, 76–84 (2009)
20. Kabbedijk, J., Jansen, S.: Steering insight: An exploration of the ruby software ecosystem. In: Regnell, B., van de Weerd, I., De Troyer, O. (eds.) ICSOB 2011. LNBIP, vol. 80, pp. 44–55. Springer, Heidelberg (2011)
21. Iyer, B., Lee, C.H., Venkatraman, N.: Managing in a small world ecosystem: Some lessons from the software sector. Calif. Mgmt. Rev. 48, 28–47 (2006)
22. Bosch, J.: From software product lines to software ecosystems. In: Proc. 13th Int. Softw. Prod. Line Conf., pp. 111–119 (2009)
23. Popp, K.M.: Goals of Software Vendors for Partner Ecosystems–A Practitioner's View. In: Tyrväinen, P., Jansen, S., Cusumano, M.A. (eds.) ICSOB 2010. LNBIP, vol. 51, pp. 181–186. Springer, Heidelberg (2010)
24. Viljainen, M., Kauppinen, M.: Software ecosystems: A set of management practices for platform integrators in the telecom industry. In: Regnell, B., van de Weerd, I., De Troyer, O. (eds.) ICSOB 2011. LNBIP, vol. 80, pp. 32–43. Springer, Heidelberg (2011)
25. Den Hartigh, E., Tol, M., Visscher, W.: The health measurement of a business ecosystem. In: Proc. of the ECCON 2006 Annual Meeting, pp. 1–39 (2006)
26. Meyer, R.: Business Models for Software Companies. BoD, Hamburg, Germany (2008)
27. Popp, K., Meyer, R.: Profit from Software Ecosystems: Business Models, Ecosystems and Partnerships in the Software Industry. BoD, Hamburg, Germany (2010)

Towards a Typification of Software Ecosystems

Jens Knodel[1][(✉)] and Konstantinos Manikas[2]

[1] Fraunhofer Institute for Experimental Software Engineering (IESE),
Fraunhofer-Platz 1, 67663 Kaiserslautern, Germany
jens.knodel@iese.fraunhofer.de
[2] Department of Computer Science (DIKU),
University of Copenhagen, Copenhagen, Denmark
kmanikas@di.ku.dk

Abstract. Traditionally, software engineering has been dominated by stand-alone development organizations and collaborations between contractors, integrators and suppliers. In the last decade, the notion of software ecosystems has been established as a new paradigm in software engineering. In its essence it proposes participative engineering across independent development organizations centered on a common technology.

This paper reviews the current state-of-the-art and presents a first step towards a typification of successful software ecosystems. We discuss key characteristic of the ecosystem types and present a set of example cases. The characterization reviews and consolidates existing research and discusses variations within the key building block of a software ecosystem. It further enables sharpening the borders of what an ecosystem is (and what not) and how the individual types can be differentiated. Thus, this paper contributes to widening the understanding of software ecosystems and serves to prepare a software ecosystem taxonomy.

Keywords: Software ecosystems · Software engineering · Ecosystem types · Ecosystem taxonomy

1 Introduction

Software systems have been traditionally developed by a single organization in isolation and within a collaboration of several organizations, whereby one organization subcontracted other suppliers to deliver parts of or whole software systems according to some kind of specification. Today, we can observe an increasing number of software systems that strongly gain value by contributions added by other organizations - without being bound to contracted specification of what to deliver at what point in time. Prominent examples of such so-called software ecosystems (SECOs) are for instance, Eclipse an open platform with plugins for all kinds of purposes or mobile device platforms like iOS or Android which are enriched by millions of apps.

The term software ecosystem was first coined more than a decade ago [1]. The research community has been successful in scattering various definitions

© Springer International Publishing Switzerland 2015
J.M. Fernandes et al. (Eds.): ICSOB 2015, LNBIP 210, pp. 60–65, 2015.
DOI: 10.1007/978-3-319-19593-3_5

of software ecosystems[1] since then. Those partially overlapping definitions define the space and the borders of the current shared understanding of software ecosystems in the research community.

In this paper, we argue for a having wider understanding on the range of existing kinds of software ecosystems. We derive our observations from ecosystems in operation (either by analysis of open, active ecosystems or of closed ecosystem where we had insights due to collaborations with industrial partners). We distill the key building blocks of software ecosystems observed and provide a first set of ecosystem types. By this we aim at paving the way towards an ecosystem taxonomy in order to enable a better understanding of ecosystems in general and its research challenges and implication in particular.

2   Setting the Scene

The work by Manikas and Hansen [7] analyzed the definitions in the literature (published until 2012). They propose a definition of software ecosystems by analyzing the existing definitions and identify three main elements that form software ecosystems: (i) common software and (a) technological platform(s), (ii) business or interests, and (iii) connecting relationships or interaction. However, today there exists a number of examples of ecosystems that fail that definition, as much as several of the alternatives definitions for software ecosystems, because although they demonstrate actor interaction that results in software solutions or services, they are not structured on top of a common platform. Examples of such types of ecosystems emerged around OSGi, Open Design Alliance, or BitTorrent.

The lack of technological platform in ecosystems has been recognized as well by Jansen and Cusumano in their survey on software ecosystems [8] where they identify that a type of "underpinning technology" for software ecosystems can also be a standard apart from a (service) platform. Similarly, Manikas and Hansen [9], examine the Danish telemedicine ecosystem as a software ecosystem although the lack of a common technological platform identifying that the ecosystem under study demonstrates symbiotic relationships in actor and software level, motivated by a set of business models, and resulting in software products or services. Knodel et al. [10] report on an example of smart ecosystems in the agricultural domain based on a standard without a common platform. Thus, the concept of software ecosystems is evolving and we perceive the need to redefine the borders of software ecosystems. In this study we focus mainly on the common software (in particular the common technological platform) and reveal that there are different types of software ecosystems that do not necessarily include a common platform (at least in the traditional sense of a software platform).

---

[1] For instance, [2,3,4,5,6,7], please note that the list is not complete.

3   Ecosystem Building Blocks

We propose the meta-model of generic ecosystem building blocks depicted in Fig.
1 as the basis of our subsequent analysis of ecosystem types. The meta-model
has been derived on the one hand from the analysis of existing literature and on
the other hand from observations made in software ecosystems in practice. The
building blocks are the following:

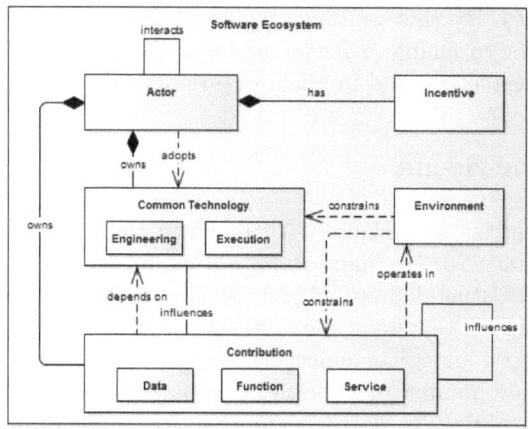

Fig. 1. Metamodel of ecosystem building blocks

- **Actor:** Ecosystems are driven by multiple actors interacting directly or indi-
  rectly with each other in collaborative or competitive nature. Actors provide
  a contribution to the ecosystem thus, the union of all contributions consti-
  tutes the moving target "ecosystem continuum". The number of actors is
  directly dependent on how open the ecosystem is to new actors, i.e. the entry barriers to the ecosystem. Typical instances of actors of an ecosystem
  may be individuals (developers, contributors, users, customer), commercial
  organizations, governmental entities, non-profit associations, and social communities.
- **Incentive:** Actors pursue some kind of incentive, which motivates their participation in the ecosystem. Typical instances comprise personal or business interest, fame, legal or standard regulations, legal or commercial forces,
  shared market needs or requirements.
- **Common Technology:** Ecosystems emerge around a shared technology.
  Instances of this technical linchpin can be twofold: (1) at engineering time
  (e.g., infrastructure, IDEs, SDKs, APIs, or standards) or (2) at execution
  time while the ecosystem is in operation (RTEs, platforms, frameworks, or
  protocols).
- **Contribution:** Actors provide contributions (with the linchpin being a special contribution as it is the key enabler of the ecosystem). Typical contribution may be software (functionality in form of apps, software service, or

stand-alone solutions; data in its raw form, aggregations, or context information) or services (management, integration, customization, etc.).
- **Environment:** The environment of the software ecosystem can be physical (interacting with the real world) or digital (IT only). It sets constraints for the software it is operating. Constraints may be imposed by special hardware, physical laws, social rules, or legal policies.

4   Analysis of Ecosystem Types

In this section we present different types of software ecosystems identified while discuss their characteristics according to the software ecosystem building blocks.

- **Cornerstone Ecosystems**
  Cornerstones are the more "traditional" types of software ecosystems: actors develop contributions on top of a common software platform typically extending the platform's functionality. Thus the existence of a technological platform is of central importance for the ecosystem of this type. The literature provides a number of examples of ecosystems of this kind like the iPhone AppStore, Android, or Eclipse. Cornerstone ecosystems and different perspectives of ecosystems of this type have been in focus of the research so far.
- **Standard-based Ecosystems**
  Compliance to standards is the key requirement for contribution in this kind of ecosystem. The standards replace a common technological platform and provide rather a specification of desired and required behavior of contributions, independent from their concrete realization as long as compliant. Standard-based ecosystem was initially proposed by Jansen and Cusumano [8]. Ecosystem standards usually are maintained and evolved organized by consortia with (paid) memberships. Standards often define rules to guarantee certain non-functional properties across individual contributions (e.g., safety in the ISOBUS standard in agricultural domain).
- **Protocol-based Ecosystems**
  Protocols are a less restrictive and more flexible technical linchpin of ecosystems. They provide a predefined specification of interaction of contributions with each other (e.g., exchange of data, call of software services).
- **Infrastructure-based Ecosystems**
  Infrastructure-based ecosystems share the same technical environment or tools at development time, but at the same time they provide independent contribution (e.g., Gnome, Github). The interactions between actors across individual contributions are often on a social level. Contributors themselves share their output and dedicate their efforts towards more than just one contributions (e.g., see [6] or [11]).

Table 1. Analysis of software ecosystem types

Category	Cornerstone	Standard	Protocol	Infrastructure
Emergence	successful product or actor(s)	specifications	need for use	successful product
Leadership	often run by single organization	often run by consortia	often run by community or organization	often run by (open source) community or company
Structure (Execution)	centralized, close collaboration, platform provides for governance, common technology part of the product	high level of actor & product independence, commitment to specific version	actor & product independence	different products, common technology not part of the product
Structure (Engineering)	cornerstone SDK shared across all actors	specification shared across all actors	API shared across all actors	common technology shared across all actors
Governance (common tech-nology)	monarchic or aristocratic decisions about products (few decide, others have to follow)	federal decisions (no one can't do anything without shared agreement of all (key) parties)	democratic decisions (anyone can do anything, as long as the majority agrees	monarchic, democratic, or federal decisions about shared infrastructure
Governance (contribution)	obey the integrator (threat of being overruled)	stick to the rules	follow the guidelines	freedom of choice (anything possible)
Changeability (common tech-nology)	orchestration dependent	slow, common agreement, backwards compatible	slow, common agreement, backwards compatible	orchestration dependent
Change Adoption (contribution)	orchestration dependent	painless (as long compliant)	painless (as long compliant)	independent of common technology

5   Discussion

The four types of software ecosystems are our starting point towards a typification of software ecosystems. In Table 1 we present the initial results on analyzing the major differences among the four types. In future work we aim at formalizing and extending the analysis and as well as adding a comparison to classical software product development outside an ecosystem.

We believe that the typification of software ecosystems must consider two distinct viewpoints: engineering and execution. Depending on its type, ecosystem expose different characteristics in their structure, governance, and the adoption of changes. Further, the leadership and emergence are key differentiators of ecosystem types. Based on these findings we argue that software ecosystem research has to adopt a broader view. In particular, the commonalities and specialties of each type should be analyzed to push software ecosystem research forward.

Goal of our future work is to come up with a well-defined taxonomy of software ecosystems and their characteristics. The taxonomy shall serve to guide researchers to focus on open challenges on the one hand and practitioners to learn from typical patterns and anti-patterns when participating in a software ecosystem on the other.

References

1. Messerschmitt, D., Szyperski, C.: Software ecosystem: understanding an indispensable technology and industry. MIT Press Books 1 (2003)
2. Jansen, S., Finkelstein, A., Brinkkemper, S.: A sense of community: A research agenda for software ecosystems. In: 31st International Conference on Software Engineering - Companion, ICSE-Companion 2009, vol. 2009, pp. 187–190 (May 2009)
3. Bosch, J.: From software product lines to software ecosystems. In: Proceedings of the 13th International Software Product Line Conference, SPLC 2009, Pittsburgh, PA, USA, pp. 111–119. Carnegie Mellon University (2009)
4. Bosch, J., Bosch-Sijtsema, P.M.: Softwares product lines, global development and ecosystems: Collaboration in software engineering. In: Mistrik, I., van der Hoek, A., Grundy, J., Whitehead, J. (eds.) Collaborative Software Engineering, pp. 77–92. Springer, Heidelberg (2010), doi: 10.1007/978-3-642-10294-3_4
5. Bosch, J., Bosch-Sijtsema, P.: From integration to composition: On the impact of software product lines, global development and ecosystems. Journal of Systems and Software 83(1), 67–76 (2010)
6. Lungu, M., Lanza, M., Gîrba, T., Robbes, R.: The small project observatory: Visualizing software ecosystems. Science of Computer Programming 75(4), 264–275 (2010); Experimental Software and Toolkits (EST 3): A special issue of the Workshop on Academic Software Development Tools and Techniques (WASDeTT 2008)
7. Manikas, K., Hansen, K.M.: Software ecosystems – A systematic literature review. Journal of Systems and Software 86(5), 1294–1306 (2013)
8. Jansen, S., Cusumano, M.A.: Software ecosystems – analyzing and managing business netowrks in the software industry. In: Jansen, S., Brinkkemper, S., Cusumano, M.A. (eds.) Software Ecosystems – Analyzing and Managing Business Netowrks in the Software Industry, pp. 13–28. Edward Elgar, Cheltenham (2013)
9. Manikas, K., Hansen, K.M.: Characterizing the danish telemedicine ecosystem: Making sense of actor relationships. In: Proceedings of the Fifth International Conference on Management of Emergent Digital EcoSystems, MEDES 2013, pp. 211–218 (2013)
10. Knodel, J., Naab, M., Rost, D.: Supporting architects in mastering the complexity of open software ecosystems. In: Proceedings of the 2014 European Conference on Software Architecture Workshops, ECSAW 2014, pp. 1–13. ACM, New York (2014)
11. Mens, M.G.T., Goeminne, M.: Analysing ecosystems for open source software developer communities. Software Ecosystems: Analyzing and Managing Business Networks in the Software Industry. Edward Elgar (2013)

A Survey on the Perception of Innovation in a Large Product-Focused Software Organization

Johan Linåker[✉], Husan Munir, Per Runeson, Björn Regnell,
and Claes Schrewelius

Software Engineering Research Group, Computer Science, Lund University, Lund, Sweden
{johan.linaker,hussan.munir,per.runeson,bjorn.regnell}@cs.lth.se

Abstract. Context. Innovation is promoted in companies to help them stay competitive. Four types of innovation are defined: product, process, business, and organizational. **Objective.** We want to understand the perception of the innovation concept in industry, and particularly how the innovation types relate to each other. **Method.** We launched a survey at a branch of a multi-national corporation. **Results.** From a qualitative analysis of the 229 responses, we see that the understanding of the innovation concept is somewhat narrow, and mostly related to product innovation. A majority of respondents indicate that product innovation triggers process, business, and organizational innovation, rather than vice versa. However, there is a complex interdependency between the types. We also identify challenges related to each of the types. **Conclusion.** Increasing awareness and knowledge of different types of innovation, may improve the innovation. Further, they cannot be handled one by one, but in their interdependent relations.

Keywords: Product innovation · Process innovation · Business innovation · Organizational innovation · Software engineering · Software business · Survey · Case study · Empirical investigation

1 Introduction

In recent years, the focus on innovation has increased in many lines of business. Novel products and services have always been important, while with an increasing pace of change, new technologies and market concepts being launched, with small vendors coming up and changing the scene in very short time, the need for continuous innovation is stressed in larger companies. Internet technologies for communication and distribution, and products and services primarily differentiated with respect to software, enables this shift by lowering the thresholds for new actors, and thereby threatening the position of existing ones.

Innovation is not only bringing new products to the market. The Organisation for Economic Co-operation and Development (OECD) Oslo manual [1], which is used to guide national statistics collection on innovation, distinguishes between four categories of innovation, i) product, ii) process, iii) marketing, and iv) organizational. These categories are defined as follows: *A product innovation is the introduction of a good or service that is new or significantly improved with respect to its characteristics or intended uses* [1, §156], while a *process innovation is the implementation of a*

© Springer International Publishing Switzerland 2015
J.M. Fernandes et al. (Eds.): ICSOB 2015, LNBIP 210, pp. 66–80, 2015.
DOI: 10.1007/978-3-319-19593-3_6

new or significantly improved production or delivery method [1, §163]. In the context of software engineering, we also count software development processes and practices as "production" methods in the process innovation category. *A marketing innovation is the implementation of a new marketing method involving significant changes in product design or packaging, product placement, product promotion or pricing* [1, §169]. Note that this involves the whole concept of bringing a product or service to the market, a kind of innovation we have seen in the software and internet domain, for example, using information or advertising instead of money as a trade for services. Finally, an *organisational innovation is the implementation of a new organisational method in the firm's business practices, workplace organisation or external relations* [1, §177]. This is also prevalent in software, where for example open source software, outsourcing and offshoring significantly has changed the game in many lines of business.

Given these categories of innovation, we were interested in studying to what extent these were known and integrated in the culture of a large company, which is under rapid change, and where innovation is a key survival factor, due to the volatility of the market. In particular, we wanted to study the awareness of the innovation concepts, and the interplay between the four types of innovation; which types precedes the other? There is a similarity to the software process improvement trinity of people, process and technology, much discussed in the 1990's [15]. More specifically, this study formulates three research question:

RQ1 What are the general perceptions of the term *innovation*?
RQ2 What relations are assumed between *product* innovation and *process, organizational* and *marketing* innovation, respectively?
RQ3 Which challenges exist with respect to the four types of innovation?

To address the research questions we launched an internal online survey [11] in a local branch of a multi-national corporation. The target population consisted of approximately 900 employees. On a global level the company employs approximately 5,000.

We found that the understanding of the innovation concept is somewhat narrow, and mostly related to product innovation. A majority of respondents indicate that product innovation triggers process, business, and organizational innovation, rather than vice versa. However, there is a complex interdependency between the types.

The paper is outlined as follows. In Section 2 we summarize empirical studies on people's attitudes to innovation in software engineering. Section 3 describes the methodology and design of the survey, as well as threats to validity and a characterization of the case company. In Section 4, we report our findings from the survey, and analyze the data. Section 5 concludes the paper.

2 Related Work

Innovation related to information technology (IT) has become vital part of most organizations' success, primarily for two reasons: i) growing importance of innovation for organizational life, and ii) the introduction of IT into almost every business unit of organizations [10]. Lee and Xia [21] addressed the process bottlenecks to innovation, where development teams are inefficient and reactive in most cases. Consequently, this causes problems with lack of support for business adaptions to shifting demands. Agile development seem to offer remedy to make the whole process more innovative for product development and help development teams to quickly deliver innovative, high quality solutions to an ever increasing demand of business innovation [14].

On the other hand, research evidence [7] also suggest that agile could also be a hindrance for product innovation. It creates barrier in transferring the ideas outside the team boundaries due to short iterations and feature backlog reduced the amount of time that teams could spent trying new things or sharing new ideas across different teams. Wnuk et al. [30] also hinted the fact that existing requirements processes are designed to handle mature features and consequently, raises the question of process innovation by having a separate requirements engineering process to make room for innovative features (other than featured backlog) in the products.

Lund at al. [23] conducted a survey to explore the effects that reutilization have on innovation. Results revealed that standardization of process will free up time for innovation and most interestingly, routines are capable of having positive impact on occurrence of ideas and follow through on ideas. Furthermore, paring routines with openness to continuously improve the existing routines leverage positive effects on innovation. Therefore, take away from the study for managers is to take a look at existing routines with the spectacle of improving them, which will not only improve the efficiency but also the innovation aspect.

Moreover, another study was found where Harrison et al. [12] conducted a survey with 170 Finnish software organizations to explore the impact of human capital on open innovation. Therefore, it can be used as an example where people are affecting the innovation activities in the organization. The study findings suggest that software companies with the larger academically educated staff are more likely to apply open innovation business strategies to accelerate their internal innovation process. The study further argued that this could be due the strong ties between communities and universities. Similarly, Nirjar [25] also performed a survey with 121 software companies across India to explore the impact of workforce commitment on the innovation capability of the software enterprises. The study findings highlighted that the commitment of the managers of software firms can significantly enhance the innovation productivity by creating certain policies (i.e. open business model) [6] and practices/processes.

3   Methodology

In this section we describe the surveyed company more thoroughly and elaborate on the survey design, analysis and threats to validity.

3.1   About the Company

The company, which is a multi-national corporation with approximately 5,000 employees globally, develop embedded devices and the studied branch is focused on software development for communication hubs and additional connected devices in an internet of things (IoT) fashion. We consider the studied company a representative case [29] for similar ones, and hypothesize that the findings have a much broader generality than just this company. The studied branch of the company has 1,600 employees, of which 800 work on software development for the devices, and 100 work on connected devices.

The company develops software in an agile fashion and uses software product line management (SPL) [26]. The company has defined more than 20,000 features and system requirements across all the product lines. Considering the innovation aspect, the company is moving from a closed innovation model to an open innovation model [6], through the use of open source software to exploit the external resources to accelerate their innovation process. The open source solution, referred to as *the platform*, is the base for their software product line projects and derived products. New projects on the product line typically entails 60 to 80 new features with an average of 12 new system requirements per feature. There are more than 20 to 25 development teams develop these features.

3.2 Survey Design

An internal online survey [11] was designed in collaboration between the researchers and company representatives, running an internal project, aimed at assessing and improving the innovation climate in the company. The questionnaire is composed of three major parts:

1. Factors that contribute to the innovation climate, based on Ekvall's scheme [9].
2. Questions on the four types of innovation (product, process, organizational and marketing) and their relation, based on the OECD model [1].
3. Factors that hinder and help innovation, based on Jansen et al.'s Open Software Enterprise model [16].

In addition to ranking and preference questions, the survey had fields for free input for most questions. The questions were defined in several iterations between researchers and company representatives, particularly to make the terminology of the survey understandable for the participants. Further, the survey was piloted to a small group of company representatives before the final launch.

One particular term was given certain care, namely *marketing innovation*. The original definition is that a *marketing innovation is the implementation of a new marketing method involving significant changes in product design or packaging, product placement, product promotion or pricing* [1, §169]. However, in the company context, the term was perceived to be only related to what the marketing department was responsible for, and thus too narrow. Therefore, we replaced the term with *business innovation* and extended it to cover the process where the needs of the customers are captured as input for the product planning. This extends business innovation into the area of Requirements Engineering, which can be seen as a software engineering process, i.e. is covered by the process innovation definition. This area is therefore somewhat overlapped, but with the general distinction that high level capturing of requirements is mainly covered by the business innovation definition.

The survey was launched via the company intranet in October and November 2013 to about 900 employees via a census sampling, most of them being developers, of which 229 responded, i.e. a response rate of 25%.

3.3 Survey Analysis

As the surveyed company is product-focused the surveys had a main focus on deter-mining the level and perception of product innovation. Due to the attempt to address the more general innovation questions, the analysis focuses on three of the questions, connecting product innovation to process, business and organizational innovation.

The respondents were asked to "select the more likely scenario" in the following questions:

- The product innovation triggers the process innovation, or vice versa
- The product innovation triggers the business innovation, or vice versa
- The product innovation triggers the organizational innovation, or vice versa

This gave an ordinal scale with two options to answer which makes any attempt of drawing conclusions limited, although a general pattern was observed, as shown in Figure 1. The survey generated 469 free text comments. Except for the three earlier mentioned questions, comments were mainly gathered from four questions where the respondents were asked how innovative (s)he perceived the organization to be with respect to the four types of innovation.

Qualitative analysis with a thematic approach [8] was used to analyze the data, which was codified in up to three levels. Based on the codified data and the comments in gen-eral, perception of innovation concepts were analyzed (Subsection 4.1) and the connec-tions between product innovation and process, business and organizational innovation, respectively were identified (Subsections 4.2–4.4). Further on, based on the themes and comments in general, challenges were then identified and generalized in regards to the four types of innovations (Subsections 4.5–4.8).

3.4 Threats to Validity

The construct validity [18], refers to whether the survey measured what it was intended to. This can be addressed through e.g. pilot studies, which was performed before the official launch. Further on, the questions were developed iteratively and based on estab-lished literature.

In regards to the analysis, a threat to the construct validity is the risk of researcher subjectivity as the first author performed the mapping and main analysis. This was addressed by having the second and third authors perform their own individual analysis of the data, and could compare their findings with that of the first author.

External validity regards whether the results be generalized to outside of the surveyed sample [29]. In this paper, we analyze the questions, which can be published from the company's confidentiality perspective. Thus, we do not focus on their perceived current innovation status, but rather on the general understanding of innovation factors and their relations. Thereby, we also focus on the most generalizable aspects, which we hypothesize are valid for other companies of similar characteristic to the studied one, as a representative case [29].

A surveys reliability [18] concerns whether the same results can be obtained if the survey process was repeated. As the sample was obtained through a census sampling frame and had a response rate of 25% we regard this optimistically. Although, this

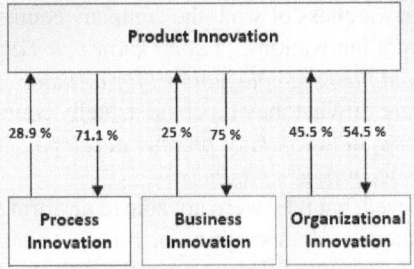

Fig. 1. Triggering relation between the four types of innovation: product, process, business and organizational. Percentage value shows the share of respondents that select X → Y as the most likely scenario.

cannot be strengthened until follow-up surveys are performed. This is something that will be done in the future as the company wants to measure how the internal perception of innovation develops over time.

4 Results

In this section we present our findings from the qualitative analysis of the survey responses. First the general perceptions of innovation is presented based on survey responses in 1. Then connections between product innovation and process, business and organizational innovation is presented respectively. Direction of arrows show the innovation type triggering the leading innovation (see fig. 1). For instance, the arrow from process innovation to product innovation shows that 28.9% respondents think that process innovation leads to product innovation. Similarly, the arrow from product innovation to process innovation suggest that 71.1% respondents think that product innovation lead to process innovation and the same arrow pattern applies for other innovation types. Finally, the challenges identified in regards to each innovation type is listed. As the types of innovation relate to each other, the challenges are structured accruing to the type where it relates the most, although a challenge may affect more

4.1 Perceptions of Innovation

Although not general, it was observed among the comments that some had trouble relating to the term innovation as such. The borderline between when something goes from being an improvement or common functionality to an innovation is fluid. *"I recognize that [company] does this often [. . .] But I'm not sure if it's really innovative or just mindless changes."*

Some respondents consider innovation as part of their everyday work, while others are a bit more unclear on the distinction between their everyday work and innovative activities, or just creativity as a process. *"As a designer the largest part of the task when bringing forward is to be creative. However there is a difference between being creative and being innovative."*

A reason could be unawareness of what the company counts as innovations and examples of different types of innovations. *"I don't know much about the innovations that we do. I didn't know about the [example feature] for instance"*.

Some may not be aware of what they do could actually count as an innovative activity. *"I work with support systems and not product development. Some part of the time goes into improving how we produce products."*

Further on, some believed that they were not able to perform any innovative activities as it was not a part of their work description or role. A tester expressed how he was not able to innovate as he assumed this was a task dedicated to developers. Another tester reasoned similarly. *"Working with testing so not much improvement in the product besides some ideas that pops up occasionally."*

This thinking was present on a general level in connection to all of the four types of innovation. As mentioned, this could be due to that the awareness is limited of how and where they can innovate. A better understanding needs to be achieved for the different types of innovations and how these interplay. *"Most of all, I would say that I have only minor insight and understanding of this field [of organizational innovation]."*

A consequence may be that some believe innovation is not possible. *"I don't think it is possible to be innovative in this area [organizational innovation]."*

Apart from spreading awareness and knowledge, another important factor that needs consideration is the mindset. *"Since I'm not involved in this part of our business then it's not in my mindset, but when you now mentioned it I will take it into my consideration of innovation."*.

4.2 Product Innovation vs Process Innovation

On the question whether product innovation triggers process innovation, or the other way around, 71 percent answered the former (see fig.1). Although the percentage points in one direction, it is clear from the free text answers that this question is more complex than so.

Processes can be strict and complex, creating overhead and distraction, occupying time that could have been focused on creative thinking, as pointed out by a respondent. *"If the development process is driven as a rigid framework that is complex and difficult to understand who decides what and why, then you do not get in the dynamics of ideas."*

This is also identified as a challenge of process complexity in Subsection 4.6. Although processes can force a static frame on employees, it can help to bring structure to the innovation process and thereby still encourage innovation and creative thinking. *"... well defined and established processes leads to innovative products."*

Another challenge is idea tracing and execution uncertainty (see Subsection 4.5), which is an area where we hypothesize that well-designed processes can help to clarify what happens to ideas and the roadmap for how innovations can be pushed through. Similarly, processes can also help to increase the awareness of the product scope and the innovation strategies in the organization.

Process innovation may help the organization become more efficient and reduce waste as can be interpreted by the OECD definition [1] and as pointed out by a respondent: *"... process innovation improve performance, simplifies and speeds-up development process - thus allowing to have more resources in true product innovation"*.

This aligns with the area of Software Process Improvement [13], which includes possible implications from new or improved tools and techniques. As put by another respondent: *"... We need to have the proper techniques, equipment and SW in order to develop new and improved products."*

The resources made available can be defined as freed-up budget-hours, which can be used for other purposes, such as time dedicated to activities focused on rendering product innovation. An organizational and cultural challenge in this case is to actually make this dedication which demands a committed management. *"The process innovations are often meant to make development faster with more quality, but I'm not sure the gained resources are spent on product innovation."*

Beneficial factors from a process change, other than freed up resources, may also include an increase in performance and quality as confirmed by the respondents. Although, it is a matter of definition how software quality relate to product innovation [27], this will hopefully render in a better product offering which further down the release ladder may prove to be a trigger of future product innovations.

Hence, by innovating and improving the processes in the correct way and dedicating the freed up resources to product innovation, process innovation can be seen as a trigger for product innovation. This is in line with findings by Lund and Magnusson [23]. On the other hand, processes are not decoupled from the products. There needs to be an awareness of product roadmaps and an adaptive mindset as some processes may require continuous tailoring as a consequence. *"I think the general mindset is "keeping the eye on the prize", you see the upcoming releases in the horizon and you adjust the process to meet those releases."*

The need to adapt is not a simple task and requires both resources and dedication. Keeping pace with new features and products can be very demanding for an organization as pointed out by the respondents. Process changes needs to be quickly adopted for the organization not to fall behind or get confused, as described in the process innovation challenges (Subsection 4.6).

Just as new products may create a demand for new processes and tools, they can also be an inspiration for new techniques and solutions. *"On the other hand, new products can also inspire new techniques and HW/SW solutions.".*

4.3   Product Innovation vs Business Innovation

On the question whether product innovation triggers business innovation, or the other way around, 75 percent answered the former (see fig.1). As with the previous question, although there is a clear majority in one direction, this does not give the complete answer.

Some see product innovation as the driver with respect to business innovation due to that *"Innovative products are a great source for new business opportunities and marketing"*. Innovative features affects which consumer groups that should be targeted, and in effect which marketing channels that can be used. The nature of the innovative features also has implications on how the marketing message can be phrased and communicated. From this point of view, the products both enable and set a demand for a continuous business innovation that can adapt to changing functionality and feature sets. A good product as foundation, can even be seen as a source of inspiration to excel business innovation as hinted by the following respondent. *"I think everything starts with the product. If you are a company with "Wow!"-products then the rest will come. A consumer will see through (eventually) if the company is only selling a mediocre product but have brilliant marketing. However, if we have good products, it will be more motivating bringing it to the market, which will inspire us to excel also in business innovation"*

From the other perspective, innovative marketing may be a requirement for what otherwise would be considered a normal product. Competitive products, which are technically inferior, may very well prove more popular compared to a technically superior product, due to the awareness and visibility towards the customers, as identified by the respondents. Business innovation can create the hype needed to tell about what the innovative features are, how they differentiate and how they fit in the customers' context. However, as pointed out by the previous quote, if the product does not fill the expectations, innovative marketing will not be a viable solution in the long run.

New innovative ways are continuously needed to keep pace and capture the demands from the existing and emerging customer channels, e.g. through end-user feedback [2]. An awareness of what needs the customers have today and will have tomorrow, is an important input from business and marketing to push the product innovations forward in the right directions. *"Because business innovation brings in new experience directly from market, new demands and requirements and thus giving a product a right direction"*

This creates a challenge for the organization in terms of synchronization. The view of what features are to be considered game-changers and prioritized in the release planning process [5], may prove troublesome due to internal communication gaps between marketing and product development [17], which may lead to wrong features being promoted as a consequence. *"Scope/product planning, business side and development [should be] in sync regarding both our innovation initiative [...] and how to drive innovations all the way to product."*

As explained, there is a dual sided relationship. There is a dependency going in both directions where one can trigger the other. One respondent provided a concrete example which summarizes the relationship. *"It is pretty much both. Look at the music and film business which has invented new ways of marketing and distribution, but I believe the wish of distribute TV via satellite has created new products for making it possible and to get paid for it. Then again we have the Google glasses. Right now they are cool, but not very useful until we find a useful feature for them and that itself will create a business for them."*

4.4   Product Innovation vs Organizational Innovation

On the question whether product innovation triggers organizational innovation, or the other way around, 55 percent answered the former (see fig.1). Opposed to the previous questions, this was not as clear majority for the product innovation centric view.

Improving and innovating the way in which a company collaborates and interacts with external parties and stakeholder, can trigger product innovations in several ways.

Application of open innovation business strategies is one way to accelerate their internal innovation process [12]. Crowdsourcing ideas, engaging in Open Source communities, welcoming third-party developers, acquiring promising startups and starting joint-ventures or ecosystems are a couple of activities that falls into the open innovation paradigm originally defined by Chesbrough [6], that may render in new product innovations.

Creating a more innovative organizational environment with committed employees is another way that can lead to more product innovations [25], as described by a respondent: *"With a flexible and happy organization that makes people get looser boundaries I believe we can get a more innovative climate"* Bringing people from different backgrounds and functional areas creates diversity and enables for new discussion to arise and to discuss ideas from new angles [4, 19], or as put by the following respondent: *"Connecting colleagues which hadn't possibility to communicate before allows to discuss more problems and ideas.".* Calantone et al. [4] adds that this cross-functional integration also allows for the employees to evolve their skills by learning and sharing knowledge amongst each other, which is important for product development.

This connects to a need for a general awareness of what has been done, and what is being worked on. *"... more often than not these innovations are "hidden" in small segments of the company, not actively promoted and spread (and that's both good and bad, many projects dies when they need to become too big)."* By communicating items such as features, functionality, experienced problems and related solution across internal borders, cross-functional views can be established more automatically. A solution in one project may turn out to solve the same issue or create new ideas in another project, which could either be considered a process or a product innovation. This relates to the concept of inner source [22] and how it can help organizations work more open and cross-functional, and in the end become more innovative [24].

Organizational barriers and communication issues is another area, where organizational innovation may trigger product innovation in the long term perspective. When products or processes stretch over multiple business units or projects, this can create room for bureaucracy, different prioritization schemes, culture and politics, to mention a few factors [19]. *"Some sections within the company are quite innovative, but when it comes to cross-functional agreements and alignment, there always seems to be a resistance to change and adapt to new ways of working and safeguarding what seems to the best for "me/my team" is more important than what's best for the company."*

Pushing through and spreading an idea across these borders require a high level of internal permeability. *"Organization organized for better collaboration (=no filtering, no proxies, smaller proximity, time zone, etc...) is more likely to produce more innovative ideas. Layering, direct reporting, micro management, and similar old-school practices are killing innovation."*

Looking from the other perspective, new product innovations will create new demands and implications which will give rise for possibilities and triggers for organizational innovation [4]. *"New and exciting products means we have to adapt how we work to support these in the best-possible, not only from an engineering or software perspective, but for example from the launch projects etc."*

As has been discussed in regards to previous sections on the matter of product innovation versus process and business innovation, there exists a dual relationship here as well as exemplified by the response: *"Organizational innovation increases our capability to handle new and complex tasks. Innovative products will require us to handle new or more complex tasks and without room for growth, product innovation will fizzle."*

4.5 Product Innovation Challenges

In the responses, several aspects were mentioned as challenges to the product innovation.

a) *Idea tracing and execution uncertainty* – Even though there may be a rich pool of innovative ideas being produced and a general will to contribute, it is important to maintain and support it. Knowledge and awareness of what happens to ideas contributed to the innovation development process is important for the contributors to feel that they are taken seriously and that it is worth to continue contributing, which in turn gives an increased innovation capacity for the company [19]. When the ideas come bottom-up there needs to be a feedback loop top-down that stimulates this need of information as confirmed by Koc and Ceylan [20], and Wnuk et al. [30].

b) *Short term perspective* – By having a narrowed foresight, release planning tend to prioritize non-unique features which renders in low diversity in the product range, thus making the company being a follower of competitors rather than a leader. A longer time perspective needs to be integrated into the company culture, together with a positive mindset for game changers and innovative features to be created.

c) *Product scope and innovation strategy* – Uncertainty about the product roadmap and feature scope leads to risks that the creative minds of the company are misdirected. A common and established innovation strategy can help defining the product scope and frame where ideas are needed suggested by Koc and Ceylan [20], and Wnuk et al. [30].

d) *Limiting environment and mindset* – Soft factors such as employees feeling that they can have a free mindset and share ideas openly is important for an innovative environment. It must be okay to test new ideas, but also to fail. These are factors, triggered by Ekvall's innovation climate model [9].

e) *Restriction by external stakeholders* – A commercial product company can have many stakeholders, some not being the end customer. This may include distributors and service providers further down the value chain, adding value and modifications to the product before they reach the final buyers. These stakeholders put requirements that may prevent and limit the feature scope possible to address. This filter risks to kill ideas inside the company and ignore needs, both identified and unidentified, from the end customers. This challenge is in line with Conboy and Morgan's findings [7].

f) *Limited time for innovation activities* – Tight project budgets and short deadlines are two factors that can restrict time available for idea creation. Developers usually have pet projects and ideas they would like to work on, some even dedicate their spare time for this purpose. By allowing the time, this can prove a valuable source of product innovation as suggested by Conboy and Morgan [7].

g) *Cross-functional resources* – Bringing new people together creates new product ideas and can boost innovation development. Cross-functional labs-sections and dedicated innovation team are two examples suggested by Conboy and Morgan [7], and Koc [19].

4.6   Process Innovation Challenges

This section presents the challenges, directly related to process innovations.

a) *Process change too slow* – The introduction of a new process may be cumbersome for several reasons, with the effect that the changes are implemented slowly. This can cause confusion for employees being caught between two states – before and after the change – and also result in an unsynchronized organization as different parts may adapt faster than others.

b) *Process change too often* – Another issue with respect to process change is that they may happen too often. This can be a cause effect relationship with an adoption process, as old processes risk being outdated once introduced if done in a too slow and inefficient manner. When the environment changes, for example technology and dependencies towards partner's progress, so does the requirements on the internal tools and processes have to change at the same pace. This can also relate to organizational innovation.

c) *Process change top down* – Problems can arise when a process is introduced top-down instead of bottom-up. Managers may not always know what is the most efficient way to work compared to those actually performing the work. This challenge is also in line with the findings of Qin [28], and Wnuk et al. [30].

4.7   Business Innovation Challenges

Challenges related to business innovation are about alignment with the market and end users.

a) *Reaching the end-customers* – When there are layers between the producer and end-customer, for example, distributors and service providers, promotion of new ideas and product innovations to end-customers gets complicated. As technology and social habits evolve, new innovative ways are needed to keep pace with the different forums for communication used by the end-customers of today and tomorrow. Examples of such phenomena are software ecosystems [31].

b) *Product and marketing synchronization* – The views on what the top innovative features are may differ between different parts of the company. A misalignment like this can create confusion between marketing and product development. This could render in the wrong features being promoted. The suggested needs of the end customers should be communicated and synchronized to all relevant parts of the organization, e.g. product planning, marketing and development.

4.8   Organizational Innovation Challenges

Organizational innovation challenges relate to collaboration, communication and change.

a) *Closed organizational borders* – If the organization is too introvert and closed, opportunities, possible collaborations, sources of ideas and other possible inputs to their internal innovation process might be missed. By opening up the company borders for external collaboration and influence, new possibilities can arise both in regards to new innovations and markets, as described by the Open Innovation paradigm [6].

b) *Intra organizational collaboration* – Barriers and layers can prevent otherwise prosperous and potential collaborations between business units in organizations.

Examples may be different sub-priorities of features between projects and multiple number of mangers creating a complex and bureaucratic hierarchy as identified among the respondents and confirmed by Koc [19]. These are related to what Bjarnason et al refer to as "gaps" [3]. Koc further points out that such cross-functional integration demands a high level of coordination, otherwise it will rather have a negative impact on the product innovation.

c) *Intra organizational learning* – Unawareness of what has been done in other parts of the company can create inefficiency and missed possibilities. In regards to process innovation, tools, technologies and processes from one part may prove its self superior or complementary to those used in other parts. And in regards to product innovation, a commoditized good or service from one business unit may turn out as innovative if added to the value proposition in another business unit's product chain. This is a challenge in-common with inner source [22], but also one of the ways in how it can help organizations become more innovative by using it as a type of intra-organizational open innovation [24].

5   Conclusions

The view on what innovation is and where it can be performed is a diversified topic. OECD [1] differentiates between four types: product, process, market and organizational innovation. These were adopted in the survey on which this paper is based on, with a redefinition of market innovation into business innovation. The original definitions are general and applicable on a multiple number of fields. This paper puts them in the context of software engineering characterized by the opinions of people involved in different levels of a large software development organization.

The perception of the term *innovation*, to answer the first research question (See **RQ1**, Section 1), is diversified. Even though it is not general, some had trouble relating to the term innovation as such and when a feature or certain work can be classified accordingly. Some believed that they were not able to perform any innovative activities as it was not a part of their work description or role, which was present in connection to all of the four types of innovation. Apart from awareness and knowledge, another important factor that also needs consideration is the mindset of the employees that innovation is possible and something that they can help to create.

The different types cannot be considered isolated or decoupled which answers the second research question (See **RQ2**, Section 1). Connections between product innovation and process, business and organizational innovation exists in both directions. Introduction of product innovations creates demand and possibilities for processes, marketing and organization to adapt and optimize as the conditions has been changed. Interdependencies may require tailoring being done, either as a direct consequence or as a side effect. On the other way around, introduction of a process, business or organizational innovation can change the environment and conditions for how product development is being done. Inputs such as new technologies, ideas, resources and know-how are example factors which can be considered a cause behind a product innovation effect. Open innovation could be classified as an organizational innovation that can render inputs to the internal innovation process [6].

Challenges correlated to the different innovation types were also identified, with respect to the third research question (See **RQ3**, Section 1). These give a context to the term of innovation that covers parts other than the more normal conception of innovation in regards to just products. Some challenges may target more than one type of innovation, e.g. internal communication which can cause issues for introduction on new processes and organizations as well as hinder ideas to be spread and discussed.

For future research it would be interesting with studies confirming and exemplifying the connections described, for example how process innovation could trigger product innovation. An anticipated challenge will be to trace a cause effect relationship and connecting the two areas. Another area also includes confirming the challenges identified, and further characterizing the innovation types from a software engineering perspective.

References

1. Oslo Manual – Guidelines for collecting and interpreting innovation data. OECD and Eurostat, 3rd edn. (2005)
2. Bano, M.: Aligning services and requirements with user feedback. In: 2014 IEEE 22nd International Requirements Engineering Conference (RE), pp. 473–478 (2014)
3. Bjarnason, E., Wnuk, K., Regnell, B.: Requirements are slipping through the gaps - A case study on causes & effects of communication gaps in large-scale software development. In: 19th IEEE International Requirements Engineering Conference, RE 2011, Trento, Italy, August 29-September 2, pp. 37–46 (2011)
4. Calantone, R.J., Tamer Cavusgil, S., Zhao, Y.: Learning orientation, firm innovation capability, and firm performance. Industrial Marketing Management 31(6), 515–524 (2002)
5. Carlshamre, P.: Release planning in market-driven software product development: Provoking an understanding. Requirements Engineering 7(3), 139–151 (2002)
6. Chesbrough, H.W.: Open innovation: the new imperative for creating and profiting from technology. Harvard Business School Press, Boston (2003)
7. Conboy, K., Morgan, L.: Beyond the customer: Opening the agile systems development process. Information and Software Technology 53(5), 535–542 (2011)
8. Cruzes, D.S., Dybå, T., Runeson, P., Höst, M.: Case studies synthesis: A thematic, cross-case, and narrative synthesis worked example. Empirical Software Engineering (2014)
9. Ekvall, G.: Organizational climate for creativity and innovation. European Journal of Work and Organizational Psychology 5(1), 105–123 (1996)
10. Fichman, R.G.: Going beyond the dominant paradigm for information technology innovation research: Emerging concepts and methods. Journal of the Association for Information Systems 5(8), 11 (2004)
11. Fink, A.: The Survey Handbook, 2nd edn. Sage (2003)
12. Harison, E., Koski, H.: Applying open innovation in business strategies: Evidence from finnish software firms. Research Policy 39(3), 351–359 (2010)
13. Harter, D.E., Krishnan, M.S., Slaughter, S.A.: Effects of process maturity on quality, cycle time, and effort in software product development. Management Science 46(4), 451–466 (2000)
14. Highsmith, J., Cockburn, A.: Agile software development: The business of innovation. Computer 34(9), 120–127 (2001)
15. Humphrey, W.S.: Managing the software process. SEI Series in Software Engineering. Software Engineering Institute (1989)

16. Jansen, S., Brinkkemper, S., Souer, J., Luinenburg, L.: Shades of gray: Opening up a software producing organization with the open software enterprise model. Journal of Systems and Software 85(7), 1495–1510 (2012)
17. Karlsson, L., Dahlstedt, Å.G., Regnell, B., Natt och Dag, J., Persson, A.: Requirements engineering challenges in market-driven software development an interview study with practitioners. Information and Software Technology 49(6), 588–604 (2007)
18. Kitchenham, B.A., Pfleeger, S.L.: Personal opinion surveys. In: Guide to Advanced Empirical Software Engineering, pp. 63–92. Springer (2008)
19. Koc, T.: Organizational determinants of innovation capacity in software companies. Computers & Industrial Engineering 53(3), 373–385 (2007)
20. Koc, T., Ceylan, C.: Factors impacting the innovative capacity in large-scale companies. Technovation 27(3), 105–114 (2007)
21. Lee, G., Xia, W.: The ability of information systems development project teams to respond to business and technology changes: a study of flexibility measures. European Journal of Information Systems 14, 75–92 (2005)
22. Linåker, J., Krantz, M., Höst, M.: On infrastructure for facilitation of inner source in small development teams. In: Jedlitschka, A., Kuvaja, P., Kuhrmann, M., Männistö, T., Münch, J., Raatikainen, M. (eds.) PROFES 2014. LNCS, vol. 8892, pp. 149–163. Springer, Heidelberg (2014)
23. Lund, K., Magnusson, M.: The delicate coexistence of standardized work routines and innovation. In: Proceedings of the 19th International Product Development Management Conference, Manchester, UK (June 2012)
24. Morgan, L., Feller, J., Finnegan, P.: Exploring inner source as a form of intraorganisational open innovation (2011)
25. Nirjar, A.: Accruing innovation in software firms through employees commitment. International Journal of Indian Culture and Business Management 6(4), 391–409 (2013)
26. Pohl, K., Böckle, G., van der Linden, F.J.: Software Product Line Engineering: Foundations, Principles and Techniques. Springer-Verlag New York, Inc., Secaucus (2005)
27. Prahalad, C.K., Krishnan, M.S.: The new meaning of quality in the information age. Harvard Business Review 77(5), 109–118 (1998)
28. Qin, S.: Managing process change in software organizations: Experience and reflection. Software Process: Improvement and Practice 12(5), 429–435 (2007)
29. Runeson, P., Höst, M., Rainer, A., Regnell, B.: Case Study Research in Software Engineering – Guidelines and Examples. Wiley (2012)
30. Wnuk, K., Pfahl, D., Callele, D., Karlsson, E.A.: How can open source software development help requirements management gain the potential of open innovation: an exploratory study. In: Proceedings of the 2012 6th ACM-IEEE International Symposium on Empirical Software Engineering and Measurement (ESEM), Piscataway, NJ, USA, pp. 271–279 (2012)
31. Wnuk, K., Runeson, P., Lantz, M., Weijden, O.: Bridges and barriers to software ecosystem participation - a case study. Information and Software Technology 56(11), 1493–1507 (2014)

Ecosystems and Open Innovation for Embedded Systems: A Systematic Mapping Study

Efi Papatheocharous[1(✉)], Jesper Andersson[2], and Jakob Axelsson[1]

[1] Swedish Institute of Computer Science (SICS), SE-164 29 Kista, Sweden
{efi.papatheocharous,jakob.axelsson}@sics.se
[2] Department of Computer Science, Linneaus University, SE-351 95 Växjö, Sweden
jesper.andersson@lnu.se

Abstract. This paper surveys work on ecosystems and open innovation of systems in the context of software engineering for embedded systems. The primary research goal is to develop a research agenda based on the topics identified within the research publications on the topic. The agenda is based on a systematic mapping study of 260 publications obtained from digital libraries and is influenced by a set of areas of interest, i.e., product lines, open source, third party, business models, open innovation, and strategy. The results from the study include analysis of the type of research conducted in the field, its origin and research contribution. The study identifies the need for more solutions to specific open innovation problems such as mapping business models to technical platforms; defining open ecosystem processes that foster open innovation; and improving how ecosystem players can leverage on tool support for open innovation. A direction for future research is also provided.

Keywords: Software ecosystems · Open innovation · Embedded systems

1   Introduction

Technological advances allow more and more systems to be connected to one another nowadays. The technology is straightforward and flexible and removes several impediments for innovation and new business opportunities. It has already been recognised in the software domain, that an increasing number of companies make their products and services available to offer opportunities for extended services and increase the value of existing products to customers that exceeds the typical company boundaries [1].

From the engineering perspective however, the challenge is larger and it involves to satisfy the compelling needs for more flexibility, shorter time-to-market, and greater ability to build systems of systems. We have introduced in our previous work [2] a specific form of these systems where plug-ins can be installed in different products (i.e., embedded systems) giving them the opportunity to collaborate for higher-order functionality or with data-intensive applications. We have highlighted the need for new or innovative business models, sustainable networks, ecologies or federations in the embedded systems domain, as they are less flexible and resilient to

J.M. Fernandes et al. (Eds.): ICSOB 2015, LNBIP 210, pp. 81–95, 2015.
DOI: 10.1007/978-3-319-19593-3_7

change, than for example in comparison to other domains, like pure software products. Some connected topics that both interest us as researchers and the industrial community we have interviewed, are software ecosystems, open innovation processes methods and tools, organisational and business architectures, product lines, open source and third party options for collaborations and sustainability [2].

Much of the research related to the open-innovation part of ecosystems of embedded systems is empirical, and drawn from specific domains, such as mobile phones [3] or the automotive [4]. To the best of our knowledge no domain-independent study exists that aims at understanding the quantities and trends of research, types of existing research and contributions on innovation for embedded software, its origin and application domains. Conducting research on this topic is challenging and no mature examples have been made available to the public or reported in scientific publications. The reasons for this are many, for instance that these systems are difficult to investigate empirically due to the number of stakeholders involved. Therefore, some of the definitions do not have much theoretical support and current research is still explorative.

This paper summarises the results from a systematic mapping study [5] on aspects of ecosystems, product lines, open source or third party collaborations and business models, open strategic innovations in product development of embedded systems and software. The aim is to identify what there is already research on (which research domains) and pro-actively explore prospective venues of research. Thus, the study maps the existing research and practice in the literature providing a foundation for where does the research originate from, what are the trends during the last years, which are the main application domains and what kind of research and research contributions exist. This information can enhance the researchers' understanding of the quantities and trends in the literature of the area. The mapping study provides an overview and quantification of the research contributions in the field, and as reported in [5], systematic studies are considered necessary to conduct especially when researchers are entering a new or unknown field of research, which is true for the field we are interested in. The results help us to define a direction for future research on open innovation for embedded systems' software and their ecosystems.

The interest in ecosystems and in particular the software ecosystem, has expanded beyond company platforms, business models and definitions. The systematic literature by Manikas and Hansen [6] focuses primarily on definitions in this context from a software engineering perspective. The authors conclude that analytical descriptions and monitoring of real-world ecosystems is limited. The consequences are that research results do not feed from industry and vice-versa, and that industry misses out on innovation improvements and efficiency when is not influenced by research. The objective of our research is to improve our understanding on the nature of existing research on ecosystems of open innovation and connections between different types of research and contributions, primarily from academia and practitioners. Our study uses a different strategy and scope compared to study [6]. It examines the literature body that includes these notions and the primary contribution is a research agenda that can direct future research towards challenges relevant for industry and academia and leverage on existing research in the field.

The remainder of this paper is organised as follows: the next section summarises the design of the study, Section 3 describes the findings, Section 4 presents analysis of the results, a research agenda, and Section 5 concludes the paper and describes of our future work.

2   Research Method

A modified version of the systematic mapping process described in [5] was used for the study. The process steps and the results (marked in grey) are illustrated in Fig. 1. The process contains five distinct steps: planning, scoping (including searching), selecting, classifying and mapping. This section is structured according to these steps.

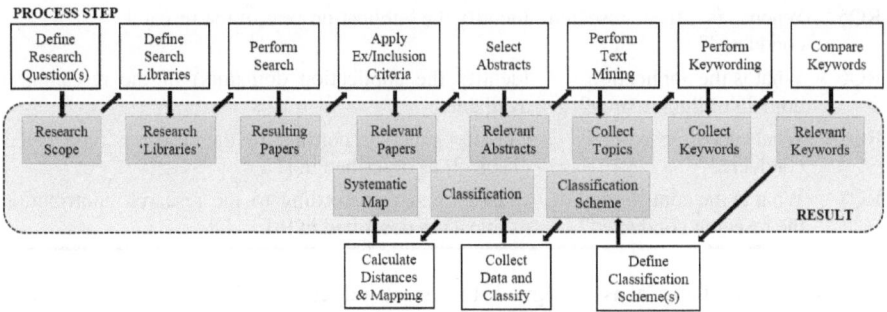

Fig. 1. Systematic mapping process and results of the study

2.1   Planning

In the planning phase, we defined the research scope by a set of Research Questions (RQ), which is summarised in Table 1. They aim at collecting fundamental demographic information that characterises the field.

2.2   Scoping

The research questions guided the second phase (scoping) where the search scope was defined. The search scope included a set of scientific databases as data sources, namely ACM, Springer Link, Engineering Village, Science Direct and IEEE Explore digital libraries. As recommended in [5] we defined the search string by performing iterative search of publication databases and evaluating the results each time. The search string was revised and modified accordingly based on the quality of the results obtained.

The final search string was: *"embedded AND (software OR system) AND ("product development") AND (ecosystem OR "eco system" OR "eco-system" OR "product-line" OR "product line" OR productline OR "open-source" OR "open source" OR "third party" OR "third-party") AND ("business model" OR "business-model" OR businessmodel OR "innovation system" OR "open innovation" OR "strategic innovation")"*.

Table 1. Research Questions of the study

RQ #	Description	Evidence
RQ1	What is the origin of the research?	Identify the affiliations of the authors and specify the country from which the publication originates.
RQ2	Which are the main publication venues of the research?	Identify the publication type of the research (book chapter, conference paper, journal paper or standard), and the primary venues that publish the research.
RQ3	What is the affiliation of the researchers?	Identify the affiliations of the authors either as academia, industry, professional organisation, or governmental.
RQ4	What is the research domain of the research conducted?	Classify the primary research domain(s) where research is conducted (many times more than one domain applies and domains are identified using the abstract keywords).
RQ5	When is the research conducted?	Identify the publication year of the research.
RQ6	What is the application domain of the research?	Identify the application domain(s) of the research, if available.
RQ7	What type of research is conducted?	Classify papers according to the research type facets (Table 3) as described in [7].
RQ8	What is the contribution of the research conducted?	Classify papers according to the research contribution (Table 4) as described in [8].

This search string was designed to target papers in the domain of product development embedded systems, dealing with software-related systems, and then qualify them in aspects of ecosystems, product lines, open source software, third party or business models, or innovation. The same search string was applied to the selected databases, where we searched the full paper, abstract and keywords. In total we identified 73 papers from ACM Digital library, 294 papers from Springer Link, 5 papers from Engineering Village, 558 papers from Science Direct and 192 papers from IEEE Xplore digital library. The search scoping data is summarised in Table 2.

Table 2. Search scoping and selection results from the study

Database	Resulting Papers	Included Papers
ACM	73	18
Springer Link	294	25
Engineering Village	5	4
Science Direct	558	109
IEEE Xplore	192	104
Total	1122	260

2.3   Selecting

As keyword searches are considered to be too coarse-grained [5], a more precise selection method must be applied to identify the most relevant publications. Two researchers carried out this step independently and any differences were discussed until an agreement was reached.

In the selection phase the primary studies were selected by the application of the following inclusion/exclusion criteria that the researchers defined together:

1. Exclude search results that contain "Table of Contents", "Contents", "Index", "Front Matter", "Proceedings", or "from the editor" in the title, or have an empty title, are duplicate results, or are interviews, standards, full books, encyclopaedia sections, dictionary sections, or written in other languages than English.
2. Include search results that contain in the title something near any of the terms "software", "development", "embedded", "product" or "system".
3. Include search results that contain in the title something near any of the terms "innovation", "business", or "market" and check if in the list of keywords of the publication any of the terms "software", "development", "embedded", "product" or "system" appear. 'Something near' here, implies a subjective selection that required discussions before an agreement could be reached.
4. Screen the abstracts of the papers that after conducting steps 1-3 a disagreement between the researchers is reached and resolve the conflict by deciding which ones to include or exclude in the final paper selection.
5. Exclude papers where the full text was not available for the synthesis part only (3 papers from Science Direct).

The searching and screening steps should include all papers that match the search criteria and exclude papers deemed as 'not relevant' for the study. Parts of the screening process was subjective and sometimes discussions where required to reach an agreement. In the screening step the disagreement level was low, less than 3%.

The process finished with 18 papers from the ACM, 25 papers from the Springer Link, 4 papers from the Engineering Village, 109 papers from the Science Direct and 104 papers from the IEEE Xplore digital library, all together 260 studies. Table 2 summarises how the number of studies evolved during the process.

2.4   Classifying

In the classification step, the abstracts were processed to validate that the search string used was meaningful and helped in the definition of the classification scheme (i.e., ensured that the scheme takes the type of words used in the studies into account). Text mining was used to derive major topic clusters and derive preliminary hierarchies, i.e., lists topics that frequently appear. Then, keywording was used to identify the primary concepts (keywords) found in the abstracts of the publications, extracting topics of interest. The papers were classified based on a set of classification schemes (related to the RQs in Table 1 and explained in the last column). Tables 3 and 4 summarise the type of research facet [7] and type of research result [8] (or contribution) in software engineering.

2.5   Mapping

With the classification schemes in place the publications were mapped on them. Again, this step was carried out independently by two researchers and any differences were discussed until an agreement was reached. On average the disagreement level was around 30% (79 studies were analytically discussed). From the studies that were analytically discussed, there were 6 papers for which classification was not possible. These papers were either part of a book (not a single book chapter and not a full book and thus were not excluded in the first step of the Inclusion/Exclusion process) or could not be analysed as stand-alone publications. Thus, these papers were reported as "None", "Other" or "NA". The map was used to create different frequency plots, to answer the RQs (Table 1) and highlight a direction for future research (Table 7).

Table 3. Type of research as described in [7]

Type	Description
Validation research papers	Techniques investigated are novel and have not yet been implemented in practice. Techniques used are for example experiments, i.e., work done in the lab. Papers investigate the properties of a solution proposal that has not yet been implemented in practice. The solution may have been proposed elsewhere, by the author or by someone else. The investigation uses a systematic, thorough, methodologically sound research setup. Possible research methods are experiments, simulation, prototyping, mathematical analysis, mathematical proof of properties, etc.
Evaluation research papers	Techniques are implemented in practice and an evaluation of the technique is conducted. That means, it is shown how the technique is implemented in practice (solution implementation) and what are the consequences of the implementation in terms of benefits and drawbacks (implementation evaluation). Papers identify problems in industry.
Solution proposal papers	A solution for a problem is proposed, the solution can be either novel or a significant extension of an existing technique. The potential benefits and the applicability of the solution is shown by a small example or a good line of argumentation. Papers propose a solution technique and argue for its relevance, without a full-blown validation. The technique must be novel, or at least a significant improvement of an existing technique. A proof-of-concept may be offered by means of a small example, sound argument, or some other means.
Philosophical papers	Papers sketch a new way of looking at existing things by structuring the field in form of a taxonomy or conceptual framework.
Opinion papers	Papers express the personal opinion of somebody whether a certain technique is good or bad, or how things should been done. They do not rely on related work and research methodologies. Papers contain the author's opinion about what is wrong or good about something, how we should do something, etc.
Experience papers	Explain on what and how something has been done in practice. It has to be the personal experience of the author. Papers' emphasis is on what and not on why. The experience may concern one project or more, but it must be the author's personal experience. The papers should contain a list of lessons learned by the author from his or her experience. Papers in this category will often come from industry practitioners or from researchers who have used their tools in practice, and the experience will be reported without a discussion of research methods. The evidence presented in the paper can be anecdotal.

Table 4. Type of research results in software engineering as described in [8]

Type	Description
Procedure or technique	New or better way to do some task, such as design, implementation, measurement, evaluation, selection from alternatives. Includes operational techniques for implementation, representation, management and analysis, but not advice or guidelines.
Qualitative or descriptive model	Structure or taxonomy for a problem area; architectural style, framework, or design pattern; non-formal domain analysis. Well-grounded checklists, well-argued informal generalisations, guidance for integrating other results.
Empirical model	Empirical predictive model based on observed data.
Analytic model	Structural model precise enough to support formal analysis or automatic manipulation.
Notation or tool	Formal language to support technique or model (should have a calculus, semantics, or other basis for computing or inference). Implemented tool that embodies a technique.
Specific solution	Solution to application problem that shows use of software engineering principles – may be design, rather than implementation. Careful analysis of a system or its development. Running system that embodies a result; it may be the carrier of the result, or tis implementation may illustrate a principle that can be applied elsewhere.
Answer or judgement	Result of a specific analysis, evaluation, or comparison.
Report	Interesting observations, rules of thumb.

3   Findings

This section reports on the study's findings obtained from the classification and mapping. The classification was based on the kind of data that we found about the publications and we present the results according to the RQs (Table 1).

RQ1: What is the origin of the research? The researchers scanned the studies and produced a list of countries based on the affiliations of all authors. The count was based on the number of papers affiliated with each one of the authors for each country (i.e., one count was made for a country per paper if one of the authors' affiliation originated from that country). 42 unique countries were identified and the top countries publishing in the area were: USA (24%), Germany (17%), Sweden (10%), UK (10%), and Finland (10%). More than 60% of the research originates from one of these countries; an indication that the field does not attract worldwide attention.

RQ2: Which are the main publication venues of the research? The researchers identified first the publication type (book chapter, conference paper, journal paper or standard) and then there the top venues publishing the research were found. The total unique publication venues found was relatively high, 112, which shows that the research is scattered in many publication venues. Most of the research is published in journals (54%) and more than one third of the papers appear in conference proceedings (36%). We collected the h5-index values as reported in Google Scholar of the top venues (accounting for 29% of the total publications). The papers' venues were highly ranked and even though no specific publication venues exist, they represent qualitative publications and results present some additional value.

RQ3: What is the affiliation of the researchers? The researchers classified the origin of the research contribution to one or more affiliation categories. The results are shown in Table 5. In total 249 papers are listed, as 2 papers included the combination of affiliations industry, academic and professional organisation and 9 papers could not be classified due to lack of information (affiliation was not reported and could not be found from searching the internet).

Table 5. Answer to RQ3: What is the affiliation of the researchers?

Affiliation	Academic	Industry	Professional organisation	Governmental
Academic	167	-	-	-
Industry	31	30	-	-
Professional organisation	5	2	7	-
Governmental	5	0	0	2
Total (249)	208	32	7	2

The majority of the affiliations are academia and the type of research they carry out is mostly evaluation research (34%) and then philosophical papers (21%). More rarely validation research (10%) and solution proposals (9%) appear in their work. As expected, academics dominate in the publications (they are typically more interested in publishing than industry), the number of authors that originate industry is considered high. The research carried out by industrial authors is distributed in various types of research. In some cases, industrial partners didn't co-author papers, i.e., they appear in the acknowledgements' section and thus the real industry participation in the field is not corresponded in our data.

RQ4: What is the research domain of the research conducted? The union of the domains listed by each researcher individually while scanning the papers is reported. A ranking scheme was used to prioritise to primary, secondary and tertiary domains. Table 6 shows the results. Innovation research is the domain that has received the least attention regarding solutions. The results have highlighted the interest in the field of research from both academia and industrial practitioners and researchers, but an indication was visible on lack of specific solutions, answers and judgements of specific questions and implementations is needed.

Table 6. Answer to RQ4: What is the research domain of the research conducted?

Domain	Primary domain	Secondary domain	Tertiary domain
Product	91	34	2
Software	88	31	5
Innovation	0	24	0
Business	0	15	0
Other	1	154	253
Total	180	259	260

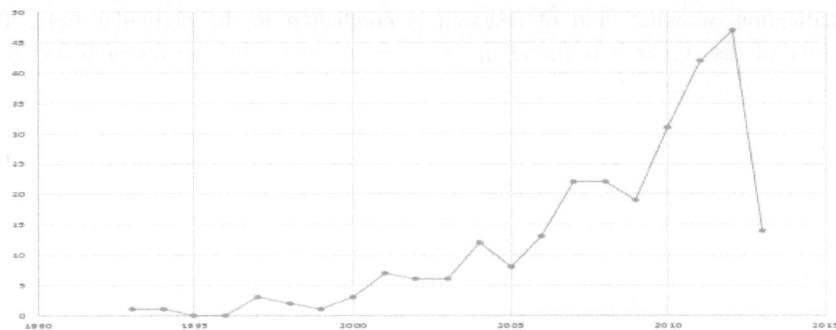

Fig. 2. Answer to RQ5: When is the research conducted?

RQ5: When is the research conducted? The researchers identified the chronological year that the publications were available. Most of the research is conducted in the past few years (2007-2013) as shown in Fig. 2. There is an increasing number of publications happening in years after 2007 on the topic, a peak was reached in 2012 and then it decreased for the next year (2013). This is primarily due to the timing of this study and the limited availability of more recent articles from the scientific databases.

RQ6: What type of research is conducted? The researchers collected all the application domains the papers belonged to. 45% of the papers belonged to 41 unique domains and the predominant domains found were 12% open source, 10% manufacturing, 8% telecom and mobile phones, 7% automotive and 6% information systems.

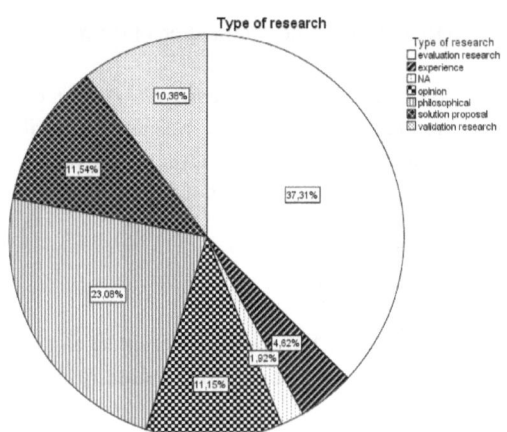

Fig. 3. Answer to RQ6: What type of research is conducted?

RQ7: What type of research is conducted? Two researchers individually classified the papers based on the type facets as described by Wieringa at al. [7]. While papers were classified individually, the researchers resolved all disagreements by thoroughly discussing the papers and the consolidated results are reported in Fig. 3 They provide an indication on what kind of research is conducted in the particular field. The majority of the research is found in the category of evaluation research and then philosophical papers follow.

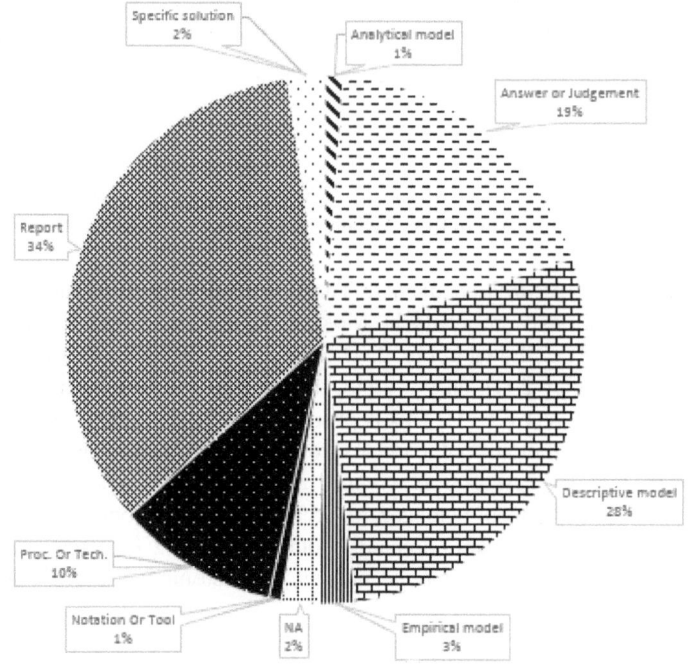

Fig. 4. Answer to RQ8: What is the contribution of the research conducted?

RQ8: What is the contribution of the research conducted? Two researchers individually classified the papers in terms of research contribution based on the categories described by Shaw [8] and any disagreements on the classification were resolved by discussing the papers. The consolidated results are shown in Fig. 4.

4   Analysis and Discussion

This section includes an analysis of the results, presented as synthesis from selected observations that lead up to an agenda for directing future research.

4.1   Analysis of the Results

The literature collected contributes mostly in identifying requirements and ways to manage change in business environments, and assess the evolution of technologies due to this change. One example, is the framework (presented in [9]) *"for understanding innovation management as digital technology is integrated in traditionally physical products"* which discusses issues like organising logic, market dynamics and architecture design. The literature study showed that product innovation and IT innovation have a significantly different and competing outlook on innovation. For instance, product innovation cultivates centralised firm control while the IT innovation ecosystem supports network centricity and creation of digital options. A consequence mentioned in horizontally structured industries, networked collaborative environments with highly non-linear open innovation processes, is that governance mechanisms are useless. The CEO of a company (co-authoring [10]) overseeing methodology, software and strategy for the company's products, confirms the theory in [11] that differentiates business for software innovation into primary and secondary innovations. Innovation is expressed as applied knowledge, and results in the following four types of innovation: new and competitive architecture, organisational capability, product platform and, finally, product family and product. These need to be aligned to become the *"source of innovation extensions that will keep the architecture alive for a realistic commercial timeframe"* [11]. An interesting observation is that *"organizational processes for the adoption of open innovation are reliant on practices for closed innovation"* [12].

The topic of innovation and performance enhancement of the offerings provided by organisations if opened to external partners is also discussed. Among the benefits, services, as mentioned in [13], are to be improved in descending order from the collective contribution of customers, suppliers and competitors. The first are the only ones to actually contribute to the development of new innovative services, while universities and consultants are reported as not likely to immediately effect innovation performance, at least in the specific services industry. In other cases, a survey conducted on software product companies [14] showed that their biggest challenge to growth was not technical, but related to management and marketing. The competence of the personnel is a contributing factor, but also the networks developed in particular for younger companies are important for improvement. Other factors that enable new product development management argued, are for example the degree of networks coupling in collaboration environments, while negative effect is attributed to high rates of entry and exit of parties [15].

Most of the research describes how a solution is implemented and what are the consequences, i.e., benefits and drawbacks, and many times industrial problems are identified. Another aspect found in the literature is that risks are highlighted for businesses opening up to outsiders, third parties, or open source communities, but also benefits from doing so. The common risks mentioned are related to intellectual property rights, interoperability, ownership, control, cost of adaptation, technology evolution and complexity, market shift, and cover legal, managerial and business aspects. Many cases report open innovation processes (e.g., outside-in, inside-out and coupled [12]), methods (e.g., agile and knowledge management [16]) or policies (e.g., selectively revealing code [17]) and tools (e.g., cloud-computing for collaboration spaces [18]). In [18] challenging new requirements for complex industrial infrastructures and products are emphasised that *"require added manufacturing know-how along the value chain to drive the next level of operational efficiency and performance. The development of these complex interlaced systems over the entire product lifecycle represents an increasing challenge for all manufacturers and their suppliers."*

In the literature we found most of the above aspects are highlighted from a single industry or company perspective and only in a few studies are ecosystems and systems of ecosystems discussed. A study [19] conducted with decision makers from European companies showed that even though they *"look to open innovation for value creation and capture, there is still a desire to remain self-reliant"* and thus limited cases exist on decision making together with value network partners. A few examples of mentioning collaborative and across-company networks with multiple players exist and we exemplify them next. The glocal enterprise notion [18] is about *"value creation from global networked operations and involving global supply chain management, product-service linkage, and management of distributed manufacturing units"*. In particular domains, even after several years of development *"the concrete result of the open innovation process seems rather scarce"* [20]. In product lines, a requirement would be that the software needs to carry more information than traditional software packages [21], and a lot of work needs to be done on the coordination and management regarding the federation aspect. In [22] it is mentioned that *"the power of the platform leader depends on the degree of dependence of other agents in the ecosystem of platform leaders"* and based on examples in the US IT industry the authors try to understand better the role of the platform leader in the business ecosystem. In [23] cases are indicated where companies became more flexible and applied more free managerial practices based on the expectations of open source communities while in [24] the theoretical gap of business ecosystems and network structures, strategy and evolution is emphasised.

4.2   Research Agenda

Based on the discussion above we have identified areas that require additional research. Clearly, ecosystems for embedded software require additional research to better understand innovation, business, and organisational aspects for that specific area. Miller and Morris [11] describe innovation in two levels; primary innovation that creates a new competitive architecture based on knowledge from existing markets and products, which requires new organisational capability to transform innovations into products. The primary innovations are prerequisites for efficient open-innovation of products, that is, secondary innovations in the ecosystem.

The product is based on a product platform, which is a reflection of the organisational capabilities and forms the basis for product families. More specifically, better understanding of the mechanisms for primary innovations, that is, the learning knowledge processes that form the innovation system, its organisational and architectural aspects in an ecosystem context, is needed and how capabilities can be transformed into supporting ecosystem platforms.

Table 7 presents an agenda with research topics that target the *primary innovations* as discussed above. The research focus is initially on learning from existing product platforms and ecosystems, which is reflected in the agenda. New knowledge is the basis for primary innovations. Based on new knowledge the community can innovate solutions, such as specific patterns, methods and techniques, which can then be validated. The items on the agenda are thus concerned with deriving knowledge about the *competitive architecture* and *organisational capability* for *open innovation*.

Table 7. Research agenda

Topic	Research need
Software innovation	In the context of software ecosystems we need to further understand the competitive architecture and organisational capabilities that foster open-innovation, for example, investigate if some specific ecosystem structures better support software innovation than the rest.
Competitive architectures for innovation	An important aspect of the innovation system is the competitive architecture. We need to better understand the transition from learning about existing products and markets to knowledge and further to the definition of a new competitive architecture in ecosystems. Beyond defining the architecture, what descriptions (e.g., technical, architectural, quality assurance) are parts of the organisational capability that enable open innovation in a software ecosystem?
Process flexibility in the ecosystem	One important aspect of the competitive architecture and organisational capability that we may learn from existing markets and product families is which kind of ecosystem processes support software innovation across domains and players. There is currently a lack of generalizable results here.
Ecosystem procedures and techniques	On a more detailed level, we may derive knowledge from studies about procedures and techniques that support innovation in ecosystems that could be part of the organisational capabilities and strengths.
Business innovation for software	The other important aspect of innovation in ecosystems is business innovation, which could be equally useful for the creation of new organisational capability. For a start we need to research best current practices for business innovation in the software domain. Currently there are no general answers to what works and what doesn't as existing knowledge is based on single data points reported by industry or academia in experience papers.
Business environments for innovation in ecosystems	On the more detailed level business agreements with respect to relationships and operations that enable software innovation and collaboration across organisational borders are currently not well understood and more research is required. Ensuring understandability and analysability require support from models and it is unclear which business environment characteristics need to be included in such models, for example size, type of offering, resources, existing and planned networks, roles.
Business processes and software innovation	The final capability we include in our agenda is concerned with understanding how ecosystem processes and practices support business innovation and software innovation combined. Jansen et al. [25] categorises processes into five core areas (i.e., governance, R&D, software product management, marketing and sales, consulting and support services). Thus, further research is needed for them to be better understood in the context of open-innovation in ecosystems.

5   Conclusions and Future Work

This paper is the first step in charting the research on ecosystems and open innovation of systems in the context of software engineering for embedded systems based on the specific research questions we posed. We have identified several areas researched and others that require additional research. The systematic map provides and overview of this field of research that includes information about the origin of the research, publication venues, and publication frequency from 1993 until when this research was conducted (early 2014). In addition the map emphasized on the type of research conducted, the research and application domains and the research results and contributions achieved. The map was analysed for trends and patterns.

Overall, the result shows that the field is an emerging field of research. The type of research is primarily explorative, that is, philosophical, experience or evaluation research producing reports, opinions, or descriptive models from specific parts of the world. Finding concrete answers to most questions the studies we found pose is very difficult, something that our analysis confirms. Here lies the community challenges and thus, we provide a research agenda based on the mapping analysis. In the future, we plan to extract more results from the systematic study conducted and present them in an extended publication.

Acknowledgments. The research was funded by VINNOVA, the Swedish Agency for Innovation Systems and Innovative Product Development (Grants No. 2012-03782 and 2013-03492).

References

1. Messerschmitt, D.G., Szyperski, C.: Software Ecosystem: Understanding an Indispensable Technology and Industry. MIT Press, Cambridge (2003)
2. Axelsson, J., Papatheocharous, E., Andersson, J.: Characteristics of Software Ecosystems for Federated Embedded Systems: A Case Study. Inform. Software Tech. 51(6), 1457–1475 (2014)
3. Trew, T., Botterweck, G., Nuseibeh, B.: A Reference Architecture for Consumer Electronics Products and Its Application in Requirements Engineering. In: Avgeriou, P., Grundy, J., Hall, J.G., Lago, P., Mistrík, I. (eds.) Relating Software Requirements and Architectures, pp. 203–231. Springer, Heidelberg (2011), http://link.springer.com/chapter/10.1007/978-3-642-21001-3_13
4. Kuschel, J., Remneland, B., Holmqvist, M.: Open Innovation and Control: A Case from Volvo. In: 43rd Hawaii International Conference on System Sciences, pp. 1–10 (2010)
5. Petersen, K., Feldt, R., Mujtaba, S., Mattsson, M.: Systematic Mapping Studies in Software Engineering. In: Proceedings of the 12th International Conference on Evaluation and Assessment in Software Engineering, Swinton, UK, pp. 68–77 (2008)
6. Manikas, K., Hansen, K.M.: Software Ecosystems – A Systematic Literature Review. J. Syst. Software 86(5), 1294–1306 (2013)
7. Wieringa, R., Maiden, N.A.M., Mead, N.R., Rolland, C.: Requirements Engineering Paper Classification and Evaluation Criteria: A Proposal and a Discussion. Requir. Eng. 11(1), 102–107 (2006)
8. Shaw, M.: What makes good research in software engineering? International Journal on Software Tools for Technology Transfer 4(1), 1–7 (2002)
9. [S55] Svahn, F., Henfridsson, O.: The Dual Regimes of Digital Innovation Management. In: 45th Hawaii International Conference on System Science, pp. 3347–3356 (2012)
10. [S42] Van Zyl, J.: Process Innovation Imperative (Software Product Development Organisation). In: Proceedings of the Change Management and the New Industrial Revolution, pp. 454–459 (2001)
11. Miller, W.L., Morris, L.: Fourth Generation R&D, Managing Knowledge, Technology and Innovation. Wiley Publishers (1999)

12. [S251] Morgan, L., Finnegan, P.: Open Innovation in Secondary Software Firms: An Exploration of Managers' Perceptions of Open Source Software. SIGMIS Database 41(1), 76–95 (2010)
13. [S70] Wagner, S.M.: Partners for Business-to-Business Service Innovation. IEEE Transactions on Engineering Management 60(1), 113–123 (2013)
14. [S72] Hietala, J., Kontio, J., Jokinen, J.-P., Pyysiainen, J.: Challenges of Software Product Companies: Results of a National Survey in Finland. In: 10th International Symposium on Software Metrics, pp. 232–243 (2004)
15. [S74] Uzuegbunam, I.S.: Managing Collaborative New Product Development of Complex Software Systems: Mythical Man-Month Re-Visited. In: IEEE International Engineering Management Conference, pp. 494–498 (2005)
16. [S91] Gourova, E., Toteva, K.: Enhancing Knowledge Creation and Innovation in SMEs. In: 2012 Mediterranean Conference on Embedded Computing, pp. 292–297 (2012)
17. [S147] Henkel, J.: Selective Revealing in Open Innovation Processes: The Case of Embedded Linux. Research Policy 35(7), 953–969 (2006)
18. [S238] Camarinha-Matos, L.M., Afsarmanesh, H., Koelmel, B.: Collaborative Networks in Support of Service-Enhanced Products. In: Camarinha-Matos, L.M., Pereira-Klen, A., Afsarmanesh, H. (eds.) PRO-VE 2011. IFIP AICT, vol. 362, pp. 95–104. Springer, Heidelberg (2011), http://link.springer.com/chapter/10.1007/978-3-642-23330-2_11
19. [S219] Morgan, L., Finnegan, P.: Deciding on Open Innovation: An Exploration of How Firms Create and Capture Value with Open Source Software. In: León, G., Bernardos, A.M., Casar, J.R., Kautz, K., De Gross, J.I. (eds.) Open IT-Based Innovation: Moving Towards Cooperative IT Transfer and Knowledge Diffusion. IFIP, vol. 287, pp. 229–246. Springer, Boston (2008), http://link.springer.com/chapter/10.1007/978-0-387-87503-3_13.
20. [S4] Tongia, R., Subrahmanian, E.: Information and Communications Technology for Development (ICT4D) - A Design Challenge? In: International Conference on Information and Communication Technologies and Development, pp. 243–255 (2006)
21. [S13] Van der Linden, F.: Software Product Families in Europe: The Esaps Cafe Projects. IEEE Software 19(4), 41–49 (2002)
22. [S73] Choi, B., Phan, K.: Platform Leadership in Business Ecosystem: Literature-Based Study on Resource Dependence Theory (RDT). In: Technology Management for Emerging Technologies, pp. 133–138 (2012)
23. [S19] Shaikh, M., Cornford, T.: 'Letting Go of Control' to Embrace Open Source: Implications for Company and Community. In: 43rd Hawaii International Conference on System Sciences, pp. 1–10 (2010)
24. [S20] Rong, K., Hou, J., Shi, Y., Lu, O.: From Value Chain, Supply Network, towards Business Ecosystem (BE): Evaluating the BE Concept's Implications to Emerging Industrial Demand. In: IEEE International Conference on Industrial Engineering and Engineering Management, pp. 2173–2177 (2010)
25. Jansen, S., Brinkkemper, S., Souer, J., Luinenburg, L.: Shades of Gray: Opening up a Software Producing Organization with the Open Software Enterprise Model. J. Syst. Software 85(7), 1495–1510 (2012)

Assessing the Value Blueprint to Support the Design of a Business Ecosystem

Luciana A. Almeida[1], Cleidson R.B. de Souza[1,2(✉)], Adailton M. Lima[1],
and Rodrigo Q. Reis[1]

[1]Universidade Federal do Pará, Belém, PA, 66075-110, Brazil
lu.abdon.si@gmail.com, {adailton,quites}@ufpa.br
[2] Instituto Tecnológico Vale, Belém, PA, 66055-090, Brazil
cleidson.desouza@acm.org

Abstract. Ecosystems are an important aspect of today's software business, and can be beneficial to companies that can create and organize such ecosystems around their products. Unfortunately, creating such ecosystems is not an easy task. The value blueprint is a tool created by Adner, that allows a company to identify the different types of risks to be faced during the establishment of an ecosystem. In this paper we describe a case study conducted to assess the value blueprint as an effective tool to help in the design of new ecosystems. This case study is based on data about the Apple Watch. We report our evaluation of the value blueprint tool and provide recommendations for practitioners interested in establishing their own ecosystems and researchers interested in the design of ecosystems.

Keywords: Business ecosystem · Ecosystem design · Value blueprint

1   Introduction

Nowadays, innovation is a key point to any companies' growth and success. In the past, innovation depended exclusively on the company itself. However, today there is a increasing recognized importance of the role of, visible or not, collaborators in a company's success. Business ecosystem is the term used to refer to this new scenario. While there are several definitions of business ecosystems, we will adopt Moore's definition: "a business ecosystem is a dynamic structure of interconnected organizations that depend on each other for mutual survival." [2] Therefore it is an economic community supported by a foundation of organizations and individuals who interact through assets and services, produces value to customers, which also belong to the ecosystem. Members of the ecosystem also include suppliers, inputs producers, competitors and other stakeholders.

The corollary of this new scenario is that companies currently need to be able to identify, understand and act upon their dependencies if they want to succeed [3]. In fact, both academics and practitioners recognize the importance of dealing with the dependencies among the different members of a business ecosystem. For instance,

J.M. Fernandes et al. (Eds.): ICSOB 2015, LNBIP 210, pp. 96–101, 2015.
DOI: 10.1007/978-3-319-19593-3_8

Gawer and Cusumano [1] discuss a framework to be used by managers to design a strategy to become leaders in their ecosystem. Similarly, Eisenmann, Parker and Alstyne [4] discuss how relationships among ecosystem members might allow one provider in one ecosystem enter another ecosystem. However, most of the research in the area is based on analysis of existing products. Only a few papers have been written about the required steps for a company to manage the dependencies among ecosystem parties *in the beginning of a process*.

In our work we are interested in developing an enterprise business ecosystem, i.e., an ecosystem that will be used solely within our organization. However, differently from other studies [5], this ecosystem will be built from the scratch. Therefore, we started to look for recommendations, guidelines or methodologies about how to manage the dependencies that should be taken into account when designing our own ecosystem. A related work we identified is the Model Business Canvas [7], a tool used to model, document and present business models. However, the business canvas does not take into account the broader "context", i.e. the ecosystem, where this business is embedded. An extension to the business canvas is proposed by Sniukas [8] who argues that the canvas should include the current business reality in which businesses are embedded including partners, suppliers and other parties. Risk, however, is not explicitly represented in the business canvas. The work that most closely reflected our interests is the work written by Adner [3]. Adner proposes a tool, called Value Blueprint, that *allows one to identify the risks associated with ecosystem design especially those risks associated with implicit and explicit dependencies*.

This paper reports on our assessment of the value blueprint [3] as a tool to support the design of software ecosystems. This assessment is done through a case study. In this case, we decided to focus on the development of innovative ecosystems, and for this reason the Apple Watch [6, 13] case has been chosen. Since we do not have access to internal Apple's employees, our data collection was based on data available in the news, articles and the product description currently available at Apple's website. Our results suggest that the value blueprint is a simple and powerful tool to design business ecosystems, but it has some limitations and requires specific background that might limit its applicability.

2   Designing Ecosystems Using the Value Blueprint

In order to identify, document and reason about risks in the context of ecosystems, Adner proposes a tool called value blueprint. This tool provides an overview of the members required to deliver the value proposal of a product as well as different types of risks associated with them. Beyond the "traditional" execution risks, there are two additional types of risks, co-innovation and adoption risks, that are essential in the context of business ecosystems. Co-Innovation risks consist of *externally* developed technologies or approaches that should exist so that the company product is successful, while adoption chain risks refer to all the participants in the value chain that should *adopt* the innovation so that the customer can have the opportunity to recognize the product's value proposal.

To express these risks, Adner uses a simple metaphor: a continuous traffic sign represented by green, yellow, or red lights, to indicate the alignment of each member. For the co-innovation risks, green means the associated members are ready and in place; yellow means that they are not yet in place, but that they have a plan for this; and red means that these parties are not in place and there is no clear plan set for them. For the adoption risks, green means that a member is looking forward to participating in the business ecosystem; yellow means that they are neutral, but open to entering it; and red means that the member has clear reasons for not joining.

Adner [3] argues that it is rare for an innovative product to start with all the lights green. That is not mandatory, either. Yellow lights are acceptable, as long as they are followed by a plan to make them turn into green. Red lights, though, are challenging. Any red light, either by lack of capacity of a collaborator to deliver or by lack of will to cooperate, or due to a problem of its own, must be addressed, for instance by creating incentives to find a way to overcome problematic connections in the project.

With the creation of the value blueprint all the components for a minimum viable ecosystem (MVE)[1] are clearly laid out. This blueprint establishes the elements needed to deliver the value proposal, how they are positioned and their relations. Once the relationships are identified and mapped, it is possible to have a vision of all the members involved in the ecosystem alongside the risk and challenges that extend beyond the company's own immediate responsibilities.

3   Method of Research

Adner presents several examples of value blueprints in his book including Apple's iPod and iPhone, Nigeria's M-Pesa, Amazon's Kindle, among other products. Adner also presents some recommendations to be used during the creation of one's own ecosystem [3, p. 64].

We followed these recommendations to be able to assess the process of creating value blueprints as well as the blueprints themselves. Therefore, we chose to create a value blueprint for the Apple Watch. Although, this is not the first of its kind, it is expected to give birth to a family of products by Apple [6]. We chose Apple due to its good track of success in the context of business ecosystems in the last years. Another reason for choosing this product is that in our own company, we are exploring the usage of wearables. Therefore, we hoped that creating such an ecosystem could provide a good starting point for our own project.

In this paper the research method applied is the case study [9], which allows the study of a contemporary phenomena in a broad and uncontrolled context (like the Apple Watch). Our data collection was exclusively performed by exploratory qualitative procedures [10], extracting data available in the Internet (especially Apple's website) and from Adner's book [3]. Other data collection methods were not viable due to

---

[1] Adner defines a minimum viable ecosystem (MVE) as "the simplest ecosystem [one can] assemble and still create some new value" [2, pg. 198].

the case selection, i.e., interviewing or observing Apple developers and management was not possible despite the potential to uncover a number answers for this study.

It is important to mention that Adner presents the value blueprint for other Apple products, including the iPod, iPad and iPhone [3]. So, we did not create the blueprint for the Apple Watch from the scratch, we used some of the ideas from other products to guide our data collection and analysis methods.

4   Results and Discussion

Figure 1 shows the value Blueprint for the Apple Watch MVE based on the material we collected and the previous Apple's ecosystems from Adner [3]. The product is clear identified, the Apple Watch. The suppliers are characterized as all those who offer inputs for the product construction, like the inputs for new technologies, the WatchKit and the investors interested in seeing the results of the product [12]. The intermediates are the retailers, like the Apple Store and the network operators. The complementors are those who many times are not in the managers' field of vision: they are the retailers who are willing to adopt the Apple Pay system, including the airline companies who enable their boarding passes through the Passbook, the developers who write apps for the product and leads the product to have even more value proposals to the users. End-users include iPhone users, as well as users of other Apple services including Apple Pay, Apple TV, and iTunes.

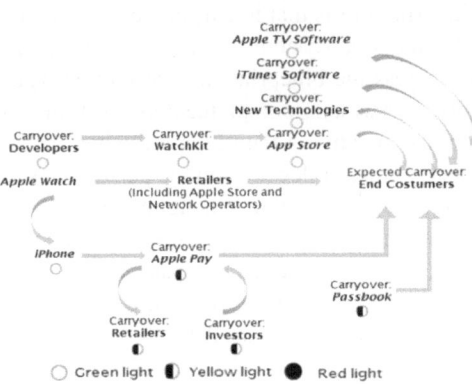

The blueprint also illustrates the co-innovation risks and adoption chain risks. For instance, we can observe that the Apple Watch is a device that is launched with a co-innovation risk [3], since it requires an iPhone 5 or 6 to unlock other functionalities. Of course, Apple is already familiar with this risk and this is definitely part of its strategy. In fact, what Apple is doing is what Adner calls *ecosystems carryover*, in which the consolidation of an ecosystem is used to create advantage over a new ecosystem.

Fig. 1. The Value Blueprint representing the Apple Watch MVE

An example of ecosystem carryover would be how the iPhone leveraged the iPod's ecosystem. In the scenario of the Apple Watch, Apple wants to use the iPhone's ecosystem to establish a new ecosystem for its watch. Apple indeed argues that an important new value proposition of the Apple Watch is that with this device the user can control all other Apple devices, like iTunes playlists, Apple's TV channels, and so on.

Other co-innovation risks we identified in the blueprint are the new technologies developed to allow the user experience including infrared LEDs; photo sensors; Touch Force; TapTic Engine; Flexible Screens; among others. Technologies like

Wi-Fi, GPS and Bluetooth are necessary to the Apple Watch value proposal [13] and therefore, are regarded as project execution risks, which are not part of the blueprint.

Adoption chain risks refer to the participants that should adopt the innovation so that the customer can have the opportunity to recognize the value proposal [3]. In this case, it is important to recognize that Apple's usual plan is to induce existing consumers to buy new products and move to the new ecosystem based on the value proposal of this new product. In our case study, we can find the Apple Pay and Apple Watch products. Apple Pay is the electronic payment system launched by Apple [11]. It is already available for the iPhone 6, i.e., an iPhone 6 user is able to perform purchases with Apple Pay-enabled retailers without an Apple Watch. In other words, Apple Watch consumers will benefit from the investors and retailers who already support the Apple Watch, which means that the Apple Watch ecosystem will *likely* carry along a number of investors and retailers from the iPhone ecosystem [11].

An example of an adoption chain risk we identified is related to the software developers who will write applications for the Apple Watch, i.e., for this watch to be successful, it is important to have developers motivated to contribute to it even before the product is released. To deal with this risk, Apple has made a number of important decisions. First of all, software for the Apple Watch will be provided through the App Store (yet another example of ecosystem carryover). In addition, Apple will provide the WatchKit with new tools and APIs that will allow developers to create Apple Watch applications [20]. By providing these, we argue that Apple expects to increase the likelihood of an ecosystem carryover among the software developers.

Our initial evaluation of the value blueprint tool is that it is a simple, easy to understand and yet powerful tool to design business ecosystems. Our assessment is based on the fact that in the notation used to express the blueprints has only three types of (graphical) components: business members (partners, complementors, etc), their status regarding the product, and the relationships among them. On the other hand, the identification of the parties is very subjective, i.e., it depends on the person constructing the blueprint. Furthermore, identifying the relationships among the different blueprint members is not as straightforward, especially for non-business professionals. Another challenge we faced was the time and effort required to create a blueprint. It is not a simple task, and required the first author four weeks to do so even though, as mentioned, the Apple's Watch blueprint was based on similar Apple's blueprints [3].

5   Final Remarks

The value blueprint [3] is a tool proposed to help innovators to design products in the modern context of business ecosystems. We conducted a case study using the value blueprint by modeling the Apple's Watch ecosystem. By modeling partners, suppliers, investors and other ecosystem members as well as the extent to which they are engaged with the Apple Watch, it was possible to identify the risks associated with this product. This blueprint, however, is a *diagnosis* tool: it allows one to identify the current status of his/her ecosystem, but does *not* suggest what (s)he needs to do in order to change this ecosystem towards a more positive outcome. Companies interested in launching ecosystems around their products still have to choose the strategy [1, 2, 4] they will adopt in their ecosystems. This also suggests that the creation of a blueprint is only the first step, since companies will need to continuously monitor their ecosystem and update their blueprint accordingly.

As for future work, we will use the lessons learned in this case study to continue the design of our enterprise ecosystem. In addition, we will also explore computational support for the creation, and analysis, of value blueprints.

Acknowledgements. Authors would like to thank the funding from CNPq (process numbers 485070/2013-8 and 310468/2014-0), Chamada 59/2013 MCTI/CT-Info/CNPq (process number 440880/2013-0) and CAPES through a M.Sc. scholarship granted to the first author.

References

1. Gawer, A., Cusumano, M.: Platform Leadership, p. 2. HBR Press, Cambridge (2002)
2. Moore, J.F.: Predators and Prey, A New Ecology of Competition. HBR (May-June 1993)
3. Adner, R.: The Wide Lens – What Successful Innovators See That Others Miss. Penguin Group (USA) Inc., USA (2012)
4. Eisenmann, T., Parker, G., Van Alstyne, M.: Platform Envelopment. Strategic Management Journal 12(32), 1270–1285 (2011)
5. Ghanam, Y., et al.: Making the leap to a software platform strategy: Issues and challenges. Information and Software Technology 54(9), 968–984 (2012)
6. TechCrunch, http://techcrunch.com/topic/product/apple-watch/
7. Osterwalder, A., Pigneur, Y.: Business Model Generation – Innovation in Business Models (2011)
8. Sniukas, M.: Take Your Business Model to the Next Level. In: Innovation Solutions from Innovation Management (2013)
9. Yin, R.K.: Case study research: design and methods. Sage Publications, Inc. (1994)
10. Strauss, A., Corbin, J.: Basics of Qualitative Research: Techniques and Procedures for Developing Grounded Theory, 2nd edn. SAGE publications, Thousand Oaks (1998)
11. The Seattle Times: Apple broadens its ecosystem with its watch, payment system (2014), Patently Apple: Apple Pay: The Digital Wallet that will Rule the World (2014)
12. Appleinsider: iPhone 6 & Apple Watch reveals lived up to the hype for Wall Street, investors have high hopes for Apple Pay (2014)
13. Apple Webpage (2015), https://www.apple.com/watch/overview/

Effects of Technological Change on Acquisition Behavior: An Empirical Analysis of Electronic Design Automation

Thomas Lücking[1] and Marcus Wagner[2(✉)]

[1] Sony Computer Entertainment Europe, 10 Great Marlborough Street,
London W1F 7LP, United Kingdom
thomas.luecking@hotmail.de
[2] Augsburg University, Universitätsstr. 16,
86159 Augsburg, Germany
marcus.wagner@wiwi.uni-augsburg.de

Abstract. This paper contains an empirical analysis of acquisition dynamics in the electronic design automation (EDA) industry. Using qualitative and quantitative data, we show that particular groups of EDA firms strongly contribute to acquisition activity in the industry at specific times. Based on this we provide empirical evidence that specialized firms pursue focused and 'defensive' acquisitions during times of uncertainty, indicating that concentration on existing competencies is preferred over diversification into promising new, but unfamiliar markets.

1   Introduction

High-technology (high-tech)[1] industries are characterized by rapid technological change during which firms have to maintain their competitive positions based on their (technological) competencies. Acquisitions (synonymous: takeovers, mergers) are a means to access such competencies and their analysis thus of high practical relevance to inform firms how to use them [1]. Although there is a large body of empirical management research literature on the acquisition phenomenon, most of this work focuses on outcomes of corporate takeovers. Researchers have acknowledged the complexity of acquisitions by looking at potential aspects that affect post-merger performance [2, 3], with factors like the targeted knowledge base, innovation type and market relatedness emerging [4, 5, 6]. It was found that inconsistency is often due to substantial lack of explanatory value of the independent variables [7].

Another reason could be simultaneous inclusion of several industries and insufficient consideration of strategies. Finally, only few studies addressed the question of why acquisitions are done at a single-industry level [8]. Yet, this is crucial given that motives behind acquisitions differ in relevance across industries and that the latter consist of different strategic groups [9]. Therefore, individual firm behavior

---

[1] Our definition refers to the North American Industrial Classification System categories high-tech manufacturing, communication services, software services, and engineering and tech services [12].

© Springer International Publishing Switzerland 2015
J.M. Fernandes et al. (Eds.): ICSOB 2015, LNBIP 210, pp. 102–116, 2015.
DOI: 10.1007/978-3-319-19593-3_9

is a function of a particular environment with specific technological changes [10], firm-specific strategic positions characterized by type and breadth of product portfolios, and institutional factors [11]. Related to the latter, work on merger waves empirically identifies drivers for temporal clustering of acquisitions, with technological shocks being a major one [13, 14, 15].

In order to assess corporate behavior appropriately it is crucial to understand the competitive environment within which the firm is primarily active. Each firm competes on the basis of its competencies, which are ultimately embodied in the specific products and services the firm offers and that its customers are willing to pay for [16]. Hence, we provide a focused analysis of firm behavior in general and of acquisition behavior in particular by concentrating on a single industry, EDA, involving detailed knowledge about that particular business and information about the types of products of each firm.

This allows to identify different strategic groups as well as relevant industry specific trends, answering the following research questions: Does technological change have a significant impact on the acquisition behavior and do firms with different product portfolios behave differently during that technological change? In answering this question whose relevance was pointed out in the beginning of the introduction and motivated further by an exposition of the literature on post-merger performance, acquisition waves and strategic groups, we contribute to the strategic management field and the above specific literatures in it.

2   Theoretical Background and Hypotheses Development

The velocity at which modern technological regimes change, makes the concept of dynamic capabilities in the field of strategic management increasingly relevant [17]. This is because not changing the resource base of a firm through them gives conservative, exploitation-oriented projects priority over longer-term, explorative endeavors [18]. In this case, firms also need to devote large amounts of managerial and financial resources to address current customers, a situation also known as *"the tyranny of the served market"* [19]. Not adapting to changing conditions becomes visible in product portfolios, since existing offerings are the outcome firm's past strategy [20].

Eventually, technological change can render existing competencies obsolete [21]. The literature on post-merger performance thus suggests technology-driven acquisitions as a means to address competency loss, which correlates with the intensity of technological change [22]. Furthermore, research on merger waves has shown that industry-specific conditions nuance wider institutional factors in their effect on acquisition behavior [23].

In order to dissect acquisition behavior for a single industry, it is necessary to go beyond a simple count of acquisitions. Instead, differences between the industry's strategic groups need to be considered. Although all firms are equally exposed to technological change some might be affected differently since firms within one industry differ [24]. Therefore, we take the structure of product portfolios into account to address individual differences across firms. This approach also address calls in prior work to address more directly the relevance and importance of within-industry diversification on performance [25]. Also, to reveal such qualitative relationships between product portfolios, technological change and acquisition patterns we need to limit the scope of our study to acquisitions in one specific industry.[2] This is further supported by benefits from diversification into industry-specific or 'related' fields being shown to be transferable to a single-industry level, and the role of acquisitions for innovation [26].

Following approaches from configuration theory, technological change is understood here as a cause of environmental turbulence beyond incremental and modular reconfigurations that implies major technological development [27, 28]. Based on this definition of technological change, we distinguish between two generic types of takeover strategies within the boundaries of a single industry. The first can be characterized as 'expansive', meaning that the acquirer extends its activities into new product-/service-categories within the boundaries of its industry. The second generic type of takeover strategy can be described as 'defensive' in that the acquiring firm purchases an organization that offers products/services in sub-categories or product segments in which the acquirer already has an established interest.

Our empirical analysis is about U.S. EDA firms. EDA is the general term for the software tools that are used to design and test semiconductors. As part of the extremely dynamic semiconductor sector, EDA firms work under a permanent pressure to innovate. The existence of the so-called 'design gap' is a good indicator of this pressure. This gap embodies the enormous challenge that chip design software firms face. Manufacturers of silicon-based chips constantly invent smaller-scale manufacturing processes, and they need corresponding design software to realize the advantages and address the challenges of miniaturization [29]. In other words, while a new smaller manufacturing process is being developed, chipmakers approach EDA software firms to incorporate corresponding features into their products. This leads to the 'design gap' in which design software has to constantly catch up with technological advancements. This permanently creates fertile niches for EDA software in which new ideas and technologies can evolve in the form of new ventures, while entry barriers in terms of required capital are low. As a consequence, we deal with an industry that is characterized by a high frequency of corporate acquisitions.

We define the type of takeover strategies that emerge from technological change by observing the targets and their particular products in relation to the introduction of the 90 nm chip scale, which is a technological change with strong implications for the EDA industry. At the beginning of 2004, Intel started to release its first 90 nm microprocessors to end customers [30]. In fact, a discussion about 90 nm can be observed starting in 2003 [31], which indicates a concern about competencies in light of this technological change. Given acquisitions can mitigate their erosion, the following hypothesis is proposed:

H1: The introduction of the 90 nm chip technology has a positive impact on the number of acquisitions by firms in the EDA industry.

---

[2] See the methodology section for more information on the set of acquisitions analyzed.

Apart from expecting a general increase in acquisition behavior, our industry knowledge and our data also allows us to differentiate between product categories within EDA. To understand EDA tool categories, it is important to understand that chip designers depend on EDA tools providing a high level of abstraction which in the end can be automatically transformed into a blueprint for physical manufacturing (including defined placements and routings).

The chip design process flow can be broadly divided into three subcategories/ phases, the Electronic System Level (ESL), IC Front-End (IC-FE) and IC Back-End (IC-BE) design [29]. ESL encompasses the most abstract software at the beginning of a design process while IC-BE is closest to the concrete physical layout of the chip. Because of the ramifications of early design choices in the beginning of the development process tools at the highest abstraction levels become more and more valuable as complexity continues to increase. This could also be observed with the introduction of the 90 nm process in mass production.

Around 2003, experts became vocal on the importance of ESL tools for coping with challenges from the introduction of 90 nm manufacturing scales [32]. Detailed product information allows us to distinguish between firms with and without ESL software in their product portfolios. We consider the acquisition of a target that offers ESL products as more unrelated or expansive compared to an acquisition of a target with non-ESL products when the acquirer has no ESL products in its product portfolio.

Since the 90 nm transition induced demand for ESL competencies, we would expect non-ESL firms to diversify into the ESL segment in their attempt to maintain competencies and therefore, to pursue expansive acquisition strategies. In addition, diversification along the value-added design chain is very feasible considering the integrated nature of the chip design flow, where ESL is a new endpoint extending the chain by one module. Since for customers, complete design suites from only one EDA supplier ensure perfect compatibility and reduce implementation efforts from interfaces with third parties [33], the following hypothesis can be stated:

H2a: Firms without ESL products react to 90 nm chip technology with an expansive strategy by acquiring targets with ESL products.

Opposed to this expansive acquisition motive, 'non-ESL firms' could also prefer defensive acquisitions in the sense of related takeovers. This would enable firms without any ESL products to strengthen their existing product lines and to increase revenue from those by acquiring (innovative) targets. In dynamic environments such a focused strategy could be more rational since business extension implies more efforts and operative friction [34]. In addition, by acquiring similar targets, competition in the industry is decreased and margins can potentially be improved. Thus, a second (competing) hypothesis can also be posed as follows:

H2b: EDA firms without ESL products react to the 90 nm chip technology through a defensive strategy by acquiring targets within product segments they already occupy.

Hypotheses 2a and 2b both imply a positive moderating effect on the total number of acquisitions by firms without ESL products of the technological change to 90 nm. Testing which of them holds based on acquisition behavior is therefore only possible using the detailed industry-level data with qualitative information that is at our disposal.

3   Methodology

To test our above hypotheses we employ a unique panel dataset of U.S. EDA firms from 1996–2006. Despite an international industry structure, the large majority of global revenue comes from EDA firms based in the U.S. [35]. This allows us to control for any country effects without losing global information about specific trends and developments. Gartner Dataquest and Gary Smith EDA published annual reports on firms in the global EDA industry for the period 1996–2006 including information about the specific sub-segments in which firms are active, allowing us to track the type and breadth of firm-specific activities within the EDA industry over time. For the U.S. firms in these reports matching financial data for all public U.S. firms from the Compustat database was obtained and patent information was sourced from the database of the National Bureau of Economic Research (NBER). Information about the takeover activity of the firms comes from the Thomson One Banker database.

An acquisition is defined here as a purchase that leads to a corporate equity stake of more than 50 percent of another company [36]. This excludes deals resulting in minority stakes and the repurchasing of a company's own shares. Also excluded are corporate deals involving non-EDA companies, such as IT service companies. Through this strict data treatment, we are able to interpret every acquisition as an event following which the acquiring party has full control over the target and full formal access to the firm's technological competencies. Starting with a sample of 468 acquisitions conducted by public U.S. EDA firms between 1996 and 2006, every acquisition entry was manually evaluated using these rules, resulting in a final set of 247 before any empirical analysis was conducted. Furthermore, qualitative triangulation through secondary sources (e.g. [32]) ensured the filtering was appropriate.

From the NBER database 16,446 patents have been extracted, of which 2,748 were applied for prior to our chosen time period (1996–2006). These latter patents are used to calculate starting patent stocks in 1996. Before the matching process, 84.2 percent of all patents are in the IPC categories 'G' (Physics) and 'H' (Electricity). Almost 13.9 percent are in the 'B' (Performing Operations, Transporting) and 'C' (Chemistry, Metallurgy) categories. Due to our narrow industry focus and to avoid any patent selection bias, we estimated all our models with two versions of our patent data. One version included only patents belonging to the more industry-related categories 'G' and 'H' and one version included all patents. The reported models in this analysis include all patents since the results do not differ significantly.

A proper selection is necessary to account for the arguments about the distinct dynamics. Since we talk about industry-specific trends we need to make sure that all included firms experience upcoming technological changes in their direct environment in a similar way. Therefore, every firm within the dataset generated has been analyzed regarding its business affiliation to the EDA industry. Thus, for a condensed set of 36 companies we identified EDA as (at least) one of its core business and kept them in the final dataset. The years 1996 and 1997 have been excluded from our analyses owing to there being too few data points. For the purpose of this analysis, our dataset is sufficiently large, since data of similar size has been used [37]. VIF values of 1.17 to 3.75 indicate that multicollinearity is unlikely to be an issue in our analysis [38].

Our dependent variable is the number of acquisitions being conducted by a given firm in a given year. Since this is a count variable, we employ a negative binomial model for our regression analysis [39]. The panel structure of our dataset allows us to address within- and between-differences in our dataset. We used the Hausman test to decide between fixed- and random effects. Based on the insignificant test results and our special interest in the behavior of a whole industry, we estimate a random effects model to also account for time-constant variables and to avoid a bias towards the subset of *"treated"* individuals.

Our first explanatory variable represents the change in microchip complexity going from 130 nm to 90 nm in mass production. The first large-scale introduction of 90 nm microprocessors happened in 2004 [30]. Considering usual lead times within the semiconductor industry, we consider this trend to have already been fully established in 2003. Further confirmation comes from publications and articles about the coming of the 90 nm chip scale and its implications for chip design in 2003. As our time period runs from 1998–2006, our new *90 nm* variable equals zero up until including 2002, and becomes unity from 2003.[3]

Utilizing our detailed product information we are able to summarize and distinguish between the different product-related EDA main categories, namely ESL, IC-FE, and IC-BE plus 'others', which represents all non-categorized product segments. To distinguish between ESL and non-ESL offering firms we employ two dummy variables. The *(Firm with) ESL products* variable is equal to equity if a respective firm offers products in the ESL sub-segment in a given year. Contrary to this, the *(Firm with) only non-ESL products* variable indicates whether a company is *only* offering IC-FE and/or IC-BE but no ESL in a given year. The residual sub-category 'others' is not included in the model, i.e. the other two dummies are to be interpreted relative to this omitted category.[4] For the two explanatory variables included, we allow for a one-year time lag to reduce endogeneity and biases from different accounting methods [36].

Our employed model controls for different levels of innovative activity, firm size, and financial performance as these factors showed significant effects on the propensity to acquire in past acquisition research. Internal R&D can be an alternative to acquisition of external know-how [40]. Therefore, we consider different levels of R&D activity, calculating the variable *R&D intensity* as the ratio of R&D expenditures to net sales [41]. In addition to R&D input, the level of past output is a well-accepted indicator of the ability to identify and absorb new intellectual property [42]. Also known as absorptive capacity, this innovative output is measured by the patent stock of a firm [43]. The standard perpetual formula is used, which is then

---

[3] Taking absolute years can be a rather rough timeframe for the described trend since high-tech industries often change quicker than years. That is why we altered the length of the time trend to check the robustness of our model, as is described in the results section.

[4] *(Firm with) ESL products* and *(Firm with) only non-ESL products* have a correlation of -0.55 at a significance level below 0.05 (see Table 2).

normalized by firm size as proxied by net sales [44, 45].[5] Normalization allows addressing the issue of size disparities between firms that could undervalue the patent stock of smaller EDA firms.

Thus, we calculate *R&D output* as the ratio of patent stock to net sales, with the depreciation rate set at 15 percent [43]. Although our data only covers the years 1996–2006 all available patent information before 1996 (2,748 patents) was used to avoid truncation bias for the calculation. To control for size related differences in firm behavior, we employ a *firm size* variable by using the natural logarithm of net sales of a firm.[6] Similarly, we use the change in annual net sales ('sales') for each firm i and year t to control for firm growth. Controlling for financial success we calculate *profitability* as EBITDA to net sales. In order to account for a company's ability to meet its short-term obligations from its current assets, *liquidity* is calculated as the ratio of current assets to current liabilities. To account for the economic and institutional environment of the industry, we include the annual *industry's annual acquisitions* as a variable gauging general, industry-wide behavioral patterns. Except for the latter, we employ a one-year time lag for all described control variables for the same reasons we lagged two of our independent variables (*[Firm with] ESL products* and *[Firm with] only non-ESL products*). Tables 1 and 2 provide the descriptive statistics and correlations as well as variance inflation factors.

Table 1. Descriptive statistics

	Variable	Mean	S.D.	Min.	Max.
1	Number of annual acquisitions	0.57	1.16	0.00	7.00
2	New 90 nm technology	0.43	0.50	0.00	1.00
3	(Firm with) ESL products	0.31	0.46	0.00	1.00
4	(Firm with) only non-ESL products	0.40	0.49	0.00	1.00
5	90 nm technology (techn.) * ESL products	0.17	0.38	0.00	1.00
6	90 nm techn. * only non-ESL products	0.11	0.32	0.00	1.00
7	R&D intensity	0.27	0.20	0.03	1.99
8	R&D output	0.34	0.46	0.00	3.32
9	Firm size	5.49	1.72	1.70	9.04
10	Growth	0.25	0.70	-0.65	6.46
11	Profitability	0.14	0.29	-1.49	0.78
12	Liquidity	2.91	1.94	0.31	14.81
13	Industry's annual acquisitions	12.65	5.65	4.00	22.00

[5] To normalize patent stock, [44] use assets and [45] uses employees to account for firm size.

[6] Compared to the often-employed value of total assets, net total sales are better suited to represent the size of software firms. The number of employees can act as an alternative to net sales and produces qualitatively similar results when used in our estimations.

Table 2. Correlation matrix and variance inflation factors

No.	1	2	3	4	5	6	7	8	9	10	11	12	13
1	1.00												
2	-0.03	1.00											
3	0.45	0.16	1.00										
4	-0.27	-0.25	-0.55	1.00									
5	0.15	0.52	0.67	-0.37	1.00								
6	-0.07	0.41	-0.24	0.43	-0.16	1.00							
7	-0.04	-0.03	-0.01	0.20	0.00	0.06	1.00						
8	-0.12	0.20	-0.04	-0.13	0.05	0.05	0.25	1.00					
9	0.22	0.14	0.17	-0.44	0.14	-0.20	-0.52	-0.31	1.00				
10	0.07	-0.21	-0.09	0.10	-0.11	-0.08	0.37	0.12	-0.32	1.00			
11	0.24	0.03	0.13	-0.27	0.07	-0.09	-0.50	-0.38	0.62	-0.19	1.00		
12	-0.17	-0.07	-0.29	0.19	-0.24	0.08	0.17	0.26	-0.27	0.10	-0.12	1.00	
13	0.22	-0.35	-0.11	0.17	-0.22	-0.07	-0.03	-0.11	-0.06	-0.04	-0.02	0.02	1.00

Note: variable numbers refer to Table 1; all correlations > |0.17| significant at $p < 0.05$

4   Results

Table 3 shows the results of our negative binomial regression models. Most obviously, our first hypothesis does not hold true in any of the employed models meaning that the introduction of the 90 nm chip production scale by itself has no significant effect on the number of acquisitions within the EDA industry. As a robustness check, we adjusted the length of the 90 nm time dummy and employed different lengths from one to three years always yielding insignificant results. Models 2 and 3 include all of our three explanatory variables, where Model 3 features additionally contingency effects (interactions) through which we can simultaneously test our first and second hypotheses.

Looking at the interaction effects, we can confirm that EDA firms without any ESL products acquire significantly more from 2003: the time when chip design became increasingly more complex and ESL products experienced strong demand due to the smaller manufacturing scale at 90 nm. So far, this empirical result confirms our reasoning for expecting higher acquisition activity levels from firms without ESL products, but it does not clarify if firms acquire more in general or with a focus on ESL targets. Yet, further support for one of our latter hypotheses comes from the fact that EDA companies that already offered ESL software products did not seem to be affected by the introduction of smaller chip scales. More precisely, these types of companies show significantly higher acquisition activities during the entire time period analyzed (significant in model 2 and 3).

Table 3. Negative binomial panel regression analyses on the number of annual acquisitions

Variable	Model 1		Model 2		Model 3	
New 90 nm technology	0.12	(0.26)	0.13	(0.27)	-0.41	(0.64)
(Firm with) ESL products			1.41***	(0.54)	1.42**	(0.56)
(Firm with) only non-ESL products			0.33	(0.56)	-0.21	(0.62)
90 nm techn. * ESL products					0.35	(0.68)
90 nm techn. * only non-ESL products					1.91**	(0.87)
R&D intensity	-0.34	(1.21)	0.07	(1.11)	0.30	(1.15)
R&D output	0.43	(0.59)	0.47	(0.50)	0.60	(0.50)
Firm size	0.22	(0.19)	0.25	(0.16)	0.32*	(0.17)
Growth	0.43**	(0.19)	0.55***	(0.19)	0.59***	(0.19)
Profitability	1.34	(0.77)	1.16	(0.75)	1.18	(0.76)
Liquidity	-0.23	(0.14)	-0.10	(0.13)	-0.11	(0.14)
Industry`s annual acquisitions	0.08***	(0.02)	0.09***	(0.02)	0.08***	(0.02)
Likelihood ratio test for nested model 1			6.06**		12.51**	
Likelihood ratio test for nested model 2					6.45**	
Wald χ^2 (df)	37.04 (8)***		42.89 (10)***		52.40 (12)***	
Log Likelihood	-138.23		-135.20		-131.98	
Observations (Groups)	178 (36)		178 (36)		178 (36)	

Notes: *** p < 0.01; ** p < 0.05; * p < 0.1 (based on two-tailed significance tests); values in parentheses refer to standard errors

To see whether hypothesis 2a or 2b hold true we provide a simple descriptive overview of all acquisitions involving ESL offering targets from 1998–2006. Although 2a and 2b are competing hypotheses, we can find good arguments for both, since they represent a typical economic trade-off decision. That is why we are interested in the actual behavior of strategic groups within the single high-tech industry setting analyzed.

As can be seen in Table 4, out of the six acquirers involved in ESL takeovers, five had already been offering ESL products prior the respective mergers. Only one company taking over an ESL target before 2003 (in 2000) did not offer any ESL related products. Conversely, firms without ESL products apparently kept acquiring within their already occupied product categories, which means that they followed a more focused acquisition strategy in relation to their core business. Therefore, we can reject hypothesis 2a and note strong support for 2b.

As concerns the control and other variables in the regression model reported in Table 3, *Growth* and *industry's annual acquisitions* continuously show significant positive effects on the number of acquisitions in all models. Their high significance levels clearly hint at a strong relationship between recent business growth and its continuation through corporate takeovers (for the *growth* variable). Moreover, unobserved general dynamics seem to play an important role in addition to our identified industry trend (for *industry's annual acquisitions*). Most other control variables (*R&D intensity, patent stock, profitability,* and *liquidity*) remain insignificant in all tested and reported models.

This can be explained by the analysis' focus on a single industry where the similarities in innovation activities, business models, and utilization of internal resources cannot explain a large portion of the differences between industry players in terms of acquisition behavior. Likelihood ratio tests confirm the superior explanatory power of the largest employed model.

Table 4. ESL deals during the analyzed period from 1998 to 2006

Target	1998	1999	2000	2001	2002	2003	2004	2005	2006	Acquirer
Analogy		1								Avant*
Avant				1						Synopsys*
Axis Systems						1				Verisity*
C Level Design				1						Synopsys*
Cascade							1			Synopsys*
Chrysalis Symbolic Design		1								Avant*
Co-Design Automa-tion					1					Synopsys*
First Earth						1				Mentor*
Get2Chip						1				Cadence*
Orcad		1								Cadence*
Summit Design									1	Mentor*
Verisity								1		Cadence*
Visual Software			1							Xilinx
Total ESL deals	0	3	1	2	1	3	1	1	1	
Total annual deals	19	24	20	10	12	19	14	6	7	
Annual share of ESL deals	0%	13%	5%	20%	8%	16%	7%	17%	14%	

Note: * = Acquirer has been offering ESL software before.

5   Discussion and Conclusion

In this study, we proposed to integrate different explanatory factors for acquisition behavior in order to better understand the dynamics in very dynamic high-tech industries. Our results show that the rise of the 90 nm process for mass production by itself had no significant influence on the number of acquisitions within the EDA industry. Despite the undeniable increase of complexity in chip design, we cannot identify a corresponding change in general EDA acquisition behavior in terms of frequency. A possible explanation could be that the constant pressure to innovate (the so called 'design gap') overshadows the specific effects coming from the described technological change.

Whilst we are far from generalizing the non-impactful nature of any industry trend on acquisition activities in high-tech industries, the insignificant effect of technological change by itself further supports our call to utilize firm-specific characteristics that allow for more differentiated empirical analysis of the acquisition phenomenon. In fact, the confirmation of one of our competing hypotheses, 2b, reveals the existence of behavioral differences coming from strategic positions as mirrored by the different product portfolios. Only by differentiating between different types of acquirers can we show a significant effect coming from a particular technological change within the industry. Moreover, the descriptive overview of ESL targets provides further insights about the takeover behavior of the different acquirers. Apparently, non-ESL firms do acquire significantly more within their already occupied product categories, namely IC-FE and IC-BE, making little attempts to diversify into the promising new ESL fields.

The confirmation of hypothesis 2b instead of hypothesis 2a is very interesting as it indicates that during times of technological change, firms seem to value their competency and expertise in already established product categories higher than any potential revenue growth in new (heavy demanded) but rather unknown product segments. Thus, we can confirm the existence of some basic principles and mechanisms of organizational learning.

More related and hence more secure investments are preferred over more explorative activities [18]. The fact that this behavior happens during a time of greater technological ferment makes sense as competition over technological leadership happens particularly during these periods [21]. The majority of corporate acquisitions take place in related industries. Thus, intra-industry acquisitions should show a similar picture, but just at a different level. Corporate acquisitions serve very well as a valid measure for this kind of conclusion especially when controlled for internal R&D as a potential supplement.

The significant effect of *industry's annual acquisitions* suggests the existence of additional institutional effects in terms of micro- or macro-economic environments even at the level of a single industry. A stronger form of 'herd behavior' could not be identified since we could not find any support for hypothesis 2a. Nevertheless, our initial statement about the complexities involved in corporate acquisition decisions is validated in this control variable. A methodological contribution of our analysis results from the utilization of detailed product information as an indicator of technological competence. Together with a comprehensive qualitative understanding about the actual value creation of the products offered along the chip design process, we were able to provide explanations for technologically motivated acquisitions that extend the literature by relating to more disaggregated levels. This more detailed level of analysis also provides more relevant practical support by acknowledging product related strategic decisions and the resulting actions on corporate acquisitions. However, in order to being able to inform these kinds of decisions, more industries need to be analyzed in a similar manner.

In summary, our analysis focuses on technology-driven acquisitions and provides empirically tested explanations for certain patterns of acquisition behavior of firms within an industry at a particular time. The methodology of a single-industry focus delivers novel insights into the logic underpinning acquisition dynamics. While such an approach is required to do justice to the complex circumstances in each individual (high-tech) industry, it also has its limitations. An analysis at this single-industry level requires detailed data that is not always available, especially in the case of industries that are larger in terms of aggregate sales volumes, less concentrated and/or more fragmented in terms of products. This also applies to a deep understanding of the actual products as well as knowledge of an industry's relationship with its customers.

Other limitations might come from the exclusion of minority stakes and venture capital or corporate venturing investments, which are known to be very common in high-tech industry environments. Although the omission of these activities may be a weakness of our approach, our strict selection criteria allow for a clearer interpretation of the included deals, which would not have been much improved by adding the aforementioned categories since minority stake investments are typically chosen when uncertainty about future developments is quite high.

Conversely, corporate takeovers that result in full formal control over and responsibility for the target can be seen as an ex-post confirmation of an already convincing performance that is worth integrating into the acquirer's existing business. Along the same lines, our analysis also leaves out any form of inter-firm cooperation because again these reflect situations of greater potential uncertainty.

Future research on acquisition behavior might involve a stronger consideration of the various strategic characteristics of industry players. Our analysis has shown that the mere existence of a technological change or trend may not be enough to show any effect on hitherto dynamic industries. We also encourage more empirical research on acquisition behavior in similar high-tech industries to further corroborate and confirm our findings, and provide evidence from beyond the EDA industry. One has to understand the complexities of a firm's business environment in order to evaluate its behavior and ultimately to offer better managerial implications. We hope that the value of following this convincing argument is apparent from this study.

References

1. Wagner, M.: Acquisition as a means for external technology sourcing: complementary, substitutive or both? Journal of Engineering and Technology Management 28, 283–299 (2011)
2. Agrawal, A., Jaffe, J.F.: The post-merger performance puzzle. In: Cooper, C., Gregory, A. (eds.) Advances in Mergers and Acquisitions, pp. 119–156. JAI Press, Stamford (2000)
3. Ahuja, G., Katila, R.: Technological acquisitions and the innovation performance of acquiring firms: a longitudinal study. Strategic Management Journal 22(3), 197–220 (2001)
4. Wagner, M.: To explore or to exploit? An empirical investigation of acquisitions by large incumbents. Research Policy 40, 1217–1225 (2011)
5. Cloodt, M., Hagedoorn, J., van Kranenburg, H.: Mergers and acquisitions: Their effect on the innovative performance of companies in high-tech industries. Research Policy 35(5), 642–654 (2006)
6. Wagner, M.: Acquisitions as a means of innovation sourcing by incumbents and growth of technology-oriented ventures. Int. J. of Tech. Management 52, 118–134 (2010)
7. King, D.R., Dalton, D.R., Daily, C.M., Covin, J.G.: Meta-analyses of post-acquisition performance: Indications of unidentified moderators. Strategic Management Journal 25(2), 187–200 (2004)
8. Schoenberg, R., Reeves, R.: What determines acquisition activity within an industry? European Management Journal 17(1), 93–98 (1999)
9. Porter, M.: Competitive Strategy: Techniques for analyzing industries and competitors. Free Press, New York (1980)
10. Ahern, K.R., Harford, J.: The importance of industry links in merger waves. Journal of Finance 69(2), 527–576 (2014)
11. DiMaggio, P.J., Powell, W.W.: The iron cage revisited: Institutional isomorphism and collective rationality in organizational fields. American Sociological Review 48(2), 147–160 (1983)
12. TechAmerica. TechAmerica's NAICS-based definition of high tech. (2013), http://www.techamerica.org/naics-definition
13. Andrade, G., Mitchell, M., Stafford, E.: New evidence and perspectives on mergers. Journal of Economic Perspectives 15(2), 103–120 (2001)
14. Gort, M.: An Economic Disturbance Theory of Mergers. The Quarterly Journal of Economics 83(4), 624–642 (1969)
15. Harford, J.: What drives merger waves? Journal of Financial Economics 77(3), 529–560 (2005)
16. Prahalad, C., Hamel, G.: The Core Competence of the Corporation. Harvard Business Review 68(3), 79–91 (1990)
17. Teece, D.J., Pisano, G., Shuen, A.: Dynamic capabilities and strategic management. Strategic Management Journal 18(7), 509–533 (1997)
18. March, J.G.: Exploration and exploitation in organizational learning. Organization Science 2(1), 71–87 (1991)
19. Hamel, G., Prahalad, C.K.: Corporate imagination and expeditionary marketing. Harvard Business Review 69(4), 81–92 (1991)
20. Garud, R., Kanøe, P. (eds.): Path Dependence and Creation. Psychology Press, Mahwah (2001)
21. Tushman, M.L., Anderson, P.: Technological Discontinuities and Organizational Environments. Administrative Science Quarterly 31(3), 439–465 (1986)

22. Dushnitsky, G., Lenox, M.J.: When do firms undertake R&D by investing in new ventures? Strategic Management Journal 26(10), 947–965 (2005)
23. Mitchell, M.L., Mulherin, H.J.: The impact of industry shocks on takeover and restructuring activity. Journal of Financial Economics 41, 193–229 (1996)
24. Stern, I., Henderson, A.D.: Within-business diversification in technology-intensive industries. Strategic Management Journal 25(5), 487–505 (2004)
25. Zahavi, T., Lavie, D.: Intra-industry diversification and firm performance. Strategic Management Journal 34(8), 978–998 (2013)
26. Henkel, J., Rønde, T., Wagner, M.: And the Winner is – Acquired. Entrepreneurship as a Contest yielding Radical Innovations. Research Policy 44, 295–310 (2015)
27. El Sawy, O.A., Malhotra, A., YoungKi, P., Pavlou, P.A.: Seeking the Configurations of Digital Ecodynamics: It Takes Three to Tango. Information Systems Research 21(4), 835–848 (2010)
28. Furlan, A., Cabigiosu, A., Camuffo, A.: When the Mirror Gets Misted up: Modularity and Technological Change. Strategic Management Journal 35(6), 789–807 (2014)
29. Birnbaum, M.D.: Essential Electronic Design Automation. Prentice Hall International, Upper Saddle River (2004)
30. Intel: Microprocessor quick reference guide. Intel Corp. (2013), http://www.intel.com/pressroom/kits/quickreffam.htm
31. EE Times: ESL tools: Are EDA giants in the game? EETimes.com (2004), http://www.eetimes.com/document.asp?doc_id=1151215
32. International Business Strategies: Analysis of the relationship between EDA expenditures and competitive positioning of IC vendors for 2003. A custom study for EDA consortium and edacentrum e.V (2003), http://www.edac.org/downloads/04_05_28_IBS_Report.pdf
33. Sperling, E.: Experts at the table: Changing design. System-Level Design Community (2012), http://chipdesignmag.com/sld/blog/2012/02/10/expertsat-the-table-changing-design-3/
34. Grant, R.M., Jammine, A.P., Thomas, H.: Diversity, diversification, and profitability among British manufacturing companies, 1972-84. Academy of Management Journal 31(4), 771–801 (1988)
35. Lebret, H.: Start-up: What we may still learn from Silicon Valley. CreateSpace, Lausanne (2007)
36. Desyllas, P., Hughes, A.: Sourcing technological knowledge through corporate acquisition: Evidence from an international sample of high technology firms. Journal of Technology Management Research 18(2), 157–172 (2008)
37. Soh, P.: Network patterns and competitive advantage before the emergence of a dominant design. Strategic Management Journal 31(4), 438–461 (2010)
38. Kleinbaum, D.G., Kupper, L.L., Muller, K.E., Nizam, A.: Applied Regression Analysis and Multivariable Methods. Duxbury Press, Washington (1998)
39. Cameron, C.A., Trivedi, P.K.: Regression analysis of count data. Cambridge University Press, Cambridge (1998)
40. Hitt, M.A., Hoskisson, R.E., Ireland, R.D.: Mergers and acquisitions and managerial commitment to innovation in M-form firms. Strategic Management Journal 11(summer special issue), 29–47 (1990)
41. Blonigen, B.A., Taylor, C.T.: R&D intensity and acquisitions in high-technology industries: Evidence from the US electronic and electrical equipment industries. Journal of Industrial Economics XLVIII(1), 47–70 (2000)

42. Cohen, W.M., Levinthal, D.A.: Absorptive capacity: A new perspective on learning and innovation. Administrative Science Quarterly 35(1), 128–152 (1990)
43. Kleer, R., Wagner, M.: Acquisition through Innovation Tournaments in High-Tech Industries: A Comparative Perspective. Economics of Innovation and New Technology 22(1), 73–77 (2013)
44. Grimpe, C., Hussinger, K.: Pre-empting technology competition through firm acquisitions. Economics Letters 100(2), 189–191 (2008)
45. Hussinger, K.: R&D and subsidies at the firm level: An application of parametric and semiparametric two-step selection models. Journal of Applied Econometrics 23(6), 729–747 (2008)

Hitting the Target: Practices for Moving Toward Innovation Experiment Systems

Teemu Karvonen[1(✉)], Lucy Ellen Lwakatare[1], Tanja Sauvola[1], Jan Bosch[2],
Helena Holmström Olsson[3], Pasi Kuvaja[1], and Markku Oivo[1]

[1] University of Oulu, Oulu, Finland
{Teemu.3.Karvonen,Lucy.Lwakatare,Tanja.Sauvola,Pasi.Kuvaja,
Markku.Oivo}@oulu.fi
[2] Chalmers University of Technology, Göteborg, Sweden
Jan.Bosch@chalmers.se
[3] Malmö University, Malmö, Sweden
Helena.Holmstrom.Olsson@mah.se

Abstract. The benefits and barriers that software development companies face when moving beyond agile development practices are identified in a multiple-case study in five Finnish companies. The practices that companies need to adopt when moving towards innovation experiment systems are recognised. The background of the study is the Stairway to Heaven (StH) model that describes the path that many software development companies take when advancing their development practices. The development practices in each case are investigated and analysed in relation to the StH model. At first the results of the analysis strengthened the validity of the StH model as a path taken by software development companies to advance their development practices. Based on the findings, the StH model was extended with a set of additional practices and their adoption levels for each step of the model. The extended model was validated in five case companies.

Keywords: Software development · Agile development · Feedback loops · Innovation experiment systems · Continuous deployment

1   Introduction

Traditionally, R&D's assumptions about desired product functionality are based on a list of requirements or product backlog items that are gathered by product management. However, customer needs might change very rapidly, and they are often difficult to identify. This may lead to a situation in which R&D spends time and effort on developing product functionality that doesn't add value for customers. To solve this problem, agile methods [1] offer a set of practices that allow for shorter development cycles and more frequent interaction with customers. In conjunction with agile methodologies, approaches, such as innovation experiment systems (IES) [2] and continuous experimentation [3], emphasise data collection practices and continuous validation with customers in order to improve R&D accuracy and

© Springer International Publishing Switzerland 2015
J.M. Fernandes et al. (Eds.): ICSOB 2015, LNBIP 210, pp. 117–131, 2015.
DOI: 10.1007/978-3-319-19593-3_10

customer responsiveness. However, while these approaches are attractive to companies in the software industry, they require an evolution of the company's current ways of working. Typically, and as recognised by Olsson et al. [4] in the Stairway to Heaven (StH) model, software development companies most often evolve from traditional development to agile R&D, from agile R&D to continuous integration (CI), from CI to continuous deployment (CD) and from CD to R&D as IES. While the first step in the StH model is characterised by long feedback loops and slow cycles, the later steps enforce fast feedback, rapid cycles and data-driven development practices in which feature value is continuously validated with customers. As recognised in this research [4], a number of opportunities and challenges are associated with the evolution from one step to the next.

In this study, and based on multiple-case study research, we investigate how five Finnish software development companies evolve their software development practices according to the steps in the StH model. In particular, we identify the benefits and the barriers they experience when moving beyond agile practices and towards IES. Therefore, our research questions are:

RQ1 What are the benefits and barriers that software companies experience when moving towards IES?

RQ2 What are the key practices that software companies need to adopt in order to evolve their software development practices according to the StH model?

The contribution of this paper is threefold. First, we strengthen the validity of the StH model, as introduced by Olsson et al. [4], in terms of the typical evolutionary path that software development companies take when advancing their development practices. Second, we extend the model with a set of practices required for climbing the steps in the StH model. We also identify the four levels at which these practices can be adopted. Third, we validate the extended model in five Finnish software development companies using a multiple-case study approach involving qualitative interviews at each company.

The rest of the paper is structured as follows. Section 2 introduces related work that is relevant to this study and, most importantly, we present the StH model. In Section 3, we extend the StH model and introduce the practices that companies apply when evolving towards IES. Section 4 presents our case study design and research method. In Sections 5 and 6, we validate the extended model and discuss the case study findings. Section 7 concludes this paper and suggests topics for future research.

2   Related Work

Today, most companies have adopted agile methods, and different flavours of the methods have become the *de facto* way of working in the software industry [5]. In allowing for more flexible ways of working with an emphasis on customer collaboration and speed of development, agile methods help companies address many of the problems associated with traditional development [6]. As a way to further advance agile development practices, companies are moving from release cycles of 6 to 12 months to more frequent software releases [7, 8, 9, 10]. To achieve this, companies increasingly adopt practices such as CI [11], continuous delivery [12] and CD [13]. In empirical studies, Claps et.al [13] and Leppänen et al. [14] recently identified multiple benefits and challenges associated with the adoption of CD. They noted that some of the benefits include faster feedback, more frequent releases, reduced risk for each release and improved productivity and quality; some of the challenges include customer preferences to non-frequent release, domain constraints and manual testing. The adoption of these practices reflects an evolution in which companies move beyond agile practices towards R&D practices characterised by short release cycles, frequent customer validation and fully automated testing and deployment practices. Although the same agile R&D principles apply, moving beyond agile practices means: a) integrating business strategy planning, operations and other corporate functions into shorter development and release cycles [4], [15]; b) utilising automated testing practices that allow for frequent builds [12] and c) implementing continuous experimentation and innovation with customers [2, 3, 4] to better understand real customer needs. The specific aspects involved in going beyond agile as well as more holistic views of agility have been discussed in recent SE studies [15, 16] and especially in the context of lean software development [17]. As recognised in these studies, the main motivation for companies moving beyond agile is that, even though agile practices can improve R&D efficiency and product quality, they are insufficient for achieving benefits in a business ecosystem [18] and at the enterprise level [16]. To realise benefits at these levels, companies need to scale the benefits they experience at a team level, that is shorter development and feedback cycles, to include product management and customers. In order to better understand this evolutionary path, we outline the StH model below. The model describes the steps that companies may take when moving towards IES and it works as the basis for our discussion on how to improve company competitiveness and customer responsiveness.

Based on significant empirical experience as well as numerous studies that have described the transition from traditional development to more agile ways of working and beyond, the StH model [4] describes the typical evolution path for software development companies that are evolving their ways of working. In capturing this transition in five steps, the model reflects much of the prominent research in the field, and it helps understand the way in which most companies advance their software development practices. Based on empirical research as well as the authors' previous experiences of working with software development companies, the model also outlines the actions that companies need to take when climbing the different steps and advancing their ways of working. In previous research [4], the model has been used as a tool to identify where the company is in its evolutionary path and what actions it needs to take to advance. It has also been useful for describing the fundamental change that software development goes through when a company attains the final step on the stairway and when R&D is viewed as an experiment system in which customers are involved in continuous, real-time validation of software functionality [19].

The StH model views evolution from the point of view of four stakeholders: 1) the R&D organisation, 2) the validation and verification organisation, 3) the customers and 4) the product management organisation. In the StH model, the 'traditional development', step A, is characterised by long development cycles. Development processes are sequential and teams are typically large and separated into disciplines

[20]. In step B, the R&D organisation starts adopting agile development practices, typically by introducing smaller cross-functional development teams that work in shorter cycles [1]. However, at this step, product management and system verification still work according to the traditional development approach. In step C, practices for CI are adopted, including automated builds and automated testing [11]. In this step, both R&D and system verification work in short cycles and there is always a shippable product. In step D, CD is adopted and the customers are involved in short cycles with frequent software releases [13]. Code changes are pushed to the customer allowing instant feedback on new functionality. In step E, companies adopt data collection mechanisms to continuously learn about customer behaviour and product use. Feature experiments are run on a continuous basis and the collected data steer the R&D organisation [2, 3]. Rather than being specified by the product management in the early phase of development, requirements evolve based on data collected from real-time customer use. In this step, the entire organisation, including product management, is involved in short feedback cycles. In each of the steps, the level of integration of and interaction between company functions increases. Thus, steps D and E cannot be achieved without R&D, product management and customers that work in short development cycles. One implicit premise of the StH model is that evolution starts from traditional development. While this is typically the case for large-scale software development companies, it might not be the situation for smaller companies and new software start-up companies. As described by Ries [21], those types of companies are typically created much closer to the last steps in the model, i.e. the CD and the IES steps. However, as a model that pictures the general evolution path, StH depicts the different steps that are relevant for most companies and the evolution that most often occurs between those steps.

In this study, we use the StH model as the theoretical basis from which to explore the benefits and barriers experienced by five Finnish companies as they climb the steps described in the model. The StH model is outlined in Fig. 1. Although the StH model has been widely used in many software development companies, and it has been referred as 'the typical evolution path', so far the validation of the model has been limited to use of the multiple-case study method. However, in the absence of research that can validate the typical evolution steps towards IES, the assumptions that the StH model makes about companies that take those steps seem to be well aligned with recent SE literature and practitioner reports describing the companies' strategic goals and experiences in adopting agile and CI practices. According to Claps et al. [13], so far only a few companies have succeeded in deploying software continuously to their customers. At Gap Inc. [7], the transformation to agile was started by first selecting a pilot project that made a big investment in the company's CI system. At Conject AG [8], the transition from the traditional six-month release cycle to the continuous flow of small releases was enabled by aligning coding and testing activities to the same short cycles, by test automation and by implementing the CI system. At Rally Software [9], the transition from an eight-week release cadence to continuous delivery of software was enabled by abandoning time-boxed Scrum sprints and by adopting lean practices, such as Kanban and Kaizen. By first developing a better understanding of the entire process, the company was able to make many changes to the development process. In addition, the company's Sales, Marketing, Support, Technical Account Managers and User Learning teams were affected. NASA Ames Research Center [10] was able to move from a six-month delivery cycle to a three-week cycle within two years due to the evolution of its development practices. This two-year evolution process was described as a journey from traditional to lean and then to agile.

3   Extending the Stairway to Heaven Model

In this section, we extend the StH model by integrating it with practices that are important for companies that are evolving towards IES (Fig. 1). Those practices are suggested based on empirical research as well as the authors' previous experiences of working with software development companies. To categorise the practices, we use the Business, Architecture, Process, Organisation (BAPO) approach, i.e. interdependent software development concerns as outlined by Linden et al. [22]:

- **Business:** How to make a profit from your products;
- **Architecture**: The technical means to build the software;
- **Process:** The roles, responsibilities and relationships within software development;
- **Organisation**: The actual mapping of roles and responsibilities to organisational structures.

The purpose of this extension is to allow for a more precise analysis of both the company's current ways of working and the practices they may need to adopt to further evolve. There are four levels at which the adoption of these practices can take place.

- **Not adopted**: The practice is not adopted or it is abandoned.
- **Team**: The practice is adopted in some teams. Some teams inside the organisation can be ahead of the rest of the organisation.
- **Product**: The practice is adopted at the product organisation/program level. Some product organisations can be ahead of the rest of the organisation.
- **Institutionalised**: Practice is fully adopted; it is the standard way of working throughout the entire organisation.

The application of the extended StH model in five case companies is demonstrated in Section 5. It should be noted that there is no "one and right" way for companies to evolve towards IES. Different software engineering processes have to be tailored to fit the particular business goals of the organisation, the specific context of the organisational culture, etc. Thus, we don't consider the practices we present below as prescriptive in that they have to be deployed in a certain way in a company. Rather, they are descriptive, and they suggest actions that are needed when advancing between the different steps in the model. However, when implemented in a company context they require careful adjustment to fit the particular company context.

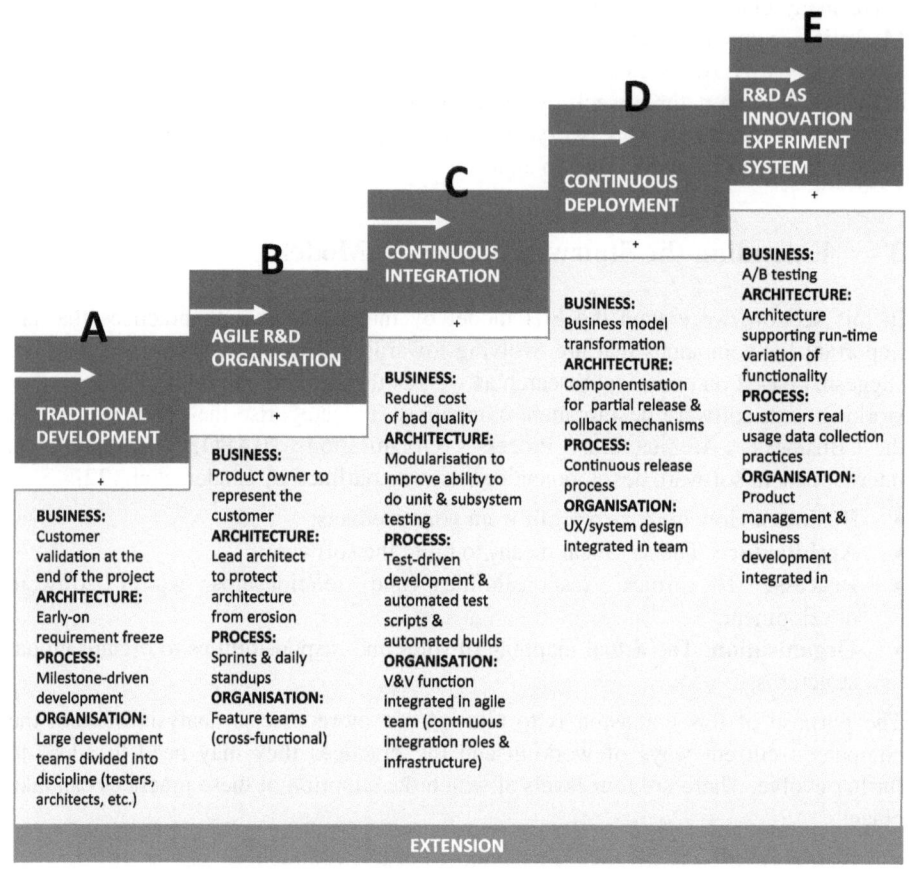

Fig. 1. The Stairway to Heaven model [4] and (+) the extension

4   Research Design

4.1   Research Method

This study is an in-depth multiple-case study that adopts an interpretive approach [23]. It includes empirical data from five case companies in the ICT sector in Finland, allowing for a cross-case analysis of the data. The case study method is a suitable research approach for an overall study in which researchers act as investigators and control over the context is not possible [24]. The case study approach is also beneficial for creating a rich understanding of people's experiences.

4.2   Data Collection and Analysis

This paper reports on a three-month (November 2014–January 2015) multiple-case study involving five Finnish software development companies that are moving towards IES. The main data collection method used was semi-structured individual interviews with open-ended questions [23]. Altogether, the study included 24 interviews. In all of the interviews, we reused the original StH study [4] set of interview questions. The interviews had four main themes: (1) organisation and current way of working, (2) customer interaction mechanisms/models, (3) strengths and weaknesses in ways of working and (4) benefits and barriers as experienced when moving towards IES. In companies A, B, C and D, we conducted five interviews in each company and, in company E, we conducted four interviews. In companies A, B, C and D, the interviews were conducted face-to-face and in company E the interviews were conducted via videoconference. The data collection involved case company stakeholders from Product Management, R&D, Validation & Verification and Sales & Marketing (Table 1). All of the interviews were held in English. The duration of the interviews ranged from 90 to 120 minutes; the interviews were recorded and transcribed. During the interview, the three researchers shared the responsibilities; one researcher mainly asking the questions and two researchers took notes. Section 4 describes the case companies that participated in the study in more detail as well as their position in relation to the StH model.

Table 1. Case companies and interviewees' roles

Case	Industry	Interviewees' roles
A	Embedded systems and R&D services	1) Special device senior manager, 2) Special device product owner, 3) Sales and account manager, 4) Senior specialist in software, 5) Quality manager in wireless segment
B	Telecommunications	1) Test automation manager, 2) Senior developer, 3) Program manager, 4) Operations manager of the local site, 5) Technical coordinator
C	Telecommunications	1) System verification engineer, 2) Program manager, 3) Software architect, 4) Product line manager, 5) Software engineer
D	Factory automation	1) Project manager, 2) Program manager, 3) User experience (UX) designer, 4) Product manager, 5) Developer
E	IT services	1) Product owner, 2) Project manager, 3) Technical service owner, 4) Technical lead

The data analysis was performed by three researchers in continuous collaboration, following the general techniques for case study analysis suggested by Runeson et al. [23] using the QSR NVivo tool.[1] During the analysis, all of the materials, including transcripts, field notes, audio files and other related material, were stored in NVivo. All of the transcribed interviews were carefully read and coded by themes. For this study, three main levels of codes were applied for each of the 24 interviews: 1) 'barriers' (barriers that prevent companies from moving towards IES), 2) 'benefits' (anticipated or identified benefits of moving towards IES) and 3) 'practices' (practices

---

[1] Qualitative data analysing software (http://www.qsrinternational.com/).

for moving towards IES). The results were synthesized in two phases by adopting within-case analysis and cross-case analysis, as described by Yin [24].

4.3   Validity and Generalisation of the Results

Generally, in case study research, there are different threats to validity, such as researchers' biases, that can limit the trustworthiness of the results. In our study, we assess three aspects of validity, i.e. construct validity, external validity and reliability, as identified by Runeson et al. [23]. Prior to data collection, the research design that also included the data collection process was carefully considered. The activity involved acquiring the original interview guide, selecting appropriate companies and roles for the interviews and providing all interviewees with introductory materials (e.g. study objectives, the structure of the interview, etc.). This was done to address construct validity, which is concerned with a clear representation of the studied constructs. However, company transition may take even several years. Therefore, interviewees' memories about transition may not be as accurate as they are for more recent events in the company. The companies were selected from a group of leading-edge companies that were participating in a large national research program that aimed to enhance Finnish ICT companies' capability to deliver value in real-time. Convenience sampling was applied. Threats to the reliability of the study findings were mitigated by having at least three researchers involved in all phases of the research, particularly in the data collection and analysis phases. This practice helped reduce the research bias that could arise from having only one researcher participate in data collection and analysis. Additionally, to lower the risk of errors in the interviews, the transcripts that were used for data analysis were sent to the interviewees for review. External validity is mostly concerned with the generalisability of a study's findings. The findings of our study are meant to provide software companies with insights with the intention of helping them move beyond agile practices.

5   Case Study

This section presents the case companies and main findings, individually, for each case company by applying the extended StH model introduced in Section 3. We report benefits (RQ1), barriers (RQ1) and key practices (RQ2) for each company and analyse them in the StH model. Table 2 summarises the findings for each company by applying the StH model and extension. Section 6 presents the cross-case analysis based on the data collected from all five case companies. Three researchers collectively compiled the information presented in Table 2 and analysis was based on the researchers' common interpretation of how practices were adopted in each case company.

Table 2. Adoption of the extended StH model practices. Not adopted (NA), Team (TE), Product (PR), Institutionalised (IN).

		Traditional	Agile	CI	CD	IES
Company A	**Business**	NA	IN	IN	NA	PR
	Architecture	NA	IN	IN	PR	PR
	Process	NA	IN	IN	TE	NA
	Organisation	NA	IN	IN	PR	NA
Company B	**Business**	NA	IN	TE	NA	NA
	Architecture	NA	IN	TE	PR	TE
	Process	NA	IN	TE	NA	NA
	Organisation	NA	IN	NA	NA	NA
Company C	**Business**	NA	IN	PR	NA	NA
	Architecture	NA	IN	IN	PR	PR
	Process	NA	IN	PR	NA	NA
	Organisation	NA	PR	PR	NA	NA
Company D	**Business**	NA	PR	PR	NA	NA
	Architecture	IN	PR	PR	NA	NA
	Process	IN	PR	PR	NA	NA
	Organisation	NA	PR	NA	NA	NA
Company E	**Business**	IN	TE	NA	NA	NA
	Architecture	IN	TE	NA	NA	NA
	Process	IN	TE	TE	NA	NA
	Organisation	IN	TE	TE	NA	NA

5.1   Company A

Company A is developing embedded software solutions for specialised markets in the wireless and automotive industry as well as providing R&D services. The focus is on customisable software solutions for the automotive industry and the wireless connectivity of special devices used by specialised market segments such as public safety. As shown in Table 2, Company A is best described as a company with institutionalised practices for CI. Architecture, process and organisation practices were already established in CD in some teams and product programs. We could see that this company as a whole is moving towards CD. Experiences and lessons learned from these practices were proactively used to coach other parts of the organisation in this transition to CD. Interestingly, although this company had not yet institutionalised CD practices, some product programs had already applied IES practices in some selected customer cases. According to the interviewees, the main benefit of moving towards CD is to improve customer feedback cycles and project transparency. The main barriers are considered to be the lack of a suitable business model, test automation and common practices for CD. As identified by the interviewees, in order for the organisation to move forward, management must invest more in CI build systems and test automation.

5.2   Company B

Company B is a telecommunications equipment manufacturer that also provides services for managing network operations. In this company, we interviewed employees from the R&D organisation who are responsible for developing a compact mobile broadband solution. Company B has institutionalised agile practices, and several teams within the company have already adopted CI practices. According to the interviewees, the main benefit of moving towards CD is that product quality will improve due to frequent and automated test suits. The main barrier is considered to be the issue of how to adjust and align internal and external stakeholders to shorter development cycles. As identified by the interviewees, in order to move forward the level of test automation must be increased, which will require additional resources and investments.

5.3   Company C

Company C is a manufacturer of data and telecommunication network equipment that also develops a variety of supporting tools for the management of mobile broadband networks. In this company, interviews were conducted with employees involved in the development of a network traffic-monitoring tool. As illustrated in Table 2, Company C can be best described as a company that has well-established agile practices and that has adopted CI and CD practices in parts of the organisation. According to the interviewees, the main benefit of moving towards IES is to improve competitiveness and product quality, as customer feedback would increasingly impact product development. The main barrier for CD is that some company functions still work according to pre-defined milestones, and those functions still support a six-month release cycle. As identified by the interviewees, in order to move forward the current product architecture must be updated from a PC platform to a virtualised cloud computing platform.

5.4   Company D

Company D is developing minerals processing solutions and flow control technology for its customers in the mining, construction, oil and gas industries. In addition, the company develops advanced automation solutions, i.e. distributed control systems for its customers in pulp, paper and power. For the purpose of this study, we interviewed employees involved in the development of a factory automation platform solution. Table 2 illustrates the current situation of how Company D has recently adopted both agile and CI practices in one product program. However, the rest of the company is still primarily using traditional practices. According to the interviewees, it is not possible to move towards CD and IES because their systems are performance- and safety critical. However, while this is the general view, some parts of the systems, e.g.

the user experience (UX) parts, could be improved by applying CD and IES practices. Thus, in order for Company D to move forward, it must identify which modules or parts of the system could be deployed and experimented with in a continuous manner.

5.5   Company E

Company E provides product engineering and IT services to a variety of customers from the telecommunications and consumer electronics industries and the semiconductor industry. In Company E, we interviewed the employees responsible for developing the company's public website. The team is using Scrum as a project management framework with no CI system or automated test cases. Table 2 illustrates how Company E is still mostly applying traditional development practices. However, some teams have adopted agile and CI practices with the intention of having these practices adopted by more teams. According to the interviewees, moving forward would improve product quality and reduce time-to-market. The main barrier for moving forward is the difficulty of aligning the globally distributed development teams. As identified by the interviewees, in order to move forward employees must increase their awareness of and competence in agile software development and the number of cross-functional teams must increase.

6   Discussion

In the previous section, and by using the five steps in the StH model, we identified the current position and practices of each case company. In addition, the extended model was used to identify the practices that companies may apply to advance their practices further. This section summarises and further discusses the benefits, barriers and key practices as identified from the case study interviews and addresses how the interviewees in this study have experienced the evolution. As shown in Table 3,we found multiple similar benefits and barriers that were also identified in earlier studies [4], [13, 14]. Additionally, the table presents the key practices that are needed to move to the next step in the StH model.

In our study, all five companies (A-E) have established agile software development practices within the R&D organisation. Companies A, B and C had already been using agile practices for a couple of years, whereas D and E had only been using them for approximately one year. All of the companies held the opinion that the primary benefit of an agile R&D organisation was that incremental and iterative development allows for more efficient and flexible product development.

Companies A, B, C and D have advanced their software development practices by introducing CI practices, i.e. building and testing software functionality automatically. None of the companies claimed to have achieved fully automated testing. The main benefit of CI is that production quality software is always available internally. The main barrier to moving forward to CI and CD seems to be the high investment and significant effort required to ensure adequate test automation.

Table 3. Summary of benefits, barriers and key practices for moving towards IES

	Traditional -> Agile R&D	Agile R&D -> CI	CI -> CD	CD -> R&D as an IES
Benefits	Short sprints provide the possibility of quickly changing the course of product development.	Provides the ability to build and test products incrementally. Provides high-quality software functionality with production quality.	Customers get fast and incremental delivery of relevant functionality. Customers can perform their own testing and business activities on top of deliveries.	The innovation validation is fast. Immediate feedback is obtained. New business opportunities are identified and development resources are focused
Barriers	It is difficult (complex process) to align different cross-functional teams within the R&D organisations.	There is a lack of team discipline, Test Driven Development (TDD) and module tests for CI test automation.	The shortening of the Validation and Verification (V&V) cycle is complex and expensive. The lack of trust in software quality and missing functions may cause a negative impression.	Customer feedback is integrated into the short development and business planning cycle. It is difficult to conduct experiments in safety-critical systems.
Key practices				
Business	Incorporate product owner to represent customer in development team.	Incorporate supply chain (component and technology suppliers) in the development cycle.	Incorporate lead customers in development. Renew business model, contracts, marketing and sales strategies	Adopt data-driven strategic decision-making model. Implement A/B testing with the customer.
Architecture	Architects monitor and safeguard the integrity of the product architecture in feature-driven development.	Provide modular architecture that can be integrated and tested continuously.	Provide architecture where software functionality can be deployed independently.	Adopt product platform (e.g. virtualisation, cloud technologies) that enables flexible experimentation.
Process	Develop features in sprints, frequent (daily) team meetings.	Adopt test-driven development and daily build practices.	Improve automated system testing and adopt a continuous release process.	Establish a short customer feedback loop and process for data-driven decision making.
Organisation	Adopt and empower cross-functional/feature teams.	Integrate validation and verification (V&V) in cross-functional/feature teams.	Ensure that System/UX design and business development work in short cycles and in alignment with R&D.	Synchronise supplier and customer organisation in short development cycles.

In our study, only Company A has evolved its software development practices to CD at the product and team levels. Therefore, our findings rely on the interviewees' views of what that transition might require and how it effects the organisation. The main anticipated benefit of CD is that customers receive relevant software functionality faster and incrementally. However, moving to CD seems to require renewing traditional business models as well as identifying customers that are willing to have continuous releases of software functionality. It also seems that the transition from CD to IES might not be feasible for all products and business segments. Interviewees in Company B and Company D consider their current products to be too safety-critical for introducing any experiments with their customers. This finding confirms what earlier research has suggested, i.e. that IES may not be feasible for all products and business segments, and that if pursued, the evolution towards IES requires changes in both the product and business portfolio.

7   Conclusion, Limitations and Future Research

In this paper, we identify the benefits and barriers that software development companies face when moving beyond agile development practices. In particular, and based on a multiple-case study in five Finnish companies, we identify the practices that companies adopt when moving towards IES. Our findings show that all of the interviewed companies have established agile software development practices within their R&D organisations. The primary benefit of doing so is that incremental and iterative development allow for more flexible product development projects in which customer feedback informs the organisation's development efforts and investments. When moving from agile practices to implementing CI at the team level or product level, companies A, B, C and D have improved their R&D capability to continuously integrate and validate software changes at a team and/or component level, and in some cases even at a system level. In this way, the R&D organisation gets faster feedback about functionality and they can avoid the many challenges related to integration of functionality. However, and as recognized by the interviewees, CI is not free. The main barrier is considered to be the high investment and significant effort that are required to ensure adequate test automation and the development of automated test cases. In our study, only Company A has evolved its software development practices to CD, and then only in some of its products and teams. Company A has made initial attempts to transition further to IES by experimenting with customers to validate new software functionality

The contribution of the paper is threefold. First, we apply the StH model in five Finnish case study companies. This strengthens the validity of the model and describes the evolution path that software development companies may take when advancing their development practices. Second, we extend the model with a set of practices that companies adopt at each step of the StH in order to advance further. In our case studies, we see that companies tend to institutionalise practices in the lower steps of the StH, adopt practices at the product level at the step at which they currently operate, and explore next step practices in individual development teams.

Finally, we validate the extended model and its practices in five Finnish software development companies using a multiple-case study and interpretive approach.

The main limitation of our study is related to the generalisability of the results. Although case study findings may provide important information regarding typical patterns and a set of practices, they cannot be generalised to the entire software development domain.

For future research, we suggest additional case studies that focus on stakeholders, such as customers, suppliers, subcontractors, platform providers, development partners, etc. This might broaden the understanding of the company's evolution path towards IES and expand the StH model view from an internal company perspective to an external ecosystem perspective.

Acknowledgements. This work was supported by TEKES as part of the Need for Speed project (http://www.n4s.fi/) of DIGILE (Finnish Strategic Centre for Science, Technology and Innovation in the field of ICT and digital business). This work was done in co-operation with the Software Center (www.software-center.se), a Nordic collaboration initiative between eight companies and three universities.

References

1. Highsmith, J.: Agile Project Management: Creating Innovative Products. Addison-Wesley Professional, New York (2009)
2. Bosch, J., Eklund, U.: Eternal Embedded Software: Towards Innovation Experiment Systems. In: Margaria, T., Steffen, B. (eds.) ISoLA 2012, Part I. LNCS, vol. 7609, pp. 19–31. Springer, Heidelberg (2012)
3. Fagerholm, F., Guinea, A.S., Mäenpää, H., Münch, J.: Building Blocks for Continuous Experimentation. In: 1st International Workshop on Rapid Continuous Software Engineering, pp. 26–35. ACM Press, New York (2014)
4. Olsson, H.H., Bosch, J., Alahyari, H.: Towards R&D as Innovation Experiment Systems: A Framework for Moving Beyond Agile Software Development. In: IASTED Multiconferences - Proceedings of the IASTED International Conference on Software Engineering, pp. 798–805 (2013)
5. Rodríguez, P., Markkula, J., Oivo, M., Turula, K.: Survey on Agile and Lean Usage in Finnish Software Industry. In: ACM-IEEE International symposium on Empirical Software Engineering and Measurement, pp. 139–148. ACM Press, New York (2012)
6. Dybå, T., Dingsøyr, T.: Empirical Studies of Agile Software Development: A Systematic Review. Information and Software Technology 50, 833–859 (2008)
7. Goodman, D., Elbaz, M.: "It's Not the Pants, it's the People in the Pants" Learnings from the Gap Agile Transformation What Worked, How We Did it, and What Still Puzzles Us. In: Agile Conference, pp. 112–115. IEEE Press, New York (2008)
8. Marschall, M.: Transforming a Six Month Release Cycle to Continuous Flow. In: Agile Conference, pp. 395–400. IEEE Press, New York (2007)
9. Neely, S., Stolt, S.: Continuous Delivery? Easy! Just Change Everything (Well, Maybe It Is Not That Easy). In: Agile Conference, pp. 121–128. IEEE Press, New York (2013)

10. Trimble, J., Webster, C.: From Traditional, to Lean, to Agile Development: Finding the Optimal Software Engineering Cycle. In: 46th Hawaii International Conference on System Sciences, pp. 4826–4833. IEEE Press, New York (2013)
11. Ståhl, D., Bosch, J.: Modeling Continuous Integration Practice Differences in Industry Software Development. Journal of Systems and Software 87, 48–59 (2014)
12. Humble, J., Farley, D.: Continuous Delivery: Reliable Software Releases through Build, Test, and Deployment Automation. Addison-Wesley Professional, Boston (2010)
13. Claps, G.G., Berntsson Svensson, R., Aurum, A.: On the Journey to Continuous Deployment: Technical and Social Challenges Along the Way. Information and Software Technology 57, 21–31 (2015)
14. Leppänen, M., Mäkinen, S., Pagels, M., Eloranta, V.-P., Itkönen, J., Mäntylä, M.V., Mannisto, T.: The Highways and Country Roads to Continuous Deployment. IEEE Software 32, 64–72 (2015)
15. Fitzgerald, B., Stol, K.-J.: Continuous Software Engineering and Beyond: Trends and Challenges. In: 1st International Workshop on Rapid Continuous Software Engineering, RCoSE 2014, pp. 1–9. ACM Press, New York (2014)
16. Karvonen, T., Rodriguez, P., Kuvaja, P., Mikkonen, K., Oivo, M.: Adapting the Lean Enterprise Self-Assessment Tool for the Software Development Domain. In: 38th Euromicro Conference on Software Engineering and Advanced Applications, pp. 266–273. IEEE Press, New York (2012)
17. Poppendieck, M., Poppendieck, T.: Implementing Lean Software Development. Addison-Wesley, New York (2006)
18. Bosch, J., Bosch-Sijtsema, P.: From Integration to Composition: On the Impact of Software Product Lines, Global Development and Ecosystems. Journal of Systems and Software 83, 67–76 (2010)
19. Olsson, H.H., Bosch, J.: From Opinions to Data-Driven Software R&D: A Multi-case Study on How to Close the "Open Loop" Problem. In: 40th EUROMICRO Conference on Software Engineering and Advanced Applications, pp. 9–16. IEEE Press, New York (2014)
20. Pressman, R., Maxim, B.: Software Engineering: A Practitioner's Approach. McGraw Hill Education, New York (2014)
21. Ries, E.: The Lean Startup: How Today's Entrepreneurs Use Continuous Innovation to Create Radically Successful Businesses. Crown Publishing, New York (2011)
22. van der Linden, F.J., Dannenberg, R.B., Kamsties, E., Känsälä, K., Obbink, H.: Software Product Family Evaluation. In: Nord, R.L. (ed.) SPLC 2004. LNCS, vol. 3154, pp. 110–129. Springer, Heidelberg (2004)
23. Runeson, P., Höst, M., Rainer, A., Regnell, B.: Case Study Research in Software Engineering: Guidelines and Examples. John Wiley & Sons, New Jersey (2012)
24. Yin, R.K.: Case Study Research: Design and Methods. SAGE Publications Inc., California (2009)

Communication in Firm-Internal
Global Software Development with China

Bilal Zaghloul[1]([envelope]), Dirk Riehle[2], and Minghui Zhou[3]

[1] Friedrich-Alexander University Erlangen-Nürnberg, Information Systems Department,
Lange Gasse 20, 90403, Nuremberg, Germany
bilal.zaghloul@fau.de
[2] Friedrich-Alexander University Erlangen-Nürnberg, Computer Science Department,
Martenstr. 3, 91058, Erlangen, Germany
dirk@riehle.org
[3] Peking University, School of Electronics Engineering and Computer Science,
100871, Beijing, China
zhmh@pku.edu.cn

Abstract. Globally distributed software development projects are on the rise. However, 69% of cross-regional projects fail completely or partially, because of lack of cross-cultural understanding. This paper presents a qualitative study of the impact of communication on Global Software Development (GSD) within firms due to cultural differences. In particular, we provide a model of problems and solutions related to communication of German/Chinese and American/Chinese collaborations in GSD. The model was derived using grounded theory to study six globally distributed software development projects. The results may not only help companies understand cultural problems, but also help them overcome these problems. To this end, we discuss the solutions adopted by the multinational software companies that we studied.

Keywords: Global software development · Cultural differences · Communication · Qualitative research · China collaboration

1   Introduction

Globally distributed software development, also called global software development (GSD), is growing as the software industry is experiencing an increase in globalization of business [1]. The reasons motivating GSD are reduction of costs, access to skilled labor, getting closer to customers, time difference utilization, and improving the quality of work [2]. Yet, according to a study by a major auditing firm, 69% of all outsourcing projects fail completely or partially [3]. Main reasons are the lack of cultural harmony between the vendor and the client and poor relationship management. In this paper, we present the results of a qualitative study on how to address cultural differences in GSD. We interviewed six project managers from six different globally distributed software development projects. All projects were firm-internal projects, with at least one team on each project

© Springer International Publishing Switzerland 2015
J.M. Fernandes et al. (Eds.): ICSOB 2015, LNBIP 210, pp. 132–138, 2015.
DOI: 10.1007/978-3-319-19593-3_11

being based in China. We applied a Grounded Theory (GT) approach to analyze the interviews and related data and to develop the model.

The two central categories that emerged from our GT-based analysis are communication and trust, of which this paper reviews the communication category. As a key result, we present the solutions as best practices, which practitioners in large multinational corporations can adopt to address problems of GSD.

2   Related Work

The existing literature provides a number of relevant studies that explore the impact of communication on GSD.

For example, Persson et al. [4] discover a set of challenges related to the lack of face-to-face communications in agile distributed software development. Damian & Zowghi [5] present a model of how remote communication and knowledge management, cultural diversity and time differences negatively impact requirements gathering, negotiations and specifications. Holmstrom et al. [6] find that temporal, geographical, and socio-cultural distances have an impact on communication, and present solutions based on qualitative interviews of American and Irish companies.

There are also studies that try to understand the reasons of communication issues. For example, Bjørn & Ngwenyama [7] investigate communication breakdowns that can be attributed to differences in life world structures, organizational structures, and work process structures within a virtual team. Keil et al. [8] investigate the effect of culturally constituted views of face-saving on the willingness to communicate bad news regarding a software development project in the USA and in South Korea.

Most studies investigate communication issues in GSD, and very few present solutions for the discovered issues. In our study, we show the issues related to communication and their particular solutions in the projects. Although some of the communication problems have been already mentioned in other studies, such as, the problem of the lack of face-to-face communication, the face-saving problem, and the language barriers [4, 6, 8], our study does not describe only problems, but also solutions from industry.

Our findings improve or extend prior work due to different contexts, difference in data collection, different way of analysis, and novel results.

3   Study Preparation

We use a Grounded Theory (GT) approach for our research [9].

We chose interviews as the main method of data collection. Our interviewee sample included six individuals in German and American multinational software companies. Two of them were Germans representing German companies, and four were Chinese representing American and German companies. All participants held managerial roles with direct engagement in the development process. Moreover, they have between four to ten years of cross-cultural experience in the field.

Our research process started by reviewing the existing literature including papers, articles, books, etc. This allowed us to form the initial research question that served as a starting point for interview preparation. For each interview, we prepared open-ended questions on various areas of the effects of cultural differences in GSD to be addressed during the interview. These questions were used solely to navigate the interview, and were not given to the interviewee beforehand. Furthermore, we refined questions after each interview based mainly on the analysis results of the previous interview, as well as the existing literature. The analysis provided us with focus areas that we could address further in the next interview. After six interviews, we reached data saturation, i.e. we did not receive new information, rather interviewees were repeating each other. At this point, we decided to move forward towards forming the model.

We interviewed six individuals in multinational software companies. The interviews were divided equally between German and American companies. Moreover, we interviewed industry partners from different sectors in the software industry, for example electronics, energy, or enterprise solutions. This variation allowed us to gain more knowledge about the effects of culture in software development from different angles and also to see if different sectors have different problems or not. We had two personal face-to-face interviews that took place in China, and four interviews over the phone. "American" person in this paper means a person from the U.S.A. Each interview took around 1 – 1.25 hours.

4   Research Results

The result of our analysis is a model (or theory), consisting of two main categories *Communication* and *Trust*. *Communication*, in turn, is based on the key concepts *Reporting Failure*, *Communication Behaviors*, and *Collaboration across Regions*, while *Trust* is based on the key concepts *Transparency* and *Delegation and Traveling*. For reasons of brevity, we omit Trust from the discussion. The interested reader is referred to the first author's Master Thesis [10].

Our data analysis uncovered fourteen problems and eighteen solutions related to *Communication*. All problems and solutions were explicitly mentioned by our interview partners.

4.1   Communication

Data analysis showed that 153 out of 199 quotations are related to Communication, i.e. 77% of all quotations relate to Communication. Table 1 shows additional details for each of concept.

4.1.1   Reporting Failure

Half of our participants (3, or 50%) mentioned explicitly some situations where they encountered this problem. Table 2 shows a list of the encountered problems.

Moreover, the analysis revealed six solutions that were used to overcome some of the encountered problems in table 2. Table 3 presents a list of these solutions

4.1.2   Communication Behaviors

The majority of our interview partners (4, or 67%) observed several differences in the communication styles of Chinese developers in comparison with their American or German peers. Table 4 presents a list of related problems.

Moreover, the analysis revealed three solutions that were used to overcome some of the encountered problems in table 4. Table 5 illustrates a list of these.

Solutions "SL2" and "SL4" that are listed in table 5 were also mentioned to overcome problems "PR4" and PR5".

4.1.3 Collaboration Across Regions

This concept presents problems that may occur in managing the collaborations across regions, as well as some suggested solutions. The majority of our interview partners (5, or 83%) mentioned repeatedly several differences in capturing requirements, defining tasks, language barriers, and so on. Table 6 presents a list of related problems that were explicitly mentioned by our interview partners.

Moreover, the analysis revealed nine solutions that were used to overcome some of the problems in table 6. Table 7 shows a list of related solutions.

Table 1. Percentage of participants for each concept in "Communication" category

Concept	Participants		Quotations	
Reporting Failure	3 (P1,P3,P4)	50%	34	17%
Communication Behaviors	4 (P1,P2,P3,P5)	67%	37	19%
Collaboration across Regions	5 (P1,P3,P4,P5,P6)	83%	82	41%

Table 2. Problems related to "Reporting Failure"

ID	Problem	Participants
PR1	Chinese developers are more reluctant than German and American developers to report mistakes during projects.	2 (P1,P3)
PR2	Chinese make late notifications if not being able to meet the deadline. Yet, they are willing to spend long after work hours to finish the task.	1 (P3)
PR3	Strictness of Chinese team leaders makes it difficult for some developers to report mistakes or delays.	1 (P4)

Table 3. Solutions related to "Reporting Failure"

ID	Solution (Best Practice)	Problem ID	Participants
SL1	Ask management to appreciate reporting mistakes during projects.	PR1	1 (P1)
SL2	Create workshops to articulate ideas with anonymous identities, because anonymity helps Chinese avoid sharp direct feedback.	PR1	1 (P1)
SL3	Use a progress-tracking system, where a developer updates the status of his task daily to avoid late notifications.	PR2	1 (P3)
SL4	Choose software development method that encourages communication, e.g., Scrum, or other agile methods.	PR1	1 (P1)
SL5	Assign a local Chinese expert to get back to in case of problems.	-	1 (P4)
SL6	Bring up the message that delays are acceptable in presence of a strong justification.	PR2	1 (P3)

Table 4. Problems related to "Communication Behaviors"

ID	Problem	Participants
PR4	Chinese developers have less tendency than Germans and Americans towards asking questions in group meetings.	3 (P1,P5,P3)
PR5	Chinese developers seldom discuss their tasks with their superiors.	2 (P1,P2)
PR6	Chinese' "yes" or "no" has a different meaning for Americans.	1 (P3)
PR7	Chinese have a formal communication style, while Americans have an informal style.	1 (P5)

Table 5. Solutions related to "Communication Behaviors"

ID	Solution (Best Practice)	Problem ID	Participants
SL7	Ask the management to bring up repeatedly the message of the importance of open conversation.	PR4,PR5	2 (P2,P5)
SL8	Do not take "yes" or "no" for an answer. Chinese developers should write a document of their opinion after important sessions.	PR6	1 (P3)
SL9	Create a relaxing work environment for Chinese developers, where you can speak freely and informally with colleagues, and formally only with clients.	PR7	1 (P5)

Table 6. Problems related to "Collaboration across Regions"

ID	Problem	Participants
PR8	Chinese developers need detailed requirements about their tasks.	3 (P1,P3,P4)
PR9	Chinese cannot easily talk in English due to language barriers.	3 (P3,P4,P6)
PR10	Chinese are detail-oriented, while Americans and Germans see the big picture.	3 (P1,P3,P4)
PR11	The U.S.A. and China have different holidays. For example spring festival in China, and Christmas in the U.S.A.	1 (P4)
PR12	Chinese developers omit context when discussing tasks.	1 (P5)
PR13	Chinese developers like to be challenged.	2 (P3,P5)
PR14	The terminology is documented only in the country's language, i.e. Chinese in China and German in Germany.	1 (P6)

Table 7. Solutions related to "Collaboration across Regions"

ID	Solution (Best Practice)	Problem ID	Participants
SL10	Create smaller and deeper tasks deliberately and associate them with specs and context.	PR8	1 (P1)
SL11	Split up the development cycle across regions, where you can exploit the benefits of each one, for example Americans deal with customers, Chinese design, and Indians implement.	-	1 (P3)
SL12	Pay more attention when defining requirements in order not to leave any space for guessing.	PR8	2 (P1,P3)
SL13	Use a wiki-like system for technical discussions. Yet, it is not useful in case of urgent issues.	PR9	1 (P4)
SL14	Remind Chinese developers repeatedly of the importance of providing context when discussing tasks.	PR12	1 (P5)

Table 7. (*continued*)

SL15	Create discussion groups, where Chinese developers discuss technical problems with their American colleagues.	PR13	1 (P5)
SL16	Provide Chinese developers with challenging tasks.	PR13	1 (P5)
SL17	Create English training sessions in both sides. The training focuses on business terms used in the industry.	PR9	1 (P6)
SL18	Unify the terminology by creating a map table in the three languages: English, Chinese, and German, where each term is associated with its corresponding in English.	PR14	1 (P6)

5   Conclusion

In this research, we present a grounded-theory-based study of problems and solutions of German/Chinese and American/Chinese collaborations. Our data was gathered through six interviews with six participants in multinational software companies that have development centers in China.

As a result, a model with two main categories emerged: Communication and Trust. In this paper, we reviewed the Communication category for reasons of brevity. Each category contained a number of concepts, where each concept identified a set of problems and corresponding solutions. The resulting concepts in the Communication category pinpoint major areas where communication problems are likely to occur.

All problems and solutions were explicitly mentioned by our interviewees. Although some of the problems were already mentioned in other studies like the problem of face-to-face communication and language barriers, our model does not describe only problems, but also solutions from the industry.

This model provides companies with in-depth insights about the problems they might encounter, and they can turn to the specific solutions adopted by multinational software companies that we report about.

References

1. Herbsleb, J.D., Moitra, D.: Global software development. IEEE Softw. 18, 16–20 (2001)
2. Carmel, E.: Global software teams: collaborating across borders and time zones. Prentice Hall PTR (1999)
3. OSF Global Services: Overcome cultural differences in the outsourcing process (2012)
4. Persson, J.S., Mathiassen, L., Aaen, I.: Agile distributed software development: enacting control through media and context. Inf. Syst. J. 22, 411–433 (2012)
5. Damian, D.E., Zowghi, D.: RE challenges in multi-site software development organisations. Requir. Eng. 8, 149–160 (2003)
6. Holmstrom, H., Conchúir, E.Ó., Ågerfalk, P.J., Fitzgerald, B.: Global Software Development Challenges: A Case Study on Temporal, Geographical and Socio-Cultural Distance (2006)

7. Bjørn, P., Ngwenyama, O.: Virtual team collaboration: building shared meaning, resolving breakdowns and creating translucence. Inf. Syst. J. 19, 227–253 (2009)
8. Keil, M., Im, G.P., Mähring, M.: Reporting bad news on software projects: the effects of culturally constituted views of face-saving. Inf. Syst. J. 17, 59–87 (2007)
9. Glaser, B.G., Strauss, A.L.: The discovery of grounded theory: Strategies for qualitative research. Transaction Books (2009)
10. Zaghloul, B.: A Theory of Problems and Solutions in German/Chinese and American/Chinese Software Engineering Collaborations (2014), http://goo.gl/1Zcnp7

Customer Feedback and Data Collection Techniques in Software R&D: A Literature Review

Aleksander Fabijan[1]([✉]), Helena Holmström Olsson[1], and Jan Bosch[2]

[1] Malmö University, Faculty of Technology and Society, Östra Varvsgatan 11,
205 06 Malmö, Sweden
{Aleksander.Fabijan, Helena.Holmström.Olsson}@mah.se
[2] Chalmers University of Technology, Department of Computer Science & Engineering,
Hörselgången 11, 412 96 Göteborg, Sweden
Jan.Bosch@chalmers.se

Abstract. In many companies, product management struggles in getting accurate customer feedback. Often, validation and confirmation of functionality with customers takes place only after the product has been deployed, and there are no mechanisms that help product managers to continuously learn from customers. Although there are techniques available for collecting customer feedback, these are typically not applied as part of a continuous feedback loop. As a result, the selection and prioritization of features becomes far from optimal, and product deviates from what the customers need. In this paper, we present a literature review of currently recognized techniques for collecting customer feedback. We develop a model in which we categorize the techniques according to their characteristics. The purpose of this literature review is to provide an overview of current software engineering research in this area and to better understand the different techniques that are used for collecting customer feedback.

Keywords: Customer feedback · Data collection · The 'open loop' problem · Qualitative feedback · Quantitative data

1 Introduction

Although the opportunities to learn about customers and customer behaviors are increasing, most software development companies experience the road mapping and requirements prioritization process of features as complex. Product management often finds it difficult to get timely and accurate feedback from customers [2], [20]. Typically, feedback loops are slow and there is a lack of mechanisms that allow for efficient collection and analysis of customer feedback [1], [2]. Usually, confirmation of the correctness of product management decisions takes place only after the finalized product has been deployed to customers, and when there is little opportunity to adapt to changes. In previous research, we coined the term the 'open loop' problem, referring to the challenges for product management to receive accurate customer feedback to use as a basis in their decision-making processes [2]. Despite the availability of sophisticated customer feedback techniques, our research shows

J.M. Fernandes et al. (Eds.): ICSOB 2015, LNBIP 210, pp. 139–153, 2015.
DOI: 10.1007/978-3-319-19593-3_12

that these are still difficult to apply in a way that improve decision-making processes in software R&D. As a result, and despite that significant data is being collected, companies have insufficient knowledge about how their products are used and what features the customers actually appreciate and desire to use in the future. This means that there is typically a weak link between customer data and product management decisions, and no accurate way in which the organizations can assess whether the features that were prioritized during the road mapping process are also the features that are appreciated and used by customers and that generate revenue to the company [4], [17].

In the context of this, we conduct a literature review in the area of customer feedback and data collection techniques. In our review, we let the basic principles of the systematic literature review method guide us [5], and we adopt a structured approach to literature search and selection. The purpose of our review is to provide an overview of current software engineering research in this area and to better understand the different techniques that are used for collecting customer feedback in different stages of the software development process. We summarize our findings in a model in which we categorize all customer feedback and data collection techniques, as well as present in what stages of the development process they are typically used. While this topic has been carefully studied within research domains such as e.g. information systems (IS), human computer interaction (HCI) and management literature, it has not been widely recognized in the software engineering (SE) domain [31].

The contribution of the paper is twofold. First, we provide a 'state-of-the-art' overview of software engineering research within the area of customer feedback and data collection techniques. While the attention for this topic is gaining increasing interest also in the software engineering research community, there is no literature review that provides an overview of the research reported in this community. Second, we present a structured model that provides an overall understanding for existing feedback and data collection techniques, and that works as a support for selecting the appropriate feedback technique in a specific stage of the software development process.

The remaining of this paper is structured as follows. In section 2 we present the background and the motivation for this study. In section 3, we describe the systematic literature review (SLR) method from which we use the basic principles when collecting the papers. In section 4, we present the results from the literature review. In section 5, we discuss the results and we present a model in which we categorize the techniques according to their main characteristics and map them to the development stages in which they are typically used. Finally, in section 6, we present the conclusions.

2   Background

Software development in general, and how to involve and learn from customers in particular, has been a topic of intensive research for a long time [25], [38]. Recently, and as a means to solve the many challenges with how to involve customers, many companies have adopted agile development methods. For more than a decade, agile development methods have demonstrated their success in establishing flexible development processes with short feedback loops and consideration taken to evolving customer needs [1], [11]. However, and as recognized in this paper, despite recent methods and sophisticated techniques, there still exist major problems in how to learn from customers, i.e. how to efficiently collect customer feedback and customer data. In our previous research, we described this situation as the 'open loop' problem referring to a situation in which product management has difficulty in getting access to customer feedback that can help them in e.g. feature prioritization processes [2]. In related research, similar problems have been identified [34], [36] and many are those that look for the 'silver bullet' that will help solving the issue with how to best involve customers, and learn from their feedback.

The issue of how to involve customers and how to collect customer feedback has gained much attention and is a well-established topic within research traditions such as e.g. information systems (IS), human computer interaction (HCI) and participatory design (PD). In information systems research, it has been a prominent research topic for decades, with a special focus on the organizational and social contexts that influence customers and customer behaviors [31], [32]. In human computer interaction research, as well as in participatory design research, the focus is primarily on methods, activities and distinct techniques for improving usefulness, ease of use and user satisfaction [34], [35]. Also, the innovation management literature provides interesting insights in the area of customer involvement and feedback techniques. In a recent paper, Bosch-Sijtsema and Bosch [4] present a model in which they identify a number of customer involvement techniques in high-tech firms, and they categorize these according to what type of data that is collected, to what extent customers are actively or passively involved in data collection, and in what stage of the development process the technique is typically used.

However, although of critical relevance for any software development process, the topic has not gained much attention in the software engineering (SE) research domain. While there is significant research on e.g. requirements engineering and elicitation [3] techniques, there are few studies that recognize the many additional opportunities that exist to involve and learn from customers during the development process. Therefore, and as a way to assess the current 'state-of-the-art' in software engineering research, we conduct a literature review focusing on customer feedback and data collection techniques. In the best of our knowledge, such a literature review has not been conducted in the SE domain before and hence, our review addresses a gap at the same time as it creates a better understanding of recent software engineering research with relevance for this particular topic of interest.

3   Method

This literature review is our first step towards conducting a 'Systematic Literature Review' (SLR), method presented by Kitchenham [5]. As a systematic approach to searching, selecting and reviewing papers, this method provided us with a basic structure for identifying recent research with relevance for exploring our research questions. As their main characteristic, systematic literature reviews are formally planned and methodically executed. Initially developed in medicine, the method has been widely adopted in other disciplines such as criminology, social policy and economics, and recently it has gained momentum also in research domains such as e.g. information systems and software engineering [27], [28]. The purpose of our literature review is to provide an overview of recent software engineering research in the area of customer feedback and data collection techniques. In our overview, we address the following research questions:

- *RQ1.* What are the existing customer feedback techniques as reported in software engineering literature?
- *RQ2.* What are the existing customer data collection techniques as reported in the software engineering literature?
- *RQ3.* In what stages of the development process are the identified techniques used?
- *RQ4.* What are the main challenges and limitations of the identified techniques?

3.1   Search Process

In our search process, and in order to provide a 'state-of-the-art' review of customer feedback techniques in the software engineering research domain, we selected the highest ranked software engineering journals. Our search process started with selecting relevant terms such as 'customer feedback', 'customer involvement', 'customer participation', and continuing with 'data collection' and 'customer data' in order to also target non-physical collection of feedback. The journals that were included in our search process are the top ten software engineering journals, namely IEEE Transactions on Software Engineering (TSE), Communications of the ACM (CACM), Springer Empirical Software Engineering, IEEE Computer, IEEE Software, ACM Transactions on Software Engineering and Methodology, MIS Quarterly, Empirical Software Engineering, Information and Software Technology, SW Maintenance & Evolution - Research & Practice and databases [30]. In addition, we used the same queries to search for conference papers in the library of the Institute of Electrical and Electronics Engineers (IEEE), ACM, Science Direct, Scopus and on Google Scholar.

3.2   Inclusion and Exclusion Criteria

Each paper that matched the search criteria was reviewed by at least one of the researchers, and as suggested by the SLR [5], we reviewed the keywords, we read the abstract and we identified customer feedback and data collection techniques in the body of the paper. We selected the papers that recognize at least one technique for customer feedback and data collection with the purpose to use this data to improve and innovate software products, e.g. develop a new feature or a new product. In our review, we included papers where customer feedback techniques were the main purpose of the paper, as well as papers where such techniques were only one element of the paper.

3.3   Data Collection

The data extracted from each study were:

- The source (conference or a journal name)
- Classification of the study Type (customer involvement, customer data collection, new product innovation)
- Summary with main focus of the paper
- Main findings of the paper
- Main challenges

Table 1. Software engineering papers that were selected as relevant for our literature review on customer feedback and data collection techniques

ID	Authors	Title of the publication	Date	Topic Area
P1	Kabbedijk et al	Customer Involvement in Requirements Management: Lessons from Mass Market Software Development	2009	Customer involvement
P2	Chen et al.	A novel virtual design platform for product innovation through customer involvement	2011	Customer involvement
P3	Chen et al.	How customer involvement enhances innovation performance: The moderating effect of appropriability	2014	Customer involvement
P4	Wang	Facilitating customer involvement into the decision making process of concept generation and concept evaluation for new product development	2012	Customer involvement
P5	Burns and Halliburton	Tackling productivity and quality through customer involvement and software technology	1989	Customer Involvement
P6	Cohan	Successful Customer Collaboration Resulting in the Right Product for the End User	2008	Customer participation
P7	Martin et al.	XP Customer Practices: A Grounded Theory	2009	Customer Involvement
P8	Jin et al.	New Service Development Success Factors: a Managerial Perspective	2010	Customer Involvement
P9	IEE Colloquium	IEE Colloquium on `Customer Driven Quality in Product Design' (Digest No.1994/086)	1994	Customer data
P10	Yang and Chen	Customer Participation: Co-Creating Knowledge with Customers	2008	Customer Participation
P11	Bhatia et al.	Monitoring and analyzing customer feedback through social media platforms for identifying and remedying customer problems	2013	Data Collection
P12	Pang et al.	Opinion mining and sentiment analysis	2008	Customer data
P13	Bosch	Building products as innovation experiment systems	2012	Customer data

3.4   Results

This section summarizes the results of our literature search process. Although there were about 147 different papers that initially matched the search criteria entered in the search engines of the individual journals and conferences, we found only 13 papers with direct relevance to the research questions we specified. These were the papers that mentioned at least one method of customer feedback in the abstract or in the body of the paper. We present the papers that we collectively selected in Table 1.

4   Results

In accordance to the research questions (RQ 1-4), we present the existing customer feedback and data collection techniques, in what stages of the development process they are used, what characteristics they have, and what challenges and limitations that are associated with the techniques.

4.1   Customer Feedback Techniques

Most often, and as recognized in several of the papers we found, the initial source of customer feedback originates from direct interaction with the customer by using techniques based on active customer involvement [6], [7]. Typically, feedback is collected using techniques such as customer interviews, customer questionnaires and customer surveys. As recognized by Yiyi et al. [7], customer questionnaires and surveys are given to customers to have them express an idea or an opinion, in order to provide the company with a basic understanding of their needs and desires, as well as their expectations of the product. Also, and as suggested by Olsson & Bosch [25], observation of customers is a common technique to learn about their behaviors. This technique allows for follow-up questions on certain behaviors that were identified during the observation. As a more interactive approach, Kabbedijk et al. [6] suggest having 'theater sessions' together with several customers to have them express e.g. a feature request and provide input on how a certain feature would be used in their context.

Also, and as one of the most common techniques, the evaluation of prototypes is conducted in close collaboration with customers [26]. Sampson et al. [9] suggest rounds of prototype testing in which feedback is collected to support developers on a continuous basis. Such testing and evaluation activities can be internal and include developers that built the product, as well as external including beta users that agree to try the product for a limited period of time. Martin et al. [14] support the idea of having internal evaluation with developers being the first "customers", and suggest a second step in which developers coach the customers for a couple of iterations. This way, the product use is observed by its' creators while in use by the customer. As a result of this, the developers collect information about customers' experience of the product and spot issues that might not have been revealed differently. Additionally, and when having a prototype or an early version of a product, in-product surveys and web polls are important techniques for collecting feedback that helps in understanding the customer appreciation of a current and future products. Martin et al. [14] also recommend customer pairing and customer 'boot camps' as one technique to not only collect feedback from one customer, but to have customers share this feedback with other customers with similar experiences.

Burns and Halliburton [12] suggest continuous customer review of products, and customer involvements that concludes with an approval or a rejection of an idea or product concept. In their experience, operational 'walk-throughs', i.e. end-to-end tests by various customer groups should be presented to the customer, and that developers should be the first "customers" of the product. In similar, Cohan et al. [13] note that for a successful project, the customers should provide feedback on a continuous basis, and that several iterations in which the minimal product functionalities are evaluated is a beneficial way of ensuring the collection of accurate customer feedback and in a timely manner. Jin et al. [15] confirm this when recognizing that the higher the customer's involvement is, the higher the success rate will be for the product that is being developed. Finally, and as identified by Bosch [17], customer interest can also be measured by a method known as 'BASES' testing. The method was originally introduced by Nielsen [8] and measures customer interest in new product concepts in order to identify the potential of a new product or improvement of an existing one.

4.2   Data Collection Techniques

As a result of products being increasingly software-intensive, and with the opportunity to have these products connected to the Internet, companies are experiencing novel opportunities to learn about customer and product behaviours. As products go on-line, companies can monitor them, collect data on how they perform, predict when they break, know where they are located, and learn about when and how they are used or not used by customers. Typically, this form of customer and product data collection takes place when the products have been deployed and being used in real-time by its customers. In this context, Chen et al. [16] recommend to collect both customer data, e.g. demographic, psychographic, and behavioral data, as well as product data, e.g. operation, performance, responsiveness. This data can be used to generate models of product use and customer behaviors as a basis in direct interactions with customers. For example, product data reveals what features are used, how often they are used, and what point in time they are used etc., and can be used as a means for having customers rank individual features and this way directly steer product development [6].

Bosch [17] describes several techniques for customer data collection. He suggests advertising new products via online ads and having in-product surveys to identify potential interest in new products. Also, he notes that some companies display different versions of the same product or feature to customers, and have mechanisms in place to collect data on how customers respond to these different versions. In this way, companies learn about what is the preferred version of the product. This is known as A/B testing [11], and is a common data collection technique in the web 2.0 and in the software-as-a-service (SaaS) domain. Additionally, and as recognized by Kohavi et al [26], an early version of the product can be given to a sample of customers to test the functionality, where operational data, event logs and usage data are retrieved in order to identify performance issues, errors and other usability problems. Furthermore, this data can be complemented with geological data and time zone information in order to segment the customers.

In addition to the data collection techniques above, external data sources such as social media e.g. Twitter, Instagram and Facebook consist of millions of connected customers that are located around the world and that share their experiences of products. Bathia et al. [24] recognize these data sources as increasingly important sources of information where companies can learn about customer behaviors and customer opinions [29]. Similarly to social networks, crowd-funding platforms such as Kickstarter provide a source of data that reveals products that succeeded or failed in collecting the community support.

4.3   Development Process Stages

In reviewing the selected papers, we see that different customer feedback and data collection techniques are deployed depending on what development stage the product is in. In the pre-development phase, software development companies collect customer feedback in requirements specifications, through questionnaires and surveys and by engaging customers in solution jams or theater sessions where different ideas are proposed, ranked and discussed [6], [7]. Also, customer interest in this early stage can be investigated with techniques such as BASES testing [17].

During development, customer feedback is collected in prototyping sessions in which customers test the prototype, discuss it with the developers, and suggest modifications of e.g. a user interface [9], [26]. As a result, developers get feedback on customer behaviors and ways-of-working, as well as on product usefulness, ease of use etc. This feedback serves as important input in further improvement of the product. Additionally, in-product marketing and in-product surveys can be performed at this stage to get the feedback data about a product's version and potential interest in other features [17].

In the post-deployment stage when the product has been released to its customers, a number of techniques are used to collect customer and product data. First, and since the products are increasingly being connected to the Internet and equipped with data collection mechanisms, operational data, performance data and data revealing feature usage is collected. If customer experience problems with the product, they generate incident reports, support data, trouble tickets etc. that are important sources of information for the developers when troubleshooting and improving the product [10]. Often, and as recognized in previous research (see e.g. Bosch [17]), A/B testing is a commonly deployed technique in order to optimize an existing feature, introduce a new one or when building a new product.

4.4   Challenges and Limitations

There are several challenges and limitations associated with the techniques as identified in the literature review. For example, theatre sessions, or similar requirements gathering methods, require sophisticated technology implemented at the location where the customers meet [6]. This reduces the amount of available venues for such an event. Second, the customers need to be present at the same time at the same location, which might be difficult to achieve due to tight schedules in the companies and inconvenient to handle if frictions between customers are present [6].

Questionnaires, interviews, surveys, site visits and face-to-face interaction with customers are time-consuming techniques [6], [7], and therefore challenging to make happen in a fast-moving business environment in which process efficiency is key [7], [17]. Also, our review identifies challenges and limitations associated with testing of prototypes. When presenting a prototype, only parts of the product is developed. Therefore, customers are not able to test the full product, and they might misinterpret the intention with the early version of the product. This might lead the customer to believe that the product is not developed as agreed [9], [14].

A/B testing, i.e. showing different versions of the same product to different customer groups, pose numerous challenges. For example, there might be the risk that customers that get used to one version of the product get hesitant when exposed to a different version of the same product [29], [39]. Second, customer segments need to be carefully chosen in order to prevent revenue loss in case of operational problems or product expectations that do not match with the experimental version [39].

Finally, on-line ads and in-product surveys can be experienced as disturbing by customers if not presented correctly [17]. Often, customers prefer to express their opinions on social networks such as e.g. Twitter and Facebook etc., which produces similar outcomes as product surveys. However, social networks typically generate large amounts of data that is difficult to analyze [29].

4.5 Summary of Results

Table 2. Summary of literature review results

Customer feedback technique	Development stage	Challenges/limitations	Noted in paper
BASES testing	Pre-development	Potential bias of panel members	P13
Interviews	Pre-development	Time consuming	P1, P10, P2, P3
Questionnaires	Pre-development	Time consuming	P1, P10
Surveys	Pre-development	Time consuming	P1, P2, P3, P4
Observations	Pre-development	Time consuming	P1, P10
Theater sessions	Pre-development	Availability of technical infrastructure, physical presence of participants in the same location	P1
Prototype testing	Development	Only partially developed interfaces and functionality	P6, P7, P8, P13
Incident Reports	Post-development	Available only after an incident	
Developers as customers	Development	Time consuming for developers	P7
Customer pairing and boot camps	Post-development	Physical presence of participants in the same location	P7
Walk-throughs	Post-development	Time consuming for developers and customers	P5

Table 2. *(Continued)*

Customer data collection technique	Development stage	Challenges/limitations
Online ads and in-product surveys	Pre-development	Potentially disturbing for customers P13
Beta testing	Development	Only partially developed interfaces and functionality
Operational and event data	Development	Security issues when such data is P13, P11 transmitted, potentially high amounts of data
A/B testing	Post-development	Potentially confusing for customers P13 when exposed to different versions
Social networks	Post-development	Numerous sources, large quantities P11, P12 of data for analysis
Crowd-funding platforms data	Pre-development	Large quantities of data for analysis P11, P12

5   Discussion

The purpose of this study is to provide a 'state-of-the-art' review of software engineering research in the area of customer feedback and data collection techniques. In this section, we discuss the results of the review. As a structure for our analysis, we use the *qualitative* and *quantitative* categorization as suggested by Bosch-Sijtsema and Bosch [4]. In the qualitative category, we place the feedback techniques that require active participation from customers and where a smaller amount of data is collected. The quantitative category, on the other hand, represents data collection techniques where customers are only passively involved and where large amounts of data is collected. Also, we note the emerging trend of social networks as a data source for collecting customer feedback with inherent characteristics of both a qualitative and quantitative nature. Finally, we summarize our findings in a structured model that provides an overall understanding for existing feedback and data collection techniques.

5.1   Qualitative and Quantitative Feedback Techniques

When analyzing the papers and the different techniques they identify, we see two main characteristics that distinguish the different techniques from each other. First, and as traditionally used as the main approach to involve customers in software development, we identify a number of *qualitative* customer feedback techniques. These are techniques that require active participation from customers, that generate a small amount of qualitative feedback, and that are typically used in the early stages of development. The strength of such qualitative research methods is its ability to provide complex textual descriptions of how people experience a given research issue. It provides information about the 'human' side of an issue [21]. In our case these are the methods of customer feedback that we identified in section 4.1. Second, and as a result of products being increasingly software-intensive and having connectivity capabilities, we identify a number of *quantitative* data collection techniques. These are techniques that focus on product data such as performance data, error logs and other techniques of data collection that we identified in section 4.2. With quantitative techniques the order of 'questions' asked does not matter, design and results are subject to statistical assumptions and they seek to confirm hypotheses rather than explore opinions [22], [23].

5.2   Emerging Customer Feedback Techniques

In addition to the qualitative and quantitative techniques identified above, we see a tremendous growth and popularity of social network platforms such as Twitter, Instagram and Facebook as additional data sources for learning about customers. Interestingly, these data sources provide companies with additional opportunities to collect both qualitative feedback from individual customers expressing their experiences of the products, and quantitative data in terms of the large amounts of data that is generated and that represents a large customer base. Data retrieved from these networks is used to improve the products, detect errors, take decisions and trigger corrective measures [37]. For example, Bhatia et al. describe a system that automatically monitors social networks such as Facebook and Twitter [24]. It analyzes the data from the platforms and triggers events that lead to corrective actions. For this purpose, platforms known as 'sentiment monitoring systems' help companies in collecting comments from the customers, in analyzing the data generated, and in identifying major problems and to automatically trigger corrective response actions [29], [33]. In addition to social networks, crowd-funding platforms such as Kickstarter offer an insight into which products receive support and which ones failed to succeed. Such information can be used to further improve the understanding of the market desires and needs.

5.3   Summary

In this paper, and based on a literature review of recent software engineering research, we identify existing customer feedback and data collection techniques. From the pre-development stage, through the development process and also after the product is deployed to customers, each of these techniques provides companies with the opportunity to collect customer and product data. In Figure 1 below, we present our findings in a structured model that works as a support for selecting the appropriate feedback technique in a specific stage of the software development process.

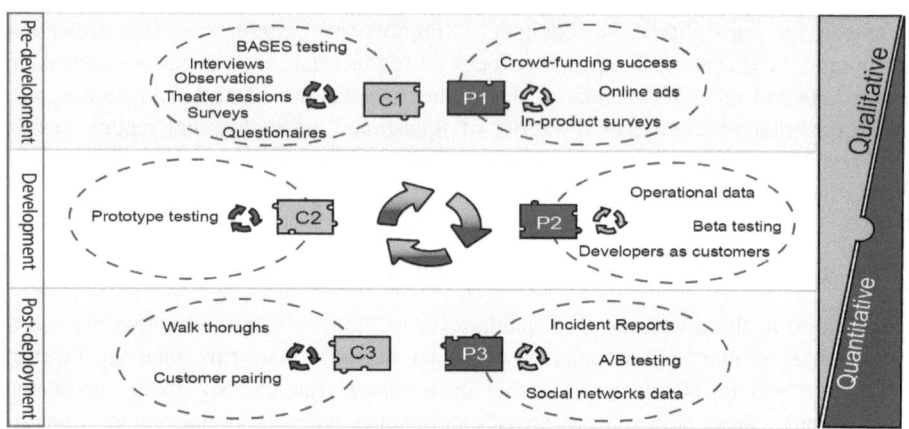

Fig. 1. Qualitative and quantitative feedback techniques

In our model, we distinguish between three development stages, i.e. pre-development, development and post-deployment. Although we recognize that this is a simplified view, and that most development processes are of an iterative nature, we define these stages as they typically involve different techniques for collecting customer feedback. First, and as shown in the pre-development phase in the model, companies aim at identifying market interest in a new product. They interview customers, they observe them while using the products, and they might even meet with them in theatre sessions to learn more about their preferences. This first iterative loop to learn about customers is defined with 'C1' in the model, with 'C' denoting 'customer' and '1' the first loop of data collection. This process usually takes several iterations and generates limited amounts of qualitative customer feedback such as interview notes, survey results, observation documentation etc. In parallel to this, companies use e.g. online surveys and in-product ads to collect quantitative data from a larger customer group. This parallel loop of collecting data is defined as 'P1' in the model, with 'P' denoting 'product' and '1' the first loop of collecting data from the product in order to improve the initial understanding for product interest and use. The C1 and P1 processes feed into each other, allowing companies to learn from both qualitative and quantitative data in an early stage of the development process.

Second, and as shown in the development phase in the model, companies aim at testing and evaluating early product concepts by using techniques such as prototyping, beta testing and by collecting operational product data. In similar with the pre-development stage, these processes are referred to as 'C2' and 'P2' with 'C2' denoting existing techniques for customer feedback and 'P2' existing techniques for data collection in this second stage of development. Again, these processes run in parallel and they complement each other with qualitative and quantitative customer and product data.

Finally, and as shown in the post-deployment stage in the model, companies use techniques to learn about customer behavior and product use when the product is commercially deployed to customers. Here, the data that is being collected is transitioning from being qualitative e.g. interview notes and observation reports, to being primarily quantitative e.g. operational data, social network data and experimental data reflecting A/B testing results. As recognized in our research, the C1- C3 techniques are typically expensive, as they require physical interaction with customers. The P1-P3 techniques, on the other hand, are typically cheaper to conduct as they use automatically generated data as input. Together, the processes and the techniques outlined in the model comprise a compelling approach for companies to collect customer feedback and data throughout the product development process.

6   Conclusion

To stay competitive, software companies need to continuously collect feedback and data from customers. However, although there are increasing opportunities for doing this, many companies struggle with how to learn from customers and what techniques to apply [2], [20]. In this paper, and in order to assess the current 'state-of-the-art' in software engineering research, we conduct a literature review focusing on customer feedback and data collection techniques. The purpose of this literature review is to provide an overview of current software engineering research in this area and to better understand the different techniques that are used for collecting customer feedback. Our research reveals a compelling set of customer feedback data collection techniques that can be used throughout the different development stages of software products. Also, we note the emerging trend of social networks as an important data source for both qualitative and quantitative data collection. We summarize our findings in a structured model that works as a support for companies when selecting the appropriate technique. In our future work, we plan to expand this review to include closely related, and highly relevant research domains. Also, we plan to validate our model in empirical contexts in order to provide also a state-of-practice view on customer feedback and data collection techniques.

References

1. Olsson, H.H., Alahyari, H., Bosch, J.: Climbing the "Stairway to Heaven". In: 2012 38th EUROMICRO Conference on Software Engineering and Advanced Applications Software Engineering and Advanced Applications (SEAA), Izmir, Turkey (2012)
2. Olsson, H.H., Bosch, J.: From Opinions to Data-Driven Software R&D. In: Proceedings of the 40th Euromicro Conference on Software Engineering and Advance Applications, Verona, Italy (2014)
3. Sommerville, I., Kotonya, G.: Requirements engineering: processes and techniques. John Wiley & Sons, Inca. (1998)
4. Bosch-Sijtsema, P., Bosch, J.: User involvement throughout the innovation process in high-tech industries. Journal of Product Innovation Management (October 2014)
5. Kitchenham, B.: Procedures for Performing Systematic Reviews (2004)
6. Kabbedijk, J., Brinkkemper, S., Jansen, S., van der Veldt, B.: Customer Involvement in Requirements Management: Lessons from Mass Market Software Development. In: Requirements Engineering Conference (2009)

7. Yiyi, Y., Rongqiu, C.: Customer Participation: Co-Creating Knowledge with Customers. In: Wireless Communications, Networking and Mobile Computing (2008)
8. Nielsen Holdings Winning with Innovation. An Introduction to BASES, http://en-ca.nielsen.com/content/nielsen/en_ca/product_families/nielsen_bases.html
9. Sampson, S.E.: Ramifications of Monitoring Service Quality Through Passively Solicited Customer Feedback. Decision Sciences 27(4), 601–622 (1996)
10. Axelos Global Best Practice – ITIL, https://www.axelos.com/itil
11. Christian, B.: The A/B Test: Inside the Technology That's Changing the Rules of Business, http://www.wired.com/2012/04/ff_abtesting/
12. Burns, H.S., Halliburton, R.A.: Tackling productivity and quality through customer involvement and software technology. In: Global Telecommunications Conference and Exhibition 'Communications Technology for the 1990s and Beyond' (1989)
13. Cohan, S.: Successful Customer Collaboration Resulting in the Right Product for the End User. In: Conference, AGILE 2008, August 4-8, pp. 284–288 (2008)
14. Martin, A., Biddle, R., Noble, J.: XP Customer Practices: A Grounded Theory, Agile Conference. In: Conference, AGILE 2009, August 24-28, pp. 33–40 (2009)
15. Jin, D., Chai, K.H., Tan, K.C.: New service development success factors: A managerial perspective. In: 2010 IEEE International Conference on Industrial Engineering and Engineering Management (IEEM), pp. 2009–2013 (2010)
16. Chen, X.Y., Chen, C.H., Leong, K.F.: A novel virtual design platform for product innovation through customer involvement. In: 2011 IEEE International Conference on Industrial Engineering and Engineering Management Industrial Engineering and Engineering Management (IEEM), December 6-9, pp. 342–346 (2011)
17. Bosch, J.: Building Products as Innovations Experiment Systems. In: Proceedings of 3rd International Conference on Software Business, Cambridge, Massachusetts, June 18-20 (2012)
18. Chen, H., Chiang, R., Storey, C.: Business intelligence and analytics: from big data to big impact. MIS Q. 36(4), 1165–1188 (2012)
19. Westerlund, M., Leminen, S., Rajahonka, M.: Designing Business Models for the Internetof Things. Technology Innovation and Management Review, 5–14 (July 2014)
20. Markey, R., Reichheld, F.: Dullweber. A.: Closing the Customer Feedback Loop. Harvard Business Review (2009)
21. Mack, N., Woodsong, C., Macqueen, K.M., Guest, G., Namey, E.: Qualitative Research Methods: A Data Collector's Field Guide. Family Health International (2005)
22. Balnaves, M., Caputi, P.: Introduction to Quantitative Research Methods. SAGE Publications Ltd. (2001)
23. Corbin, J., Strauss, A.: Basics of qualitative research, 3rd edn. Sage, Thousand Oaks (2008)
24. Bhatia, S., Li, J., Peng, W., Sun, T.: Monitoring and analyzing customer feedback through social media platforms for identifying and remedying customer problems. In: 2013 IEEE/ACM International Conference on Advances in Social Networks Analysis and Mining (ASONAM), August 25-28, pp. 1147–1154 (2013)
25. Olsson, H.H., Bosch, J.: Towards Data-Driven Product Development: A Multiple Case Study on Post-deployment Data Usage in Software-Intensive Embedded Systems. Springer, Heidelberg (2013)
26. Kohavi, R., Longbotham, R., Sommerfield, D., Henne, R.M.: Controlled experiments on the web: survey and practice guide. Data Mining and Knowledge Discovery 18(1), 140–181 (2009)

27. Manikas, K., Hansen, K.M.: Software ecosystems - A systematic literature review. Journal of Systems and Software 86(5), 1294–1306 (2012)
28. Zarour, M., Abran, A., Desharnais, J., Alarifi, A.: An investigation into the best practices for the successful design and implementation of lightweight software process assessment methods: A systematic literature review. Journal of Systems and Software 101(0), 180–192 (2015)
29. Pang, B., Lee, L.: Opinion mining and sentiment analysis. Foundations and Trends in Information Retrieval 2(1-2) (2008)
30. ISI Listed SE Journals, http://www.robertfeldt.net/advice/isi_listed_se_journals.html
31. Iivari, J., Venable J.R.: Action research and design science research – Seemingly similar but decisively dissimilar. In: ECIS 2009 Proceedings, paper 73 (2009)
32. Henfridsson, O., Lindgren, R.: User involvement in developing mobile and temporarily interconnected systems. Information Systems Journal 20(2), 119–135 (2010)
33. Zhao, J., Dong, L., Wu, J., Xu, K.: MoodLens: an emoticon-based sentiment analysis system for chinese tweets. In: Proceedings of the 18th ACM SIGKDD International Conference on Knowledge Discovery and Data Mining (KDD 2012), pp. 1528–1531. ACM, New York (2012)
34. Hess, J., Randall, D., Pipek, V., Wulf, V.: Involving users in the wild—Participatory product development in and with online communities. International Journal of Human-Computer Studies 71(5), 570–589 (2013)
35. Molnar, K.K., Kletke, M.G.: The impacts on user performance and satisfaction of a voice-based front-end interface for a standard software tool. International Journal of Human-Computer Studies 45(3), 287–303 (1996)
36. Hilbert, D.M., Redmiles, D.F.: Large-scale collection of usage data to inform design. In: Human-Computer Interaction—INTERACT 2001: Proceedings of the Eighth IFIP Conference on Human-Computer Interaction, Tokyo, Japan, pp. 569–576 (2001)
37. Antunes, F., Costa, J.P.: Integrating decision support and social networks. Adv. Adv. in Hum.-Comp. Int. 2012, Article 9 (2012)
38. Lagrosen, S.: Customer involvement in new product development: a relationship marketing perspective. European Journal of Innovation Management 8(4), 424–436 (2005)
39. The Ultimate Guide To A/B Testing, http://www.smashingmagazine.com/2010/06/24/the-ultimate-guide-to-a-b-testing/

Towards Continuous Customer Validation: A Conceptual Model for Combining Qualitative Customer Feedback with Quantitative Customer Observation

Helena Holmström Olsson[1(✉)] and Jan Bosch[2]

[1] Department of Computer Science, Malmö University, Malmö, Sweden,
helena.holmstrom.olsson@mah.se
[2] Department of Computer Science and Engineering, Chalmers University of Technology,
Gothenburg, Sweden
jan.bosch@chalmers.se

Abstract. Software-intensive product companies are becoming increasingly data-driven as can be witnessed by the big data and Internet of Things trends. However, optimally prioritizing customer needs in a mass-market context is notoriously difficult. While most companies use product owners or managers to represent the customer, research shows that the prioritization made is far from optimal. In earlier research, we have coined the term 'the open loop problem' to characterize this challenge. For instance, research shows that up to half of all the features in products are never used. This paper presents a conceptual model that emphasizes the need for combining qualitative feedback in early stages of development with quantitative customer observation in later stages of development. Our model is inductively derived from an 18 months close collaboration with six large global software-intensive companies.

Keywords: Customer feedback techniques · Qualitative feedback · Quantitative observation · Continuous customer validation · Data-driven development

1   Introduction

Recently, and due to trends such as big data [1] and the Internet of Things [2], software-intensive product companies are experiencing a fundamental shift in how software products are developed. As a result of the increasing amount of software and the capability to have products connected to the Internet, new ways to engage with customers emerge and there is the opportunity for companies to collect customer feedback not only in the early stages of development, but also after the product has been commercially deployed to customers [3, 4, 5, 6, 7].

However, and as experienced in our previous research, product companies struggle with how to include customer feedback into their development processes, and how to find efficient mechanisms for combining different feedback techniques [5, 6]. Typically, and as advocated by many of the agile development methods [8, 9, 10], the solution is to have a product owner representing the customer. This has proven useful for capturing customer requirements, and for early customer validation of product concepts. Still, difficulties arise in large-scale product development where the product owner can no

© Springer International Publishing Switzerland 2015
J.M. Fernandes et al. (Eds.): ICSOB 2015, LNBIP 210, pp. 154–166, 2015.
DOI: 10.1007/978-3-319-19593-3_13

longer represent the many different needs of such a large customer base. As the common method to address this problem, the product owner talks to a selected number of representative customers [11]. Also, and as another common solution, customer-specific teams are introduced in order to take care of the particular needs of selected and highly prioritized customers [12]. This feedback is then used to inform the product development process with the assumption that what a selected number of customers want is also what other similar customers want. These approaches, however, suffer from a number of problems. For example, and as highlighted in research on user involvement and customer feedback, what customers say they want very seldom represents what they really need [3, 13]. As recognized in this research, customer interviews and direct customer interaction capture only parts of customer behaviors and needs and therefore, need to be complemented with indirect customer observations and customer data collection in order to fully understand behaviors and patterns that customers might not be aware of themselves. Furthermore, if customer feedback that is collected in the early stages of development is not validated in the later stages, there is the risk that large amounts of the development efforts lack customer value [11]. To cater for this, companies need to continuously combine different feedback techniques, and to find ways in which early customer feedback can be evaluated and tested in later development stages and even after commercial deployment of the products.

In this paper, and based on our experiences from working closely with six large software-intensive companies, we develop a conceptual model in which we identify qualitative customer feedback techniques as typically used in the early stages of development, and quantitative customer observation techniques that are used in the later stages of development. The model emphasizes the wide range of available feedback techniques, and helps companies understand the importance of these as complements to each other. Our model suggests an approach in which development and improvement of products is seen as a continuous activity where hypotheses are continuously validated. As a result, product development shifts from being driven by early-stage requirements specification, to becoming an activity in which hypotheses form the basis for continuous validation of new product functionality.

The paper is organized as follows. In section 2, we discuss literature relevant for our research. In section 3, we describe our research method and the six case companies. Section 4 presents the empirical findings. In section 5, and based on the empirical findings, we present the problem statements that we address. In section 6, we develop a conceptual model that addresses the problems, and in section 7 we discuss our model. Finally, in section 8 we present the conclusions.

2   Background

2.1   Product Development

In product development processes, ideas are collected and prioritized during the requirements engineering process in which customers are involved [14]. Typically, ideas are generated either internally at the company and validated by having internal and/or external customers involved in early prototyping or concept validation, or they are generated in close collaboration with customers with product owners as the main customer contact. As recognized in Scrum [10], the product owner is a key stakeholder with the responsibility to have a vision of what products to build. The vision is reflected in the product backlog, which is a prioritized list of features for the product. During development, the product owner acts as the proxy to customers to make sure that their interests and needs are reflected in the development of new functionality.

Often, and as can be seen in our previous research, the selection of what ideas to include is based on previous experience and domain-specific skills, but often also on opinions and "gut feelings" held by product management. Although the decisions that are taken form the basis for significant development efforts and investments, there is little data to help product management in confirming whether decisions taken during feature prioritization were actually the right ones. In our previous research [11], and based on empirical research in a number of software-intensive companies, we coined the term the 'open loop' problem, referring to the situation in which product management has difficulties in getting accurate and timely customer feedback to help them in prioritizing new features, and where there is only a weak link between customer feedback and product management decisions. For many of the companies we work with, huge amounts of data is available, but the mechanisms to analyze this data are insufficient. Typically, challenges arise when trying to combine and make sense of feedback obtained in the early stages of development and feedback received in later stages of development. Feedback loops are slow, and very often the confirmation of the correctness of the decisions takes place only after the finalized product has been deployed to customers. As a result, there is the risk of lack of alignment of product and customer needs [5, 6] and that R&D investments are spent on product functionality that is not appreciated or used by its intended customers.

2.2   Qualitative and Quantitative Customer Feedback

Qualitative customer feedback techniques require active participation from customers, generate small amounts of data, and are typically used in the early stages of the development process [13]. The strength of such techniques is their ability to provide rich textual descriptions of how individuals experience a specific situation. As such, they provide in-depth information about the 'human' side of a situation and they reveal peoples' perceptions of a given phenomenon [15]. Qualitative customer feedback techniques focus on how to involve customers to help define the problem and evaluate proposed solutions. Typically, customer interviews, customer surveys and different types of participant observations are used to collect feedback [13, 16, 17, 18]. In face-to-face meetings and during site visits, companies ask how customers experience the product and what they would like to see in future products.

Quantitative customer observations, on the other hand, focus on data from products in the field. As a result of products being increasingly software-intensive, and with the opportunity to have products connected to the Internet, companies are experiencing novel opportunities to learn about customer and product behaviours. As products go on-line, companies can monitor them, collect data on how they perform, predict when they break, know where they are located, and learn about when and how they are used or not used by customers [5, 6]. Typically, this form of data collection doesn't involve the customer. Instead, this form of data collection takes place when the products have been commercially deployed and used in real-time by its intended customers. This situation brings with it fundamentally new engagement models with customers [2, 19], where companies can run feature experiments [10], and A/B testing of product versions [7], to continuously observe customers and validate product functionality and product concepts. A/B testing is a common data collection technique in the Web 2.0 domain and in the software-as-a-service (SaaS) domain, and it has recently gained attention also in the embedded systems domain [4]. Also here, companies realize the many benefits with having different customer groups try out different versions of the same product and collect data on what version that works the best. Additionally, and as recognized by Kohavi et al [7], an early version of the product can be given to a sample of customers to test the functionality, where operational data, event logs and usage data are retrieved in order to identify performance issues, errors and other usability problems.

As one attempt to capture the wide range of available customer feedback techniques, Bosch-Sijtsema and Bosch [13], present a model in which they identify different techniques, the type of data that is collected and the development phases in which the techniques are typically used. They picture the early development stages as characterized by direct customer feedback, and with small amounts of qualitative data being collected. In later stages, and after commercial deployment of the product, companies observe customers and use indirect feedback techniques to collect large sets of quantitative data.

Based on our experiences from an 18 months close collaboration with six software-intensive product companies, we identify the need to better understand what customer feedback techniques that are available. In what follows, and based on case study research in these companies, we develop a conceptual model that provides companies with (1) a better understanding for available feedback techniques, and (2) emphasize the importance of combining early stage qualitative customer feedback with later stage quantitative customer observation.

3   Research Approach

The conceptual model presented in this paper is developed based on an 18 months (July 2013 – December 2014) longitudinal multi-case study in six global software-intensive companies. We adopt an interpretive case study approach [20], and we work inductively in our development of the model. Typically, case study research focuses on providing a deeper understanding of a particular situation, and is used to explore contemporary phenomenon [20, 21]. The companies involved in this study use qualitative as well as quantitative customer feedback techniques to learn about their customers and how they use their products. Although in different domains, the companies face similar challenges in relation to how to combine different techniques, and how to better capitalize on the customer feedback that they collect. In Table 1, we present the case companies and the feedback techniques they currently use:

Table 1. The six case companies involved in our study

Case company	Domain	Qualitative CFT's	Quantitative CFT's
A	Software company specializing in navigational information, operations management and optimization solutions.	Site visits Customer surveys Customer interviews Yearly customer conferences Prototyping	Feature experiments Support logs Trouble reports Google Analytics
B	A pump manufacturer producing circulator pumps for heating and air conditioning, as well as centrifugal pumps for water supply.	Site visits Customer surveys Customer interviews Prototyping	Support logs Trouble reports
C	A network video company offering products such as network cameras, video encoders, video management software and camera applications for video surveillance.	Site visits Customer surveys Customer interviews Prototyping	Feature experiments Support logs Trouble reports
D	A manufacturer and supplier of transport solutions for commercial use.	Customer test labs Customer surveys Customer interviews Prototyping	A/B testing Support logs Diagnostic data Failure reports
E	An equipment manufacturer developing, manufacturing and selling a variety of products within the embedded systems domain.	Customer test labs Customer surveys Customer interviews Prototyping	Support logs Diagnostic data Failure reports
F	A provider of telecommunication systems and equipment, communications networks and multimedia solutions for mobile and fixed network operators.	Customer-specific teams Site visits Customer surveys Customer interviews	Support logs Trouble reports Customer satisfaction index Event monitoring data

The research reported in this paper is part of a larger research collaboration involving three universities and eight software development companies. The project was conducted in six months sprints with every sprint involving data collection, data analysis and results reporting. For each sprint, we conducted group interviews in each company, joint workshop sessions and validation sessions to which all companies were invited to discuss and evaluate our research results. In total, our collaboration with the companies involved twelve group interviews at the different companies with 5-8 people participating in each group, four joint workshops with 4-8 people from the different companies attending each workshop and a survey which was distributed to key stakeholders in the six companies. In addition, all sprints included one kick-off workshop, one validation workshop, and one results reporting workshop with all companies attending. All group interviews and workshops were conducted in English and lasted between 2-3 hours. The results reporting workshops were full day events including project presentations and in-depth group discussions.

Throughout the project, the two researchers carefully documented interviews and workshops. All notes were shared between the researchers to allow for in-depth analysis. During analysis, and inspired by open coding principles [22], we categorized our empirical data and phenomena found in the text. To strengthen the validity of our research, we used data triangulation, i.e. more than one data source, and observer triangulation, i.e. more than one observer in the study [23]. In addition, methodological triangulation was applied in that we use a combination of data collection methods e.g. group interviews and workshop sessions in order to avoid having one data source influence us to heavily. Also, we used a 'venting' method, i.e. a process whereby interpretations are discussed with professional colleagues [24, 25].

4   Empirical Findings

All companies involved in this study collect large amounts of customer feedback as part of their product development processes. In early development stages, product owners work closely with a selected number of customers to collect feedback, and in some companies there are customer-specific teams that serve the needs of a particular customer. Typically, techniques such as alpha- and beta testing, customer interviews, surveys, participant observations, expert reviews, and prototyping are used to obtain qualitative customer feedback on product concepts and ideas. The intention is to have customers try out early versions of a product and provide feedback on interfaces, design choices and product functionality. In most companies, product owners work closely with customers and act as a proxy towards the development organization.

In addition to qualitative feedback, all case companies collect large amounts of data revealing product operation and performance. This data is collected post-deployment and allows for quantitative analysis of e.g. features used or not used, information on system re-starts, outage, faults, re-booting, upgrade success etc. Dimensioning data such as CPU load, licenses sold etc., serve as important input for system configuration and capacity, as well as for producing sale statistics and market assessments etc. In the automotive domain, performance data such as speed, fuel efficiency, energy consumption, acceleration, and road conditions is continuously collected from the vehicle. In addition to product data collection, two of the companies have on-going feature experiments in which customers try different versions of software features. In their experiments, and as suggested in research in this area [10], they develop only small slices of functionality that can be easily validated with customers before developing the full feature. In this way, the companies avoid spending R&D efforts on developing software functionality that customers don't appreciate and use.

While all companies have well-established techniques for collecting qualitative customer feedback, they experience problems when asking customers what they want. Typically, customers are not aware of the many technological opportunities that exist.

Moreover, to provide input on existing ways-of-working might imply identifying your own weaknesses or mistakes. As a result, qualitative customer feedback techniques typically capture "ideal" customer situations and behaviors rather than the "actual" state and "real" use of a product. Finally, all companies report on the lack of validation of qualitative customer feedback in later stages of development. In relation to quantitative customer observation, we see a number of challenges. First, although the companies have access to large data sets, this is only used for troubleshooting and support, and for answering customer queries when problems occur. What is not common is to have this data inform the development organization. Also, challenges arise in relation to data quality. There is no way to ask the "right" questions, and most interviewees feel that the data collected is not helping them in their roles as developers and product managers.

5   Problem Statement

Based on the experiences in the six companies, the problems we identify are the following (Table 2):

Table 2. Key problems identified in the case companies

Problem identified:	Description:
The 'open loop' problem	The situation in which product management experience difficulties in getting accurate customer data. This leads to a situation in which decision-making is made based on opinions and "gut feeling" rather than customer data, and there is the risk that the decisions that are taken are not aligned with actual customer needs.
Large amount of unused features	Research shows that most software systems have a large amount of unused features [26], and that investments are put on functionality that are not proven valuable to customers [11]. Our interviewees are convinced that a large number of features are never used.
Wrong implementation of features	There are different ways in which a certain feature can be implemented. However, there is no efficient way in which the companies can continuously validate these alternatives with customers to decide which alternative that is the most appreciated one.
Requirements are seen as "truths"	A common view in all companies is that requirements are regarded as the "truth". However, and as shown in a number of studies [14], requirements specification is one of the most challenging tasks, and projects often fail due to their inability to cope with changing requirements.

Table 2. *(Continued)*

Problem identified:	Description:
Lack of feature optimization	In the Web 2.0 domain, the majority of the development efforts are allocated to optimization of existing features [7]. In the companies we study, with the majority in the embedded systems domain, the situation is the opposite. As a result, time is spent on adding functionality instead of re-implementing features that don't work well.
Misrepresentation of customers	In large-scale development of software for a mass-market, customer representation is difficult. Typically, and as reported in the interviews, the customers that "scream the loudest" get recognized while other customers get forgotten.
Lack of validation of feedback	Qualitative customer feedback is never validated in later stages, causing a situation in which vast amounts of development takes place although it has never been proven valuable.
Large amounts of (useless) data	All companies have significant data available that could be used to direct their development efforts, but they are unable to capitalize on this data. While big data offers great potential, there is the risk of useless data if the wrong questions are asked.

6   Qualitative and Quantitative Customer-Driven Development

In response to the problems experienced in the case companies, we developed a model that emphasizes the importance of combining qualitative and quantitative feedback techniques. We call the model the 'Qualitative/quantitative Customer-driven Development' (QCD) model (Figure 1), and it was inductively developed based on the generalization of approaches in the six case study companies. The QCD model is a conceptual model in which requirements are treated as hypotheses that are validated with customers before forming the basis for development. In contrast to specifying requirements early in the development process, the model advocates an approach in which hypotheses derived from business strategies, innovation initiatives, customer feedback and from on-going validation cycles form the basis for continuous customer validation.

As revealed in our case companies, the selection of a hypothesis is typically based on uncertainty of how to implement a new feature, what alternative way of implementation is most appreciated by customers or how to satisfy new customer segments and new markets. If a qualitative CFT is selected, the validation cycle consists of e.g. customer interviews, surveys and observations in which customer feedback is collected. If a quantitative CFT is selected, the validation cycle consists of e.g. feature experiments or A/B testing, in which functionality is deployed to the product and/or selected customers and in which product data is collected. The CFT validation data is used to decide whether to run another validation cycle (using potentially another CFT), whether to have the hypothesis put back into the backlog, or whether to abandon the hypothesis. It should be noted that qualitative and quantitative validation cycles feed into each other. While quantitative techniques might be easier to initiate since they don't require any instrumentation of code, quantitative techniques are efficient in that large amounts of data is collected with little effort. To combine different techniques allow companies to learn from a wide range of data. For example, qualitative techniques can be used to make sense of quantitative data. In similar, and as emphasized in this study, quantitative techniques can be used to validate qualitative data with a larger customer group in the later stages of development. Below, we present how the model addresses the problems identified in the case companies (Table 3):

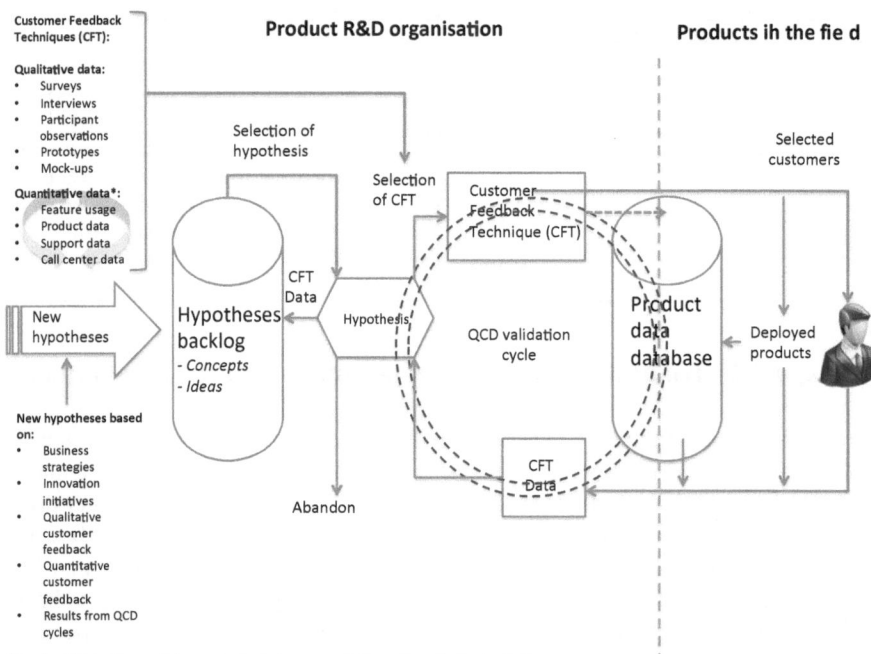

Loop in which decisions are taken on whether to do more qualitative customer feedback collection.

Fig. 1. The Qualitative/quantitative Customer-driven Development (QCD) model

Table 3. Key problems in the case companies, and how the model addresses these

Problem identified:	QCD model:
The 'open loop' problem	Requirements are treated as hypotheses that are continuously validated with customers. In this way, the model helps companies close the 'open loop' and have customer feedback inform the development process.

Table 3. *(Continued)*

Problem identified:	QCD model:
The 'open loop' problem	Requirements are treated as hypotheses that are continuously validated with customers. In this way, the model helps companies close the 'open loop' and have customer feedback inform the development process.
Large amount of unused features	Features are before it is fully developed. The model helps companies reduce effort put on unused features. Also, hypotheses can target existing features to help reveal use/non-use.
Wrong implementation of features	The model suggests iterative cycles in which implementation alternatives are continuously evaluated to confirm which implementation alternative that is the most appreciated one.
Requirements are seen as "truths"	Requirements are treated as hypotheses that are continuously validated. Only after iterative validation cycles, decisions are made whether to continue development, put it back into the backlog, or abandon the hypothesis.
Lack of feature optimization	By continuous data collection revealing feature usage, the model helps companies identify what features and what behaviors that can be optimized.
Misrepresentation of customers	A wide range of CFT's are used allowing companies to learn from a larger set of customer data.
Lack of validation of feedback	Qualitative and quantitative CFT's are combined, with qualitative feedback used as input for quantitative validation cycles and vice versa.
Large amounts of (useless) data	Frequent validation cycles and different CFT's are used to help companies refine their hypotheses and ask the right questions.

7   Discussion

As recognized in previous research [13], there exist a number of techniques for collecting customer feedback. While those used in early development stages typically include direct interaction with customers, and with small amounts of qualitative data as feedback, techniques used in later stages include indirect observation of customers, and with large amounts of quantitative data as feedback. As experienced in our research, most companies both qualitative and quantitative feedback techniques, and they have access to large amounts of customer data. However, they hardly ever use this data to inform on-going development of features [5, 6]. In accordance with research on big data [1, 2], we see a situation in which large sets of data offers great potential, but where the challenge is to ask the "right" questions in order to avoid useless data. Recently, the challenges associated with collecting customer feedback have been addressed by proposing a number of experiment models influenced by the lean startup concept of 'build-measure-learn' [11, 27, 28, 29]. In this concept, ideas are quickly turned into testable products, data is collected by measuring how the product is used, and ideas for product improvement are based on what is learned from this data [29, 30]. Typically, these models target primarily the later stages of development in which techniques for quantitative data collection are used. As a result, they lack the synergies that can be obtained when combining qualitative and quantitative customer feedback, and an understanding for how these techniques can influence each other in continuous validation cycles.

In the QCD model, qualitative and quantitative customer feedback techniques are used to validate hypotheses derived from a backlog representing product concepts and ideas. In offering support for qualitative and quantitative validation of features, the model helps companies more carefully decide whether a feature in the backlog is still interesting. Also, the model suggests an approach in which items in the backlog are regarded as hypotheses rather than requirements, and represent items that can potentially become valuable for customers. In this way, the model offers a new approach to requirements specification and validation. Instead of regarding qualitative requirements as "truths" that can be specified in the beginning of the development cycle, the model suggests an approach in which requirements are treated as hypotheses that are continuously validated with customers, and only those that prove customer value throughout the development cycle are fully developed and deployed. In combining qualitative customer feedback with quantitative customer observation, the model addresses the concern with having customers say what they think they want – but not being able to express what they really need.

8   Conclusions

In this paper, we present the 'Qualitative/quantitative Customer-driven Development' (QCD) model. The model is a conceptual model that presents available customer feedback techniques and emphasizes the importance of combining qualitative customer feedback with quantitative customer observation. By recognizing the synergies between qualitative and quantitative customer feedback, and by emphasizing continuous data collection and validation, the model helps companies improve their data-driven development practices.

In future research, we aim to validate the model to provide further details on how and when different techniques can be combined. Also, we aim at capturing different customer segments to have the conceptual model support validation cycles with different customer segments in order to maximize the value in each of these.

References

1. Chen, H., Chiang, R., Storey, C.V.: Business intelligence and analytics: From big data to big impact. MIS Quarterly 36(4), 1165–1188 (2012)
2. Westerlund, M., Leminen, S., Rajahonka, M.: Designing Business Models For The Internet of Things. Technology Innovation and Management Review, 5–14 (July 2014)
3. Bosch, J.: Building Products as Innovations Experiment Systems. In: Proceedings of 3rd International Conference on Software Business, Cambridge, Massachusetts, June 18-20 (2012)
4. Bosch, J., Eklund, U.: Eternal embedded software: Towards innovation experiment systems. In: Margaria, T., Steffen, B. (eds.) ISoLA 2012, Part I. LNCS, vol. 7609, pp. 19–31. Springer, Heidelberg (2012)
5. Olsson, H.H., Bosch, J.: Post-Deployment Data Collection in Software-Intensive Embedded Products. In: Herzwurm, G., Margaria, T. (eds.) ICSOB 2013. LNBIP, vol. 150, pp. 79–89. Springer, Heidelberg (2013)
6. Olsson, H.H., Bosch, J.: Towards Data-Driven Product Development: A Multiple Case Study on Post-Deployment Data Usage in Software-Intensive Embedded Systems. In: Fitzgerald, B., Conboy, K., Power, K., Valerdi, R., Morgan, L., Stol, K.-J. (eds.) LESS 2013. LNBIP, vol. 167, pp. 152–164. Springer, Heidelberg (2013)
7. Kohavi, R., Longbotham, R., Sommerfield, D., Henne, R.M.: Controlled experiments on the web: survey and practice guide. Data Mining and Knowledge Discovery 18(1), 140–181 (2009)
8. Highsmith, J., Cockburn, A.: Agile Software Development: The business of innovation. Software Management, 120–122 (September 2001)
9. Larman, C.: Agile and Iterative Development: A Manager's Guide. Addison-Wesley (2004)
10. Schwaber, K., Beedle, M.: Agile software development with Scrum. Prentice Hall (2002)
11. Olsson, H.H., Bosch, J.: From Opinions to Data-Driven Software R&D: A Multi-Case Study On How To Close The 'Open Loop' Problem. In: Proceedings of EUROMICRO, Software Engineering and Advanced Applications (SEAA), Verona, Italy, August 27-29 (2014)
12. Olsson, H.H., Sandberg, A., Bosch, J., Alahyari, H.: Scale and responsiveness in large-scale software development. IEEE Software 31(5), 87–93 (2014)
13. Bosch-Sijtsema, P., Bosch, J.: User involvement throughout the innovation process in high-tech industries. The Journal of Product Innovation Management (2014) (online version published October 13, 2014)
14. Hofman, H.F., Lehner, F.: Requirements engineering as a success factor in software projects. IEEE Software 18, 58–66 (2001)
15. Mack, N., Woodsong, C., Macqueen, K.M., Guest, G., Namey, E.: Qualitative Research Methods: A Data Collector's Field Guide. Family Health International (2005)
16. Kabbedijk, J., Brinkkemper, S., Jansen, S., van der Veldt, B.: Customer Involvement in Requirements Management: Lessons from Mass Market Software Development. In: Requirements Engineering Conference (2009)
17. Yiyi, Y., Rongqiu, C.: Customer Participation: Co-Creating Knowledge with Customers. In: Wireless Communications Networking and Mobile Computing (2008)
18. Iivari, J., Isomäki, H., Pekkola, S.: The user – the great unknown of systems development: reasons, forms, challenges, experiences and intellectual contributions of user involvement. Editorial in Information Systems Journal 20, 109–117 (2010)

19. Ritala, P., Agouridas, V., Assimakopoulos, D., Gies, O.: Value creation and capture mechanisms in innovation ecosystems: a comparative study. International Journal of Technology Management 63(3) (2013)
20. Walsham, G.: Interpretive case studies in IS research: Nature and method. European Journal of Information Systems 4, 74–81 (1995)
21. Runesson, P., Höst, M.: Guidelines for conducting and reporting case study research in software engineering. Empirical Software Engineering 14 (2009)
22. Strauss, A.C., Corbin, J.M.: Basics of Qualitative Research. Sage Publications, Thousands Oaks (1990)
23. Stake, R.E.: The art of case study research. SAGE Publications (1995)
24. Kaplan, B., Duchon, D.: Combining qualitative and quantitative methods in IS research: A case study. MIS Quarterly 12(4), 571–587 (1988)
25. Goetz, J., LeCompte, D.: Ethnography and Qualitative Design in Educational Research. Academic Press, Orlando (1984)
26. Backlund, E., Bolle, M., Tichy, M., Olsson, H.H., Bosch, J.: Automated User Interaction Analysis for Workflow-Based Web Portals. In: Proceedings of the 5th International Conference on Software Business, Paphos, Cyprus, June 16-18 (2014)
27. Fagerholm, F., Sanchez, G., Mäenpää, H., Münch, J.: Building blocks for continuous experimentation. In: The Proceedings of the RCoSE 2014 Workshop, Hyderabad, India, (June 3, 2014)
28. Bosch, J., Olsson H.H., Björk, J., Ljungblad, J.: Introducing Early Stage Software Startup Development Model: A Framework for Supporting Lean Principles in Software Startups. In: Proceedings of the Lean Enterprise Software and Systems Conference (LESS), Galway, Ireland, December 1-4 (2013)
29. Ries, E.: The Lean Startup: How Constant Innovation Creates Radically Successful Businesses. Penguin Group, London (2011)
30. Blank, S.: The Four Steps to the Epiphany: Successful Strategies for Products that Win, 3rd edn. (2005) http://Cafepress.com

Business Model Patterns for the Connected Car and the Example of Data Orchestrator

Martin Mikusz[1,2(✉)], Christopher Jud[1], and Tobias Schäfer[1]

[1] Department VIII, Chair of Information Systems II, Prof. Dr. Georg Herzwurm,
Keplerstraße 17, 70174 Stuttgart, Germany
[2] FOM University of Applied Sciences, Rotebühlstr. 121, 70178 Stuttgart, Germany
{mikusz,jud,schaefer}@wius.bwi.uni-stuttgart.de

Abstract. Along with the connected car, previously isolated business models of traditional goods-producing industry melt together with those of software businesses. It is becoming apparent that software businesses may have to play an important role, provided that they are capable of building up competencies in engineering business models for this emerging and converged market. We identify and cluster business model patterns that we rate as being capable of transforming product innovations, enabled by abilities and characteristics of cyber-physical systems and the underlying technical platforms, into business model innovations. We discuss further the pattern cluster Data Orchestrator.

Keywords: Business model patterns · Connected car · CPS · Platform ecosystems

1 Introduction

There is barely another industry that illustrates the potential of cyber-physical systems (CPS) clearer than the automotive sector [1]. This potential is especially expressed in smart services for the connected car, enabled by abilities and characteristics of CPS and the underlying technical platforms. Smart services offer valuable benefit for consumers through intelligent connection of the vehicle with its environment (transportation infrastructure, other vehicles, driver etc.). Along with the connected car, the automotive value chain transforms into a cross-domain value network of manufacturers and their previous suppliers and service providers, with ICT providers, smartphone manufacturers and other actors, not least software businesses. It is becoming apparent that software businesses will have a key role to play [1], provided that they are capable of building up competencies in engineering business models for this emerging, converged market. Our contribution is threefold in this regard.

First, to identify potentials for business model innovation for the connected car, we systematically select 16 especially applicable business model patterns from the set of 55 patterns that are repeatedly at the core of new, successful business models and thus constitute the core of the Business Model Navigator [2]. According to our analysis, these 16 patterns are capable of transforming product innovations, enabled by abilities

© Springer International Publishing Switzerland 2015
J.M. Fernandes et al. (Eds.): ICSOB 2015, LNBIP 210, pp. 167–173, 2015.
DOI: 10.1007/978-3-319-19593-3_14

and characteristics of CPS and the underlying technical platforms, into business model innovations. Second, to reveal patterns that are mutually reinforcing, we cluster patterns that work in a similar way. I.e., we propose combinations of patterns or composite patterns on which, if applied to smart services for the connected car, similar abilities and characteristics of CPS and the underlying technical platforms have a constitutive effect. Third and based on our results so far, we systematically analyze the three platform ecosystems Audi Connect, BMW ConnectedDrive, and Mercedes Connect Me, whether and to what extent they solely or in combination apply the identified business model patterns. Due to limited space, we will only discuss further the pattern cluster Data Orchestrator.

2   Cyber-Physical Systems and Industrial Platforms as Basis for Smart Services for the Connected Car

We exhibit abilities and characteristics of CPS from three perspectives: 1) CPS as physical goods improved by properties of software; 2) CPS as opened and linked-up systems in contrast to embedded systems with controlled behavior; 3) CPS as software-enabled product service systems or solutions.

1) Research in the field of software business has pinpointed the specific economic properties of software for a long time. There is broad consensus about the dissimilarity between software and its value chain on the one hand, and services or physical goods on the other hand [e.g. 3]. Now, CPS or previously pure physical goods at least partially exhibit those characteristics. A considerable part of CPS' overall customer value proposition can therefore be directly attributed to software, e.g. CPS' configuration and individualization capabilities [1].

2) CPS enable a wide range of novel functions, services, and features that are far beyond the scope of today's capabilities of externally non-networked embedded systems with controlled behavior [1]. All in all, the networked vehicle, which in turn is interpreted as a CPS and thus provides the basis for smart services, includes
- connected (sub)systems (telematics components, navigation etc.),
- that immediately collect physical data by means of sensors (GPS position data, vehicle condition-based sensor data, sensor data of driver assistance systems etc.),
- combine those data with additional available data and services (e.g. real time traffic information, car repair shop information etc.),
- and interact on this basis actively or reactively with the physical and the digital world, including interaction with other CPS (e.g. dynamic routing or eCall);
- this interaction takes place by means of actuators acting on physical processes (e.g. (un)lock doors, controlled cooperative brake application, perspectively etc.), via system interfaces (e.g. remote maintenance), and via human machine interfaces (e.g. permanently installed and accident-proof telephone, navigation device, smart phone etc.).

3) A product service system or solution is a combination of products and services that offers value to customer beyond the sum of its parts. Solutions are co-produced

by cross-industry cooperating business networks and tailored to customers' needs. As a consequence, new forms of cooperation and competition as well as new shapes of solutions with declined share of mechanics and hardware on the overall customer value proposition are emerging [4, 5]. We understand CPS as such software-enabled solutions, i.e. combinations of software, services and tangible product parts, generated through hybrid value creation.

Both, from technical and business perspective, smart services for the connected car require platform constructs or conceptualizations. Here, we refer to Gawer's [6] classification of technological platforms and adopt the industry platform conceptualization. Gawer defines industry platforms as products, services, or technologies developed by one or more firms, that serve as a foundation upon which a larger number of firms organized as a business ecosystem can build further complementary products, technologies, or services. With slight modifications to Gawer [6], we exhibit abilities and characteristics of industrial platforms from four perspectives: 1) network affected ecosystem governance, 2) platform leader and complementors as constitutive agents, 3) open interfaces and potentially unlimited pool of accessible innovative capabilities, 4) modular design with core and periphery.

1) Industry platforms operate within the broad organizational setting of the ecosystem, whereby coordination is ensured by ecosystem governance. In this regard, platforms are distinct in that they are associated with network effects. I.e., there are increasing incentives for more developer of complementary products and users to adopt a platform and join the ecosystem as more users and complementors join [6].

2) Besides complementors, the second constitutive agent of an industry platform is the platform leader or owner of a platform who drives industrywide innovation for an evolving system of separately developed complementary components [6].

3) Industry platforms have opened technological interfaces, whereby there are variations within the spectrum of how open these interfaces are. Potential innovators of complementary products can utilize information on the platform's technological interfaces that are disclosed by the platform leader to build compatible complements. Industry platforms therefore extend the pool of accessible innovating agents and their innovative capabilities to a potentially unlimited extent [6, 7].

4) All kinds of platforms have a modular architecture organized around a core and a periphery from which a stream of derivative or complementary products, technologies, or services can efficiently be developed and produced [6]. I.e., (industry) platforms provide a foundation of modular and systematic reusable common components. The objective is to improve efficiency and reduce cost [7].

3   Methodology

In order to rate and select our subset of patterns, we have consequently drawn on the abilities and characteristics of CPS respectively of technological platforms exhibited in section 2. We have directly transferred the three CPS and four platform perspectives into selection criteria and chose only those patterns that can be assigned to both, abilities and characteristics of CPS and of technological platforms from at least one perspective, respectively—since smart services for the connected car are solely enabled in interaction between both. Overall, we rate the selected patterns as being capable of transforming product innovations, enabled by abilities and characteristics of CPS and the underlying technical platforms, into business model innovations. To reveal patterns that are mutually reinforcing, we clustered patterns that work in a similar way. A smart combination of business model patterns is crucial for their successful use. Other business model approaches or conceptualizations besides the Business Model Navigator consider the principle of combination crucial as well [8-10]. Here, we have drawn on the overall assignment of the 16 selected patterns to the seven selection criteria in sum and applied Agglomerative Hierarchical Clustering [11] to make up homogeneous groups.[1] Based on our results so far, we analyzed the introductory mentioned platform ecosystems whether and to what extent they solely or in combination apply the identified business model patterns. We gained data by structured analysis of publicly available documents (online available product information, press releases etc.). We focused on smart services enabled by abilities and characteristics of CPS and the underlying technical platforms, and largely neglected pure infotainment, as well as non-networked driver assistance systems.

4   Results and Implications

Table 1 shows our identified set of patterns that promise potentials for business model innovation for the connected car. We offer five combinations of patterns or composite patterns. These patterns work in a similar way and thus are mutually reinforcing.

Due to limited space, we only discuss further the pattern cluster Data Orchestrator.

The Leverage Customer Data pattern benefits from present-day technological progress and the consequential ability to systematically collect and process big amounts of data. It focuses on the collection of customer data and its profitable usage in real time [2]—the latest often in strong interaction with network effects (2.1). Leverage Customer Data can be interpreted as collecting, processing and selling of sensor data, and thereby, as in Fleisch et al. [12], tightly bound to the internet of things business model pattern Sensor as a Service [12] (1.2).

---

[1] A table similar to table 1 (obviously without clustering) served as the variable table. Filled/ empty cells were coded as 1/0. Due to both, the binary character of the data and the fact, that 0 gives no information about (dis)similarity between the objects (patterns), but only 1 does, we chose the Jaccard and the Dice similarity coefficients. We applied both to check the stability of our results—with the same result. In order to balance the focus on the unequal number of CPS and platform criteria, we inversely weighted both criteria subsets. We agglomerated using the weighted and the unweighted pair-group average linkage method— again with stable results. Both methods tend neither to very long and less homogeneous clusters, nor to dilated data space and compact clusters. The scree plot clearly determined an optimum of five clusters. In line with this result, we have considered five clusters, each with three or four elements, very useful for our purposes. This truncation level decomposes the entire variance into 36,36% within-class variance and 63,64% between-class variance.

Table 1. Business Model Patterns for the Connected Car

Composite Pattern / Cluster	Business Model Pattern	1.1 CPS as physical good improved by software	1.2 CPS as opened & linked-up system	1.3 CPS as software-enabled solution or PSS	2.1 network affected ecosystem governance	2.2 platf. leader & comple-mentors as constitutive agents	2.3 open interf. & unlimited innovative capabilities	2.4 modular design to improve efficiency & reduce cost
Complemen-tary Solution	Add-On	✓		✓		—		
	Cross-Selling			✓		✓		
	Solution Provider			✓		✓	—	
Digital Customiza-tion	Digitalization	✓					—	✓
	Layer Player			—			✓	✓
	Long Tail	—		—			—	—
	Mass Customization	—		—				—
Open Commerce	E-Commerce		✓				✓	
	Open Business Model	—				—	—	
	Revenue Sharing	—		—		—	—	
Digital Lock-In	Freemium	—			—			
	Lock-In	—			—			
	Razor and Blade	✓		—	—			
Data Orchestrator	Leverage Customer Data		✓		—			
	Orchestrator		✓					✓
	Two-Sided Market		✓		✓			

Filled cell: The pattern is able to transform a product innovation, coming from the respective ability or characteristic of CPS / industry platform, into a business model innovation; Ticked / "—" cell: Transformation of product innovation into a business model innovation is already in practical use / no example of application could be found so far.

We have identified the pattern Leverage Customer Data in practice, especially in the sense of Sensor as a Service: To be able to use most of the smart services weanalyzed, car owners have to agree on permanent sensor data transmission to others, not mentioned by name (1.2). Further telematics services or pay-as-you-go insurance models or scenarios on the basis of these data are imaginable or already in service. Telematics services register automatically when a service is required and transfer all state related sensor data relevant for the service to the (external) service provider. In certain cases, even a remote repair of malfunctions via software interface is possible. Telematics services can just as well end up in a classic on-site roadside assistance. However, we could not find any evidence that platform leaders try to interrelate profitable usage of customer data in real time with network effects (2.1).

In the Orchestrator pattern, a focal company—here the platform leader—only focuses on its core competencies, while any other activity along the value network is being outsourced to specialized service providers and actively coordinated by the focal company. Focusing on core competencies enables to benefit from partners' specific skills and by that leads to increased performance and reduced costs [2] (2.4). In so doing, openness plays an important role in order to render or orchestrate ad-hoc cooperation between electronic service providers, on-site local service providers and other cyber-physical systems (1.2)—similar to the Open Business Model.

Within all three analyzed platform ecosystems, the respective platform leader acts as orchestrator—related to almost all examined smart services. E.g., eCall (based on sensor data that also allow a remote analysis of accident type and severity, eCall can automatically execute an emergency call) as well as telematics services can end up in a classic on-site roadside assistance (1.2). By concierge services, the driver can receive a remote and location independent assistance around the clock, among others enabled by interlinked and intelligent vehicular sensors and actuators, and eventually brought out by specialized service providers (e.g. hotel booking etc.). Mercedes integrates TomTom navigation services; Audi those of Google. DoubleSlash develops apps for BMW's

ConnectedDrive platform ecosystem, while BOSCH is a specialist supplier for emergency call management (2.4).

The Two-Sided Market pattern enables interaction between two independently acting user groups via an intermediary or a platform. Network effects are central to this business model pattern—i.e., the more users from one group use the platform, the more attractive it becomes to users from the other group, and vice versa [2] (2.1). As already mentioned, leveraging customer data in the sense of collecting, processing and selling of sensor data closely interacts with network effects (1.2, 2.1).

At the present, we rate the three platform ecosystems as closed to some extent—that is probably why we could not find the Two-Sided Market pattern visibly addressing two-sided network effects. However, we identified one-sided network effects connected with traffic information services: BMW's traffic information system takes GPS data among others also from movement profiles of other networked vehicles (ConnectedDrive-enabled BMW vehicles) in real time. In this way, a system of systems of many vehicular CPS is created and all of them function as resource integrators by supplying the necessary sensor data (1.2). I.e., the more users use this smart service, the better it functions and the more attractive it becomes to further users (2.1).

Overall, the three business model patterns discussed in this section can potentially transform product innovations into business model innovations, mainly coming from the understanding of CPS as opened and linked-up systems (1.2) in combination with platform-based network effects (2.1). As this cluster focuses on customer data, collected and processed by opened and linked-up systems, we name it Data Orchestrator. We consider this cluster important, since it is the only one that applies the full potential coming from criterion 1.2 in practice, and the only one that applies platform-based network effects in practice in case of the Two-Sided Market pattern.

5   Limitations and Future Research Directions

Our results are limited by its exploratory nature and need further elaboration, scrutiny, and competing views. Further empirical studies, now beginning, are needed and are to go far beyond our first exploratory study. In addition, further empirical work should provide a deeper evaluation.

References

1. Broy, M., Cengarle, M.V., Geisberger, E.: Cyber-Physical Systems: Imminent Challenges. In: Calinescu, R., Garlan, D. (eds.) Monterey Workshop 2012. LNCS, vol. 7539, pp. 1–28. Springer, Heidelberg (2012)
2. Gassmann, O., Frankenberger, K., Csik, M.: The Business Model Navigator: 55 Models that will Revolutionise your Business. Pearson, Harlow (2014)
3. Schief, M., Buxmann, P.: Business Models in the Software Industry. In: 45th Hawaii International Conference on System Sciences, pp. 3328–3337 (2012)
4. Galbraith, J.: Organizing to deliver solutions. Organizational Dynamics 31, 194–207 (2002)

5. Velamuri, V.K., Neyer, A.-K., Möslein, K.M.: Hybrid value creation: a systematic review of an evolving research area. J. Betriebswirtschaft 61, 3–35 (2011)
6. Gawer, A.: Bridging differing perspectives on technological platforms: Toward an integrative framework. Research Policy 43, 1239–1249 (2014)
7. Gawer, A., Cusumano, M.A.: Industry Platforms and Ecosystem Innovation. Journal of Product Innovation Management 31, 417–433 (2014)
8. Amit, R., Zott, C.: Value creation in e-business. Strateg. Manag. J. 22, 493–520 (2001)
9. Timmers, P.: Business Models for Electronic Markets. Electronic Markets 8, 3–8 (1998)
10. Osterwalder, A., Pigneur, Y.: Business model generation. Wiley, New Jersey (2010)
11. Everitt, B.S., Landau, S., Leese, M.: Cluster analysis, 4th edn., Arnold, London (2001)
12. Fleisch, E., Weinberger, M., Wortmann, F.: Business Models and the Internet of Things (2014), http://www.iot-lab.ch/wpcontent/uploads/2014/11/EN_Bosch-Lab-White-Paper-GM-im-IOT-1_3.pdf

Business Models for Platform-Based Digital Services: Stakeholder Expectations

Christopher Jud(✉)

University of Stuttgart, Keplerstr. 17, 70174 Stuttgart, Germany
jud@wius.bwi.uni-stuttgart.de

1 Problem and Research Question

The transformation of physical products into product service systems offers possibilities for delivering benefits to customers and increases the value for them to use the products. Therefore these products are charged with services [1]. This transformation is not only a chance but also a challenge for several industries – not only but especially in Germany where automotive manufacturers and machine manufacturers as long as the ecosystems of these industries account for a huge part of the gross national product (GNP) [2].

The originally business model (BM) of for example automotive Original Equipment Manufacturers (OEMs) is changing. The portfolio contains different BM starting with selling cars to car sharing, where the product is not the car itself but instead offering the service to use a car for driving from one point to another by paying only for the time the car is used [3]. Next to this example there is a bunch of services which further increase the value of the product for the customer by adding features like music streaming or the delivery of different kinds of information. Also the usage of the product can be improved by offering services like telematics services or additional features like concierge services. Via the concierge service a user i.e. in a car can contact a call center to book hotels or flights etc. All these BM strongly depend on information technology and corresponding digital services. The benefit of some of these services is questionable. Some of them strongly bounded to the product (services of automotive OEMs) or the added value is questionable (In-car e-mail function). For others, the benefit for the customer is uncertain (monitoring the temperature of a refrigerator via an app as example for an application in the domain of Internet of Things (IoT)). These points are very rarely concerned within the literature. The question is what kinds of services are meeting the users' expectations. Further need to be examined, how developers and suppliers can be attracted by service platforms.

But not only the range of BM is changing, also does the structure of suppliers and partners. The portfolio of digital services created and offered i.e. by automotive OEMs for example for their in-car platforms are challenged. The commitment of IT-companies like Apple or Google to offer software solutions for cars challenge the platforms of the OEMs. Apps and services, which have been offered for their ecosystems for devices like Tablet-PC and smartphones, open new possibilities for extending the offerings to further devices like cars or other IoT-devices. Former suppliers (of interfaces) now influence innovations and decisions concerning digital services for the platforms and product development. The threat for OEMs is that they are demoted to "hardware suppliers"

© Springer International Publishing Switzerland 2015
J.M. Fernandes et al. (Eds.): ICSOB 2015, LNBIP 210, pp. 174–178, 2015.
DOI: 10.1007/978-3-319-19593-3_15

because the digital services are created for and delivered by the ecosystem of the IT companies. The automotive industry is one example where a physical product is charged with digital services to enhance the users benefit while using the product. Other examples are machine or tool manufacturers as well as manufacturers of consumer products like refrigerator or watches.

This dissertation investigates the upcoming changes from the OEMs stakeholders' point of view. Furthermore the gaps found in creating services that meet the stakeholders' expectations are addressed. The different ecosystems and BM regarding digital services will be reviewed. The following research questions will be examined within this dissertation: How do platform-based digital services affect the expectations of stakeholders regarding physical products enhanced by digital services? Which factors influence these stakeholders' expectations?

2   Related Work

This dissertation builds upon previous literature regarding service platforms and ecosystems, business models and digital services like in [5,6,7]. In [6] different characteristics of software ecosystems and views on such platforms are discussed. The authors also mention embedded ecosystems. This concept is one idea for companies to circumvent the lock-in to one platform-vendor. [7] discusses the distinction between internal and external platforms as well as the network effects on platforms and multi-sided markets. Especially multi-sided markets represent a concept which will be important for this dissertation because of the stakeholder view of this dissertation. Also the governance of ecosystems and platforms are discussed in these papers. The governance of ecosystems and platforms is one point which need to be discussed also in the topic of this dissertation because governance structures also influence the perception of platforms or ecosystems by the stakeholders.

New BM in IoT, mobility (with focus on the car as the product) and others are discussed in literature. For example in [4,5,6,7,8]. This literature builds the theoretical foundation for the dissertation. Next to these sources, literature from the domain of requirements engineering and stakeholder theory will be used to examine requirements of stakeholders regarding digital services bundled with physical products. These findings will be extended by empirical studies during this dissertation.

3   Methods

The dissertation is based on a reference framework, in which the roles, relationships and artifacts are put into relation. This reference frame will be created by findings and results of existing literature. The theoretical background of the dissertation will therefore be done via a qualitative literature review supported by an analysis of the current market situation. In qualitative surveys with experts from domains of digital services and related research fields, the fundamental assumptions of this dissertation will be examined and validated. The results of the surveys will be aggregated and summarized and refined in several iterations (Delphi method).

The requirements of the stakeholder will be raised by quantitative surveys of (potential) users of digital services, developers etc. Therefore an online questionnaire will be sent among others to a selection of potential users differenced by age, income level, education and geographical region etc. To get in touch with potential users and other stakeholders, different sources like social media, online forums etc. will be used. Also conferences and manufacturers could be another possible source to collect empirical data.

The key findings of the different parts of research should be brought together and design advices will be developed. The results of this dissertation should help to understand the requirements of the stakeholders better, especially of the user, and offer possibilities to transfer these insights to the research fields that explore the development of digital services and technical creation of them. The criteria that will be worked out during this dissertation address professionals that work in the field of digital service design or business development. Another target group for the results are researchers that work in the field of digital services.

4   Preliminary Results

The author worked in a research group which published preliminary work in this field where BM with regard of digital services of German premium car manufacturers have been examined [10]. Here, the increasing importance of in-car service platforms have been analyzed and the types of BM have been described. Key findings have been that all the examined companies offer digital services for their products. But the strategy and invests vary. BMW and Daimler build up ecosystems for their products which can be seen as offerings of services available for a broad range of models in the portfolio of the companies. BMW and the ConnectedDrive platform has a high maturity level from the authors' point of view and offers for example an in-car store, where the user can buy additional services to extend the feature set of the car by a Real-Time Traffic Information (RTTI) service or a navigation function. Audi hesitates out of the authors' point of view and has a comparable range of services only for a very limited number of models. Another finding is that the kinds of BM of the companies related to the digital services are very comparable over the portfolio of the three companies. But not all patterns which have been suggested by the authors for digital services are used in the current services.

A second paper [11] builds upon that and refines the findings of [10]. The BM patterns have been clustered using criteria basing on properties of cyber-physical systems and technological platforms. The clustering gives an overview, which of the patterns show a coherence in the CPS- and platform-criteria. Clustering the patterns regarding to that criteria gives evidence which pattern is appropriate to be combined and can be used to generate BM out of them. Based on public available information and data, the findings show that some of the patterns are already in use. For others, no evidence for an application could be found.

But this previous work has only been the first step into a more in-depth analysis of BM in digital services and is based on documents, publications, web pages and data the authors found during the analysis phase. A validation of the findings and the extension to other domains is necessary and already in progress.

During the work on these papers the upcoming changes by the offerings and announcements of IT-companies and publications of other sources regarding this subject also have been monitored. During the research phase many announcements with regard to the future of the car had been made. Some of them cover the upcoming possibilities of digital services and the issues the current automotive OEMs have with this development.

5   Next Steps

This paper is a first summary of the research targets of the underlying work. In the next step, the relevance of the research target will be proofed via qualitative interviews of experts which work in departments of firms developing new services as well as researchers who are doing research in this field as explained above. For the interviews respective experts are necessary. The creation of a list with experts is already in preparation.

Next to that a literature analysis will be done to get an overview of the publications done in this area of research. After that a quantitative analysis will be done to validate the finding of the previous steps.

References

1. Isaksson, O., Larsson, T.C., Rönnbäck Öhrwall, A.: Development of Product-Service Systems: Challenges and Opportunities for the Manufacturing Firm. Journal of Engineering Design 20(4), 329–348 (2009)
2. Statistisches Bundesamt: Anteile starker Branchen am Bruttoinlandsprodukt (BIP) in Deutschland im Jahr 2010. In: Sueddeutsche Zeitung, vol. (158), p. 18 (2013)
3. Shaheen, S.A., Cohen, A.P.: Carsharing and Personal Vehicle Services: Worldwide Market Developments and Emerging Trends. International Journal of Sustainable Transportation 7-1, 5–34 (2013)
4. Zolnowski, A., Böhmann, T.: Formative Evaluation of Business Model Representations - the Service Business Model Canvas. In: Twenty Second European Conference on Information Systems, Tel Aviv (2014)
5. Gawer, A.: Bridging differing perspectives on technological platforms: Toward an integrative framework. Research Policy (43), 1239–1249 (2014)
6. Jansen, S., Brinkkemper, S., Finkelstein, A.: Business Network Management as a Survival Strategy: A Tale of Two Software Ecosystems. In: Proceedings of the First International Workshop on Software Ecosystems, pp. 34–38 (2009)
7. Gawer, A., Cusumano, M.A.: Industry Platforms and Ecosystem Innovation. Journal of Product Innovation Management (31), 417–433 (2014)
8. Gassmann, O., Frankenberger, K., Csik, M.: The Business Model Navigator: 55 Models that will Revolutionise your Business. Pearson, Harlow (2014)

 9. Fleisch, E., Weinberger, M., Wortmann, F.: Business Models and the Internet of Things Bosch Internet of Things & Services Lab (February 24, 2014), `http://www.iot-lab.ch/wp-content/uploads/2014/11/EN_Bosch-Lab-White-Paper-GM-im-IOT-1_3.pdf`
10. Schäfer, T., Jud, C., Mikusz, M.: Plattform-Ökosysteme im Bereich der intelligent vernetzten Mobilität: Eine Geschäftsmodellanalyse. In: HMD Praxis der Wirtschaftsinformatik(2015), doi: s40702-015-0126-4
11. Mikusz, M., Jud, C., Schäfer, T.: Business Model Patterns for the Connected Car and the Example of Data Orchestrator. In: ICSOB 2015 (2015)

Development of a Method for the Economic Evaluation of Predictive Maintenance

Tobias Tauterat[✉]

Graduate School of advanced Manufacturing Engineering (GSaME),
Universität Stuttgart, Chair of Information Systems II,
Keplerstraße 17, 70174 Stuttgart, Germany
Tobias.Tauterat@gsame.uni-stuttgart.de

1   Motivation

The High-Tech Strategy which was developed by the German Federal Government in 2011 including the future project Industry 4.0 was initiated to promote informatization of manufacturing technology and to pave the way for intelligent production and thus intelligent factories. The goal of Industry 4.0 is to ensure the future viability of the German manufacturing economy through digitization, so that this economy plays a leading role in the international environment in the future [1].

Various new technologies are the foundation of an interconnected and intelligent manufacturing that consists of interconnected and intelligent products, plant and machinery. Based on these new technologies, new concepts in manufacturing can be realized and new business models can be developed [2]. That includes for example the Internet of the Things, which allows an interconnection of physical objects, cyber-physical systems to enable intelligent objects, and machines as well as the "Appization", and the digital shadow of manufacturing [2-7].

These different technologies and concepts have an impact on plant and machinery in manufacturing companies. Particularly machines are able to capture their current states precisely and to forward them to other machines and/or software systems in order to be analyzed, if necessary. However, for this purpose machines need to become more intelligent by the integration of sensors and actuators as well as the connection to the corporate network or directly to the Internet. Based on their states, those intelligent machines are able to control or to react to several states within a defined framework [4, 8].

Regarding the life cycle of a machine the biggest added value of an intelligent machine emerges at the operating stage as data about the machine and the environment can be collected, evaluated and - based on these evaluations - actions can be performed. Such a use case at the operating stage is maintenance. Maintenance is defined as the "combination of all technical, administrative and managerial actions during the life cycle of an item intended to retain it in, or restore it to, a state in which it can perform the required function" [9]. Over time several maintenance types were established. For example corrective maintenance is carried out if an object e.g. a machine is not working anymore or an error occurs. Another example is preventive maintenance, which is time-controlled or interval-controlled and performed based on

© Springer International Publishing Switzerland 2015
J.M. Fernandes et al. (Eds.): ICSOB 2015, LNBIP 210, pp. 179–185, 2015.
DOI: 10.1007/978-3-319-19593-3_16

the manufacturer's data over the life of a machine component by an employee [9, 10]. The concept of Industry 4.0 includes intelligent machinery respectively production plants. It is imaginable that by real time collection of data about the machines and the environment and their evaluation by a software system the process of maintenance can be improved [8] as well as new business models can be developed [2]. So as part of Industry 4.0 including the transition to intelligent factories with intelligent machinery maintenance also becomes intelligent. Thus, the manufacturer's stated durability is not crucial for the execution of the maintenance in the case of Predictive Maintenance (PdM) [9]. Maintenance is rather adequately initiated by the so-called Condition Monitoring, by which the condition of the machine components is captured by appropriate sensors [11]. Based on the condition of a machine component the point of time for maintenance is predicted. As a requirement for the application of PdM it is necessary that the machines have the ability to capture the conditions of their components via Condition Monitoring and to forward these data to the corporate network respectively directly to the Internet with integration. The processing of these data is executed by software systems, which are located either in the in-house data center or in a cloud solution [12, 13]. Nowadays different technical possibilities are used to capture the condition of machine components. For instance, infrared cameras can reveal the heat development or vibrations analyzer can determine the deterioration of ball bearings [14].

Regarding the current situation of technology a technological realization of new concepts of maintenance is unproblematic, as technologies for this purpose already exist [8]. However, for companies, which perform maintenance, the question arises, whether it is reasonable from an economic point of view to introduce maintenance in terms of Industry 4.0. So far there are no specific methods to evaluate this kind of predictive maintenance.

This contribution presents the state of the art concerning methods to evaluate predictive maintenance from an economic point of view in chapter 2. Based on these findings the research objective and research questions are derived in chapter 3. Finally chapter 4 presents the research approach to achieve the research objective.

2   State of the Art

For capturing the **state of research** two literature reviews were carried out; firstly a rather unstructured literature review in order to identify methods of general economic evaluation and secondly a systematic literature review to identify and analyze methods for economic evaluation of software systems.

In contrast to an unsystematic literature review a systematic literature review should ensure that the transparency and the intersubjective traceability is increased by the systematic documentation of the individual processing steps [15, 16]. For this research project an approach consisting of five stages was chosen, based on different scientific publications regarding the conception and execution of systematic literature reviews (see e.g. [17-19]); 1) Preparation of the analysis, 2) Execution of the analysis, 3) Data extraction and analysis, 4) Conclusion, and 5) Documentation.

For this literature review following inclusion criteria were used: •Literature databases: ACM Digital Library, EBSCOhost Business Source Premier, IEEE Xplore, ScienceDirect and SpringerLink; •Publication types: Article, book; •Quality of publication: Peer-Review; •Languages: English, German; •Search space: Title, abstract; •Search term: See [1]

Within the literature review 225 publications were identified. Based on these publications 37 publications were rated as relevant. The relevance evaluation considered the publications´ content, e.g. if qualitative or quantitative factors are addressed or if the method is supporting the decision concerning investments.

From a qualitative point of view the review shows that there are different generic methods for economic evaluation in the field of investment appraisal (see e.g. [20, 21]) as well as methods for technology assessment (see e.g. [22]). However, because of their generic structure and the strong concentration on specific individual factors for the economic evaluation these methods are only partly suitable for the evaluation of PdM in machinery and plant engineering. Looking at the software specific methods for economic evaluation nine publications could be found, which consider the development or adjustment of an economic evaluation method. Two of these publications address qualitative and quantitative factors and seven publications only consider quantitative / monetary factors (see e.g. [23-25]). The application of an economic method was described and performed in 13 publications (see e.g. [26-28]). In total nine publications served as decision support of investments (see e.g. [29, 30]) and two publications addressed the introduction and/or development of software (see e.g. [31-33]). Several publications addressed the different contents only partially. At the end no method for economic evaluation of PdM can be identified.

In addition to the state of research the **state of practice** was recorded through expert interviews. These interviews served to expose if evaluation methods for investments in new technologies already exist in companies, if they already have methods to evaluate software-intensive technologies, and if there are methods to evaluate PdM, in order to prove practical relevance of this research project.

The expert interviewees have to work in a company within the machinery and plant engineering on the one hand and on the other hand to possess knowledge about the evaluation of technologies, specifically regarding the maintenance process. Five expert interviews were conducted. Each interview took 15 to 25 minutes and was recorded.

Based on these interviews it can be concluded that the subject Industry 4.0 is highly relevant to companies within the machinery and plant engineering. Especially the evaluation of technology for specific solutions regarding Industry 4.0 is highly relevant, as the companies explicitly want to know which added value they can expect

---

[1] ("efficiency analysis" OR "economic feasibility study" OR "profitability analysis" OR "calculation of profitability" OR "capital budgeting" OR "cost effectiveness study" OR "economic calculation" OR "economic efficiency calculation" OR "economy calculation" OR "efficiency calculation" OR "evaluation of economic efficiency" OR "investment appraisal" OR "viability study" OR "economic evaluation" OR "cost effectiveness assessment" OR "cost-benefit analysis" OR "cost-effectiveness analysis" OR "value analysis" OR "efficiency measurement") AND (software OR "condition monitoring" OR "predictive maintenance") AND (method OR procedure OR approach)

before investing. Looking at the maintenance of plan and machinery, currently it is realized time-controlled and based on the failure probability, which is communicated by the manufacturer of the individual machine components. The concept of PdM is highly relevant, as the needed technologies already exist. However, there are no methods to evaluate these technologies and their application from an economic point of view in the specific use case of PdM to support an investment decision based on this evaluation.

According to the findings of the state of the art there is no scientifically justified and broadly accepted method which combines the following aspects: support for investment decisions, process analysis, quantitative and qualitative economic efficiency analysis, domain of machinery and plant engineering. Based on these findings the **research deficit** is:

There is no scientifically justified and broadly accepted method for the economic evaluation of PdM for plant and machinery that supports the investment decision of companies that perform maintenance.

3   Research Objective and Research Questions

Building on the findings of chapter 2 the objective of this research project is to develop a method, which allows plant and machinery engineering companies to estimate the economic efficiency whether PdM should be deployed. The focus is on the perception of the provider of the PdM service, who wants to modify its maintenance process through an increase of software usage and who needs a better base for decision-making concerning an investment decision, based on the outcomes of such a method. Thus for the method it is insignificant, if machine manufacturer, machine operator or a third party company, which is exclusively responsible for maintenance, uses it. The object of observation is the service of maintenance and the increased usage of software for its processes. For this research project the **research objective** is:

Development of a method for the economic evaluation of PdM for plant and machinery to support the investment decision for companies that perform the maintenance.

Based on this research objective the **research questions** are:

- Which requirements should be considered for an economic evaluation method of PdM of plants and machinery in order to support investment decisions of companies that perform maintenance?
- Which existing economic evaluation methods can be used for PdM?
- How far do existing economic evaluation methods for PdM meet the requirements of a found decision support for companies that perform maintenance (see research question 1)?

- How should economic evaluation methods for PdM of plants and machinery be designed in order to support an investment decision of companies that perform maintenance?

By answering the different research questions the **expected result** of this research project can be seen in the fact that companies which discuss an investment in PdM and thus an implementation of PdM will have a method which supports the decision making, based on the outcomes of the economic evaluation method. Due to the service-oriented nature of PdM it is conceivable that trough the method on the one hand the current state is captured and on the other hand the target situation is theoretically worked out and evaluated. Based on these situations the management can be supported in the decision making afterwards, e.g. by revealing the advantages and disadvantages of the different situations or by a detailed cost-benefit comparison. To reach that expected result partial result are defined additionally, which in total represent the expected result. These partial results are: 1) Catalogue of requirements; 2) Overview of economic evaluation methods, which can be used for the evaluation of the economic efficiency of PdM; 3) Methods-Requirements Matrix; 4) Method for the evaluation of the economic efficiency for specific cases of PdM in machinery and plant engineering.

4   Research Approach

For this research project an approach consisting of five phases has been chosen, which is based on different approaches from the subject areas "Method Engineering" and "Situational Method Engineering" (see e.g. [34-37]):

1) Requirements elicitation, 2) Search for existing methods, 3) Review of existing methods based on the collected requirements, 4) Method development, 5) Validation of the developed method.

In the first phase "requirements elicitation" requirements, which are important for a method for an economic evaluation of PdM, are collected through interviews with experts. After the requirements have been collected and structured within a requirements catalog, a systematic search for existing methods for an economic evaluation for PdM starts. Following this, the existing methods, found in phase two, will be reviewed concerning the collected requirements based on the methods properties and purposes. At the end of the third phase, a methods-requirements matrix should be created in order to show the different components of each method in summary. Based on the review of the different methods in phase three, a method will be developed which considers all the requirements collected in phase one to be able to support the investment decision optimally. The artifact of this phase is a specific method to support the investment decision for PdM. Finally this developed method should be validated through the exemplary application by an industrial partner in phase five. By doing so it should be ensured that all of the important requirements for an economic evaluation of PdM are considered by the developed method and the investment decision for companies, which want to implement PdM, is facilitated. To reach the goal of validation the different requirements within the requirements catalogue must be prioritized by the industrial partner before the application of the method starts to obtain the importance of each requirement in the specific application case. Afterwards the economic evaluation is performed and the industrial partner evaluates whether the different steps of the method process and their results consider the requirements as required and whether the steps are suitable for the evaluation of the economic efficiency of PdM.

References

1. Federal Ministry of Education and Research: Project of the Future: Industry 4.0 (2015), http://www.bmbf.de/en/19955.php
2. Arbeitskreis Smart Service Welt: Smart Service Welt, Berlin (2014)
3. Acatech: Cyber-Physical Systems, München, Berlin (2011)
4. Geisberger, E., Broy, M.: Integrierte Forschungsagenda Cyber-Physical Systems, Berlin (2012)
5. Heuser, L., Wahlster, W.: Internet der Dienste, Berlin (2011)
6. Communication Promoters Group of the Industry-Science Research Alliance: Recommendations for implementing the strategic initiative INDUSTRIE 4.0, Berlin (2013)
7. Taisch, M., Majumdar, A.: ICT for Manufacturing, Milan, Dresden (2013)
8. Güntner, G., Eckhoff, R., Markus, M.: Instandhaltung 4.0, o.O (2014)
9. European Committee for Standardization: EN 13306:2010 - Maintenance - Maintenance terminology, Berlin (2010)
10. Mustakerov, I., Borissova, D.: An intelligent approach to optimal predictive maintenance strategy defining. In: Proceedings 2013 IEEE International Symposium (2013)
11. Isermann, R.: Fault-Diagnosis Systems, Berlin, Heidelberg (2006)
12. Weiss, H.: Predictive Maintenance (2012), http://www.ingenieur.de/Themen/Forschung/Predictive-Maintenance-Vorhersagemodelle-krempeln-Wartung-um
13. N.N.: Condition Based Maintenance (2015), http://www.maintenanceassistant.com/condition-based-maintenance/
14. Bengtsson, M., Olsson, E., Funk, P., Jackson, M.: Technical Design of Condition Based Maintenance System. In: Proceedings 8th Conference of Maintenance and Reliability, Marcon, pp. 95–106 (2004)
15. Petticrew, M., Roberts, H.: Systematic Reviews in the Social Science, Malden, Oxford, Victoria (2006)
16. Peine, K.: Situative Gestaltung des IT-Produktmanagements, Lohmar, Köln (2014)
17. Rowley, J., Slack, F.: Conducting a literature review. Management Research News 27(6), 31–39 (2004)
18. Kitchenham, B., Charters, S.: Guidelines for performing Systematic Literature Reviews in Software Engineering (2007)
19. Vom Brocke, J., Simons, A., Niehaves, B., Riemer, K., Plattfaut, R., Cleven, A.: Reconstructing the giant: on the importance of rigour in documenting the literature search process, Verona (2009)
20. Andree, U.: Wirtschaftlichkeitsanalyse öffentlicher Investitionsprojekte, Freiburg (2011)
21. Kruschwitz, L.: Investitionsrechnung, Berlin (2014)
22. Verein Deutscher Ingenieure: VDI 3780 - Technology Assessment Concepts and Foundations, Berlin (2000)
23. Badri, M.A., Davis, D., Davis, D.: A comprehensive 0–1 goal programming model for project selection. Journal of Project Management 19(4), 243–252 (2001)

24. Karat, C.-M.: A Business Case Approach to Usability Cost Justification for the Web (2005)
25. Taudes, A., Feurstein, M., Mild, A.: Options Analysis of Software Platform Decisions: A Case Study. MIS Quarterly 24(2), 227–243 (2000)
26. Ioannou, G., Sullivan, W.G.: Use of activity-based costing and economic value analysis for the justification of capital investments in automated material handling systems (2010)
27. Röthing, P.: Empfehlung zur Durchführung von Wirtschaftlichkeitsbetrachtungen in der Bundesverwaltung, insbesondere beim Einsatz der IT, Berlin (2007)
28. Wolf, P., Krcmar, H.: Prozessorientierte Wirtschaftlichkeitsuntersuchung für E-Government Wirtschaftsinformatik 47(5), 337–346 (2005)
29. Bernroider, E., Koch, S.: Entscheidungsfindung bei der Auswahl betriebswirtschaftlicher Standardsoftware. Wirtschaftsinformatik 42(4), 329–339 (2000)
30. Kohonen, T.: CAD-Handbuch. Auswahl und Einführung von CAD-Systemen, Berlin, Heidelberg, New York, Tokyo (1984)
31. Kazman, R., Asundi, J., Klein, M.: Quantifying the costs and benefits of architectural decisions. In: Proceedings 23rd International Conference on Software, May 12-19, pp. 297–306 (2001)
32. Soares, J.O., Fernandes, A.V.: Economic evaluation of software projects - A systematic approach. Computers & Industrial Engineering 37(1-2), 169–172 (1999)
33. Lee, T., Baik, D., In, H.P.: Cost Benefit Analysis of Personal Software Process Training Program (2008)
34. Harmsen, F., Brinkkemper, S., Oei, H.: Situational Method Engineering for Information System Project Approaches, In: Verrijn, Olle (hg.) 1994 – Methods and Associated Tools, pp. 169–194 (1994)
35. Brinkkemper, S., Lyytinen, K., Welke, R.J.: Method Engineering, London, New York (1996)
36. Mayer, R.J., Crump, J.W., Fernandes, R., Keen, A., Painter, M.K.: Information Integration for Concurrent Engineering (IICE) Compendum of Methods Report, Ohio (1995)
37. Ralyté, J., Mirbel, I., Deneckère, R.: Engineering Methods in the Service-Oriented Context, Heidelberg (2011)

Towards Standardization of Custom Projects via Project Profile Matching

Axel Hessenkämper[1(✉)] and Barbara Steffen[2]

[1] GEA Westfalia Separator Group GmbH, Werner-Habig Str. 1, D-59302, Oelde, Germany
Oeldeaxel.hessenkaemper@gmx.de
[2] University of Twente, Enschede (NL), Drienerlolaan 5, NL-7522,
NB Enschede,The Netherlands
b.r.r.steffen@student.utwente.nl

1   Problem and Research Question

Most enterprises producing and offering high-end customized products face major internal communication and alignment issues. Typically, these occur in the context of individual projects within the organization consisting of various sites, plants or other points of operation (e.g., engineering companies, customer sites,...) where valuable experience and knowledge is gained. The source of the issues is that projects are conducted within a project team's horizon and are not supported by a systematic and easy-to-use way of reusing knowledge gained in the past. This is confirmed by the statement of Mr. Banus, Country Business Unit Head Compression at Siemens Nederland NV, saying that "[Every project] has to start from an empty paper towards a package, but following a formalized procedure". Especially in customisation projects, where every project team is continuously developing new product features, new processes, or handling the use of diverse materials, the knowledge alignment issue leads to the frequently occurring problem of re-inventions and re-developments [2]. Referring to Nonaka-Takeuchi's SECI model [8], there are established theories of how to improve and persist organizational knowledge. However, in the large organizations we visited there is currently no satisfactory systematic way to store existing knowledge gained in previous projects. For example, files are often stored in a variety of ways, and most of the company's intellectual capital is under-used or even lost. There are existing content management systems (CMS) like Livelink [4], Microsoft SharePoint [5] and ShareNet [10] that have already existed for years, but none meets and exploits the needs of global enterprises. This mismatch leads to the conclusion that organizations face the central problem of poor knowledge sharing, leading to repetitive and costly re-inventions of the wheel [2].

This problem cannot be easily overcome as the apparent loss of a subsidiary's power when providing its unique knowledge is a key managerial hurdle to introducing global knowledge sharing in multi-national corporations [6]. At this moment with the current lack of satisfactory, systematic, and tangible ways for storing knowledge, a suitable aggregation of the distributed intellectual capital enterprise-wide in a way that can be used for concrete decision making in future projects seems almost impossible. This is confirmed by observations made in three different business

© Springer International Publishing Switzerland 2015
J.M. Fernandes et al. (Eds.): ICSOB 2015, LNBIP 210, pp. 186–191, 2015.
DOI: 10.1007/978-3-319-19593-3_17

scenarios as they show that the current practice of information technology is still not mature enough for a wider adoption, and that only extremely aggregated (thinned) knowledge is used [3]. Current practices are by no means a truly efficient or helpful way of storing and building upon existing knowledge and capabilities in future projects. The consequence is a significant detrimental impact on the *time* and *quality to market* of customized projects leading to huge amounts of redundant work.

The lack of a shared knowledge base additionally undermines any attempt to standardize the development process e.g., by standardizing the used (customized) components, approaches to specific sub-solutions, and the involved external partners and suppliers. We interviewed a representative of a leading supplier for railway control systems who stated that "not only reinventing the wheel costs unnecessary resources, but also overlooking already found and better solutions leads to inconsistent products. (...) Whenever this happens it leaves an inconsistent and unprofessional impression at the customer", a problem that needs to be overcome.

In summary, the main problem is that organizations often do not have a single access point for project related information that is searchable throughout the whole enterprise, which results in essential information being distributed, hidden and too context specific, with limited reuse and sharing. This problem has the following consequences:

1. *Misalignment:* There is little inter- and intradepartmental coordination resulting in faulty budget and timespan planning.
2. *Difficult team composition:* There is no systematic support to match project profiles with employees' competence profiles.
3. *Non-conformity:* Previously developed (project) solutions are overseen.
4. *Education of staff:* New employees need long training before they achieve sufficient knowledge.
5. *Knowledge gets lost:* On-site work remains undocumented and/ or information is distributed over various types of files or sources making it unclear where to retrieve information.

The problems of the internal communication could be prevented if the experience gained and the knowledge arisen through each customisation project is systematically characterized and pervasively shared throughout the whole enterprise, enabling *cross-site synergies*. Leveraging knowledge appropriately would decrease the amount of inefficient technological development and testing whilst enabling successful and adequate solutions and designs to be fine-tuned over time, becoming part of the corporate culture. As several interviewed representatives posed it, if the corporation would systematically exploit internal expertise to the fullest that quality would be improved incrementally, especially with regard to customization, which seems to be right now a widespread weak point. As a consequence, *time to market* would also decrease, because similar problems would be treated efficiently, avoiding unnecessary 'reinvention of the wheel'.

The resulting research question is therefore: How can a pervasive cross-site knowledge synergy within global enterprises be enabled by information technology?

2   Related Work

Today, advanced organizations use different variations of CMS and interact with these for information sharing. One interviewee stated that in their organization "the CMS allow employees to retrieve about 80% of the required information for custom projects". However, they lack a decent relevance-based prioritization. While these CMS allow querying for knowledge gained in previous projects, they lack a semantic characterization and any matching technology based on it. Being capable to 'transform' project profiles directly into information correspondingly ordered by relevance is in fact a must if one e.g. wants to adequately support sales people, informing and guiding their negotiations. Modern solutions based on corporate wikis and blogs [1], [9] and [11] are still insufficient: even modern tagging based on content analysis for unstructured content does not deliver a knowledge profiling good enough for systematic retrieval and reuse.

The Global Communication Infrastructure - GCI
In contrast, the results presented by the Global Communication Infrastructure (GCI) we propose strongly base on relevance-based prioritization: the GCI is envisioned to be seen as CMS enhanced with the essential functionality of a recommender system. An arising question is why solutions such as ShareNet do not live up to the customers' expectations. The answer is stated in a paper by Young [12] that hints at the impossibility of globalising knowledge making it available to all stakeholders along a products' lifecycle: the heterogeneity of the data and systems as well as the lack of coordination of the involved parties are, at least today, prohibitive. This is not only a problem of size, but also a conceptual problem, as a true integration of all this heterogeneous knowledge would require a common semantic framework and therefore a mathematical rigor absent in most of the currently proposed (ontological) knowledge representation solutions. This observation supports the decision to 1) consider classes of production processes as the "thing" to be properly described and widely shared within an organization for this custom project business; 2) (dynamically) establish domain-specific solutions tailored to the individually considered classes of production processes, and 3) do this in a fashion that can be organized as a product line of tailored, multi-context knowledge representation systems.

The GCI approach allows an organization to tailor the complexity of the knowledge modelling problem to the considered class of production problems, and to slowly increase its complexity at need, in a controlled fashion.

3   Methods

We developed a proposal for a GCI prototype, based on requirements arising from interviews, and we validate it again with relevant stakeholders. The basis of the GCI is the knowledge-driven requirement specification. Users are any professional involved in a custom project's lifecycle, from the acquisition to the implementation and maintenance. The GCI supports in a requirement driven fashion, meaning that searches rely on the question *What* (requirements) rather than *How* (potential solutions). This declarative querying is typical of semantic (or property-based and profile-driven) approaches, and it is the key to directly involve technologically less advanced stakeholders like outside and inside sales people.

Enabled through the requirement specification, the GCI' solution eases the exchange of knowledge and experience, standardisation and process optimisation by enforcing **structured reporting**, combined with **rule-based retrieval mechanisms** that provide links to fitting reports on prior projects ordered by relevance according to the profiles of the project and the situation..

By systematically leveraging product and process knowledge gained during customisation projects throughout the product lifecycle (e.g. commissioning, service, optimization,...), it additionally leads to an automatic increase of standardisation within the organizations, despite the focus on individual projects and customisation. The GCI grows with every continued project this way enhancing the organization's retrievable intellectual capital.

Dually, it is also possible to discontinue or take out types/categories and data whenever they become obsolete due e.g. to technological discontinuities or strategic changes, ensuring that the knowledge base is kept up-to-date in *real-time*. This systematic approach to knowledge gathering, management, and reuse decreases the amount of technological development spent on re-inventing and testing, and, at the same time, it reduces *time-to-market* and increases the *quality-to-market*: as GCI's rule-based retrieval function helps professionals to systematically exploit the internal expertise previously gathered at other sites and plants.

4   Preliminary Results

The GCI is intended to be itself a customized product, created as a flexible platform with all the functionalities that then need to be customized and implemented for each specific company in collaboration with their domain experts. This customisation process ensures an excellent fit of the categories/requirements in the GCI with those actually present in the product portfolio of the customer. Fig. 1 shows how the GCI supports a continuous improvement cycle of the organisation's intellectual capital: Whenever the organisation receives a customisation request the user may start an internal search for knowledge across the previously conducted projects available in the GCI. The (customisation) project is then developed and implemented leveraging this internal knowledge as its foundation, and entering into the GCI the knowledge gained throughout its lifecycle. The following is the prototype description of the GCI.

The requirement specification (step 1) starts by defining the product category and determining some important primary parameters. For example, based on the choices for 'pipeline' and 'water' the system automatically asks the user to refine the water type (drink, or wastewater) as this is crucial information for other requirements later on in the search (e.g. which category of material has to be taken into account). This assisted refinement functionality is possible because of GCI's knowledge-driven requirement specification: the GCI asks the user step by step to further refine the project specifications based upon the knowledge already stored in the GCI. One can also further refine the profile (e.g. when picking 'oil', it can be specified as 'raw' or 'semi-refined'), thus adding categories the GCI does not yet comprise.

Based on the project profile the GCI retrieves a list of projects relevant to the search, ordered by relevance via the rule-based retrieval mechanism with best fitting projects marked green (step 2). The relevance is based on ontological information in terms of classifications and rules that depends on the current requirement profile.

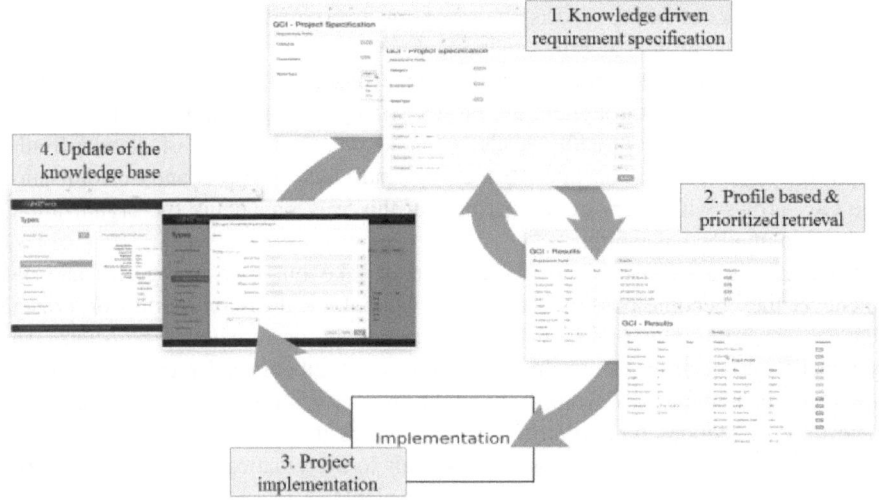

Fig. 1. GCI - Continuous Improvement Cycle

After the subsequent step 3 in the GCI cycle in which the project is implemented, all the gained knowledge is entered into the GCI.

Depending on whether the project handled already existing requirements or introduced new requirements the concrete way to save the knowledge differs. However, it is also very simple to introduce new requirements/specifications, because within the GCI the structure of the data can be easily adapted by the user. Thus the GCI allows for user-level standardized enterprise-wide knowledge updates comprising structural changes and consistent archiving.

5   Next Steps

The GCI's simplicity-driven approach is based on ontological domain modelling and weighted rules that allow one to retrieve best fitting project knowledge even without specific technological expertise. This intuitive approach provides a solid basis for an increased mutual and company-wide understanding. Thus the simplicity-oriented approach not only requires but also supports the corresponding cultural change towards a more global and shared thinking, which is very beneficial for the overall organizations. To explore the full potential for customer value we aim at introducing the product in a real use context, in close cooperation with early adopters.

A key step at the technical side is the adoption of the DyWA technology [7] to instantiate, customize and grow the GCI knowledge base for each organization. DyWA provides web based user-friendly definition of domain entities as well as their corresponding API's for a seamless integration into available business processes (e.g. Enterprise Resource Planning Systems). In particular its potential to easily create executable prototypes seems ideally suited to support the above mentioned cultural change. We are planning to evaluate this potential via concrete user-stories' of a first mover that are created for different stakeholders to allow a high degree of usability for each target professional group.

Acknowledgement. We would like to thank Jarno Bredenoord, Carolina-Marjolijn Klaus and Tobias Vermeer for early discussions of the economic aspects, and Johannes Neubauer and Stefan Windmüller for their help concerning technological questions.

References

1. Andrus, D.C.: The Wiki and the Blog: Toward a Complex Adaptive Intelligence Community. The Social Science Research Network (SSRN) (2005)
2. Ekambaram, A., Langlo, J.A., Johansen, A.: Knowledge Transfer - A Study on Construction Projects in a Norwegian Public Sector Organization. In: Proceedings of the 11th European Conference on Knowledge Management (2010)
3. Kasper, H., Lehrer, M., Mühlbacher, J., Müller, B.: Thinning knowledge: An interpretive Field Study of Knowledge-Sharing Practices of Firms in Three Multinational Contexts. Journal of Management Inquiry (2010)
4. Livelink, http://www.opentext.com/what-we-do/products/opentext-product-offerings-catalog/rebranded-products/livelink-is-now-part-of-the-opentext-ecm-suite
5. Microsoft SharePoin, https://products.office.com/en-us/sharepoint/ sharepoint-2013-overview-collaboration-software-features
6. Mudambi, R., Navarra, P.: Is knowledge power? Knowledge flows, subsidiary power and rent-seeking within MNCs. Journal of International Business Studies (2004)
7. Neubauer, J., Frohme, M., Steffen, B., Margaria, T.: Prototype-Driven Development of Web Applications with DyWA. In: Margaria, T., Steffen, B. (eds.) ISoLA 2014, Part I. LNCS, vol. 8802, pp. 56–72. Springer, Heidelberg (2014)
8. Nonaka, I., Takeuchi, H.: The Knowledge-creating Company: How Japanese Companies Create the Dynamics of Innovation. Oxford University Press (1995)
9. Remidez, H., Jones, J.B.: Developing a Model for Social Media in Project Managemnt Communications. Int. Journal of Business and Social Science (2012)
10. ShareNet, http://www.share-netinternational.org/
11. Stenmark, D.: Knowledge sharing through increased user participation on a corporate intranet. In: Proceedings of OKLC 2005. Bentley College, Waltham (2005)
12. Young, R.I.M., et al.: Manufacturing knowledge sharing in PLM: A progression towards the use of heavyweight ontologies. International Journal of Production Research 45(7), 1505–1519 (2007)

To Develop or to Reuse? Two Perspectives on External Reuse in Software Projects

Anisa Stefi[✉] and Thomas Hess

Institute for Information Systems and New Media, Ludwig-Maximilians-Universität München,
Ludwigstrasse 28, 80539, Munich, Germany
{stefi,thess}@bwl.lmu.de

Abstract. Using existing software components is a key factor when it comes to increasing productivity and improving the quality of software. It can be regarded as a mean to manage the increasing complexity of software, as software has become prevalent in most areas of our life. Thus, this study seeks to better understand the reuse of external software components. Based on two different theoretical lenses, non-rational effects on decision-making and the transaction cost theory, we analyze the degree of external reuse in software development projects. We tested our theoretical model empirically, with data collected in Germany. The empirical evidence is generally supportive of the theory with some exceptions. We find out that the not-invented-here bias plays the most important role in this strategic decision. Whereas, transaction cost constructs show mixed results. For example, technical uncertainty does not play a role, whereas business uncertainty positively influences the degree of external reuse.

Keywords: Transaction cost · Theory · Not-invented-here bias · External software reuse

1   Introduction

In the recent years, we have been witnessing software platforms on the consumer side opening up and taking advantage of external software extensions, such as plug-ins or apps, like for example in the Apple iOS ecosystem. From the provider perspective, the concept of integrating external software components which are purchased on the market, or adopted from the open source community is not a new phenomenon. This idea has been presented with the introduction of the software reuse concept in 1969 by McIlroy, who envisioned software systems composed of already existing software components, similar to other mature engineering disciplines [1]. Research on software reuse has focused on both creating reusable software assets and addressing the challenges that organizations face, when they are systematically reusing software internally. However, little research considers the reuse of software assets that are not developed inside the firm. Research on software reuse within organizational context, has not explicitly addressed this, leading to ambiguous results that show a high software reuse within the open source community [2, 3], whereas organizations struggle to implement a successful reuse

© Springer International Publishing Switzerland 2015
J.M. Fernandes et al. (Eds.): ICSOB 2015, LNBIP 210, pp. 192–206, 2015.
DOI: 10.1007/978-3-319-19593-3_18

program [4, 5]. In this study, we refer to the reuse of artifacts developed outside the organization as external software reuse.

Reusing software components can decrease the time-to-market as well as lessen uncertainty associated with internal development [6]. Despite these benefits and advances in software development, external software reuse has not been very prominent in research [6]. From a management perspective, reusing external software is a make-or-buy decision. One of the theoretical approaches to explain make-or-buy decisions, is the transaction cost theory (TCT), which is based on the assumptions of bounded rationality [7]. This theory argues that rational decision makers will choose internal development, if the costs of the transaction are high. The costs associated with external reuse are related to searching, integrating, or maintaining the components. Nevertheless, research has often shown that decision makers deviate from the rational behavior [e.g. 8]. Research on software reuse has suggested that the not-invented-here (NIH) bias could be one of the inhibitors [see 9, 10]. This bias reflects the tendency to favor in-house development, independent of other factors. Whereas existing research has found contradictory evidence about the effect of the NIH bias [see 9, 10], research has not explicitly distinguished whether the reused software artifact were developed within the firm, or acquired from outside. Especially when considering software developed by external providers, this bias can play a more important role. It can be perceived by the organization as a degradation of its own in-house expertise, and competence [11].

Therefore, we address this research gap by analyzing the degree of external reuse in organizations based on the non-rational factor of the NIH bias, as well as bounded-rational factors of the transaction cost theory. The key goal of our study is to contribute to a heightened understanding of the decision to reuse external software components from a management perspective. More specifically we look at the following research questions: (1) Does the not-invented-here bias influence the degree of external software components reused within a project? (2) How do transaction cost factors such as asset specificity and environmental uncertainty explain the degree of external software components reused within a software project?

Our goal is not to evaluate the effectiveness of the decision but rather to explain its drivers. Therefore, to address these questions we analyze the degree of external components reused within software projects. We focus on companies that have the capability to develop software internally, and also choose to acquire software components developed by external providers in order to develop their software product. External providers could be software companies developing commercial components, or the open source community. Thus, as software development becomes more complex, firms might choose to avoid the "reinvent the wheel" concept, by acquiring software components, although they have the capability to develop software on their own. A software component is defined as a software product, or part of a software product that provides an interface, which allows its functionalities to be integrated in other software products [12]. Different from the service integration, which uses remote synchronous or asynchronous calls to the API, components are used locally. Ravichandran and Rothenberger [13] identify two types of software reuse, black-box reuse where the source code of the component is not available and white-box reuse where the source code is modifiable. Black-box reuse can be achieved by creating within-code references to the functional interfaces provided by the component [14]. White-box reuse can be realized by adopting, modifying, linking, and integrating the code of an external component to the project code [14]. An analogous concept is that of commercial off-the-shelf (COTS) software components, that are black-box components where the software developer does not have control over its evolution [15]. Moreover, software developers are able to integrate software components independently of the platform they were implemented in, by using software wrappers [16]. As external software artifacts, are widely available, they provide an interesting opportunity for improving productivity. Thus, this study contributes to the existing research by providing a theoretically grounded empirical analysis of the degree of external software reuse, in software development projects.

The rest of the paper is structured as follows. After having presented the motivation for this study in the first section, we will describe the theoretical background in the second section. In section three we will develop and ground the hypotheses, as well as integrate them in a research model. The design of the empirical study will be presented in the fourth section. The data analysis will be presented in the subsequent section. We will conclude the paper by presenting our key findings, addressing potential limitations and suggesting areas for future research.

2   Related Work

There has been limited research considering make-or-buy decisions in software development. The concept of make-or-buy was first introduced by Culliton [17] in the area of production, and manufacturing. In IS research, the most discussed make-or-buy decision is that of the information technology outsourcing (ITO). A plethora of studies have analyzed this concept through different theoretical lenses, and based on the specific artifact outsourced. Theoretical underpinnings cover the classical transaction cost theory, resource view, agency theory, etc., and even considered the effects of non-rational decision making [e.g. 8]. One of the outsourced activities discussed within this research stream, is that of software development [e.g. 14, 18]. Therefore, in analyzing the decision to reuse external components within software projects we relate to existing research in outsourcing software development activities. With technical knowledge being comprised of software packages, libraries, and frameworks [18], there is little literature analyzing the degree of external software artifacts in software development from the management perspective. Most of the studies on the reuse of software components focus on the general issues related to using existing software components [19, 20] or the individual perceptions of software developers [10] or are specific to the open source research [2, 3]. There is no study known to the authors that quantitatively analyses the degree of external software reuse from the behavioral, and transaction cost perspective, which will be introduced below.

2.1   The Role of Non-Rationality in Decision Making

Research in decision making has shown that individuals systematically deviate from the laws of statistics and Bayesian updating when it comes to judgment of probabilities [21].

One of the most known works in this area, is that of Kahneman and Tversky [22], leading to the development of the prospect theory, which models decision making under risk. As Camerer [21] acknowledges, "some research has pointed towards a systematic departures, or biases, which spring from a small number of heuristics" [21 p.171]. In the last decade, research in decision making has further focused on analyzing the occurrence and the effect of the cognitive biases in different contexts.

In the IS discipline there is a number of articles that have focused on the cognitive biases in decision making [see 20]. Moreover, cognitive biases have also been discussed and analyzed in the context of software development processes [e.g. 23, 24]. In order to fully understand and capture the managerial decision making process, it is important to address such deviations from the rational behavior. The bias analyzed in this paper is the NIH bias or syndrome. Katz and Allen (1982) define the NIH bias "as the tendency of a project group of stable composition to believe it possesses a monopoly of knowledge of its field, which leads it to reject new ideas from outsiders to the likely detriment of its performance" [25 p. 8]. Thus, the NIH bias leads to the rejection, or the underutilization of external ideas and technologies, which has negative effects on the performance of projects [26, 27]. According to the knowledge management research, the NIH bias exists because of cultural aspects, inappropriate incentive systems, difficulties in intra-organizational communication, and status issues [26]. Moreover, Wastyn and Hussinger [11] found that the NIH bias is more likely to be influenced by external knowledge sources, rather than from other sources within the firm. Even from a practical perspective the NIH bias has caught some attention. For example, to lessen the effect of the NIH bias, Texas Instruments offered a "not invented here, but I did it anyway" award [28]. With regard to software reuse, previous studies have found out contradictory results when analyzing software developers perceptions on reuse [see 9, 10]. On the contrary, within the open source community, developers reuse software, without the need of extra incentives [2]. Different from the previous studies, we focus on external software reuse and we empirically analyze this bias at the project level.

2.2   Transaction Cost Theory

Transaction cost theory addresses make-or-buy decisions and has been used in various disciplines in both theoretical and empirical research [29-31]. It was initially introduced by Coase [32], who discussed the concept of firms and the limitations of price mechanisms, and was further developed by Williamson [7, 33-35]. The basis of the TCT are assumptions of bounded rationality and opportunism [36]. Bounded rationality refers to the fact that the human mind is limited, and cannot process all the information involved in an economic transaction. Opportunism is described by Williamson as "self-interest seeking with guile" [7 p. 554]. The basic idea of TCT is that, when buying a product or a service, the purchasing organization has to perform a series of activities related to this transaction, such as monitoring whether the supplier acts accordingly to the contractual specifications. These activities come at a price, and if the costs in addition to the purchase price become larger than internal production costs, self-production is the best option.

The three characteristics of a transaction which affect its costs are asset specificity, uncertainty, and frequency. Asset specificity, as pointed out by Williamson [7], is one of the most important dimensions of a transaction, and refers to the "degree to which the assets used to conduct an activity can be redeployed to alternative uses and by alternative users without sacrifice of productive value" [37 p. 105]. Uncertainty refers to the fact that the information regarding the transaction is not always known. Williamson acknowledges two types of uncertainty: behavioral and environmental [38]. Behavioral uncertainty is attributed to opportunism, and is related to the fact that actors may strategically non-disclose, alter, or disguise information. Environmental uncertainty, on the other hand, is attributed to bounded rationality and can be a result of factors such as technology, demand, local factor supply conditions, inflation, etc. [38]. The last dimension, asset frequency, refers to "the level of recurrence of the activities needed by the firm for the transaction" [39 p. 127].

In IS research, TCT has been widely used for analyzing make-or-buy decisions and especially ITO decisions [29, 36, 39, 40]. For example, Lacity et al. [29] identify 73 empirical findings using TCT. Despite a wide body of research drawing on TCT, there is no empirical research known to the authors that analyses the degree of external software component reuse on a project level. However, with increasing speed of environmental changes and the increasing number of available components, the decision to use existing components can be crucial to create a competitive advantage. Explaining the degree of external software component reuse based on TCT, could lead to a better overall understanding. Moreover, TCT has been shown to possess explanatory power regarding ITO decisions, which we would also expect in this study.

3   Research Model and Hypotheses

The level of analysis in this research is a software project. This is an adequate level of analysis as projects within an organization can have different requirements. In the following, we consider the non-rational effect of the NIH bias and TCT constructs.

3.1   Not-Invented-Here Bias

The most important inhibitor discussed in the software reuse literature is the NIH bias or syndrome [5, 41-44]. The NIH bias "refers to a negative attitude to knowledge that originates from a source outside the own institution" [26 p. 368]. This negative attitude has been suggested to influence the adoption or the usage of external technologies, ideas, or knowledge. In the context of software reuse, research has argued about a general preference towards internal development but the NIH has not been the focus of extensive research. Additionally, existing studies focus on the developers' perception and provide conflicting results [see 9, 10, 28]. By reusing existing software, "people may feel hindered in their creativity and independence by reusing someone else's software" [45 p. 16]. Thus, both managers and developers might tend to overvalue their work as well as to underestimate the benefits of external software components, and would therefore prefer internal development over the usage of external software components.

Based on this reasoning, the NIH bias in the organization is negatively associated with the degree of external software reuse in the software development process. In the case of external software reuse we conceptualize the NIH bias through two aspects. The first one is a general preference for internal development, which influence the reuse of software artifacts in general. Therefore, managers who favor internal development will reuse external software components to a lesser degree. The second aspect, which is conceptualized based on the knowledge reuse research, is the reluctance to collaborate with other software providers. Thus, managers of software projects choose not to use external software components as they do not want to be dependent, or cooperate with other software providers. Thus, we can state the following two hypotheses with respect to the influence of the NIH bias on the degree of external software used within a project.

H_{1a}: *The preference for internal software development in the organization will have a negative effect on the degree of external software reuse, within the software development process.*

H_{1b}: *The reluctance to collaboration with external providers will have a negative effect on the degree of external software reuse, within the software development process.*

3.2   Transaction Cost Constructs

In the context of ITO decision, TCT constructs have shown ambiguous results. In a lot of cases transaction frequency did not turn out to be a significant predictor [29, 39]. As software projects are specific and vary in complexity, they are considered a one-time event [18]. Therefore, since we focus on software projects, we can exclude transaction frequency construct without contradicting the TCT logic.

Project Specificity

TCT claims that the higher the specificity of an asset, the higher the transactions costs will be due to the risk of opportunistic behavior from the supplier. Therefore, in such cases firms could develop the software in-house more effectively. Research in the context of ITO decisions has found mixed empirical results [29, 39]. In this study, as most software companies work at a project level, asset specificity refers to the degree that the project fits the individual requirements of the company, or its customers, making the project a highly specific investment. A very specific software project also has specific software requirements. According to TCT, identifying relevant, external software components for a specific project is more difficult. This is because other companies or developers are not motivated to develop software components, which are difficult to use in alternative ways. Therefore, in the case of external software components reuse, we argue that a specific software project requires higher transaction costs in order to meet the desired requirements [46]. Thus, based on the TCT, it can be argued that the higher the level of software project specificity, the higher the willingness of software companies to produce the assets completely in-house rather than adapt existing external solutions. Therefore, we propose the following hypothesis:

H_2: *The degree of software project specificity will have a negative effect on the degree of external software reuse, within the software development process.*

Environmental Uncertainty

Similarly to specificity, when acquiring external software components, environmental uncertainty will play a role in the decision. There are two types of environmental uncertainty in software development projects. First, there is the uncertainty related to the technology, and second the uncertainty related to business development. In ITO research, the construct of environmental uncertainty is conceptualized considering the two aspects, business and technical uncertainty. In the case of software projects, we explicitly differentiate between the two as technology influence the core competences of the company. Thus, technical uncertainty is specific to the technology used, and is affected by the software systems, programming languages, etc., whereas business uncertainty is related to the changes in business priorities [47].

We argue that in uncertain business environments, managers might fear that the desired project might induce extra costs, and buying software components will be thus more expensive, also because requirements might change. Therefore, they will engage in acquiring less external software components, also due to the extra cost related to finding and acquiring external software components. Thus, in line with TCT, business uncertainty is likely to have a negative impact on the level of external software reuse. We can state the following hypothesis:

H_{3a}: *Business uncertainty will have a negative effect on the degree of external software reuse, within the software development process.*

Similarly, as technology is changing with a very fast pace, there is a high risk that the technology might not be adequate in the future. Thus, the more technical uncertain a project is, the more difficult it is to assess the software components that could be used in the project. Thus, the higher the perceived uncertainty associated with the technology of a software project, the more likely mangers will choose internal software development instead of looking for external components. Hence, we posit the following:

H_{3b}: *Technological uncertainty will have a negative effect on the degree of external software reuse, within the software development process.*

3.3   Research Model

Figure 1 depicts the hypotheses which are integrated into one research model.

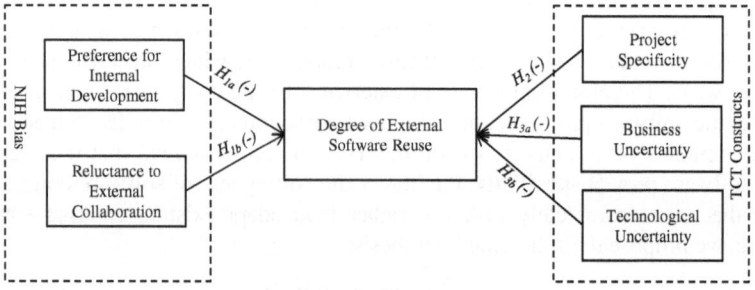

Fig. 1. Research Model

4   Research Methodology

4.1   Data Collection and Sample

In order to test our hypotheses, we collected data using the key-informant approach, which is widely adopted in organizational research [48]. The key-informant method is a technique for collecting information on organizations and collectives based on chosen informants that have particular qualifications such as specialized knowledge, or a certain position in an organization [48]. For this purpose, we developed an online questionnaire targeting people in management positions at software companies. At the beginning of the survey, the goal and the relevant definitions of the study were introduced. The participants were then asked about the usage of external software components in their company. Further, they were asked to evaluate a project in which external software components were used and to answer a number of questions based on this specific project. The survey was conducted at the project level, to allow the company to better estimate the usage of external software components.

After several pretests with researchers and managers, the questionnaire was distributed to German companies in October 2013. An invitation email was sent to 2000 decision makers in German companies. After removing incomplete answers, a total of 79 answers were analyzed giving a response rate of approx. 4%. Our sample was comprised of 76.6% top-management (CEO), 16.9% middle management (Product Managers) and only 5.2% in lower management (Engineering team-leader), 1.3% preferred not to provide details. We tested for a nonresponse bias by analyzing early and late respondents. A t-test provided no indication for the presence of a nonresponse bias at the level of 99.9%. We additionally tested for the common method bias by using the Harman's single-factor test. The first factor explained only 13.8% of the total variance, which suggests that there is no support for the common method bias [49].

4.2   Operationalization of Constructs

Most of the measurements were operationalized based on a multi-item and a 7-point Likert scale. Only the uncertainty constructs are based on single-item scale. Research has shown that single-items exhibit the same predictive validity as multiple-items (e.g. [50]). Measurement items for the constructs were adapted from previous related studies (see Table 1). Due to the novelty of our research model, we had to develop a new construct to measure our dependent variable, the degree of external software component reuse available in the market place. Therefore, we measured this degree through the two sourcing options available which are: commercial software components [51] and open source software components [52].

Table 1. Operationalization of constructs

Constructs	Items	Adapted from
NIH - Preference for Internal Development (PID)	3	[27]
NIH - Reluctance to External Collaboration (REC)	3	[27]
Asset Specificity (AssetSpec)	3	[40]
Environmental Uncertainty (EnvUnc)	1	[40]
Technological Uncertainty (TechUnc)	1	[40]
External Software Reuse (ExtSW)	2	Own development

4.3   Instrument Validation

Before testing our hypotheses, we assessed the reliability and validity of the measurement model. Content validity was established through the pre-test and the adoption of constructs that were used in the former studies as shown in Table 1. The reflective measurements were validated as suggested by the literature [53]. First we tested for the internal consistency by looking at Cronbach's alpha which should be greater than the critical value of .70. Further, we checked for composite reliability, and found that all construct are above the desired value of greater than .70. Moreover, the item loadings on their constructs should be greater than .70. The values of the average variance extracted (AVE) greater than .05 assess the convergent validity of the measurements. The results are presented in Table 2.

Table 2. Instrument validation

	AVE	Composite Reliability	Cronbachs Alpha
PID	0.671	0.858	0.774
REC	0.649	0.847	0.728
AssetSpec	0.707	0.878	0.792

Discriminant validity is also assumed as for all constructs the indicator loadings are higher than all its cross loadings. Moreover, the Fornell-Larcker criterion which says that the AVE of each latent construct should be higher than the construct's highest squared correlation with any other latent constructs [54], is fulfilled (see Table 3).

Table 3. Fornell-Larcker criterion

	PID	REC	AssetSpec	TechUnc	EnvUnc
PID	0.819*				
REC	0.473	0.805*			
AssetSpec	-0.125	-0.112	0.840*		
TechUnc	-0.098	-0.030	0.219	1	
EnvUnc	-0.012	0.130	0.041	0.278	1

*: Values of the square root of the average variance extracted (AVE)

For the formative construct, the degree of external software component reuse, validity is established by looking at the significance of the indicators' weights and the presence of multicollinearity [54]. The results are summarized in Table 4.

Table 4. Validation of formative measures

ExSW:	Degree of open source software component reuse	Degree of commercial software component reuse
Indicators Weights	0.92***	0.72***
Variance Inflation Factor (VIF)	1	1

Notes: *p < 0.10; **p < 0.05; ***p < 0.01

5   Empirical Analysis

Although the sample size fitted the "10 times" rule, which state that a minimal sample size of 10 times the largest number of predictors for any latent variable in the model, we conducted a post-hoc power analysis as suggested by Cohen [55]. For the power analysis, we used the G*Power 3.1 Software [56]. The post-hoc power analysis exhibited a power above the cut-off threshold of 0.8 [55] at the 95% confidence interval. Therefore, our sample size is adequate to test the developed model. Moreover similar datasets are also found in other studies such for example in [57].

To test the proposed hypotheses, the collected data was analyzed using structural equation modeling. The software SmartPLS 2.0.M3 [58], based on the partial-least-squares (PLS) algorithm, was used for this analysis. This method is known to perform well with small sample sizes which makes it highly appropriate for our study [53, 54]. With SmartPLS no further sample distribution assumption are necessary. In this case, the software was used to calculate path coefficients and to determine the paths' significance in the model using the bootstrapping function. The results of the analysis are presented in Figure 2.

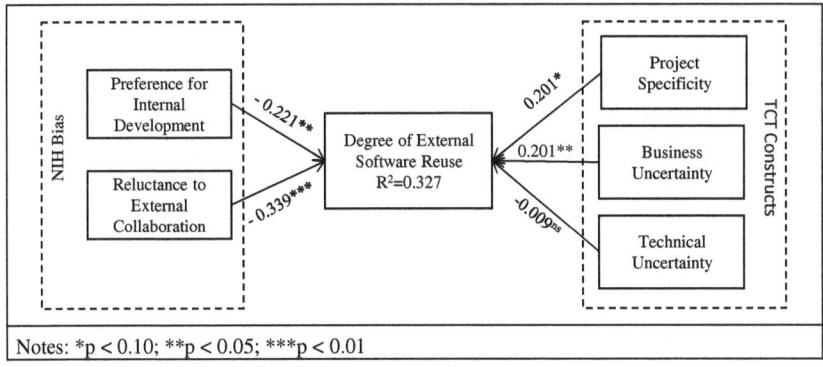

Notes: *p < 0.10; **p < 0.05; ***p < 0.01

Fig. 2. Results of the regression model

Overall, our five main constructs can explain more than one-third of the variance of the dependent variable ($R^2 = 0.327$). The NIH bias constructs, both the preference for internal development and reluctance to collaborate have a negative significant effect, thus supporting H_{1a} and H_{1b}. Moreover, reluctance to external collaboration construct has the strongest effect ($\beta = 0.339$, t = 3.223). We find that project specificity does have a slightly positive effect on external software reuse, different from expected. Thus, we have to reject hypothesis H_2. Technical uncertainty does not have an effect although the sign is as hypothesized. Business uncertainty has a significant effect on our dependent variable but with a different sign from our hypothesis H_{3a} ($\beta = 0.201$). The results of the analysis are summarized in Table 4.

Table 5. Overview of the results

Hypothesis	Sign	t-Statistics	β	Results
H_{1a}	-	2.131	-0.221	Supported
H_{1b}	-	3.223	-0.339	Supported
H_2	+	1.883	0.201	Not Supported
H_{3a}	+	2.002	0.201	Not Supported
H_{3b}	-	0.071	-0.009	Not Supported

6   Conclusions, Implications and Limitations

In this study, we looked at the relationship between the NIH bias and the transaction cost constructs on the degree of external software reuse, within software projects. As expected, we found a strong negative relationship between the NIH bias and the external software reuse. The strongest relation was found between the degree of external reuse and the reluctance to collaborate with external providers. The preference for internal development construct has a negative significant effect, which stresses that influence of NIH bias at the project level choices, and it is not only the perceptions of individual developers. Different from what TCT suggests, we find that specificity of a project has a positive, slightly significant effect on the extent of external software reuse. Asset specificity has shown contradictory results also when it comes to the outsourcing decision. Wang [18] also found a positive relationship between software projects' specificity and outsourcing success. Thus, it might be the case, that in the context of software development, specificity has a positive influence on external software reuse due to a lower risk of opportunisms from other vendors. More interestingly, we found the results within environmental uncertainty construct. We find that technical uncertainty does not influence the degree of external reuse within the project. On the contrary, business uncertainty seems to positively influence the degree of external software reuse. Thus, in uncertain business environment, reusing existing software allows mangers to mitigate possible losses. Although, we do not have the typical integrator companies as in other mature engineering disciplines, we do see   potential for a software component market which could be specialized for different industry types. This trend could be observed within game or web development, where already a large number of software components facilitate the software development process.

From the theoretical perspective, this study is the first to analyze the factors affecting the degree of external reuse within software development projects. Similar to outsourcing decisions, we could show that the factors influencing this decision can be non-rational. Thus, we found out that the NIH bias was the strongest factor influencing the degree of external software reuse. TCT provided little explanation for this make-or-buy decision. Additionally, within software development projects this study could show contradictions with the TCT logic, which need to be further investigated. Moreover, we could also observe that business and technical uncertainty behave differently and research needs to separately account for these two aspects.

With regard to practical implications, managers should be conscious of possible biases in their decision-making. First, software companies could mitigate such biases by providing a better culture, in order to take advantage of the sourcing opportunities available. Second, companies should establish clear processes and performance metrics when considering developing software artifacts in-house or reusing external ones. Specific processes based on specific metrics can mitigate the effect of the NIH bias. Third, companies could provide incentive programs that encourage managers to reuse external artifacts, when valuable for the company. The external software reused, both open source and commercial, can provide a competitive advantage for a firm, especially in the short-term. Thus, companies should adopt architectures that facilitate the integration of external components. Additionally, software component providers should increase the trust of their customers, as reluctance to collaborate is the strongest inhibitor of external reuse.

The results of the study should consider the following limitations. First, the sample size does not allow using inferential statistics for the different types of software projects. Second, since we use cross sectional data, we can only show associations, not causality. Third, the data is self-reported and consists of companies based in Germany. Nevertheless, the investigation of the degree of external software reuse turned out to be a relevant and appropriate approach to gain concrete insights into the sourcing strategies, in software development. Accordingly, future research directions are to increase the sample size and to explore other factors or use other theoretical explanations that could contribute to the usage of software components developed externally. Therefore, we would suggest extending this framework with other theories that could contribute to gaining further insights. Future research could further investigate the concept of external reuse by focusing on different levels of granularity, in order to provide a better explanation power.

References

1. McIlroy, D.: Mass-produced Software Components. In: Proceedings of Software Engineering Concepts and Techniques, Garmisch, Germany, pp. 138–155 (1969)
2. Haefliger, S., Von Krogh, G., Spaeth, S.: Code reuse in open source software. Management Science 54, 180–193 (2008)
3. Sojer, M., Henkel, J.: Code reuse in open source software development: Quantitative evidence, drivers, and impediments. Journal of the Association for Information Systems 11, 868–901 (2010)

4. Sherif, K., Appan, R., Lin, Z.: Resources and incentives for the adoption of systematic software reuse. International Journal of Information Management 26, 70–80 (2006)
5. Sherif, K., Vinze, A.: Barriers to Adoption of Software Reuse: A Qualitative Study. Information & Management 41, 159–175 (2003)
6. Keil, M., Tiwana, A.: Beyond Cost: The Drivers of COTS Application Value. IEEE Software 22, 64–69 (2005)
7. Williamson, O.E.: The Economics of Organization: The Transaction Cost Approach. American Journal of Sociology 87, 548–577 (1981)
8. Vetter, J., Benlian, A., Hess, T.: Setting Targets Right! How Non-rational Biases Affect the Risk Preference of IT-Outsourcing Decision Makers-An Empirical Investigation. In: Proceedings of the 19th European Conference on Information Systems, Helsinki, Finland (2011)
9. Frakes, W.B., Fox, C.J.: Sixteen Questions about Software Reuse. Communications of the ACM 38, 75–87 (1995)
10. Mellarkod, V., Appan, R., Jones, D.R., Sherif, K.: A Multi-level Analysis of Factors Affecting Software Developers' Intention to Reuse Software Assets: An Empirical Investigation. Information & Management 44, 613–625 (2007)
11. Wastyn, A., Hussinger, K.: Search for the Not-invented-here Syndrome: The Role of Knowledge Sources and Firm Success. In: DRUID Conference, Denmark (2011)
12. Brereton, P., Budgen, D.: Component-based Systems: A Classification of Issues. Computer 33, 54–62 (2000)
13. Ravichandran, T., Rothenberger, M.A.: Software reuse strategies and component markets. Communications of the ACM 46, 109–114 (2003)
14. Zargar, M.S.: Reusing or Reinventing the Wheel: The Search-transfer Issue in Open Source Communities. In: Thirty Fourth International Conference on Information Systems, Milan, Italy (2013)
15. Megas, K., Frakes, W.B., Belli, G., Urbano, J., Anguswamy, R.: A Study of COTS Integration Projects: Product Characteristics, Organization, and Life Cycle Models. In: Proceedings of the 28th Annual ACM Symposium on Applied Computing, pp. 1025–1030. ACM, Coimbra (2013)
16. Voas, J.M.: Certifying Off-the-shelf Software Components. Computer 31, 53–59 (1998)
17. Culliton, J.W.: Make or Buy: A Consideration of the Problems Fundamental to a Decision whether to Manufacture or Buy Materials, Accessory Equipment, Fabricating parts, and Supplies. Harvard University, Graduate School of Business Administration, Bureau of Business Research (1942)
18. Wang, E.T.G.: Transaction Attributes and Software Outsourcing Success: An Empirical Investigation of Transaction Cost Theory. Information Systems Journal 12, 153–181 (2002)
19. Li, J., Conradi, R., Bunse, C., Torchiano, M., Slyngstad, O., Morisio, M.: Development with Off-the-shelf Components: 10 Facts. IEEE Software 26, 80–87 (2009)
20. Ayala, C., Hauge, Ø., Conradi, R., Franch, X., Li, J.: Selection of third party software in Off-The-Shelf-based software development—An interview study with industrial practitioners. Journal of Systems and Software 84, 620–637 (2011)
21. Camerer, C.: Bounded Rationality in Individual Decision Making. Experimental Economics 1, 163–183 (1998)
22. Kahneman, D., Tversky, A.: Prospect Theory: An Analysis of Decision Under Risk. Econometrica: Journal of the Econometric Society 47, 263–292 (1979)
23. Mohan, K., Jain, R.: Using Traceability to Mitigate Cognitive Biases in Software Development. Communications of the ACM 51, 110–114 (2008)

24. Stacy, W., MacMillan, J.: Cognitive Bias in Software Engineering. Communications of the ACM 38, 57–63 (1995)
25. Katz, R., Allen, T.J.: Investigating the Not Invented Here (NIH) syndrome: A Look at the Performance, Tenure, and Communication Patterns of 50 R & D Project Groups. R&D Management 12, 7–20 (1982)
26. Lichtenthaler, U., Ernst, H.: Attitudes to externally organising knowledge management tasks: a review, reconsideration and extension of the NIH syndrome. R&D Management 36, 367–386 (2006)
27. Kathoefer, D.G., Leker, J.: Knowledge Transfer in Academia: An Exploratory Study on the Not-invented-here Syndrome. Journal of Technology Transfer 37, 658–675 (2012)
28. Agresti, W.W.: Software Reuse: Developers' Experiences and Perceptions. Journal of Software Engineering and Applications 4, 48 (2011)
29. Lacity, M.C., Willcocks, L.P., Khan, S.: Beyond Transaction Cost Economics: Towards an Endogenous Theory of Information Technology Outsourcing. The Journal of Strategic Information Systems 20, 139–157 (2011)
30. Klein, P.G.: The Make-or-Buy Decision: Lessons from Empirical Studies. In: Menard, C., Shirley, M. (eds.) Handbook of New Institutional Economics, pp. 435–464. Springer US (2005)
31. Lyons, B.R.: Specific Investment, Economies of Scale, and the Make-or-buy Decision: A Test of Transaction Cost Theory. Journal of Economic Behavior & Organization 26, 431–443 (1995)
32. Coase, R.H.: The Nature of the Firm. Economica 4, 386–405 (1937)
33. Williamson, O.E.: Markets and Hierarchies: Antitrust Analysis and Implications. Free Press, New York (1975)
34. Williamson, O.E.: Transaction-cost Economics: The Governance of Contractual Relations. Journal of Law and Economics 22, 233–261 (1979)
35. Williamson, O.E.: Transaction Cost Economics: How it Works; Where it is Headed. De Economist 146, 23–58 (1998)
36. Aubert, B.A., Rivard, S., Patry, M.: A Transaction Cost Model of IT Outsourcing. Information & Management 41, 921–932 (2004)
37. Williamson, O.E.: The Mechanisms of Governance. Oxford University Press on Demand, Oxford (1996)
38. Williamson, O.E.: The Economic Institutions of Capitalism Firms Markets Relational Contracting. Free Press, New York (1985)
39. Karimi-Alaghehband, F., Rivard, S., Wu, S., Goyette, S.: An Assessment of the Use of Transaction Cost Theory in Information Technology Outsourcing. The Journal of Strategic Information Systems 20, 125–138 (2011)
40. Benlian, A.: A transaction Cost Theoretical Analysis of Software-as-a-Service (SaaS)-based Sourcing in SMBs and enterprises. In: Proceedings of the 17th European Conference on Information Systems (2009)
41. Fichman, R.G., Kemerer, C.F.: Incentive Compatibility and Systematic Software Reuse. Journal of Systems and Software 57, 45–60 (2001)
42. Griss, M.L.: Software Reuse: From Library to Factory. IBM Systems Journal 32, 548–566 (1993)
43. Chapman, M., van der Merwe, A.: Contemplating Systematic Software Reuse in a Projectcentric Company. In: Proceedings of the 2008 Annual Research Conference of the South African Institute of Computer Scientists and Information Technologists on IT Research in Developing Countries: Riding the Wave of Technology, pp. 16–26. ACM, Wilderness (2008)

44. Biggerstaff, T., Richter, C.: Reusability Framework, Assessment, and Directions. IEEE Software 4, 41–49 (1987)
45. Sametinger, J.: Software Engineering with Reusable Components. Springer-Verlag New York Incorporated (1997)
46. Nelson, P., Richmond, W., Seidmann, A.: Two Dimensions of Software Acquisition. Communications of the ACM 39, 29–35 (1996)
47. Nidumolu, S.R.: Standardization, Requirements Uncertainty and Software Project Performance. Information & Management 31, 135–150 (1996)
48. Bagozzi, R.P., Yi, Y., Phillips, L.W.: Assessing Construct Validity in Organizational Research. Administrative Science Quarterly 36, 421–458 (1991)
49. Podsakoff, P.M., MacKenzie, S.B., Lee, J.-Y., Podsakoff, N.P.: Common Method Biases in Behavioral Research: A Critical Review of the Literature and Recommended Remedies. Journal of Applied Psychology 88, 879–903 (2003)
50. Bergkvist, L., Rossiter, J.R.: The Predictive Validity of Multiple-item versus Single-item Measures of the Same Constructs. Journal of Marketing Research 44, 175–184 (2007)
51. Hissam, S.A., Seacord, R.C., Lewis, G.A.: Building Systems from Commercial Components. In: Proceedings of the 24th International Conference on Software Engineering (ICSE), pp. 679–680 (2002)
52. Ajila, S.A., Wu, D.: Empirical Study of the Effects of Open Source Adoption On Software Development Economics. Journal of Systems and Software 80, 1517–1529 (2007)
53. Chin, W.W.: The Partial Least Squares Approach for Structural Equation Modeling. Lawrence Erlbaum Associates, Mahwah, NJ (1998)
54. Hair, J.F., Ringle, C.M., Sarstedt, M.: PLS-SEM: Indeed a Silver Bullet. The Journal of Marketing Theory and Practice 19, 139–152 (2011)
55. Cohen, J.: Statistical Power Analysis for the Behavioral Sciences. L. Erlbaum Associates (1988)
56. Faul, F., Erdfelder, E., Buchner, A., Lang, A.-G.: Statistical Power Analyses using G* Power 3.1: Tests for Correlation and Regression Analyses. Behavior Research Methods 41, 1149–1160 (2009)
57. Tiwana, A., Bush, A.A.: A Comparison of Transaction Cost, Agency, and Knowledge-Based Predictors of IT Outsourcing Decisions: A US-Japan Cross-cultural Field Study. Journal of Management Information Systems 24, 259–300 (2007)
58. SmartPLS, http://www.smartpls.de

Internationalization and Export of Software Products

Maarten Huijs[✉], Slinger Jansen, and Sjaak Brinkkemper

Utrecht University, The Netherlands
email@maartenhuijs.nl,{slinger.jansen,s.brinkkempe}@uu.nl

Abstract. Independent software vendors need to grow beyond their domestic markets. Software producing organizations are faced with a great number of options and opportunities on how they choose to conduct internationalization. Interestingly, efforts conducted have a high failure rate and software companies rarely succeed at first. In this paper we present a systematic mapping study and the results of 20 interviews with CEOs in the Dutch software sector. This study highlights the most important decisions made during the process of internationalization: the drivers, the process planning, market selection, and the followed market entry strategy. The choices available to the key decision makers in the right market selection and entry strategy are most strongly influenced and limited by the product architecture, characteristics of the product and company, and the level of internationalization experience located within the independent software company. The findings from this research support decision making in internationalization projects by software firms and policy makers in finding support strategies for export missions.

1   Introduction

No industry has profited more from globalization than the IT industry. IDC [1], a global provider of market intelligence, estimates that for 2015 IT spending in emerging markets will grow in excess of 8.8%, and represents 34% of worldwide IT spending. This growth accounts for 51% of all new growth in the IT marketplace, resulting in a rising number of IT companies seeking opportunities outside of their domestic markets.

The phenomenon of companies expanding to markets outside the domestic market is formulated under a wide array of classifications. Moen et al. [2] described internationalization as: "*Internationalization is the process, strategy and decisions of exporting to foreign countries*". The profits envisioned from an internationalization initiative are often uncertain [3]. Sheng-yue and Ru [4] find a dramatic failure rate; 50% of all internationalization attempts made by companies fail, resulting in a loss of valuable time and resources. There is no reason to believe that the failure rate for Independent Software Vendors (ISVs) is any lower.

Managers in charge of implementing internationalization are challenged with the daunting task of successfully guiding the internationalization process. These managers are faced with a myriad of options and opportunities on deciding how they choose to implement a successful internationalization. Research by Bell [5] suggests

© Springer International Publishing Switzerland 2015
J.M. Fernandes et al. (Eds.): ICSOB 2015, LNBIP 210, pp. 207–222, 2015.
DOI: 10.1007/978-3-319-19593-3_19

that software companies generally experience great difficulties with the export of their products and points out that problems experienced by companies selling domestically amplify with a international exposure. Currently there is no clear study linking internationalization theories to evidence found in the field.

In the Netherlands, international IT sales are largely dominated by product software sales, not custom software, services, or consultancy. Research aiding in the process of improving the exports of Dutch software companies could end up lowering the failure rate of internationalization attempts, saving these companies' valuable resources and time. This could, in turn, translate into better-performing companies and a higher GDP. The main research goal is to provide key decision-makers within the Dutch software industry with a better insight concerning factors, company characteristics, market entry strategies, and internationalization theories. This leads to the following research question: *Which market entry strategies and methods exist in the current state-of-the-art literature and how do these theories apply to the experiences of Dutch ISVs?*

When selling physical products, an international company is more or less bound to traditional terms extensively described in the current literature such as agents, logistic operators, distributors, licensee, and foreign subsidiaries. Software is characterized by shorter life cycles and lower distribution costs, meaning it cannot be defined by the traditional terms. Software companies are faced with a great number of options and opportunities on how they choose to implement internationalization. The available market entry form and the market selection is fueled by the emergence of the internet, which allows easy distribution and connection to customers and allows supplier, producer and consumer to interact on an unprecedented level through the evolvement of e-commerce platforms [8].

In this paper we highlight the challenges and export methods available to ISVs. In Section 2, the ISV Internationalization and Export Framework for ISVs is presented, which aims at providing insight for ISVs in different phases of the internationalization process. We continue in Section 3 by highlighting the research method: 20 interviews with representatives of ISVs in different stages of the internationalization process, with a combined experience comprising horror stories, success stories, and supporting evidence. Section 4 embeds the research efforts in the literature and presents a framework outlining the different internationalization methods available to ISVs. In Section 5 the evidence is presented and analyzed. Finally, in section 6 we summarize our conclusions.

2   ISV Internationalization and Export Framework

Current research does not provide a complete overview for ISVs wanting to internationalize and export their software products. After a mapping study of the literature, a research framework has been created, as modeled in figure 1. The research framework contains different process steps, in which a strategy must be chosen. The influencing factors are listed in the boxes next to the process steps. The model should be read starting from the left top after which the process can be repeated multiple times for each specific software product, or more accurate used by the organization for each individual internationalization attempt. Organizations that follow the process illustrated in figure 1 should ultimately gain in internationalization experience.

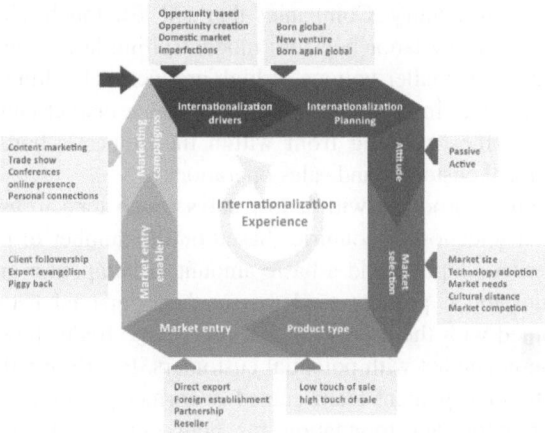

Fig. 1. ISV Product Internationalization and Export Framework

The process steps start in the top right corner, where the ISV can establish that it is time to start internationalizing and exporting software. (1) The organization must assess whether it is time for an internationalization effort and what its drivers are for doing so. (2) Secondly, the organization can start planning its efforts and basis. Is the company planning on doing international business since the first day of founding? Or is internationalization initiated after building a network of domestic customers: is it a born global? A new venture? Or does the company need to internationalize all its effort due to a previous local focus? (3) The organization must determine whether or not it will actively peruse a higher level of internationalization or if the organization will use a more passive approach. The active or passive approach influences the way the organization can determine their markets. Actively perusing internationalization can be done for instance by actively targeting international customers or hiring dedicated managers in charge of internationalization efforts. (4) Market selection focuses on how the organization will determine which markets it will target. (5) The actual strategy used by the organization to enter a market is largely dependent on the type and characteristics of the software product the organization is selling. The product type is divided in to two categories; products with a low- and products with a high touch of sale. Touch of sale describes the amount of personal intervention needed to sell a software product. (6) Market entry describes the strategy used by the organization to enter a company. (7) The market entry is followed by the market enablers, which can aid the process of market entry. Followed by the marketing campaigns or marketing methods that can be used by the organization to increase the amount of income generated from customers abroad.

Companies with a product considered to be **high touch of sale** use a different strategy to enter a foreign market compared to products with a low sales touch of sale. When support is intensive and can only by performed in person by highly trained professionals, it is less likely that the organization will use strategies with a cost-effective way to deal with support. Products with a high sales touch opt for a reseller, agent or partnership-oriented strategy or choose to open a fully owned domestic branch in the chosen country. Companies that sell low touch of sale products more often tend to select a low labor business model, selling large volumes of low priced products compare to a smaller volume of high products. This limits companies with a low sales touch product in choosing direct export as a market entry strategy, using a centralized sales force operating from within the domestic borders to service and manage international customer and sales operations.

Companies selling products with **a low sales touch** tend to use a shotgun tactic, creating an initial selection of countries based on the number of potential customers, the level of internet adoption and a basic amount of competitor analysis. Companies with a high sales touch product tend to use their personal networks to gain new business, combined with the use of content marketing, trade shows and conferences, in order to come in contact with potential customers. Identifying the level of personal experience of the management team gained in former positions, life experience and education as an important foundation for both high touch and low touch sales products. With high touch sales products, the international personal network of the company management is the primary way of building a reseller or partnership network as well as a main means of contact and creation of international business opportunities.

For companies with low touch sales products, the personal experience is mainly helpful in the creation of the "whole product", since the management with greater international experience has a better overview of all the necessary steps for building a product that is suitable for international sale. They avoid making mistakes that decrease the chances of the product appealing to an international market. The literature also sees management with a lack of international business experience as a warning sign. The research indicated the management must have traveled or studied extensively outside of the country. International experience can, however, also be gained or hired since not all decision-makers possess extensive management experience [18].

3   Research Method

The approach of this research has been, due to its exploratory nature, to first frame the research by conducting a mapping study into the literature on internationalization. The framework was used to create a structured interview protocol and a context to frame the findings of the research.

A systematic mapping study [6] has been used to identify and provide an overview of a research area. To obtain only the most influential empirical evidence to be used in this research, a filter based on the article impact was created, based on the number of citations combined with the source of the article. A manual check on the title and the abstract ensured the article focuses on the keyword combination was used. A total of 97 articles were studied. The list of articles can be found in the work of Huijs [7].

After completing the systematic mapping study a grounded theory-based method [8] was executed. The grounded theory for this research relies on 20 semi-structured interviews of 1,5 to 2 hours with CEOs of Dutch ISVs. The research identifies the various internationalization attempts undertaken by the ISVs. By performing in-depth interviews, the research aimed to identify (1) the motivation for the company to start with internationalization, (2) the selection criteria leading up to the country's entry, (3) The market entry form, and (4) the activities conducted to improve the expansion. The companies were selected based on the following criteria: (a) the headquarters are located in the Netherlands, (b) the company is active in the field of software, (c) the company sells software produced by the company or developed by a subcontractor, and (d) the company has a maximum of 100 employees worldwide. The small company size limit made sure that the companies could be considered small to medium enterprises. The primary sampling was based on convenience sampling using the Deloitte Technology Fast 500 Awards. Using the Fast 500 winners from the years 2008-2013 as a sampling frame, the list provides access into successful Dutch software companies.

The idea of grounded theory was introduced by Glasser & Strauss (2009). This method is a systematic methodology focused on discovering theory through data analysis. The grounded theory for this research relies on semi-structured interviews of the Dutch ISVs. The selected companies where selected due to the following criteria: headquarters is located in the Netherlands, active in the field of software products, the company sells software produced by the company or developed by a subcontractor, the company has a maximum of 100 employees.

Grounded theory consists of analyzing and re-analyzing the transcripts of the interviews. These interviews are recorded throughout the session and are translated into transcripts. From these transcripts, key points are extracted; these key points are called codes. The codes are grouped with similar codes in order to form categories, which form the basis for the creation of the theory and provide a validation of the theories formed during the systematic mapping study review. During the systematic mapping study, the conclusion forms a set of conceptual ideas. Ideas which provide a better insight in the internationalization theories implemented in practice by Dutch ISVs.

The research is oriented towards commercial product software. While some findings could prove useful, they may not directly address the market specifics of custom, military or embedded software. This research only focuses on ISVs, meaning the findings might not apply for large multinational companies.

Due to the difficulty in reaching companies, the choice was made to switch to a more convenient sampling strategy. However, due to switching to a non-randomized selection, this introduces a bias in the research since not all product software companies in the Netherlands are given an equal chance of being included in this study. During the grounded theory process, the researcher scanned the transcripts of the interviews and coded specific text fragments to identify important trends in the process of internationalization. By increasing the project team and performing the encoding process twice, the validity of the research would increase since the chances of incorrect coding and categorization would decrease.

4   Literature

Before getting a better understanding of internationalization and the export of software products the research started out with preforming a systematic mapping study to understand the research area of internationalization. Using a hierarchical tree map, the definitions are shown in Figure 2. The hierarchical tree map illustrates the definitions and their encapsulations. For instance, the internationalization process is part of an internationalization strategy. The categorization of topics provides insight into the number of topics in the research area of internationalization. Current literature focuses on the process and success factors of internationalization.

The main act of internationalization strategy is a term coordinating many sub activities; the actual export of virtual goods is one, the way companies enter a market is an other. After performing the empirical research we found most prominent literature position it self as internationalization theory, research often explanatory in nature with a focus on the process of internationalization and/or factors influencing the process of internationalization.

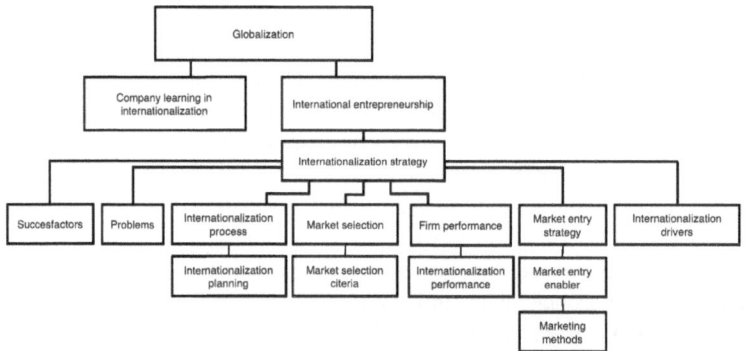

Fig. 2. Research topics breakdown

Since the mid 1900s, there have been many approaches to explain the expansion of businesses through international activities. Different theories focus on various aspects of the phenomena of internationalization. The manner in which companies conduct their business is constantly evolving: they are implementing new business models and strategies, thus changing the way they implement internationalization.

Internationalization Theories Compared. Figure 3 illustrates a collection of internationalization theories discovered by this research after performing the systematic mapping study. Each internationalization theory presents a collection of phases building up to a high degree of internationalization. The theories build up to the next phase implementing the first form of steady international activities. These theories start out with a low level of risk and commitment method using Agents to serve international customers. Three of the seven theories continue with a high-level commitment method of conducting international business.

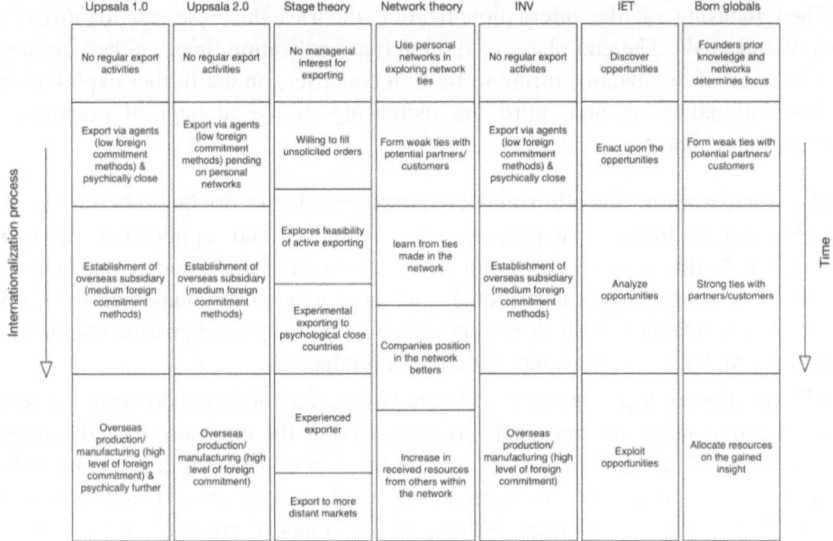

Fig. 3. Internationalization theories framed and compared

The Uppsala model, also known as the U-model or the the Stage model serves as a component of the Uppsala model, proposing an incremental approach defined in multiple stages starting in markets with the lowest uncertainty after careful calculations for the lowest cost and smallest economical and physical distance. The authors of the Uppsala model recognized the critique, since Johanson & Vahlne [9] found clear evidence supporting the importance of networks in the internationalization companies, and the Uppsala model was revised in 2009, naming the module Uppsala 2.0. An alternative coined by Oviatt & McDougall [11] is the INV theory or international new venture theory.

INV mainly ignores the fixed stages suggested by the Uppsala model, indicating the valuable contributions of SMEs to international business. The network model takes a holistic approach, researching companies combined with the influence of the relationships network surrounding the company.

Table 1. The characteristics of internationalization theories evaluated

The Internationalization theory characteristics	Uppsala 1.0	Uppsala 2.0	Network theory	INV theory	Born globals	Resource view
Psychological distance is a part of the theory	+	+	+	+	++	-
The process consist of a set of fixed steps	++	++	+	-	-	-
Includes market selection strategies	-	-	-	+	+	-
Emphasis the importance of relationships/network	-	+	++	+	++	+
Emphasis the importance resource availability	++	++	-	+	-	++

When focusing on the internationalization theories this research identified two types of end goals. The end phase of the internationalization theory either focuses on the allocating of the manufacturing to foreign countries, on the further exploitation of the internationalization and, third the increasing of the amount of countries the company can export to.

Market Orientation, Selection and Orientation. Market orientation consists of all activities aimed towards acquisition, dissemination and application of market information. Cadogan et al. [12] point out domestically focused companies are more likely less developed in a international context compared to companies with a high degree of internationalization. A market selection is the planned process of selecting a market in which a company wants to deliver a product.

Client followership consists of software companies following domestic customers who are commencing international business. Giving the company the advantage of starting out with a launching customer with strong ties. Similar the **piggyback method** first mentioned by Hollensen [14], explores the same tactic, however it chooses larger domestic partners instead of customers. Etemad et al. [15] describe 'piggy-backing' as a strategy where smaller companies rely on larger companies for the introduction to foreign markets. Although **unsolicited orders** do not qualify on their own as a market entry, the start of an internationalization process can by initiated by a unsolicited order or inquiry from a country outside the domestic market.

Sectorial focus is a strategy in which a company targets new markets based on a specific niche. Companies that are highly focused on a small niche have to take less notice of the country borders. The industry surveys of Bell [16] indicate that specific vertical sector knowledge is valuable to the degree that there is an independent of the country of origin. **Joint ventures** present a collection of strategies in which two or more parties choose to partner up. This results in a business agreement in which two or more parties agree to come together for a period of time, consisting of a set of new combined assets or resources. The level of control often corresponds to the level of shared revenue, expenses and financial assets.

Table 2. Market entry sorted low to high level of commitment

Focus	Level of commitment	Focus	Level of commitment
Direct export	Low	Client followership	Medium/High
Indirect exports	Low	Piggyback method	Medium
Licensees	Low	Agent/distributor	Medium
Unsolicited orders	Low	Industry trends	High
Export sales staff	Low/Medium	Subsidiary abroad	High
Joint ventures & strategic alliances	Medium/High	Sectorial focus	High

Indirect export is selling through an intermediate party that continues to sell the software products their customers. The intermediary can even be in the same domestic country as the ISV trying to sell the software products abroad. The **Agent/distributor** mean that in order for ISVs to sell their product, they can contract with agents and distributors to sell their products and services. **Export sales staff** can enable direct sales by directing employees to target a specific region in order to sell services and target potential new customers. **Direct export** provides a method of selling software face-to-face or buying directly via telesales or via online commerce solutions. For instance, the selling of software via the telephone is not accepted in all countries and could be seen offensive in some cultures. **Foreign establishment** researched by Lu et al. [18] tested the effectiveness of internationalization strategies, exports and foreign direct investments on the growth of an SME company. **Hybrid market entry strategies;** In the case study done by Moen [3], a researched case company chose to implement a hybrid solution, indicating that a combination of entry forms is perfectly possible.

5   Interview Results and Analysis

In the following table the companies used in this research as cases are introduced. Due to the sensitive nature of the research, most cases are presented anonymously; the research company names have been replaced by a nickname. Future plans and ideas are not included in the results, focusing on the actual activities only. Table 3 presents an overview of all case companies sorted in descending order based on degree of internationalization. The degree of internationalization of companies is measured using the measurement suggested by Ahn et al. [20], the foreign sales-to-total sales (FSTS) ratio is used resulting in a percentage indicating the dependency on foreign markets, further described as the degree of internationalization (DOI) in table 3.

During the interviews, the decision-makers were questioned on the reasons behind their choices leading up to the country or countries in which they decided to sell their products. After conducting all the interviews, the following top 5 market selection criteria were identified: (1) Sheer size (or the number of potential customers), (2) Speed of market technology adoption, (3) Based on market needs, (4) Cultural distance, and (5) Initial country selection.

One interviewee indicated hiring a market research firm to aid in the market research. The limited research could be explained by the comments of HealthComp, ImageComp and IntraComp. Indicating the fact that you can do al the desk research you want, but the actual situation at hand is too complex to fully comprehend based on desk research. The CEO of HealthComp indicated: *"When selecting the first country in the process of internationalization you can do all the desktop research you want, it will always be limited to statistics. Eventually the actual situation of selling in a foreign country is more complex and can only be discovered in practice."* The CEO indicated the level of adoption of the prospecting customers is an example of hard to measure statistics before selecting a country.

Horror story. When HealthComp originally began operating in Italy, after finding the first potential customer the company encountered a problem with the implementation of their software.*"We were unprepared for the country specific characteristics in Italy, our online software was unavailable due to the fact that many*

Italian hospitals lacked a internet connection." HealthComp CEO. This was a situation that was unimaginable when the company began exporting to Italy. The company continued by developing an offline version that could facilitate the offline use of the products in hospitals without Internet connections.

Table 3. Company cases and the degree of internationalization

Company	DOI	# FTE	# FTE int.	Year founded	Foreign customers since	Atti-tude	Application type	Presence #countries
ResearchComp	95%	12	12	2007	Day one	Active	Install based	50+
HealthComp	81%	12	0	2009	Day one	Active	SAAS	11
BiComp	81%	15	0	2005	Day one	Active	SAAS	12
MediComp	80%	35	2	2006	Day one	Active	On Premise	11
BackupComp	77%	30	0	2005	Day one	Active	SAAS	50+
ImageComp	50%	7	0	2009	Day one	Active	SAAS	16+
AppComp	40%	7	1	2009	Day one	Passive	Install based	7+
IdenComp	30%	32	2	2005	>1-2 years	Active	SAAS	5
MochaDocs	20%	3	0	2012	Day one	Active	SAAS	52
BpmComp	20%	>150	6	2006	>3 years	Active	On Premise	8
PurchaseComp	10%	25	15	2000	>10 years	Passive	SAAS	4
PersoComp	8%	40	0	2007	+/- 1 year	Passive	SAAS	5
IntraComp	4%	150+	5	1996	>10 years	Passive	On Premise	10+
FinanComp	2%	10	1	2008	>4 years	Passive	SAAS	3

To solve the problem ImageComp used a shotgun tactic, where the first step was aimed at making a selection of countries based on the number of potential customers. The product was then translated into ten languages. Combined with a multilingual marketing website with a series of landing pages optimized to entice visitors to the website, the company continues to analyze and measure the outcome, such as the number of new customers. BackupComp applied the same technique combined with a presence at foreign exhibitions: "*Especially SEO and online marketing is shooting with hail; it delivers on quantity, not quality. Therefore, the countries where we wanted to expand our operations, we started to connect with major local customers through exhibitions and conferences.*" CEO, BackupComp

IdenComp, BiComp and MediComp all displayed a selection criteria largely based on their product and the networks of partners, since the products of these three companies are implemented as add-ons – components or modules in a larger system – and simply do not function on their own. For these three companies, the customer installation base and the location of partner networks are more important. The product manager of MediComp indicated the importance of the implementation partners "*The implementation partners have a strong local network, providing in-depth knowledge on legislation, implementation, sales processes and culture.*"

None of the companies followed a determined incremental approach. The expected research for not choosing a incremental approach could be explained by the following company case decision. For one, the selection and implementation of a market entry strategy can present a sizable investment. The years it takes combined with the required resources prevent a company from quickly exchanging one market entry strategy for another. Apart from the difficulty in switching from one strategy to another, the fact remains that not all market entry strategies are suitable for every business model. The CEO of IdentComp stated some strategies can actualy only function in the country of export and not in the domestic market: *"The company experienced a situation in the Netherlands where physical meetings were always necessary from a customer perspective. The company found physical meetings less required in America due to the large size of the country."* Current theory makes no real exception for the infrastructure of the products or the nature of the company's business model.

Drivers of Internationalization. The drivers for initiating internationalization activities and the attitudes towards internationalization are based on 20 interviews with the decision-makers of the 14 case companies. The company drivers behind internationalization are largely opportunity-based. Supporting the state-of-art literature on the fact that most international undertakings start-out with an opportunity at hand and do not necessarily start out of careful planning. The initial opportunity can however provide the key decision makers of a company with the necessary persuasion that internationalization could indeed prove a successful endeavor. The drivers behind the internationalization most mentioned by the case companies are most often based on:

- **Opportunity based**; internationalization is initiated out of an opportunity at hand encountered by the company.
- **Opportunity creation**; a company starts with internationalization activities in order to create new opportunities.
- **Follow the customer**; The current customer companies are undertaking international activities, requiring the company to initiate international activities.
- **Personal motives**; presenting them self in various personal motives by key decision makers that connect to their own heritage or personal connections resulting in a willingness to relocate to a different country.
- **Personal network**; trough personal connections a company is more quickly inclined to experiment with internationalization attempts. Trough a personal network the key decision makers within a company can employ relatives to start a foreign agent or find opportunities trough personal ties with other companies abroad.

During the interview with the CEO of FinanComp the reasons and drivers for undertaking activities in context of the internationalization of their product where discussed. The first planned internationalization steps where largely devoted to personal connections proposing the implementation of a first international initiative, acting on behalf of the company as an agent. *"Very few problems occur only in the Dutch market, so why develop a product that focuses only on the Netherlands?"* CEO, MochaDocs

Barriers Encountered During Internationalization. After conducting the interviews and analyzing the case companies, this research found that surprisingly little challenges came from country-specific changes in the products. The companies that developed the product software experienced the same functionality demand from customers. The companies did not experience differences in, for instance, the wishes of a US-based marketing firm using the product software and a Dutch-based marketing firm.

After the interviews discussing the initial Internationalization drivers and the timeline of the first internationalization initiatives made by the company combined with the general attitude of the company towards internationalization. After which the interview focused on the way the company chose the initial markets to enter. The interviews indicated the actual market entry was focused on the product and the characteristics of the product that is being sold by the company. Describing the first 4 steps of the introduced ISV export framework (figure 1) explaining the relation between the market entry step and the product type step.

The product characteristics them self can turn out to be a limiting factor for the companies. The product characteristics gain little attention in the current internationalization theories, however trough the interviews they present a recurring cause of limiting or boosting the internationalization process of a company. An example of the limiting characteristics can be presented by the unpredictable circumstances of the international markets targeted by the company related to the characteristics of the company. For instance during the intervieuws the CEO of HealthComp indicated *"We were unprepared for the country specific characteristics in Italy, our online software was unavailable due to the fact that many Italian hospitals lacked a internet connection."* HealthComp CEO

Product Characteristics. The research identified three global product architectures: SAAS, installation-based & on-site. The SAAS architecture is a popular and well-published architecture implemented by organizations to build large scale multitenant software products. A single code base implementation is used to service many individual customers. Installation-based software uses a more traditional architecture where users need to install the software product on their devise, for instance a mobile devise, tablet or personal computer. In between both architectures is the on-premise architecture; a client-server architecture implemented at each specific customers company allowing all employees to use the implemented product.

During the interviews, the research identified a scale that rated the degree to which the products require human intervention for the customer to use a vendor's product software. Low sales touch products are characterized by a low level of human intervention required to sell and implement a software product. By correctly recognizing the degree of human intervention required to sell and implement the product types, this research was better able to categorize them. Products with a high sales touch require a different strategy for entering a foreign market compared to products with a low sales touch. When support is intensive, the support can only be performed in-person by highly trained professionals, providing less cost-effective ways to deal with support. The companies included in the research that chose to focus on internationalization from day on as a born global tend develop their products accordingly. Developing products with a low touch of sale with scalability in mind.

In addition to the research performed by Hasai & Almor [21] the born global is not necessarily characterized by its process alone of internationalization but rather the attitude towards the internationalization. As indicate by Madsen & sevais [22] older companies often have years of legacy in the way they do business making internationalization an endeavor that requires them to change their old ways of thinking. Born globals are companies that start with the idea of internationalization from day one. While born-again globals have the advantage of an existing customer base and a extensive personal network. Born globals have the advantage of preparation, all strategies and product characteristics are geared towards international business, often driven by the personal experience of the top managers within the these companies, the people know what decisions to increase the degree of internationalization. The CEO of ResearchComp indicated *"We are a company with no headquarters, we are a company fully distributed company not only our customers but all our employees work from all over the globe. Internationalization is in our DNA."* Companies with such a mind set and strategy present an advantage compared to companies that explore internationalization in a later stage.

Table 4. Identified product delivery mechanisms

SaaS	Installation-based	On-premise
+ Easy to update the software solution for all customers. + Easy release management + The infrastructure scales	+ Does not require an active internet connection + No data location issues + No geographic distance between vendor and customer	+ No data trust issues since all data of the product software resides within the company + Easier to implement customizations
- Difficult to implement custom customer-specific modifications - Zero or low implementation cost - Costly architecture is funded and maintained by the vendor or trusted third party - Requires reliable internet.	- Harder to test the software on all the different installation platforms with different language and region settings	- Harder to keep up-to-date by the vendor - Less control of the actual product performance by the vendor - More effort required to implement the software product.

When comparing the current state-of-art literature and our findings based on the interviews performed in the field we find a great number of decisions trough the path of internationalization are based on the characteristics of the products of the companies. For this reason we have included the product type characteristics in our main deliverable, the internationalization framework. Current state-of-art literature neglects the characteristics in for instance all of the stage models such as the Upsalla model. *"A B2B company is fundamentally different compared to the easy straightforward customer-oriented apps such as Skype or Whatsapp, since the latter do not require extensive support and training for the end users."* CEO, PurchaseComp

Based on the interviews we found that companies selling products with a high sales touch opt for reseller, agent or partnership-oriented strategies, or choose to open a fully-owned domestic branch in the selected country. Companies with products with a low sales touch more often tend to choose a low-labor business model, selling large volumes of low priced fees compare to a smaller volume of high priced fees. *"By centralizing the sales force in the same place, we are able to more easily support the personal providing necessary steering and stimulate knowledge sharing."* Product manager, ImageComp

Experience was one of the most import factors influencing the degree of internationalization. The CEO of PurchaseComp indicated public international tenders as a technique for companies without international experience to start gaining international experience: *"Entrepreneurs interested in going abroad should enroll in international tenders. Allowing the entrepreneurs to get a feel for the customer demands in a specific market. Allowing the entrepreneurs to sharpen their proposition and improving their sales messages. After enrolling and doing a few of these tenders, the odds become much higher for companies to actually win a tender."* Apart from the market entry, which presents the sizeable investment, most of the companies interviewed experienced difficulties in switching from a project-based company to a product-based company. The difficulty of switching from project to product based business models is not limited to the case-companies included in this research, the difficulties are also presented in literature [23] [24]. The ImageComp product manager stated: *"The paradigm switch from project-based software development to standard based product software was a massive overhaul, requiring an entire new set of skills."*

6   Conclusions and Future Work

While internationalization poses many challenges and pitfalls, internationalization offers great opportunities that should at least be considered by the management of all ISVs. It provides an business development opportunity for all software vendors to increase their revenue and decrease their dependence on the domestic market, whether they are in the start-up phase or have been in business for a considerable period of time. When asking which market entry strategy lead towards a successful internationalization initiative it is important to understand that there is no silver bullet. The market entry is highly dependent on a wide array of factors. Contrasting to the current literature this research advises decision makers to select the market entry strategy based on the product types, the touch of sale, the personal network and the experience located within the company.

This research concludes, based on both the results of grounded theory and the current literature, that there is no single predominant market entry strategy for Dutch ISVs. The market entry strategy depends on product and company characteristics. This research presents the fact that a market entering strategy is a sizable investment, requiring up to four years of operating without a profitable return on investment.

The years it takes combined with the required resources prevent a company from quickly exchanging one market entry strategy for another. Apart from the difficulty of switching from one strategy to another, the fact remains that not all market entry strategies are suitable for each company strategy. The research provides fertile grounds for an international study into internationalization and software export.

References

1. Insights (2013) IDC Predictions 2013: Competing on the 3rd Platform (accessed December 4, 2014)
2. Moen, Ø., Bakas, O., Anette, B., Pedersen, V.: International Market Expansion Strategies for High-Tech Firms: Partnership Selection Criteria for Forming Strategic Alliances. Int J. of Business and Management 5(1), 1–11 (2010)
3. Moen, Ø., Endresen, I., Gavlen, M.: Use of the Internet in Int'l marketing: a case study of small computer software firms. J. of International Marketing 4, 129–149 (2003)
4. Sheng-yue, H., Xu, R.: Analyses of Strategic Alliance Failure: A Dynamic Model. Paper presented at the 12th International Conference on Management Science and Engineering-ISTP. University of Incheon of Korea (July 20, 2005)
5. Bell, J., McNaughton, R., Young, S., Crick, D.: Towards an integrative model of small firm internationalisation. J. International Entrepreneurship 4, 339–362 (2003)
6. Kitchenham, B., Pearl Brereton, O., Budgen, D., Turner, M., Bailey, J., Linkman, S.: Systematic literature reviews in software engineering–a systematic literature review. Information and Software Technology 51, 7–15 (2009)
7. Huijs, M.: Exploring internationalization of Dutch independent software vendors. Msc. thesis, Utrecht University (2014)
8. Benjamin, R., Wigand, R.: Electronic markets and virtual value chains on the information superhighway. Sloan Management Review 36, 62–72 (1995)
9. Glaser, G., Strauss, C., Anselm, L.: The discovery of grounded theory: strategies for qualitative research, Chicago, Aldine (1967)
10. Johanson, J., Vahlne, J.: The mechanism of nternationalisation. International Marketing Review 7, 4 (1990)
11. Oviatt, B., McDougall, P.: Defining international entrepreneurship and modelling the speed of internationalization. Entrepreneurship Theory and Practice 29(5), 537–554 (2005)
12. Cadogan, J.W., Diamantopoulos, A., Siguaw, J.A.: Export market-oriented activities: their antecedents and performance consequences. J. of International Business Studies 12, 615–626 (2002)
13. Johanson, J., Vahlne, J.: The Uppsala internationalization process model revisited: From liability of foreignness to liability of outsidership. J. of International Business Studies 40(9), 1411–1431 (2009)
14. Hollensen, S.: Global marketing: A decision-oriented approach. Pearson, Denmark (2007)
15. Etemad, H., Wright, R.W., Dana, L.P.: Symbiotic international business networks: collaboration between small and large firms. Thunderbird International Business Review 43(4), 481–499 (2001)
16. Bell, J.: The internationalization of small computer software firms: A further challenge to "stage" theories. European J. of Marketing 29(8), 60–75 (1995)
17. Philips, R.: Guide to software export: A handbook for international software sales. International Business Press (1998)
18. Lu, J.W., Beamish, P.W.: Partnering strategies and performance of SMEs' international joint ventures. J. of Business Venturing 21(4), 461–486 (2006)
19. Reuwer, T., Jansen, S., Brinkkemper, S.: Key factors in the internationalisation process of SMEs exporting business software as a service. International J. of Business Information Systems 12(2), 140–162 (2013)
20. Ahn, S., Fukao, K., Kwon, H.U.: The Internationalization and Performance of Korean and Japanese Firms: An Empirical Analysis Based on Micro Data. Seoul Journal of Economics 17(4), 439–482 (2004)

21. Hashai, N., Almor, T.: Gradually internationalizing born global firms: an oxymoron? International Business Review 13(4), 465–483 (2004)
22. Madsen, T.K., Servais, P.: The internationalization of born globals: an evolutionary process? International Business Review 6(6), 561–583 (1997)
23. Xu, L., Brinkkemper, S.: Concepts of Product Software: Paving the Road for Urgently Needed Research. In: CAiSE Workshops, vol. 2, pp. 523–528 (2005)
24. Xu, L., Brinkkemper, S.: Concepts of product software. Eu. J. of Information Systems 16(5), 531–541 (2007)

Acquisition of Software Firms: A Survival Analysis

Marcus Wagner[✉]

Augsburg University, Universitätsstr. 16, 86159 Augsburg, Germany
marcus.wagner@wiwi.uni-augsburg.de

Abstract. This paper addresses the factors that determine the survival of young software firms and startups. It specifically focusses on the role of venture capital and organizationally radical innovation in this. The interaction of venture capital investment with the type of innovation pursued by the software firm is shown to jointly increase survival in terms of time to acquisition.

1   Introduction

Venture capital (VC) has been suggested as key for small firms and startups to financial resource access especially in technology-intensive industries [1]. Therefore, this paper addresses what affects the time until a firm is acquired, i.e. the temporal survival of a firm, what the role of VC is in this and how the latter's interaction with firm characteristics impacts on survival? The electronic design automation (EDA) segment of the semiconductor industry offers an empirical context particularly suited to analyzing these questions. Based on this, the paper contributes new empirical insights that extend the body of knowledge on this issue and especially interaction effects. The remainder of the paper is structured as follows: In the next section different theoretical perspectives on innovation and venture capital in startups are derived from the existing literature and hypotheses are introduced. Following this in the third section, data and method of the empirical analysis are detailed. The fourth section reports the findings of the analysis and the fifth section concludes. Overall, this paper in proceeding like this clarifies the role of VC based on a novel and detailed dataset of software startups.

2   Literature Review and Hypotheses

This section reviews the literature and derives hypotheses. For Anglo-American startups, survival times of at most three years for one third of the entrants in one cohort have been reported [2]. Exit (i.e. bankruptcy, not acquisition) rates are in comparison higher in recessions. For example, in the 1991-1995 recession, [3] found survival times of at most one year for 40% of the UK startups entering the market in this period. On the other end of the spectrum, [4] find that 40% of US startups survive for six years or more. High technology startups were found to have higher survival times and thus lower exit rates [5, 6]. Also the exit rate decreases with startup age and

© Springer International Publishing Switzerland 2015
J.M. Fernandes et al. (Eds.): ICSOB 2015, LNBIP 210, pp. 223–229, 2015.
DOI: 10.1007/978-3-319-19593-3_20

access to capital [2, 3], [7]. Innovation does not have a clear effect on survival times and exit rates [8, 9] except for a clearer positive effect for high technology startups and an indication that product innovation significantly increases acquisition chances for startups [10].

The motivation of venture capitalists for retaining stakes in a startup is not the same at all points of time and over time their incentives for exiting through a trade sale increase. Therefore an interaction term of venture capital provision and organisationally radical innovation included in the survival model accounts for the fact that organisational radicality makes it difficult for incumbents to imitate (which increases their acquisition need). Venture capitalists needing to "sell out" at some point to leave the investment amplifies this effect of organisational radicality. Based on these insights and those derived from the extant literature, the following hypotheses are proposed:

> *H1: VC investment makes survival more likely due to additional resources available.*
>
> *H2: Organisationally radical innovation makes survival less likely due to stronger incumbent needs for acquisition.*
>
> *H3: Joint VC investment and organisationally radical innovation make acquisition significantly more likely (i.e. a positive interaction effect of these two occurs).*

3   Methodology

Given the high industry concentration in EDA, surveying the top acquiring firms in the EDA industry to test above hypotheses seemed to make a response bias likely, since these firms may strategically misreport acquisition reasons especially if they failed in an innovation. Therefore, structured interviews were carried out, based on a short questionnaire with smaller firms in the industry. The questions were derived from the categories condensed from prior semi-structured interviews as well as from the literature. From the exhibitor list of the DATE 2006 conference which took place 6-10 March in Munich, 70 smaller and younger EDA firms were identified. These firms form the population that was approached for a structured interview during the conference.

Of the firms, 32 provided information based on a 2-page questionnaire, resulting into a 46% response rate which is deemed very high, and in turn allows drawing conclusions that are representative for the population. The survey was answered largely by general managers (n=21) and marketing and sales personnel (n=6) with the questionnaire being partly completed jointly with the respondents (n=19) and partly by the respondents on their own (n=13). There was wide variety in the primary technical design focus of the startups, ranging from e.g. analog and mixed signal design via system-on-chip design to verification. About half of the firms had more than one technical design focus.

As concerns firm size and firm age, there is a wide distribution with a median of 20 employees. Of course, surveying only 32 firms in the industry may itself introduce a response bias since in relation to the total number of firms in the industry in 2006, the response rate is only about 7%. However, given the response rate in relation to all small firms at the DATE conference (as the effectively accessible population of small firms given it was necessary to use face-to-face interviewing to survey the firms) was good, this limitation of the research was deemed acceptable since even by the standards of large scale surveys, 7% is not such a low figure. To further ascertain how representative the response sample is, variables were compared as far as possible with data from a sample of firms acquired in the EDA industry until the end of 2005 (n = 68). Based on t-tests for patenting (p = 0.67), firm age (p = 0.81) and VC investment (p = 0.30) no significant differences were found between the two samples. Given that the two sets of firms are mutually exclusive, the analysis sample is felt to be sufficiently representative for the population of all startups and small firms in the EDA industry that could potentially be acquired to continue addressing the above research questions and to derive answers that have potential to be generalised to the industry [11].

In the comparison sample of acquired EDA firms used to evaluate how representative the analysis sample is, the number of investors (r = 0.58, p < 0.01) and the diversity of different investor types (r = 0.63, p < 0.01) are both significantly associated with a binary variable of VC investment, which suggests that the latter also proxies well for more qualitative network effects. As concerns the dependent variable of the analysis, acquisition was measured as a binary variable taking the value of 1 if a firm in the sample was acquired until the end of the first quarter of 2013 (i.e. within the full seven years after the original survey) and 0 if not. Because measurement of actual acquisition was independent from the initial survey common method bias and endogeneity issues are minimised. For the multivariate survival analysis of the above hypotheses, the binary variable was transformed to a survival measure as described below. Furthermore, a number of explanatory variables were derived from the literature [12]. These include the logarithm of the number of citation-weighted patents held by the respondents, whether a startup originated out of a university research context and a binary variable of whether or not the firms perceived their innovation to be organisationally radical. Since significant positive correlation of the number of patents and a product innovation index exists, the patenting information is seen as a reliable measure with high content and discriminant validity for technological radicality [13].

Given recent methodological research has shown that an adequate sample size required for a factor analysis crucially depends on the quality of the data (in turn rendering general rules of thumb for minimum sample sizes largely invalid), we make use of an exploratory factor analysis on different items (derived from extant literature) for the reasons why larger firms did not carry out an innovation carried out by our respondents [14]. From this, factors on 'low risk-taking/day-to-day business', 'low fit/existing customers' and 'new/lacking skills' were derived and included as a control variables for differences across firms and respondents (as concerns perceptions) in different versions of the model (see [15] for details on the factors). 63% of the total variation in the data is explained by these three factors with Eigenvalues greater than unity. Other variables used in the multivariate regression are the age of the firm and its squared term, and whether or not a responding firm received VC investment. To test the above hypotheses the time until acquisition is recorded as the number of years (i.e. a discrete time interval) and the survival analysis is done using the xi:logit command of STATA, after expanding the survey. Of interest in the analysis is the probability of a firm being acquired at a time T, with the discrete time hazard rate function being:

$$h(T \mid X) = \frac{1}{1 + \exp(-\vec{\alpha}\vec{\delta} - \vec{\beta}\vec{X} - \varepsilon)}$$

With $h(T\mid X)$ being defined the hazard rate for periods T with T = 0 .. 8. $\vec{\delta}$ is a vector of period dummy variables which assume unity in the indicated year and zero in all other years, $\vec{\alpha}$ denotes the hazard rate of the corresponding period. $\vec{\beta}$ refers to a set of coefficients of the of time-constant and time-varying covariates $\vec{X}$ of the model (i.e. the explanatory control variables described earlier). Finally ε denotes the error term.

4   Results

Table 1 provides the results for the survival from applying survival models described in [16]. The models, reported in Table 1 (with robust standard errors in brackets) shows that VC investment has a significant positive and that organizational radicality has a significant negative effect on survival. This confirms H1 and H2 and also the relevance of capital access found in [2, 3], as well as the role of more radical innovation [10], as concerns the special case of organizationally radical innovation. The effect of the latter is also, as hypothesized, moderated by VC investment, i.e. venture capitalists remain invested longer in startups with organizationally radical innovation. This shows that VC investment only in combination with the latter (i.e. innovation that destroys competencies or architectural knowledge) increases time to acquisition. It also indicates a more modest role to VC and differentiates compared to earlier literature like [1], [12].

Table 1. Survival Analysis of Determinants for Time to Acquisition

Explanatory variable	Model 1	Model 2	Model 3
Year 2008	1.32 (1.26)	1.30 (1.27)	1.32 (1.25)
Year 2009	0.29 (1.35)	0.25 (1.40)	0.30 (1.40)
Year 2010	-13.34*** (1.14)	-9.17*** (1.19)	-7.67*** (1.18)
Year 2011	-13.59*** (1.15)	-9.23*** (1.19)	-7.66*** (1.18)
Year 2012	1.30 (1.33)	1.18 (1.37)	1.25 (1.36)
Year 2013	1.51 (1.42)	1.39 (1.43)	1.48 (1.40)
Age	0.01** (0.06)	0.17 (0.34)	0.11 (0.34)
Age squared	-	-0.003 (0.01)	-0.002 (0.01)
Cit.-weight. patents	-0.10 (0.23)	-0.11 (0.22)	-0.10 (0.22)
Org. radicality (yes→no)	-0.64 (1.14)	-0.60 (1.18)	-8.71*** (1.11)
New/lacking skills	0.29 (0.48)	0.32 (0.48)	0.31 (0.49)
VC (no→yes)	2.61** (1.15)	2.65** (1.15)	1.77 (1.11)
Univers. startup (no→yes)	0.42 (1.52)	0.46 (1.568)	0.69 (1.59)
VC x Org. radicality	-	-	8.56*** (1.39)
Constant	-5.47** (2.31)	-7.12 (4.41)	-5.94 (4.34)
Pseudo-R²	0.27	0.27	0.30
Wald χ^2	982.49***	528.65***	591.12***
Number of observations		190	

Notes: * $p<0.10$; ** $p<0.05$; *** $p<0.01$; n=190; years relative to 2007 as base year

Consistent with these findings, Table 2 indicates that entrants themselves only rarely are able to develop a larger market share on their own if they are not acquired at all.

Table 2. Perceived Fate of Startups not acquired in the longer Run

Variable	Frequency	% Firms	% Responses	% Choices
go out of business	17	54.8%	53.1%	50.0%
in market niche	6	51.6%	50.0%	97.1%
merger of equals	1	3.2%	3.1%	100.0%

To further corroborate these results, in a sensitivity analysis also a survival model was analysed, in which more and lesser numbers of explanatory variables were included due to conceptual considerations (specifically, these are as defined in detail in [15] the remaining factors introduced above, whether a general manager responded, firm size (measured in different categories of employee numbers), whether the innovation was economically radical/saving significant cost and the technological breadth of the startup, measured as the number of EDA sub-segments, in which it is active).

Table 3. Sensitivity Analysis of Survival Models in Table 1

Explanatory variable	Model 1	Model 2	Model 3
Year 2008	1.30 (1.28)	1.32 (1.26)	2.40* (1.34)
Year 2009	0.28 (1.44)	0.32 (1.43)	0.90 (1.62)
Year 2010	-18.59*** (1.18)	-7.75*** (1.16)	-7.94*** (2.01)
Year 2011	-8.55*** (1.19)	-7.75*** (1.17)	-9.18*** (2.20)
Year 2012	1.22 (1.39)	1.27 (1.38)	-0.51 (2.27)
Year 2013	1.40 (1.39)	1.45 (1.36)	-1.40 (2.74)
Age	-0.04 (0.33)	-0.09 (0.32)	-2.38* (1.38)
Age squared	0.001 (0.01)	-0.002 (0.01)	0.09*** (0.03)
Citation-weighted patents	-0.12 (0.15)	-0.12 (0.15)	-0.16 (0.74)
Org. radicality (yes→no)	-0.90 (0.92)	-7.95*** (1.04)	-26.41*** (8.43)
New/lacking skills	-	-	2.827** (1.20)
VC (no→yes)	2.48** (1.11)	1.84* (1.11)	15.95** (7.51)
Univers. startup (no→yes)	-	-	-6.20 (5.02)
VC * Org. radicality	-	7.30*** (1.24)	35.72*** (9.20)
Cost-saving innovation	-	-	-0.04 (3.37)
Firm size (employees)	-	-	-7.34 (1.78)
Technology breadth	-	-	-10.20*** (3.04)
General manager	-	-	17.78*** (5.84)
Low risk/day-to-day bus.	-	-	-4.22** (2.02)
Low fit/existing customers	-	-	-2.23 (1.76)
Constant	-4.44** (3.39)	-3.27 (3.31)	5.48 (23.66)
Pseudo-R²	0.25	0.27	0.59
Wald χ²	507.87***	552.08***	359.65***
Number of observations		190	

Notes: * $p<0.10$; ** $p<0.05$; *** $p<0.01$; n=190; years relative to 2007 as base year; A model corresponding to the specification of Model 1 in Table 1 is available and provided on request.

As can be seen from Table 3 reporting the results for this survival analysis, the years 2010 and 2011 have again a significant negative association with firm survival and also the other significant effects remain unchanged in all different survival model variants applied for this sensitivity test, especially the interaction effect of VC and radicality.

5   Conclusions and Discussion

The overarching question of this paper is what affects the time it takes until a firm is acquired, i.e. what affects the temporal survival of a firm? Three hypotheses on the effects of VC, organisationally radical innovation and their interaction were derived and confirmed. This suggests that venture capitalists mainly hold longer on to investments in firms that have organisationally radical innovation, whilst the latter leads to even quicker acquisition once the interaction with VC is accounted for. Additionally the years 2009 and 2010 have a significant negative association with the survival rate. The lower survival rates (i.e. increased acquisitions) in these years are due venture capitalists opting for trade sales and since large firms as acquirers are not credit rationed. As concerns threats to validity the interaction of venture capital and organizationally radical innovation could cause multicollinearity in the data. However, since its correlation with all other 13 variables used across all specifications is on all occasions below 0.52, this is not the case. Given the limits to statistical tests for representativeness, replication of the results reported here in larger EDA industry samples should be demonstrated to corroborate these. Also, whilst EDA is illustrative for pre-packaged software, analyses of other software-based sectors are desirable to confirm the generalizability of the findings reported here beyond the EDA industry.

References

1. Gans, J.S., Hsu, D.H., Stern, S.: When does startup innovation spur the gale of creative destruction? RAND J. of Econom. 33(4), 571–586 (2000)
2. Evans, D.S., Leighton, L.S.: The determinants of changes in US self-employment, 1968-1987. Small Business Economics 1, 111–119 (1989)
3. Taylor, M.P.: Survival of the fittest? An analysis of self-employment duration in Britain. Economic Journal 109, C140–C155 (1999)
4. Phillips, B.D., Kirchhoff, B.A.: Formation, growth and survival: small firm dynamics in the US economy. Small Business Economics 1, 65–74 (1989)
5. Cooper, A.C.: Entrepreneurship and high tech. In: Sexton, D., Smilor, R. (eds.) The Art and Science of Entrepreneurship, Ballinger, Cambridge, pp. 153–168 (1986)
6. Westhead, P., Cowling, M.: Employment change in independent owner-managed high-technology firms in Great Britain. Small Business Economics 7, 111–140 (1995)
7. Lin, Z., Picot, G., Compton, J.: The entry and exit dynamics of self-employment in Canada. Small Business Economics 15, 105–125 (2000)
8. Agarwal, R.: Small firm survival and technological activity. Small Business Economics 11, 215–224 (1998)

9. Audretsch, D., Mahmood, T.: New firm survival: new results using a hazard function. Review of Economics and Statistics 6, 97–103 (1995)
10. Cosh, A.D., Hughes, A., Wood, E.: Innovation in UK SMEs: causes and consequences for firm failure and acquisitions. In: Acs, Z., Carlsson, B. (eds.) Enterpreneurship, SMEs and the Macro Economy, Cambridge University Press, Cambridge (1999)
11. Lee, A.S., Baskerville, R.L.: Generalizing Generalizability in Information Systems Research. Information Systems Research 14(3), 221–243 (2003)
12. Wagner, M.: Growth of university-based start-ups and acquisition as an exit strategy in academic entrepreneurship evidence from software-based ventures. Int. J. of Entrepreneurship and Small Business 12(4), 39–412 (2011)
13. Romijn, H., Albaladejo, M.: Determinants of innovation capability in small electronics and software firms in southeast England. Research Policy 31, 1053–1067 (2002)
14. MacCallum, R.C., Widaman, K.F., Zhang, S., Hong, S.: Sample size in factor analysis. Psychological Methods 4, 84–99 (1999)
15. Wagner, M.: Acquisitions as a means of innovation sourcing by incumbents and growth of technology-oriented ventures. International J. of Tech. Management 52, 118–134 (2010)
16. Rabe-Hesketh, R., Skrondal, A.: Multilevel and longitudinal modeling using Stata. Stata Press, College Station (2008)

Lean Software Startup – An Experience Report from an Entrepreneurial Software Business Course

Antero Järvi[✉], Ville Taajamaa, and Sami Hyrynsalmi

Department of Information Technology, University of Turku, Turku, Finland
{antero.jarvi,ville.taajamaa,sthyry}@utu.fi

Abstract. This paper offers blueprints for and reports upon three years experience from teaching the university course "Lean Software Startup" for information technology and economics students. The course aims to give a learning experience on ideation/innovation and subsequent product and business development using the lean startup method. The course educates the students in software business, entrepreneurship, teamwork and the lean startup method. The paper describes the pedagogical design and practical implementation of the course in sufficient detail to serve as an example of how entrepreneurship and business issues can be integrated into a software engineering curriculum. The course is evaluated through learning diaries and a questionnaire, as well as the primary teacher's learnings in the three course instances. We also examine the course in the context of CDIO and show its connection points to this broader engineering education framework. Finally we discuss the challenges and opportunities of engaging students with different backgrounds in a hands-on entrepreneurial software business course.

Keywords: Software entrepreneurship · Education· Software business · Lean startup · CDIO

1   Introduction

Due to the global changes in business landscape, software entrepreneurship is currently a popular and an important topic to teach to students. Recent development in the industry has created the lean startup method that aims to speed up startup evolution and eliminate waste during the process. While the lean startup movement started in the software entrepreneurship domain, its principles are currently spreading to other, more tangible domains. Established companies, such as F-Secure and Tieto in Finland, have founded small startup-like teams inside the corporation to develop products and services for volatile market segments.

There is, however little evidence on how lean startup method works as a teaching tool. Thus, the research objective of this study is to evaluate the usefulness of the lean startup method in incorporating entrepreneurial, business and transferable working life skills into a software engineering project course.

In this paper, we describe the course "Lean Software Startup" that has been taught yearly in Department of Information Technology at the University of Turku, Finland

© Springer International Publishing Switzerland 2015
J.M. Fernandes et al. (Eds.): ICSOB 2015, LNBIP 210, pp. 230–244, 2015.
DOI: 10.1007/978-3-319-19593-3_21

since 2011. In addition to technical students, the course has participants from the business faculty which serves the interdisciplinary goal of the course. The paper presents the used pedagogical strategy and discusses and shares the experiences gained teaching the course during the previous three years. The course design and implementation are discussed in detail so the same principles and structure can be adapted by others.

The rest of the paper is structured as follows. The following section provides a brief introduction to the related concepts as well as motivation for the course and briefly describes related work. Sections 3 and 4 present the design of the course and its evaluation, respectively. The final section concludes the study with discussing challenges and proposing further ideas for development.

2   Background and Motivation

2.1   Customer Development and Principles of Lean Start-Up

Blank [1] presented a model that helps startups to build and improve their success by acquiring a better understanding of their customers. The model consists of the four steps as presented in Fig. 1. The first step aims to identify the customer segments and how they value the problem that the product or service proposal tries to solve (so-called Problem/Solution fit). The second step attempts to prove that there is a market for the product or service proposal that positively response to the problem (so-called Product/Market fit). The third step focuses on scaling the market by creating and driving customer demand. The fourth step aims to transform the startup firm from a learning and discovery organization to a business execution machine. During this course, only the first two steps are addressed.

Fig. 1. Customer Development model (adopted, [1])

In industry, the lean start-up method by Eric Ries [2, 3] is an extremely popular tool for technology start-ups to manage the creation of the new company. The initial model [2] was built on the top of three principles. These are: 1) the use of free and open-source software or cheap software development platforms; 2) the use of Agile software development methodologies; and 3) the use of Blank's [1] Customer Development method. The fourth basic principle to the model, the use of cheap and effective analysis tools, was added in [4]. To summarize, these principles aim to cheaply develop a 'minimum viable product' (MVP) [5] that can be used to empirically test customers' real needs.

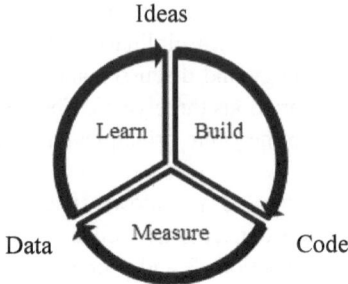

Fig. 2. The Lean Build-Measure-Learn –loop [3]

The lean start-up model has since been redefined by Ries in [3]. The basic philosophy, however, remained the same. In [3], the Build-Measure-Learn -loop (Fig. 2) is raised to a central position in the lean start-up model. The loop guides start-ups to turn ideas into products, measure the customers' response and learn from this data. This process is a fundamental part of the lean start-up method and the process is repeated over and over again. Furthermore, the same learning process is applied not only on the product but also to test the assumptions underlying the business model.

2.2   Related Work

Course, curriculum and teaching methods for research and development have long traditions [6, 7, 8]. Especially in engineering education [9], the achieved learning outcomes, implications of those to curriculum design and to teaching methods are subjects to continuous scientific discourse [10, 11]. Concerning curriculum design and development, the current study concerns a course level approach [9, 12]. With respect to teaching methods, this study focuses on transferable working life skills, action and integrated teaching methods [7, 13]. Research in the field, in this study, is often conducted using action research and case study analysis methods [14].

Related work shows that using these teaching methods that are based on social constructionism and hands on learning, do catalyze the students cognitive learning process at a deeper level [7, 8, 9, 13]. Students not only learn disciplinary knowledge but also relevant and transferable working life skills such as communication skills, teamwork skills, project management and creative product development skills. Typically the challenges in this kind of courses lie in the assessment of the learning outcomes, which are subjective and context-driven. Often the cases cannot be directly compared to other similar studies. Even if the courses share similar structure and intended learning outcomes, the teaching methods or teachers can be different and the identification of differences is difficult whether they are qualitative or quantitative [15, 16]. The value of research based on course development and assessed learning outcomes is especially relevant to practitioners who can reflect their own experiences from course planning, teaching methods development, assessment of learning outcomes and the feedback of all stakeholders to their own praxis [9, 13].

There are similar proposals for using lean start-up methodology, or respective constructions, as a base for an education design. For example, [17] proposes a design for a game development accelerator based on the method. In [18], the authors describe an incubator that, to some limit, meets the principles of lean start-up methodology. Furthermore, some experience reports exist. For example, Bosch et al. [19] tested an extended method with students in a start-up incubator.

Lean Software Startup shares similarities with Capstone courses [7,9-13,15-16]. It follows a product development process with emphasis on early phase iterations and active customer feedback through prototyping. Also the intended learning outcomes include transferable working life skills in addition to disciplinary knowledge.

There are a few proposals for innovative software engineering course with a special focus on entrepreneurship. Björkqvist et al. [20] report experiences on integrating entrepreneurship activities in a large project work course that involves both information systems and computer science students. Daimi and Rayess [21] describe a software entrepreneurship course for computer science students; however, their pedagogical approach is close to traditional lecturing while our pedagogical strategy is based on hands-on learning. Aaen and Rose [22] note that software entrepreneurship courses often utilize a plan-based approach. Thus, they developed a course that allows students to select from plan- based or agile alternatives an option to complete a software entrepreneurship course.

3   Course Design

3.1   Design Goals

The starting point for the course[1] design was to let students experience a product or service development project based on the lean startup method, as realistically as possible in the university environment. The use of a startup context where teams come up with their own business ideas is not an end in itself, but rather a means for achieving a setting where there is uncertainty and thus opportunity for innovation both in terms of product and business. If the customer and the problem were given, which is often the case in software engineering project courses, the learning would be limited to software engineering, project and teamwork skills. In this course we wanted to offer a wider scope. It must be noted that this is not an entrepreneurial course *per se*, but uses the lean startup method as a tool for creating innovative products and related business designs in a customer or user driven manner. It is clearly explained to students that the approach applies to any new product development under considerable uncertainties and risks.

A central principle in this course is that there are no explicit disciplinary knowledge learning goals for the course, thus no predetermined, planned knowledge to assimilate, and also no exam to ensure the learned substance. However, during the course the students will learn and apply theoretical knowledge, techniques and methods, and study various materials. The course has six focus areas:

---

[1] https://nettiopsu.utu.fi/opas/opintojakso.htm?id=34761&lang=en

Working with Customers/Users and Other Stakeholders. The students experience how difficult it can be to learn about customers' problems and how to help the customer understand his/her needs. . The students are responsible for finding and organizing the interaction with customers. They experience the value of talking to real customers. and learn to seek for feedback and take value also from criticism.

Lean Startup Method in Product Development. The students learn the basic ideas of the lean startup process and apply its core learning loop. The students understand that the MVP is a means for validating assumptions about the business being developed. The students experience throwing away code and changing central decisions about the customers, customer value, product and business. The students see how business and product development go forward in parallel.

Practical Software Engineering Skills. The teams choose the development tools and environments according to what is needed and put them to use. Learning new tools and languages is a normal activity during the course.

Working Life Skills. The students experience practical teamwork, will put up communication and collaboration tools as needed, learn to present and pitch their project on several occasions and to different stakeholders. Overall professionalism and taking responsibility is required.

Idea Generation and Business Development. The students learn to see opportunities and generate business ideas. They understand the importance of focusing on customers and problem first and not starting with the solution. They experience how the business idea is refined based on feedback.

Overall Business Knowledge. The students will learn overall business skills and knowledge. These are not however actively taught in the course; instead, these are discussed when the issues arise during the course.

The projects need not, and generally will not, achieve a state where they could be said to be ready and finished. It is more important that the lean startup method is used, the team experiences several rounds of its core learning cycle and the business idea as well as the product is adapted based on this feedback. In essence, the journey is important, not the endpoint.

Team formation is one of the key success factors in the course. Team size has varied during the three course instances but 4-5 members seems to work best, providing for enough skills and workforce to get things done, yet still small enough that all members are engaged, feel responsible and find a role within the team. One of the students acts as a 'team liaison' with a responsibility to keep up with the team's status and to be the connection point with the instructor. However, the team liaison is not a team leader in traditional sense as the teams will organize and manage themselves like agile teams. When the teams are formed, the instructor ensures that all teams have sufficient software engineering and business skills.

3.2   Pedagogical Setting and Learning Environment

A guiding pedagogical principle in this course is that learning happens in the context of doing and experiencing things in practice. Two central pedagogical methods to achieve this are the actual work that the students carry on in teams and weekly team mentoring sessions. Other used methods include introductory lectures, idea generation workshops, progress gates, use of supporting materials, learning logs for self-reflection and a course debriefing in the end.

Teamwork. Similar to a real software-based startup, the students have to work on a wide range of different issues. Examples of tasks that the teams typically face include configuring development environments and tools, designing and implementing the product, designing the user experience, launching the product, contacting potential customers and other stakeholders, getting customer feedback with interviews and product use analysis, learning about the business, making business and product decisions, organizing the teamwork internally, planning and allocating work, *etc*. The teams have practically full freedom to choose what they will work on and how they will work. Many of these things are new to the students and they simply need to learn for what is needed. Often, one of the students has experience in a particular area and the students learn from each other.

Mentoring. Individual one-hour mentoring sessions are held roughly once a week with each team. The sessions serve several purposes. First, in the sessions the instructor can directly give advice, teach relevant theory and point out materials to help the team go forward in a particular situation. Second, the instructor ensures that the lean startup- and customer development methods are being used. Third, the instructor helps the team resolve whatever issues there are that hinder the teamwork, especially in the beginning. It is very important that the instructor does not take the role of an authority that requires weekly progress reports, but rather the role of a more experienced team member. Unless the atmosphere is open and encouraging, the students will not present the true status of the project and ask for help with difficulties they are facing. The instructor does not interfere with the business idea and business development itself, unless it needs to be pushed to a pedagogically more fruitful direction; for instance, out of a customer segment where it would be impossible to reach customers.

Gates. There are four progress gates in the course. At each gate, each team gives a short presentation on their project, followed by comments and discussion by the other teams. The purpose of the gates is first to create structure for the four month long course, second to enable learning between teams and third to provide presentation opportunities for students. The four gates have different focuses: In the first gate the focus is on the initial business idea, team organization and technical development issues. In the second gate the teams focus on customers and stakeholders, value proposition and the first working product (MVP). In the third gate, the teams will explain what feedback they have gathered, what kind of business and product decisions they have taken based on the feedback, and present the evolved MVP. The fourth gate is similar to the third, incorporating one more lean startup learning loop. Whereas the presentations in the previous gates are more traditional, the presentation in the fourth gate is a typical startup business pitch for a wider audience than just course participants.

Lectures and Idea Generation. In the two first weeks there are three to four two hours lectures covering the overall course concept and introducing the main points of central tools used during the course – Ries' lean startup method [3], Blank's customer development [1] and Osterwalders' business model canvas [23]. Opportunity recognition and idea generation techniques are introduced and immediately used in an idea generation workshop, wherein the initial business ideas for the teams are generated.

Deliverables. There are three deliverables in the course, the learning log, the daily diary and the team log, all of them created gradually during the course. There is a checkpoint during the course to make sure all students are actively creating these deliverables. The purpose of all deliverables is explained to students.

The most important deliverable is the learning log, a semi-structured template where the students, once a week, write their perceptions on what they learned during the week (see the template in Appendix A). The primary purpose of the learning log is to make the students think back and reflect upon what they have learnt in the unstructured and sometimes messy work during the week. The secondary purpose is to provide feedback for the course instructor about what the students really learn.

The daily diary is a log where the students make a one line entry every time they work on anything in this course. The entry contains the date, number of hours worked, what did the student work on, and with whom. The primary purpose of this diary is to ensure an even workload between team members.

The team log makes the team's journey visible. Once a week, or more frequently if the team chooses to, the team writes briefly what did they do since the last log entry, what did they learn about their business case, how it affects their assumptions, and what are currently the important concerns that the team will act on next. It has turned out that reading through this log at the end of the course is an invaluable learning experience for the students. It clearly shows the 'searching by experimentation' nature of the lean startup method.

Reflection Discussion. At the end of the course, there is a moderated discussion aiming at providing final emphasis the most important learning goals of the course and providing course feedback for the instructor. This has not worked well due to lack of motivation. The students put a lot of effort into the fourth gate, and once it is passed, they feel that the course is over. This is one of the last activities before the end of semester and that might explain the lack of motivation at this point.

3.3   Course Structure

An example course structure is given in Table 1. The course consists of four parts as described in the table. At our university, a semester is divided into two periods, roughly 7-8 weeks each. The "Lean software startup" course lasts two periods, ending before the summer break. Currently, the course corresponds to 10 ECTS (European Credit Transfer and Accumulation System) credits.

Table 1. The normal structure of the course

Week	Content
Part I: Introduction (all sessions are 90 min).	
Week 1: 1st	Course introduction. Practical issues.
	Lecture: "Concurrent business and product innovation".
Week 1: 2nd	Team formation. Deadline for dropping the course!
	Lecture: "Lean startup basics", "Customer development basics".
Week 2: 1st	Lecture: "Opportunity recognition and business idea generation".
	Idea generation warm-up.
Week 2: 2nd	Idea generation workshop, presenting the ideas.
Part II: The foundations	
Week 3	Team mentoring, individually 60 min / team. Focus on business idea, team organization, project tooling, team organization and management, team roles.
Week 4	Team mentoring. Same as above.
Week 5	Emergency mentoring available by appointment if needed.
	1st Gate: Presentation of the business idea and how the team is organized.
	10 minutes presentation + group discussion.
Part III: Execute	
Week 6	Team mentoring
Week 7	Team mentoring
Week 8	Team mentoring
Week 9	Emergency mentoring available, by appointment – in case a team is in trouble.
	2nd Gate: First product (MVP) demonstration and customer acquisition, evolution of the business idea.
Week 10	Team mentoring
Week 11	Team mentoring
Week 12	Team mentoring
Week 13	Emergency mentoring, again only by appointment
	3rd Gate: Product demonstration (MVP) and customer feedback, evolution of business idea and the product.
Part IV: End game	
Week 14	Team mentoring
Week 15	Team mentoring
Week 16	**4rd Gate**: Demo Day. Business pitch, 5 min., followed by group discussion to share experiences from the last weeks.
Week 17	**Retrospective**: Moderated discussion: What did we learn. Course closing.
Week 18	Deadline for all course deliverables.

4   Evaluation

In the following, we evaluate how well the goals of the course were achieved, using the learning diaries and the self-reported data from the students. The course has been organized three times, first in the autumn semester of 2011–2012 (started in September and ended in December, 2011); second time in the autumn of the academic year 2012–2013 and third time in the spring semester of 2013–2014 (started in January and ended in June, 2014). While the structure of the course has remained the same, there were no business students in the first instance. Therefore, in the evaluation we focus only on the last two instances.

Table 2 shows the number of students that participated in the course in each instance. In addition, there were a few students who enrolled in the course but dropped out the first week of the course.

Table 2. The number of participants in the course by their major disciple

Discipline	Autumn 2012	Spring 2014
Technology	19	16
Business	10	8

To evaluate the implementation of the course, we used the semi-structured learning diaries, the 'learning logs', written by the students during the course as the primary data source. As a secondary data source, we used a questionnaire sent to the participants of the course in December 2014.

As a part of the course, the students were required to write and update a structured, weekly learning log. An example of the structure is given in Appendix A. The shortest learning diaries were 2 pages and the longest 15 pages, the average being 5 pages. The learning diaries were analyzed by the authors by reading them carefully and counting how many times the student had written about learning something in each of the six learning areas. The learning area was given the score 0 if the student had no learning experience on a learning area, score 1 for at least one reported learning experiences, score 2 for repeated reported learning experiences and score 3 for repeated and deep learning experiences. The distinction between scores 2 and 3 is subjective and reflect the difference between how strongly the students described the learning. The averages for each learning area were then calculated, for all students together and separately for technology and business students (Table 3).

Learning Logs. The findings from the learning log data indicate that a moderate to good amount of learning takes place in all learning areas. Furthermore, there was not a single student that reported not learning something in most of the learning areas. Interestingly, both technology and business students experienced the most learning in the "idea generation and business development" area. The possible reason for this is that the students had not previously participated in a hands-on business development course, even though many business students had studied the topic in previous courses. The hands-on nature of the course is seen also in high "work life skills" learning experience. As anticipated, technology students learned more about software engineering, but interestingly this was the only area where there was a notable difference between the two student groups. The "general business knowledge" learning area had the poorest learning outcome.

In the learning log, the students also reported the source of the learning experience (Table 4). These learning sources were analyzed in a similar manner to the learning areas. Unsurprisingly, the team was the most common source, reflecting the constant peer learning during the teamwork. The mentor was also a frequent source for learning which indicates that the mentoring concept is a useful and working pedagogic method. Self was the third frequent source for learning, interestingly more for business students. Two other sources that were probed in the learning logs, customers and other teams, got only sporadic mentions in the reports. It is somewhat surprising that the group discussions in the four gates and frequent contacts with customers and stakeholders did not seem to provoke learning.

Table 3. Learning experiences in learning areas

Learning area	All students	Technology	Business
Working with customers/users/ stakeholders	2.2	2.1	2.3
Lean startup method	1.8	1.9	1.8
Software engineering skills	1.9	2.2	1.5
Working life skills	2.3	2.3	2.3
Idea generation and business development	2.6	2.5	2.6
General business knowledge	1.3	1.3	1.2

Table 4. Sources of learning

Source of learning	All Students	Technology	Business
Self	2.0	1.7	2.4
Team	2.4	2.5	2.4
Mentor	2.3	2.0	2.6
Other teams	0.4	0.6	0.3
Customers	0.6	0.4	0.8

Survey. The results of the survey of the participants of the course are used as the secondary data source. The questionnaire was submitted via e-mail to students who have participated into the course during its previous instances. We targeted only students who were still active at the university and whose university email accounts were working. In total, the questionnaire was sent to 41 students (50% of the total course participants). The students had four weeks to answer the questionnaire. A reminder email was sent after two weeks. Finally, a total of seven usable answers were received, thus yielding the response rate of 17.1%.

While the learning diaries were written during the course, we were keen to see how the attitudes of the students changed awhile after the course. None of the respondents continued the project after the course. Four respondents reported that they have had discussion with their teams on the continuance of the course work towards a commercial product. However, they deemed that the idea or the team were not mature enough. Nevertheless, all answerers had a positive attitude towards founding their own software firm and working as an entrepreneur.

In almost every feedback, the teacher was mentioned as one of the most important source for learning. As noted by one business student majoring in Marketing:

> *"The thing that I liked the most in this course was how involved the teacher was in our work. This is really the only course where I think I could learn through one on one interaction if thesis courses don't count."*

Furthermore, both technology and business students praised the collaboration over the faculty borders. This was often mentioned as a learning outcome in the course.

"Teamwork with Software Engineers (it is really different than Teamwork with only other Business students)..." – Marketing major.

5   Discussion

5.1   Experiences

The overall experience of the teacher in the three course instances is positive; the course is inspiring and even fun to teach. Most students are committed, enthusiastic and hardworking, and the student feedback is good. Clearly the course succeeds in engaging the students and thus provides a good foundation for learning. However, despite the word 'startup' in the course title, and words 'entrepreneurial' and 'software business' in the title of this paper, we would not consider this as a full entrepreneurship course, nor as a software business course. Rather, the course combines some elements from both themes into an intensive, multifaceted learning experience.

On the entrepreneurial theme, the students experience working and making decisions under uncertainty, taking responsibility on issues outside of their current skills, experience failing and learning from it, and gain insight into the entrepreneurial attitude.

On the software business theme, the students get to design business models. However, the discussions, designs and experiments concerned only the value proposition, distribution and marketing channels, customer segments and revenue models, thus providing a somewhat narrow view on software business development.

As a third theme, the students get to experience on experimental, user and customer driven innovation process that we believe is becoming widely used in cases where both the product and the distribution channel are digital.

5.2   Challenges

One of the challenges, noted during the execution of the course, is the requirements that a multidisciplinary course imposes upon the primary teacher. The teacher needs to understand and be able to help both in business related and in technological issues. In our implementation, the teacher had a decade of experience of teaching software engineering as well as experience with running his own startups. This greatly helped to transfer the knowledge to the students; however, as a downside, the course is highly dependent on a single teacher and increases his workload. A second teacher with business background and specialization at software startups was also present in the four gates and gave invaluable insights – mainly on the business ideas and their potential and flaws. Getting a fresh, second opinion was clearly beneficial for the students.

This kind of course is also challenging for students, who in previous courses, have mainly been required to solve clearly defined problems. This course requires a different mindset: As a team, they need to (by themselves) identify what must be done, learn the required knowledge and skills and solve the problems. Frequent mentoring sessions with the teacher in the first weeks of the course were extremely important to the students.

Unsurprisingly, one of the major challenges in the course is the team formation. The objective is to have sufficient business and technical skills in every team. This has not always succeeded. In two cases the technical skills in a team turned out to be insufficient which was handled by swapping student volunteers between two teams. Lack of business skills has not been a problem. Either the commitment of business students has been higher or technical students have been able to learn business issues easily and contribute to business side as well.

5.3   Engineering Professional: CDIO

We also examine the Lean Software Startup course in the context of the CDIO (Conceive–Design–Implement–Operate) engineering education structure and find four shared objectives and similarities that can be explicitly identified across the two.

The CDIO engineering education framework and structure was originally designed to better equip graduating engineers with transdisciplinary and scalable working life skills such as communication, project management, teamwork, and problem solving capabilities in addition to the actual disciplinary knowledge and skills [9, 13, 24]. This structure and framework level intended learning outcome is also the first joint surface boundary with CDIO framework and Lean Software Startup course [25, 26, 27].

The CDIO framework is based on 12 standards that emphasize a focus on learning outcomes instead of taught content, versatile assessment of learning, integrated curriculum, active learning and the learning of the engineering problem solving cycle: Conceive, Design, Implement and Operate which is also where the acronym CDIO derives from [27]. Entrepreneurial practices based on iterative engineering problem solving cycles such as that used the in the course "Lean Software Startup" are very much aligned with the CDIO framework and learning philosophy with a) emphasis on integrated curriculum, b) active learning methods, which emphasizes learning by doing, c) teamwork setting, d) and design-implement experiences, which are an essential part of both the CDIO as well as the Lean Software Startup course. This is the second joint boundary surface.

The third similarity and shared objective in this course and in CDIO is the emphasis Problem Based Learning (PBL) as the learning approach. The students actively construct knowledge coached and facilitated by the teaching team in a hands-on learning environment [6, 15, 29] instead of traditional lecturing where the teacher transmits information or his own interpretations of knowledge to the passively listening students.

The fourth explicit joint surface boundary [9, 11] between CDIO and Lean Software Startup course is the societal impact at which it is targeted. Lean Software Startup course catalyzes students' innovation skills and the construction and adaption of knowledge needed in the challenges of future industries as well as the building of global societies.

6   Conclusion

This paper presented the blueprint for the "Lean software startup" course that is built upon the customer development and lean startup methods. We reported the used course design and pedagogical strategy and evaluated the course with students' learning logs and with a short survey. The results show that this kind of a course can teach software engineering, software business and entrepreneurship skills to software engineering and business students. The course design relies on hands-on learning in multidisciplinary teams, which has been praised by the participants. No course is perfect and we will continue to develop the course in future. Furthermore, we call for experience reports, course designs and education evaluation by software business and entrepreneurship teachers to share knowledge and to further develop the field of software business education.

References

[1] Blank, S.: The Four Steps to the Epiphany: Successful Strategies for Products that Win, 2nd edn. Cafepress.com, San Mateo (2005)

[2] Ries, E.: The lean startup, http://www.startuplessonslearned.com/2008/09/lean-startup.html (accessed on April 7, 2013)

[3] Ries, E.: The Lean Startup: How Today's Entrepreneurs Use Continuous Innovation to Create Radically Successful Businesses, 1st edn. Crown Business, New York (2011)

[4] Cooper, B., Vlaskovits, P.: The Entrepreneur's Guide to Customer Development. CooperVlaskovits, USA (2010)

[5] Ries, E.: Minimum Viable Product: a guide, http://www.startuplessonslearned.com/2009/08/ minimum-viable-product-guide.html (accessed on April 7, 2013)

[6] Daniels, M.: Developing and Assessing Professional Competencies: a Pipe Dream? Digital Comprehensive Summaries of Uppsala Dissertations from Faculty of Science and Technology 738, AUU (2011)

[7] Leifer, L.J., Steinert, M.: Dancing with ambiguity: Causality behavior, design thinking, and triple-loop-learning. Information Knowledge Systems Management 10, 151–173 (2011)

[8] Froyd, J.E., Wankat, P.C., Smith, K.A.: Five Major Shifts in 100 Years of Engineering Education. Proceedings of IEEE 100, 1344–1360 (2012)

[9] Crawley, E.F., Malmqvist, J., Östlund, S., Brodeur, D.R.: Rethinking Engineering Education, The CDIO Approach. Springer, USA (2007)

[10] Dym, C.L., Rossmann, J.S., Sheppard, S.D.: On Designing Engineering Education: Lessons Learned at Mudd Design Workshop IV. Int. J. Engng. Ed. 20, 470–474 (2004)

[11] Wesner, J.W.: What We Have Learned in Mudd Design Workshop V: Learning and Engineering Design. Int. J. Engng. Ed. 22, 685–688 (2006)

[12] Edström, K., Kolmos, A.: PBL and CDIO: complementary models for engineering education development. European Journal of Engineering Education 39, 539–555 (2014)

[13] Atman, C.J., Sheppard, S.D., Turns, J., Adams, R.S., Fleming, L.N., Stevens, R., Streveler, R.A., Smith, K.A., Miller, R.L., Leifer, L.J., Yasuhara, K., Lund, D.: Enabling Engineering Student Success: The Final Report for the Center for the Advancement of Engineering Education. Morgan & Claypool Publishers, San Rafael (2010)

[14] Eisenhardt, K.M.: Building Theories from Case Study Research. Academy of Management Review 14, 532–550 (1989)
[15] Taajamaa, V., Sjöman, H., Kirjavainen, S., Utriainen, T., Repokari, L., Salakoski, T.: Dancing with Ambiguity – Design thinking in interdisciplinary engineering education. In: Design Thinking Conference, Shenzhen, China (2013)
[16] Taajamaa, V., Westerlund, T., Liljeberg, P., Salakoski, T.: Interdisciplinary Capstone Project. In: 41th SEFI Conference, Leuven, Belgium (2013)
[17] Järvi, A., Mäkilä, T., Hyrynsalmi, S.: Game Development Accelerator – Initial Design and Research Approach. In: Proceedings of From Start-ups to SaaS Conglomerate: Life Cycles of Software Products Workshop, Potsdam, Germany, pp. 47–58 (2013)
[18] Callele, D., Boyer, A., Brown, K., Wnuk, K., Penzestadler, B.: Requirements Engineering as a Surrogate for Business Case Analysis in a Mobile Applications Startup Context. In: Proceedings of From Startups to SaaS Conglomerate: Life Cycles of Software Products Workshop, Potsdam, Germany, pp. 33–46 (2013)
[19] Bosch, J., Olsson, H.H., Björk, J., Ljungblad, J.: The Early Stage Software Startup Development Model: A Framework for Operationalizing Lean Principles in Software Startups. In: Fitzgerald, B., Conboy, K., Power, K., Valerdi, R., Morgan, L., Stol, K.-J. (eds.) LESS 2013. LNBIP, vol. 167, pp. 1–15. Springer, Heidelberg (2013)
[20] Björkqvist, J., Petre, L., Rönnholm, K., Truscan, D.: Integrating Innovation Activities in a Master Level Capstone Project Course. In: International Conference on Engineering Education. Research reports 38. Turku University of Applied Science, pp. 1065–1072 (2012)
[21] Daimi, K., Rayess, N.: The Role of Software Entrepreneurship in Computer Science Curriculum. In: Proc. International Conference on Frontiers in Education: Computer Science and Computer Engineering (FECS 2008), Las Vegas, Nevada, pp. 53–62 (2008)
[22] Aaen, I., Rose, J.: A Software Entrepreurship Course – Between two paradigms. In: 15th Annual Interdisciplinary Entrepreneurship Conference. St. Gallen and Zurich (2011)
[23] Osterwalder, Y., Pigneur, Y.: Business Model Generation: A Handbook for Visionaries, Game Changers, and Challengers, 1st edn. Wiley (2010)
[24] Taajamaa, V., Westerlund, T., Liljeberg, P., Salakoski, T.: Interdisciplinary Capstone Project. In: 41th SEFI Conference, Leuven, Belgium (2013)
[25] Levina, N., Vaast, E.: The Emergence of Boundary Spanning Competence in Practice: Implications for Implementation Technology 738, AUU (2011)
[26] Couto, V., Mani, M., Lewin, A.Y., Peeters, C.: The Globalization of White-Collar Work: The Facts and Fallout of Next-Generation Offshoring. Booz Allen Hamilton Inc. (2006)
[27] Levina, N., Vaast, E.: Innovating or Doing as Told? Status Differences and Overlapping Boundaries in Offshore Collaboration. MIS Quarterly 32, 307–332 (2008)
[28] http://www.cdio.org/implementing-cdio/standards/12-cdio-standards
[29] Savin-Baden, M.: Problem-Based Learning in Higher Education: Untold Stories. The Society for Research into Higher Education and Open University Press, Buckingham (2000)

Appendix A   A Template for a Structure Learning Log

Learning Log

You do not have to answer to all questions every week, only when you have something to say. However it is important that you use this learning log as a weekly "check list", think and reflect back every question.

Please start any of your comments by entry Wxx where xx is the week number. There is an example in the third question how your log should eventually look like... so you are supposed to just use a single learning log document, not one for each week.

The learning log serves two purposes:

— Thinking through what you have learned in an unstructured work amplifies your learning (there is clear scientific evidence on this :-)
— Feedback for the course instructor on how this type of course could be improved

The Questions

1. What inspired you this week?
2. What was surprising?
3. What did you learn about entrepreneurship/business development?
   W38 Business ideas need only to be good enough to get started; the idea will evolve as learning about the customers, product, markets etc. takes place.
   W39 Long and detailed business plans do not work as tools for developing a business.
   W39 Osterwalder's business plan canvas as a tool for business development, just the idea.
4. What did you learn about product development?
5. What did you learn about software technology?
6. What did you learn about software engineering development practices / tools?
7. Comments on teamwork, good or bad. Anything that worked well or did not?
8. Where did most of the learning come from, from the mentor, your team fellows or you? Anything specifically worth mentioning?
9. Free comments

Software Engineering Knowledge Areas in Startup Companies: A Mapping Study

Eriks Klotins[(⊠)], Michael Unterkalmsteiner, and Tony Gorschek

Blekinge Institute of Technology, SE-37179, Karlskrona, Sweden
{eriks.klotins,michael.unterkalmsteiner,tony.gorschek}@bth.se

Abstract. *Background* – Startup companies are becoming important suppliers of innovative and software intensive products. The failure rate among startups is high due to lack of resources, immaturity, multiple influences and dynamic technologies. However, software product engineering is the core activity in startups, therefore inadequacies in applied engineering practices might be a significant contributing factor for high failure rates. *Aim* – This study identifies and categorizes software engineering knowledge areas utilized in startups to map out the state-of-art, identifying gaps for further research. *Method* – We perform a systematic literature mapping study, applying snowball sampling to identify relevant primary studies. *Results* – We have identified 54 practices from 14 studies. Although 11 of 15 main knowledge areas from SWEBOK are covered, a large part of categories is not. *Conclusions* – Existing research does not provide reliable support for software engineering in any phase of a startup life cycle. Transfer of results to other startups is difficult due to low rigor in current studies.

Keywords: Startup · Software engineering · Mapping · Engineering practice · Agile · Lean · Small companies · Development of software intensive products

1 Introduction

Recent developments in technologies have created an increasing demand for innovative software products. Startup companies are addressing this need and gain importance as suppliers of software-intensive products and innovation. The inherent nature of software enables small companies to produce and launch software products fast with few resources. However, most of startup companies fail before realizing any significant achievements [11]. Partially this is due to market factors or financial issues, however the impact of software product engineering and inadequacies in applied engineering practices is not fully explored, and might be a significant contributing factor for the high failure rates.

Chorev et al. [8] identify 16 key factors for a successful startup, such as political and economical environment, marketing, idea, funding and product development among others. Many authors [2, 3, 8, 12, 26, 41] address general issues of startups.

© Springer International Publishing Switzerland 2015
J.M. Fernandes et al. (Eds.): ICSOB 2015, LNBIP 210, pp. 245–257, 2015.
DOI: 10.1007/978-3-319-19593-3_22

Only a few focus on how software engineering is done in startups. Yau et al. argue that scaled down engineering practices solve problems present in larger, established companies while ignoring specific challenges that emerge only in startup companies, stating that different approaches altogether are needed for software engineering in the context of startups [20].

In this paper we aim at identifying software-intensive product engineering practices utilized in startup companies and mapping them to Software Engineering Body of Knowledge (SWEBOK) [31] knowledge areas and categories, describing both state-of-the art, and gaps in research on startup software engineering. Furthermore, to analyze how identified software engineering knowledge areas support the startup life cycle we use the four phase model proposed by Crowne [11] and map identified knowledge areas to different phases in the startup life-cycle. By use of these well-established taxonomies [2], [10] we show state-of-the-art and expose gaps for further research, but with a clear and distinct focus on the software engineering perspective.

This paper is structured as follows. Section 2 gives an overview of the field and motivates the study. Section 3 details the research methodology we applied to identify and map relevant papers. Section 4 reports results from the mapping. Section 5 answers the research questions and discusses the results. Section 6 concludes the paper.

2   Background and Related Work

A startup company shares many features with small or medium enterprises such as youth, market pressure and dynamic technologies [33]. However startups are different due to their aim and the challenges they face [33]. In contrast to established companies, who regardless of their size focus on optimizing an existing business model, startups focus of finding one [26]. Sutton [33] defines a startup as an organization that is challenged by youth and immaturity, extremely limited resources, multiple influences and dynamic technologies and markets.

Crowne [11] had proposed a four phase start-up life-cycle model. Successfully transferring from first phase to the last indicates that a startup has become an established company. The model identifies distinct challenges at each phase that a start-up must address to advance to the next stage. We seek to identify knowledge areas supporting transfer trough start-up life cycle by addressing challenges identified by Crowne [11].

Paternoster et al. [23] conducted a mapping study to characterize state-of the-art research in startups. They conclude that only a minority of studies in the area are dedicated to (software) engineering, and since 2000 when this gap was first identified [33] it has been only partially filled.

Coleman et al. [9] conducted a grounded theory study to explore how software processes are formed in a startup. This study concludes that there is not enough resources to explore the best way to develop the software and startups use whatever software process that supports their immediate business objective. Consequently, the development process is heavily influenced by previous experiences of a person acting as development manager [9].

Pino et al. [25] conducted a systematic review on software process improvement (SPI) in small and medium organizations. The study is aimed at discovering what approaches to SPI in small-medium companies exist. Although their study was not aimed at startup organizations, they conclude that prescriptive approaches, such as CMM and SPICE, are not suitable for small organizations. Therefore, they emphasize the need for more lightweight and tailored approaches.

Several startup specific process models have addressed this need. For example, LIPE [40] addresses immaturity, ad-hoc approaches and scalability of engineering processes. ESSDM [4] proposes an iterative approach to build and validate multiple product ideas simultaneously. The Helical model [13] supports innovation by experimentation of multiple product ideas, frequent releases and synchronization with other organizational processes.

Software Engineering Body of Knowledge (SWEBOK) characterizes content of software engineering discipline and promotes consistent view to software engineering. SWEBOK is organized in 15 main knowledge areas; each knowledge area is organized in sub-categories. Although, SWEBOK is not specifically aimed at startups it is widely recognized within software engineering community [31].

To understand the degree to which research supports software engineering in startups, it is useful to map existing studies. One recent contribution is the mapping study by Paternoster et al. [23], describing research on startups and providing a characterization of software development in the startup context. However, their work does not classify the identified work practices such that it can be understood what software engineering problem is actually addressed. In contrast, our study aims at identifying and classifying software engineering knowledge areas in startup companies, enabling a) analysis and improvement of existing practices and b) revealing opportunities for further investigation.

3   Research Methodology

The mapping process consists of three activities: identification of relevant publications, data extraction, and data mapping. We identify relevant publications by an emerging systematic literature review method – snowball sampling [38]. For data mapping we follow the recommendations by Petersen et al. [24].

3.1   Research Questions

Our study is driven by the goal to understand to what extent engineering in startup companies is supported by research. To pursue this goal we seek answers to the following research questions:

RQ1: What is state-of-practice in terms of utilization of software engineering knowledge areas in startups?

RQ2: What is the relevance and rigor of the studies reporting experiences from software engineering in startups?

In order to structure the identified practices into knowledge areas, as well as identify gaps in knowledge (RQ1) we use SWEBOK [31] as a software engineering dictionary. Although SWEBOK was not created for startups, we lack alternatives, and SWEBOK is considered the accepted SE subject area overview [6, 28]. To provide an account whether the practices can be transferred to industry (RQ2) we assess rigor and relevance [17] of the identified studies.

3.2   Mapping Study Design Overview

Identification of Primary Studies: We used snowball sampling [38], defining the starting set from an earlier and broader mapping study on startups [23]. We performed only forward snowball sampling from the starting set, as earlier papers are likely to be covered by the previous study by Paternoster et al. [23].

We screened the sampled papers to select studies that report on primary research focused on software engineering practices in startups. At first, for each paper we applied a sanity check filtering out duplicates, non-English and non-peer-reviewed papers. We used titles and abstracts for screening; in ambiguous cases, we read the full text. The screening criteria are summarized in table 1.

Table 1. Screening criteria

Inclusion criteria	Notes	Examples of excluded papers
A paper reports primary research	With primary research we understand studies that provide direct evidence about the research question [16].	[15, 34]
A paper reports a study in a startup company	We have used definition by Sutton [33] to differentiate between startups and established companies.	[22, 32]
A paper addresses software engineering	We use SWEBOK [31] to identify software engineering topics	[34, 37]
A paper addresses a challenge or a practice	With practice we identify use of a methodology, routine, tool or framework pertaining software engineering. With challenge we understand difficulty to achieve intended product quality, scope, budget or time constraints	[10]

We used Google Scholar to identify referencing papers, i.e. to perform forward snowball sampling. The first author performed the screening of papers. Results of the process were organized in a spreadsheet that was reviewed by the second and third author.

Data Extraction: Post identification of relevant studies data extraction was performed with the primary goal to extract information indicating which knowledge areas are explored in the study. We also extracted information pertaining to rigor – context description, description of study design, validity discussion, and relevance – information on subjects, study context, scale and research method according to the assessment method by Ivarsson et al. [17].

3.3   Analysis

To answer our first research question (RQ1: What is state-of-practice in terms of utilization of software engineering knowledge areas in startups?) we map the extracted practices to SWEBOK [31]   knowledge areas and categories. In the mapping, we keep track on coverage – how many of knowledge areas and categories are covered by evidence. Coverage, or lack of it, reveals gaps in current research. We also use startup life cycle model by Crowne [11] to identify to what extent state-of-practice covers all four phases of startup life cycle.

To answer our second research question (RQ2: What is the relevance and rigor of the studies reporting experiences from software engineering in startups?) we synthesize rigor, relevance and research type, and analyze number of cases per study.

3.4   Threats to Validity

Systematic reviews have a generic bias towards positive results as they get published more often [5]. However, we do not consider this as a major threat as we especially aim to identify gaps and do not address the performance of individual practices. Another generic threat to mapping studies using snowball sampling is related to the quality of the starting set [38]. As a starting set we have selected the 43 studies identified by Paternoster et al. [23]. The set covers a rather broad period from 1994 to 2013, includes both journal and conference papers from multiple publishing venues. Thus, the starting set follows all guidelines set forth by Wohlin [38].

We focused on forward snowball sampling, as earlier studies are likely to be covered by the previous mapping study by Paternoster et al. [23]. Nevertheless, we performed a backward iteration on the final set of papers to reduce the risk of missing important studies. As a result, 241 papers were discovered. Subsequent screening identified one [20] relevant study. Furthermore, we have conducted a review of gray literature to screen further information pertaining to our research questions. This resulted in one more paper [12], which we did however not include in the further analysis because the described practices are already reported in other, peer-reviewed, studies.

Threats to study selection are addressed by explicit inclusion and exclusion criteria, and a detailed screening protocol. Explicit extraction templates guided the data extraction process, thus ensuring uniformity of the extracted data. To avoid bias set by personal opinions of the researchers executing the study, ambiguous cases were discussed among the authors.

4   Results

As a result of the snowball sampling, we identified 558 papers, 14 of them passed the screening process and were included for further analysis. The reasons for exclusion break down to the following: 80 duplicates, 17 not written in the English, 126 not peer reviewed (books, keynotes, blogs etc.), 354 not focused on startups, 50 not addressing software engineering, 7 not describing a practice or challenge, 32 not available in full text.

From the relevant papers we extracted 54 practices distributed among 11 of the 15 software engineering knowledge areas. Table 2 summarizes the identified primary studies and respective SWEBOK knowledge areas. The coverage column shows how many second level categories are covered by the papers (e.g. 6/8 means that two categories out of total of eight in SWEBOK were not covered at all).

Table 2. Knowledge areas and relevant papers

Knowledge Area (KA)	Coverage	Covered categories
Software Requirements	6/8	Requirements Process [14] Requirements Elicitation [1, 29] Requirements Analysis [35] Requirements Validation [1, 29] Practical Considerations [19, 20]
Software Design	4/8	Software Design Fundamentals [1, 14, 29] Key Issues in Software Design [18] User Interface Design [1, 21, 30, 35] Software Design Tools [1, 35]
Software Construction	3/5	Software Construction Fundamentals [7, 21, 29, 30, 36] Managing Construction [7] Practical Considerations [21]
Software Testing	2/6	Software Testing Fundamentals [18] Test Process [19, 35]
Software Maintenance	1/5	Techniques for Maintenance [29]
Software Configuration Management	3/7	Software Configuration Identification [1] Software Release Management and Delivery [1, 19, 29] Software Configuration Management Tools [29]
Software Engineering Management	3/7	Software Project Planning [18, 29] Software Project Enactment [39] Software Engineering Management Tools [27]
Software Engineering Process	2/5	Software Process Measurement Techniques [20] Software Engineering Process Tools [1]

Table 2. (*Continued*)

Software Engineering Models and Methods	2/4	Modeling [1] Software Engineering Methods [1, 13, 14, 21, 29]
Software Quality	1/4	Software Quality [18]
Software Engineering Professional Practice	2/3	Professionalism [1] Communication Skills [1, 19, 21]
Software Engineering Economics	0/5	
Computing Foundations	0/17	
Mathematical Foundations	0/11	
Engineering Foundations	0/7	

One of the main goals of research on startups is the transfer and widespread use of the results [17]. Potential for transfer can be judged by measuring rigor and relevance. The results reveal that most papers have high relevance, as they report studies performed in actual startups. However, the rigor of these papers is low as they lack contextual descriptions as well as in what manner the study was designed and executed. Figure 1 summarizes contribution type, rigor and relevance.

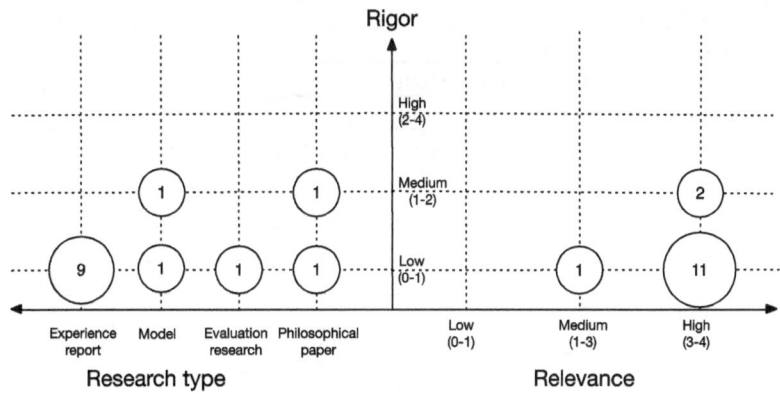

Fig. 1. Overview of research type, rigor and relevance distribution

As shown in figure 1, left side, the majority of the discovered papers are experience reports with low rigor, indicating a rather weak presentation of study design, industrial context and validity threats. The right side of figure 1 shows that the majority of the identified papers present results relevant for industry. The reported studies are conducted in a real industry environment, on a representative scale and are utilizing empirical research methods.

A study that investigates more than one case and compares findings among multiple cases provides more generalizability. We extracted the number of cases studied per paper and mapped them to publishing year in figure 2.

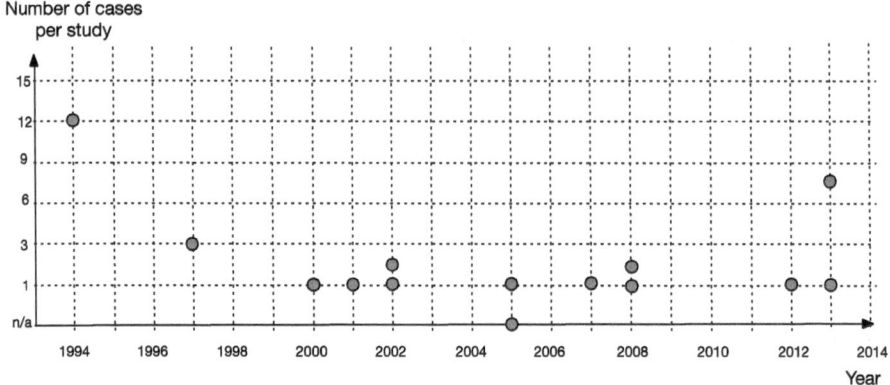

Fig. 2. Publishing years and number of cases per report

Table 3 summarizes the extracted publishing venues. A majority of the studies (60%) are published as conference papers.

Table 3. Publishing venues

Publishing venue	Papers
IEEE Software	[1, 7, 30]
XP Conference	[29]
HCI International Conference	[35]
Lean Enterprise Software and Systems	[4]
International Journal of Project Management	[13]
International Conference on eXtreme Programming and Agile Processes in Software Engineering	[14]
Canadian Society for the Study of Education conference	[19]
Pacific Northwest Software Quality Conference	[18]
Agile conference	[21]
IEEE Computer	[36]
Americas Conference on Information Systems	[27]
SOFTWARE PROCESS—Improvement and Practice	[20]

5   Analysis and Discussion

5.1   RQ1: What is State-of-Practice in Terms of Utilization of Software Engineering Knowledge Areas in Startups?

The mapping of practices to SWEBOK (table 2) shows that the majority of the main knowledge areas (11 out of 15) are addressed. However, a more detailed analysis reveals that only 28 of 62 categories from the knowledge areas are covered. One could argue that some of the knowledge areas, for example Mathematical Foundations knowledge area (KA), may be of less interest for startups or some categories could be more relevant than others. To better understand which knowledge areas and categories are more relevant for startups, we use Crowne's model of the startup life cycle [11].

We use Crowne's startup life-cycle model, in combination with the knowledge areas proposed by SWEBOK [31], to analyze whether the state-of-practice addresses software engineering challenges relevant for startups and to what extent such support is still lacking.

During the *startup* phase in Crowne's model, a company aims to build the first version of a product [11]. Understanding and communicating the needs of the target audience, and defining a development scope establish the foundation for further software engineering. The Requirements Engineering KA aims to support activities related to understanding needs and constraints placed on a software product, and is addressed by [1, 14, 19, 20, 29, 35]. Identified knowledge areas cover all categories, except Software Requirements Fundamentals and Software Requirements Tools. The Software Requirements Fundamentals category provides underlying concepts for the whole KA. For example, in this category the differentiation between functional and quality requirements is introduced. May [21] argues that a key differentiator between competitor products is an interaction experience, however the presence of specific quality requirements was not reported in his study. We argue that a lack of research in this area indicates an insufficient understanding of quality requirements' role in software engineering in the startup context.

Operating with very limited resources, a startup must carefully select the scope of the first release. Both scope definition and assessment belong to the SWEBOK Software Engineering Management KA, which is not addressed by any of identified studies. We argue that the absence of practices addressing scope definition could be a contributing factor to premature failure.

Following the *startup* phase, the *stabilization* phase [11] aims at improving the product to a level where it can be decommissioned to any number of new customers without causing any overhead on product development. The Software Design KA provides support for improving internal qualities of the product and is addressed by [1, 14, 18, 21, 29, 30, 35]. The Requirements Management category becomes relevant to maintain product integrity while adding new features [11], however this category is not addressed by any of identified studies.

After the *startup* and *stabilization* phases, the *growth* phase poses challenges like expanding the team, ensuring transfer of know-how, and managing the product. The Communication Skills category, addressing knowledge transfer within the team, is covered by [1, 19, 21].   The Product Life Cycle and Portfolio Management categories belong to the Software Engineering Economics KA, however none of the identified practices address these categories. The Software Engineering Economics KA directly addresses the relation between software technical decisions and business goals of the organization. We argue that absence of practices belonging to this area reveals a key gap in building viable software products in startups.

The *maturity* phase is the final phase on Crowne's model and it takes place when product development is robust and processes are predictable for day-to-day operations and invention of new products [11]. The Software Engineering Process KA addresses process introduction and improvement. Practices belonging to Software Process Measurement Techniques and Software Engineering Process Tools categories are reported in [1, 20]. Other categories of this KA are not covered by any of the identified practices. We argue that at this phase, startups gradually mature towards small-medium enterprises (SME), rendering research on software process introduction and improvement in SME's also relevant.

5.2   RQ2: What is the Relevance and Rigor of the Studies Reporting Experiences from Software Engineering in Startups?

Studies conducted in a realistic environment, e.g. a startup company, have a larger potential to provide useful results, compared to laboratory experiments [17]. A research method that facilitates investigation in realistic contexts, with industry professionals and on a realistic scale, contributes to industry relevance [17]. Moreover, the extent to which a study method is described contributes to the understanding of results and the evaluation of potential benefits and risks prior to application [17]. The rigor of the evaluation and presentation is also an indication to a level of trust that can be put on the results [17].

We have found that most identified studies are conducted in collaboration with actual startup companies, thus scoring high on relevance scale (figure 1). However, research type analysis suggests that most papers are experience reports (figure 1) and study only one case (figure 2). Further analysis shows that most of the papers fall into the low rigor category (figure 1). This implies that a) a majority of the studies do not compare and analyze data from multiple cases and b) results among different studies are difficult to compare due to their low rigor. Therefore, the extent to which reported results can be generalized is low, and transfer to different startup companies is difficult.

6   Conclusions

We have mapped software engineering practices from peer-reviewed scientific papers about startups to SWEBOK categories and to startup life cycle phases. This was done in order to understand to what extent software engineering in startups is supported by research. Results show that a surprisingly small number of papers address the core software engineering knowledge areas in startups. Even though this gap was first identified by Sutton et al. [33] more than a decade ago, very little has been done to address it.

By means of a literature review we have identified 54 practices that, to some extent, cover all critical knowledge areas. However, a majority of categories are not addressed by research. We analyzed whether the reported practices are actually useful for startups. Even though many knowledge areas are covered, we identified gaps in practices supporting successful transition trough the startup life cycle, particularly in market-driven requirements engineering, engineering scope definition, alignment between technical decisions and business goals, software architecture, and implementation of software engineering process.

The analysis of transferability of practices shows that the majority of studies are conducted in a realistic environment, thus providing relevant results. However the rigor of identified studies is low due to insufficient descriptions of applied research methods and poorly reported study contexts. In such an applied field as software engineering, the ability to transfer results from one environment to another is critical [17]. As a result, a lack of rigor makes this transfer difficult or even dangerous for two reasons. First, contextual information enables a company to see if a good practice or lesson reported is relevant in their context. Second, as study design details are missing the level of trust in how the study was performed is hard to judge. This result confirms similar conclusions by Paternoster et al. [23].

We conclude that existing studies, addressing software engineering in startups, are insufficient to support all engineering aspects and do not create a solid body of knowledge. Moreover, results from existing studies are hard to transfer to startup companies due to an inadequate level of reporting rigor.

While the mapping of engineering practices presented in this paper can serve as a basis, more empirical research with focus on product engineering in the start-up context is required to address the identified gap. Even though performing research in startups is difficult due to rapidly changing environment, more primary studies are needed to understand how software-intensive product engineering is performed in startups. Completing the picture on what practices are actually used in startups and what impact said practices had on product engineering process would be a first step. Identifying inadequacies in used practices and proposing remedies are our mid-term goals.

References

1. Ambler, S.: Lessons in agility from Internet-based development. IEEE Software 19(2), 66–73 (2002)
2. Blank, S.: Embrace failure to start up success. Nature 477(7363), 133 (2011)
3. Blank, S.: The four steps to the epiphany, 2nd edn. K&S Ranch (2013)
4. Bosch, J., Olsson, H.H., Björk, J., Ljungblad, J.: The early stage software startup development model: A framework for operationalizing lean principles in software startups. In: Fitzgerald, B., Conboy, K., Power, K., Valerdi, R., Morgan, L., Stol, K.-J. (eds.) LESS 2013. LNBIP, vol. 167, pp. 1–15. Springer, Heidelberg (2013)
5. Brereton, P., et al.: Lessons from applying the systematic literature review process within the software engineering domain. J. Syst. Softw. 80(4), 571–583 (2007)
6. Budgen, D., Turner, M., Brereton, P., Kitchenham, B.: Using Mapping Studies in Software Engineering. In: Proceedings of PPIG 2008, pp. 195–204 (2008)
7. Carmel, E.: Rapid development in software package startups. In: Proc. 27th Hawaii Int'l. Conf. System Sciences, pp. 498–507 (1994)
8. Chorev, S., Anderson, A.R.: Success in Israeli high-tech start-ups; Critical factors and process. Technovation 26(2), 162–174 (2006)
9. Coleman, G., O'Connor, R.V.: An investigation into software development process formation in software start-ups. J. Enterp. Inf. Manag. 21(6), 633–648 (2008)
10. Consumano, M., Yoffie, D.: Competing on Internet Time: Lessons from Netscape and Its Battle with Microsoft In This Issue. Free Press (2000).

11. Crowne, M.: Why software product startups fail and what to do about it. In: Engineering Management Conference, pp. 338–343. IEEE, Cambridge (2002)
12. Dande, A., Eloranta, V.: Software Startup Patterns-An Empirical Study (2014)
13. Deakins, E., Dillon, S.: A helical model for managing innovative product and service initiatives in volatile commercial environments. Int. J. Proj. Manag. 23(1), 65–74 (2005)
14. Deias, R., et al.: Introducing XP in a start-up. In: International Conference on eXtreme Programming and Agile Processes in Software Engineering, pp. 62–65 (2002)
15. Fayad, M.E., Laitinen, M.: Process Assessment Considered Wasteful. Commun. ACM 40(11), 125–128 (1997)
16. Group, S.E.: Guidelines for performing Systematic Literature Reviews in Software Engineering. Engineering (2007)
17. Ivarsson, M., Gorschek, T.: A method for evaluating rigor and industrial relevance of technology evaluations. Empir. Softw. Eng. 16(3), 365–395 (2010)
18. James, L., Mater, B.S.: Solving the Software Quality Management Problem in Internet Startups. In: Pacific Northwest Software Quality Conference, pp. 503–512 (2000)
19. Kajko-Mattsson, M., Nikitina, N.: From Knowing Nothing to Knowing a Little: Experiences Gained from Process Improvement in a Start-Up Company. In: 2008 Int. Conf. Comput. Sci. Softw. Eng., pp. 617–621 (October 2008)
20. Kautz, K.: Improvement In Very Small Enterprisese: Does It Pay Off? Softw. Process Improv. Pr. 226, 1988, 209–226 (2000)
21. May, B.: Applying Lean Startup: An Experience Report. In: Agile Conference (2012)
22. Mendes, E., Counsell, S.: Investigating Early Web Size Measures for Web Cost Estimation. J. Syst. Softw. 77(2), 157–172 (2005)
23. Paternoster, N., et al.: Software development in startup companies: A systematic mapping study. Inf. Softw. Technol. 56(10), 1200–1218 (2014)
24. Petersen, K., et al.: Systematic Mapping Studies in Software Engineering. In: Evaluation and Assessment in Software Engineering, pp. 68–77 (2008)
25. Pino, F.J., et al.: Software process improvement in small and medium software enterprises: a systematic review. Softw. Qual. J. 16(2), 237–261 (2007)
26. Ries, E.: The Lean Startup: How Today's Entrepreneurs Use Continuous Innovation to Create Radically Successful Businesses, 1st edn. Crown Business (2011)
27. Shakir, S., Nørbjerg, J.: IT Project Management in Very Small Software Companies: A Case of Pakistan. In: Americas Conference on Information Systems, pp. 1–8 (2013)
28. Sicilia, M., et al.: The Evaluation of ontological representations of the SWEBOK as a revision tool, 1–4 (1990)
29. da Silva, A.F., Kon, F., Torteli, C.: Xp south of the equator: An experience implementing xp in brazil. In: Baumeister, H., Marchesi, M., Holcombe, M. (eds.) XP 2005. LNCS, vol. 3556, pp. 10–18. Springer, Heidelberg (2005)
30. Jansen, S., Brinkkemper, S.: Ivo Hunink, C.D.: Pragmatic and Opportunistic Reuse in Innovative Start-up Companies. IEEE Softw. 42–49 (2008)
31. Society, I.C.: Guide to the Software Engineering Body of Knowledge Version 3.0 (SWEBOK Guide V3.0)
32. Sulayman, M., et al.: Towards a theoretical framework of SPI success factors for small and medium web companies. Inf. Softw. Technol. 56(7), 807–820 (2014)
33. Sutton, S.M., et al.: The Role of Process in a Software Start-up. IEEE Softw. 17(4), 33–39 (2000)
34. Tanabian, M.M., et al.: Building High-Performance team through effective job design for an early stage software startup. In: Engineering Management Conference, pp. 789–792 (2005)

35. Tingling, P., Saeed, A.: Extreme programming in action: a longitudinal case study. In: Jacko, J.A. (ed.) Human-Computer Interaction 2007. Part I. LNCS, vol. 4550, pp. 242–251. Springer, Heidelberg (2007)
36. Wall, D.: Using open source for a profitable startup. Computer (Long. Beach. Calif), 158–160 (2001)
37. Watson, K., et al.: Small business start-ups: implications. Int. J. Entrep. Behav. Res. 4(3), 217–238 (2006)
38. Wohlin, C.: Guidelines for Snowballing in Systematic Literature Studies and a Replication in Software Engineering. In: Evaluation and Assessment in Software Engineering (2014)
39. Yau, A., Murphy, C.: Is a Rigorous Agile Methodology the Best Development Strategy for Small Scale Tech Startups? (2013)
40. Zettel, J., et al.: LIPE: A Lightweight Process for E-business Startup Companies Based on Extreme Programming, pp. 255–270 (2001)
41. Getting Real The smarter, faster, easier way to build a successful web application, http://37signals.com/

Value Creation in SaaS Development

Ivan Aaen[1](✉) and Nikolai Gjerløff[2]

[1] Department of Computer Science, Aalborg University, Aalborg, Denmark
ivan@cs.aau.dk
[2] PathShaper Aps, Aalborg, Denmark
nikolai@pathshaper.dk

Abstract. Software as a Service (SaaS) development projects run for an unbounded amount of time, and it is important to continuously offer customers increased value from using the solution. Otherwise, a one-time payment for using a similar product would appear more attractive. Uncritically implementing value-adding ideas might however not always be in accordance with the business interests of the SaaS development company. We take a look at a small software development company with a SaaS business model and propose an approach to facilitate coordinated innovation on two levels: *Business model* and *software development*. We use the approach on an ongoing case from this company. Our results indicate that the case has benefitted from using the toolset presented here. The approach is designed for small SaaS companies with 5-10 developers using agile development methods.

Keywords: Value creation · Software innovation · SaaS · Business models

1 Introduction

Tom DeMarco [11] argues that software development today focus too much on cost and too little on value. He points out that we should first ask ourselves *is the project worth doing* and require the gain to outweigh the costs by far.

Requiring the gain to be much higher than the cost means that we can afford to aim for a great solution instead of just an adequate one. This could involve hiring a good team and letting it grow even better by leaving time for both skill and software development. Alistair Cockburn [9] argues that preparing the developers for the next challenge is the second most important activity in a project.

Increasing the gain could also involve making the software team innovative. In order to do this we need a way to catalyze and reward thinking along new paths. A methodology – *Essence* – has been proposed for this [1, 3]. This methodology focuses specifically on maximizing value creation within a software development team.

Innovation at the project or team level might interact with innovation at the business level: New features in a project might suggest changes at the business level, and changes at the business level might suggest changes in scope and focus for a software project. Osterwalder and Pigneur [13] present the *Business Model Canvas*, a tool for creating and communicating innovative business models. Where the notion of

© Springer International Publishing Switzerland 2015
J.M. Fernandes et al. (Eds.): ICSOB 2015, LNBIP 210, pp. 258–271, 2015.
DOI: 10.1007/978-3-319-19593-3_23

value is open in Essence, it tends to be more specific in the Business Model Canvas making the canvas a possible framework for aligning software innovation based on Essence with business development.

Integration of innovation on the two levels is important for SaaS projects since they run for an unbounded amount of time while constantly affecting the business model. This integration also allows the software team to view value creation from the perspective of the company's business model.

For software companies with a SaaS business model, the ability to continuously improve the value of the service for the customers is essential for customer retention and revenues:

1   *SaaS customers pay periodic fees as opposed to upfront payments at acquisition time. The amount they pay is typically proportional to how long they use the product.*

2   *A SaaS product that does not evolve may in the long run become more expensive for the customer than investing in similar software. If the SaaS software evolves, it is no longer comparable to a one-time investment but to a series of investments in consecutive versions of a similar software product. For long-term usage, this may push the total costs of ownership more in favor of SaaS products.*

3   *Usually, SaaS customers need not invest much in using a service. This is particularly true for simple services where data is easily moved. Low switching-costs make it easier for customers to try competing services in search of more desirable ones.*

This brief discussion leads us to our research question: Can the Business Model Canvas and Essence be integrated to improve value creation in small agile software development companies using a SaaS business model?

We will try to illuminate this question by first examining the two frameworks and apply a combination of the two on a practical case.

We briefly present the Business Model Canvas in *Section 2*. *Section 3* outlines key concepts in Essence. Developing business models and models for software innovation introduces a need to visualize the present, the options considered, and the current strategies at the same time. *Section 4* therefore presents color-coding as a way to keep these perspectives in one model. *Section 5* discusses strategy management based on SWOT analysis of business models. *Section 6* illustrates the approach by applying it to an ongoing project, and *Section 7* discusses the integration of the approach into the software process. *Section 8* concludes by evaluating the results and discussing if this approach is useful for small SaaS companies.

2   The Business Model Canvas

A business model describes the rationale of how an organization creates, delivers and captures value [13]. Business model should be simple enough to be easily grasped and held in our minds, and sufficiently detailed to hold the most important elements of the business. If we cannot fully comprehend it, we cannot evaluate the impact of our decisions on the business, and if we omit crucial elements, we may neglect to take important factors into account. In *Business Model Generation* Osterwalder and Pigneur propose nine building blocks for creating a business model: *Customer Segments* (CS), *Value Proposition* (VP), *Channels* (CH), *Customer Relationships* (CR), Revenue Streams (R$), *Key Resources* (KR), *Key Activities* (KA), *Key Partnerships* (KP), and *Cost Structure* (C$).

Together, these nine blocks form *The Business Model Canvas*. The canvas is used both as a business model brainstorming-tool and as a communication aid. When brainstorming with this tool, you describe each important element of the nine blocks at a high level of abstraction.

3   Essence

Whereas the Business Model Canvas is an innovation tool for the business model, Essence is specifically aimed at software development. Although it in no way precludes innovation done by other parties, the main focus is on the creative power of good software teams. We will sum up Essence as described in a number of sources [1-5].

Essence is based on four Views to help examine a problem from four basic perspectives, four Roles assigned to team members, and four Values to serve as guiding principles. The four Views are:

1   *Paradigm: The use domain view. Used to explore the problem to be solved, understand the use context of the software, and in some cases completely reinterpret a problem and/or setting.*

2   *Product: The design view. Used to explore key design options, e.g. architecture, key components, platforms, and algorithms. This is where we come up with ways to build the envisioned product using available technologies.*

3   *Project: The management view. Used to build and maintain the project vision shared among team members and communicated to external stakeholders. The vision serves to give focus and direction in a project without excessive detail to be able to embrace change even late in development.*

4   *Process: The procedural view. Used to support the working process and not least for evaluating options and results. As Essence is about innovation, the main focus is on idea generation and on evaluation and maturation of ideas.*

Each Role in Essence is associated with a View, and with the exception of the Child role, these roles stick to a team member throughout the project. The four Roles of Essence are:

1   *Child (Paradigm View): The Child role is the only non-permanent Role and is automatically assigned to anyone while working at the Paradigm View. Visitors from outsider are also invited to take on a Child Role. This role is for exploring options in the use domain while building a shared paradigmatic understanding in the team – or indeed while challenging the ruling paradigm.*

2   *Responder (Product View): Responders are the software developers of the team. They are responsible for coming up with ways to answer the challenges facing the project. They are the ones who build the product and identify new options in the design at any time.*

3   *Challenger (Project View): Similar to the Product Owner in Scrum, the Challenger is responsible for developing and maintaining project challenges for the responders in order to create the highest value in the end product.*

4   *Anchor (Process View): Similar to a Scrum master, the Anchor is responsible for representing the project to its stakeholders, for solving team-related problems, for facilitating a good work environment, and for ensuring a sound and impartial basis for decisions. An Anchor is typically also a Responder.*

As Essence is designed to fit with agile development methods like XP [7, 8] or Scrum [14], these roles are just additional hats for the team members.

The Values are dialectical transformations of the values from the Agile Manifesto [6]. Each value is tied to a specific View:

1   *Reflection (Paradigm View). In Essence, the agile manifesto value Customer collaboration over contract negotiation is replaced with Reflection over requirements. The use context, scenarios, and requirements must always be negotiated and reflected upon: Do we get it right?*

2   *Affordance (Product View). The agile manifesto value Working software over comprehensive documentation is replaced with Affordance over solution. At every stage of development, the present design offers new possibilities. The affordance of these possibilities should be explored.*

3   *Vision (Project View). The agile manifesto value Responding to change over following a plan is replaced with Vision over assignments. Assignments define tasks to do, which basically means that the time for innovation is over. The vision serves to narrow the scope enough to ensure convergence in the project while keeping the door open to change. A good team needs latitude to use the insights gained from working on a problem while still being steered by a vision.*

4   *Facilitation (Process View). The agile manifesto value Individuals and interactions over processes and tools is replaced with Facilitation over structuration. To facilitate the creative process and make the team aim for mature solutions is more important than adhering to predefined processes.*

The overview of a project shared among team members and with external stakeholders is called a Configuration. A configuration reflects *not only the software itself but the entire product; it reflects what we think that product should do, how well it should do it, and why this matters to us and other stakeholders*   [3].

Configurations – representing a status and a basis for evaluation – are represented in Essence as Configuration Tables. A configuration table consists of 4 columns and 4 rows. Each column represents an Essence View, and each row represents the Views at different levels of abstraction.

4   Color-Coding Models

SaaS projects are long-term and new ideas must take the current state of a project into account. Essence Configuration Tables are designed for incremental software development and take the current state of a project into account, as the outcome of one sprint is the starting point of the following. Likewise, Business Model Canvases can be developed in multiple iterations.

One could therefore create configuration tables and canvases for the present and an envisioned future respectively to assess which developments would move in a desirable direction. The most important information in these two models will be how they differ, and therefore it might be more optimal to combine the two tables or canvasses into one to visualize *where we are* in relation to *where we are heading*.

Such combined models would help improve or sustain the mutual fit between software development and business model. Similarly, it would also simplify updating the current and the envisioned future state.

A way to keep track of the current state in relation to the future state is shown in Figure 1 and Tables 2 and 3 where colors indicate different states. The relation between colors and states is found in Table 1.

Table 1. Color codes for states

Black	Status, what is already in place in the model
Green	Work-in-progress, items currently under development such as Sprint backlog items, or ongoing developments in a canvas building block
Blue	Opportunities and unused strengths under consideration, product backlog items, optional developments in a canvas building block
Red	Identified problems, weaknesses, threats

It should be noted that the states are seen from a development perspective. New items usually enter the models as blue or red. When updating a table or canvas, blue items can be promoted to green if the team has capacity for new challenges. Furthermore, green items can be promoted to black if they are either completely done or good enough for the team to move on to other challenges. Sometimes, development is suspended before the item is in a good enough state, and in this case the item reverts to blue.

Red items may indicate problems with the model itself. Solving them might entail a revision of the model in question or indeed of both models to get them realigned.

5   Strategy Management

Integrating Essence and Business Model Canvasses allows the company to align strategies for software development with overall business strategies: Do developments at the project level suggest favorable changes to the business model, or will developments at the business level indicate a revision of the software project?

SWOT analysis is a common and simple tool to identify *strengths, weaknesses, opportunities* and *threats* to an enterprise – a business or a project. Based on this tool, Weihrich [16] introduces the TOWS matrix and formulates four generic strategies:

1   *The WT Strategy (min-min): When weaknesses match threats, the enterprise is in trouble. This type of strategy therefore aims to minimize both to help the enterprise survive.*

2   *The WO Strategy (min-max): When weaknesses match opportunities, the enterprise has opportunities but also weaknesses that impede taking advantage of them. This type of strategy therefore aims to minimize a weakness to allow for maximizing an opportunity.*

3   *The ST Strategy (max-min): When strengths match threats, the enterprise is facing threats that might be dealt with by using strengths in the company. This strategy therefore focuses on utilizing strengths to eliminate threats by maximizing the former while minimizing the latter.*

4   *The SO Strategy (max-max): Strengths combined with opportunities is the most desirable situation an enterprise can be in. This strategy is about maximizing both and utilizes the strengths to take advantage of a situation.*

These four generic strategies combined with the Challenger and Responder Roles in Essence serve as the inspiration for the "Response/Challenge notation" or simply the RC notation. This notation is shorthand for answering a challenge with selected responses.

We will introduce this notation in Business Models Canvasses and Essence Configuration Tables. Starting with a SWOT analysis of a model, the findings are listed in relevant cells and prefixed with the letters S, W, O, or T. The findings are numbered to distinguish findings of the same type from each other. These SWOT findings form the basis for formulating strategies. The items are color-coded as described in Section 4. Red items represent threats or weaknesses, whereas blue items represent opportunities or unused strengths.

The RC notation combines the SWOT findings into strategies. A strategy here is understood as a challenge (opportunity or threat) answered by one or more responses. In our notation a strategy is written with the items responding to the challenge first followed by an arrow and then the items constituting the challenge (e.g. S1>T1 stating that a strength is used to counter a threat or even in concatenated form S1+S2>O1>T1 stating that two strengths can build a capability which in turn is used to mitigate a threat).

This notation serves to visualize possible strategies for moving a business model in a desirable direction. In other words, the notation should help clarify how to eliminate red items, and how to turn blue items into black. Green items relate to the strategy currently employed to create a new status. When a current strategy has fulfilled its purpose, the color turns from green to black to indicate what created and maintains the current status. Black strategies are deleted when the status is stable and no longer requires the strategy to be actively pursued.

6   Illustration: The AntiPage Project Case

We will illustrate the methodology by applying it to an ongoing project. The methodology was used in recurring strategy management as the project progressed.

The project concerned the development of *AntiPage*, a content management system developed by PathShaper. PathShaper is a small SaaS company named after its service. The company specializes in tools and consulting to help its customers become successful online. The company offers SaaS products based on three systems:

The *PathShaper* system is a data mining system for web server log-files. It is used for measuring the actual response times experienced by users, studying how Search Engines behave on customer websites, and more.

SEODar is a data mining system indexing pages for analytical purposes. SEODar is used for Search Engine Optimization, Website quality assurance, and studying the structure of the web in general and the nature of Search Engines in particular.

AntiPage: A Content Management System for web sites that ensures faster response times and higher revenue. The development of this system forms the basis for our case.

6.1   Early Development of AntiPage

Development of AntiPage began in 2010. PathShaper noticed that one of its customers – here called *Customer1* – had problems modifying their websites to capitalize on findings from SEODar or PathShaper. Similar problems were seen at other customer sites. The company therefore found that the value of these two data mining systems would increase, if it were easier to implement the changes identified by such findings.

Development started out with a proof-of-concept version having just enough functionality to run the company website. Customer1 was not receptive to the idea of basing their large setup on a brand new content management system, but development continued anyway as the company saw a lot of potential in the new product.

At that time, testing only on relatively trivial websites and having no real customer impeded the project. Developing software together with domain experts expecting to use the product afterwards helps a team prioritize and build the right features. Creating a profitable SaaS product is as much about knowing the problem area exceptionally well as it is about technology. Kim and Mauborgne [12] offer several examples of companies becoming successful because they understood the desires of their customers better than their competitors did.

Another problem turned out to be that several ideas were implemented but subsequently failed to see much use. A fair evaluation of the market value of each idea before implementation is important.

6.2   The Initial Project Configuration

To get an idea of the project status at this stage we developed an Essence Configuration Table (Table 2). Configuration tables serve to give an overview of key points on the four Views. This overview is used to evaluate the current status of the project, and to see if the Views are in congruence and in line with the project vision.

Table 2. Initial AntiPage Configuration Table

Paradigm	Product	Project	Process
Reflection *Challenge.* Help companies get more value out of their web sites. *Use context.* CMS for large companies.	*Affordance* Providing content management with fast load times. Allowing a lot of flexibility	*Vision* *Metaphor:* The Road Runner of CMS. A fast and flexible CMS with good SEO support.	*Facilitation* Quality focus on making AntiPage attractive to large customers.
Stakeholders *PathShaper.* Wants a marketable product (main stakeholder). *Resource it.* Wants to provide quality websites to its customers.	*Design* Engine and UI separate from webserver. Engine and UI hosting: PathShaper. Webserver hosting: Any web hotel.	*Elements* *Grounds:* Faster load times help increase conversion rates. More flexibility ease improvement work. *Warrant:* AdWords competitions make high conversion rates essential and SEO attractive. *Qualifier:* More expensive than free solutions. Many free solutions have more features. *Rebuttal:* Costs are small compared to faster response times. Small sites may not get the revenues required and are not likely customers.	*Evaluation* *Procedure:* Try to sell AntiPage to *Customer1.* *Criteria:* Will *Customer1* buy AntiPage?
Scenarios Managing a large website with custom-made functionality. Managing numerous smaller websites in different data centers and needing to share resources between them.	*Components* Page generation engine. Content mgt. UI. Synchronization component.	*Features* Content mgt. Maintenance of multiple sites. High scalability for # of simultaneous visitors per server. High flexibility in generating HTML for SEO.	*Findings* *Customer1* wanted a mature system. Small companies show an unexpected interest in AntiPage despite the poorer cost/benefit ratio. They decide based on how large they want to become.

The first row in the table describes the overall vision, the challenges to meet, the use context, key product ideas, and general qualities to pursue.

The second row describes key principles for each View, stakeholders involved, architectural foundation, why the vision is convincing (based on Stephen Toulmin's model of argumentation [15], and how to work towards the vision.

The last and most specific row describes key scenarios for using the product, main components of the product, principal features to include in it, and findings from evaluating the current configuration.

The configuration table made sense except for the serious problem identified under findings: AntiPage is targeting the high-end market without any success (the red-colored element in the Table 2). On the other hand, small companies unexpectedly showed interest in the product (the blue-colored element).

These findings conflicted with our initial understanding of how this project was related to the overall business model of the company. We therefore decided to review the business model canvas for PathShaper using the approach described in Section 5.

6.3   Revising the Business Model Canvas

PathShaper's initial Business Model Canvas is outlined in Figure 1 (the black text). The Value Propositions clearly target customers that are highly dependent on the performance of their websites. In principle, the AntiPage project is in line with the business model, but the findings in Table 2 indicates that a revised business model and/or a revised development project might align product and business model better.

The revision started with a SWOT analysis of the canvas resulting in a number of findings – among those were two findings that matched those from Table 2. In Figure 1 these findings are marked as described in Chapter 5. The market problem found in Table 2 was generalized and marked as T1 in Figure 1 to indicate that it is classified as an external threat. The interest from small companies was generalized and marked as O2 to indicate that this was classified as an external opportunity.

We then created four *Vision Scenarios*. In Essence, vision scenario development involves defining two opposite ways to handle two different aspects of the project, and then strategies are formulated for each combination. In our case we chose *Many Small Sites* vs. *Few Large Sites* and *Sale Through Partners* vs. *Direct Sales*, and drafted strategies for each of these four combinations.

Looking for ways to respond to T1, the opportunity O2 *Smaller companies than anticipated express interest in AntiPage solutions* looked interesting. If we wanted to boost sales to small companies, we should focus on the combination of sales through partners and small sites. In that quadrant we saw the opportunity O2 and two strengths that could enable O2: S2 (*More easy to use UI*) and S4 (*AntiPage contexts preloaded with simple templates that can be modified into a less ambitious website*). This suggests a simple SO strategy as described in Section 5.

Combining these two strengths to exploit O2 would be a viable and affordable way to answer T1. The strategy would essentially consist of two legs: S2+S4>O2 and O2>T1, or in concatenated form: S2+S4>O2>T1. The first leg serves to make AntiPage attractive for small sites, and the second serves to compensate for the missing sales due to T1. We consequently marked these items green in Figure 1 to indicate this as the current strategy.

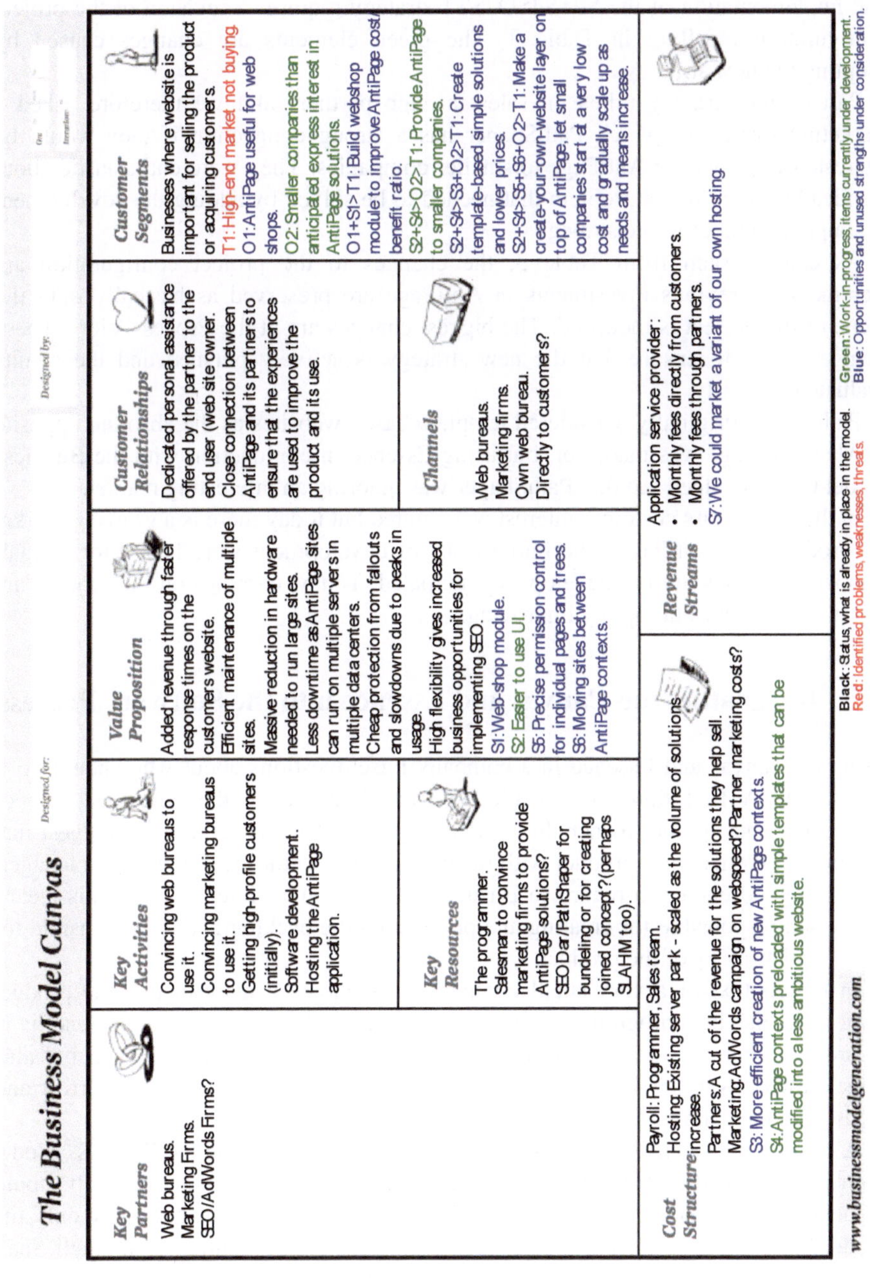

Fig. 1. Business Model during review

6.4   Revising the Project Configuration

The implementation of the S2+S4>O2>T1 strategy requires a revision of the project configuration resulting in Table 3. The green elements are changes caused by adopting the new strategy.

Part of the strategy relies on sales through partners and we therefore asked a marketing bureau to which PathShaper has a strong connection if they would be interested in providing AntiPage to smaller companies. They were enthusiastic about the idea but price was a problem that needed to be solved by adding the development of simple templates to the strategy.

As can be seen from Table 3, the changes to the project configuration are incremental. Previous investments in AntiPage are preserved as basically only the scope of the project is modified. The biggest changes are at the Process View. These changes serve to ensure that the new strategy is actively pursued and the results evaluated regularly.

PathShaper originally considered template-based websites as the absolute opposite of what AntiPage was made for, but using Essence in conjunction with the Business Model Canvas helped see that PathShaper was ignoring an interesting market.

In the early years customer interest was limited but today there is a growing market for product like AntiPage. The initial costs of development were heavy for a small company, as sales did not develop as anticipated. Today, earnings on the product are still unsatisfactory but rapidly improving.

7   Integrating the Canvas and Essence into the Software Process

Using the canvas and Essence in a company raise questions about who should do it and when? A first thing to consider is who should have the combined role of Challenger and Product owner. In the Scrum primer, Deemer et al. [10] suggest that the product owner for a product with many customers could be the product manager. This is a good choice in regard to Business Model Canvas integration as this means the person responsible for creating and prioritizing the backlog is also responsible for the overall strategy of the product.

In the context of a very small company, this choice can mean that the product owner will also be a programmer on the team. This is likely to create some benefits in regard to a shared understanding between the team and the product owner, but also some drawbacks in the form of the product owner's perspective becoming narrow and focused on the details of implementation.

A broader perspective can be achieved by making Essence and the Business Model Canvas a part of the sprint cycle. Deemer et al. [10] suggest that a workshop should be held near the end of a sprint for *product backlog refinement*. Normally only the product owner and the team would be present, but in the context of a small SaaS software development company few if any additional people will need to be invited in order to be fully able to make sound decisions on adjusting company strategy.

Table 3. Revised AntiPage Configuration Table

Paradigm	Product	Project	Process
Reflection *Challenge.* Help companies get more value out of their web sites. *Use context.* CMS for large companies or smaller and ambitious ones (O2).	*Affordance* Providing content management with fast load times. Allowing a lot of flexibility	*Vision* *Metaphor:* The Road Runner of CMS. A fast and flexible CMS with good SEO support.	*Facilitation* Quality focus on streamlining AntiPage so it becomes attractive to customers of various sizes.
Stakeholders *PathShaper.* Wants a marketable product (main stakeholder). *Resource it.* Wants to provide quality websites to its customers. *MarketingBureau1* wants to sell mid-priced solutions based on AntiPage.	*Design* Engine and UI separate from webserver. Engine and UI hosting: PathShaper. Webserver hosting: Any web hotel.	*Elements* *Grounds*: Faster load times help increase conversion rates. More flexibility ease improvement work. *Warrant*: AdWords competitions make high conversion rates essential and SEO attractive. *Qualifier:* More expensive than free solutions. Many free solutions have more features. *Rebuttal:* Costs are small compared to faster response times. Ambitious sites may not require added revenues at once.	*Evaluation* *Procedure:* Try to sell AntiPage to sites of all sizes. *Criteria:* Selling AntiPage in higher volumes.
Scenarios Managing a large website with custom-made functionality. Managing numerous smaller websites in different data centers and needing to share resources between them. Running a single simple website (S2+S4).	*Components* Page generation engine. Content mgt. UI (S2). Synchronization component.	*Features* Content mgt. Maintenance of multiple sites. High scalability for # of simultaneous visitors per server. High flexibility in generating HTML for SEO. Simpler UI (S2). Standard templates (S4).	*Findings* Sales increasing at a satisfactory rate.

If we schedule this workshop at the end of a sprint, we would start by updating the color-coding of the Business Model Canvas to reflect the new status. After having just talked through but not yet refined the strategy, we could list ideas and insights accumulated during the sprint and discuss what to do with them. A way of doing this would be to use the product backlog refinement as the transition between one Essence configuration and the next. Using a configuration table is useful here since the changes between the two tables should be checked against the current Business Model Canvas. Each change will fall into one of three categories:

1   *In accordance with the canvas*
2   *Warrants changes in the canvas*
3   *Not bringing the business in the right direction*

Essence is used for this idea evaluation with the Anchor as facilitator. Some canvas changes may not be a result of software innovation, so a periodical revision of the Business Model Canvas should be part of the process even when there are no items of the second category.

8   Conclusion

This paper has examined ways of combining the Business Model Canvas and Essence, and we have suggested an approach for small SaaS development companies.

The Business Model Canvas helped PathShaper decide where to focus efforts, and Essence helped come up with ways to improve AntiPage in this area.

By using the SWOT and RC notations in the Business Model Canvas, we have a way to facilitate the exploration of the relationship between items. In addition, the notation used makes it possible to follow the reasoning behind the proposed strategies which makes revision of the envisioned future easier: if a SWOT item is changed, all strategies depending on it must be revised.

We find it both possible and beneficial to integrate the Business Model Canvas with Essence. The proposed color-coding allows us to easily identify where different items in the Business Model Canvas are in regard to development, and this makes it easier to identify which changes should be picked for the next Essence configuration. Furthermore, our RC notation allows us to track multiple future scenarios suggested by Essence in the canvas and determine how they affect the business model. The AntiPage case points to greater clarity and growing revenues from using this approach.

The main drawback in relation to using the approach is an increased complexity of the resulting Business Model Canvasses. For larger projects, the SWOT items and RC notation items may not easily fit into the canvas.

References

1. Aaen, I.: Essence: Facilitating Software Innovation. European Journal of Information Systems 17, 543–553 (2008)
2. Aaen, I.: Software Innovation –Values for a Methodology. In: Aanestad, M., Bratteteig, T. (eds.) SCIS 2013. LNBIP, vol. 156, pp. 72–86. Springer, Heidelberg (2013)

3. Aaen, I.: Essence - Pragmatic Software Innovation. Unpublished book draft. Department of Computer Science, Aalborg University, Aalborg (2015)
4. Aaen, I.: Roles in innovative software teams: A design experiment. In: Pries-Heje, J., Venable, J., Bunker, D., Russo, N.L., DeGross, J.I. (eds.) IFIP WG. IFIP AICT, vol. 318, pp. 73–88. Springer, Heidelberg (2010)
5. Aaen, I., Jensen, R.H.: Pragmatic Software Innovation. In: Bergvall-Kåreborn, B., Nielsen, P.A. (eds.) TDIT 2014. IFIP AICT, vol. 429, pp. 133–149. Springer, Heidelberg (2014)
6. Beck, K., Beedle, M., van Bennekum, A., Cockburn, A., Cunningham, W., Fowler, M., Grenning, J., Highsmith, J., Hunt, A., Jeffries, R., Kern, J., Marick, B., Martin, R., Mellor, S., Schwaber, K., Sutherland, J., Thomas, D.: Manifesto for Agile Software Development (2001)
7. Beck, K., Andres, C.: Extreme programming explained: embrace change. Addison-Wesley, Boston (2005)
8. Beck, K., Fowler, M.: Planning extreme programming. The XP series. Addison-Wesley, Boston (2001)
9. Cockburn, A.: Agile software development. Addison-Wesley, Boston (2002)
10. Deemer, P., Benefield, G., Larman, C., Vodde, B.: The Scrum Primer. Scrum Training Institute (2010)
11. DeMarco, T.: Software Engineering: An idea whose time has come and gone? IEEE Software 26, 95–96 (2009)
12. Kim, W.C., Mauborgne, R.: Blue Ocean Strategy: How to create uncontested market space and make the competition irrelevant. Harvard Business School Press, Boston (2005)
13. Osterwalder, A., Pigneur, Y., Clark, T.: Business model generation: A handbook for visionaries, game changers, and challengers. Wiley, Hoboken (2010)
14. Schwaber, K., Beedle, M.: Agile software development with scrum. Series in agile software development. Prentice Hall, Upper Saddle River (2002)
15. Toulmin, S.E.: The uses of argument. Cambridge University Press, Cambridge (2003)
16. Weihrich, H.: The TOWS Matrix — A tool for situational analysis. Long Range Planning 15, 54–66 (1982)

Wealthy, Healthy and/or Happy —
What does 'Ecosystem Health' Stand for?

Sami Hyrynsalmi[1]([✉]), Marko Seppänen[2], Tiina Nokkala[3], Arho Suominen[4], and Antero Järvi[1]

[1] Department of Information Technology, University of Turku, Turku, Finland
{sthyry,antero.jarvi}@utu.fi
[2] Department of Pori, Tampere University of Technology, Tampere, Finland
marko.seppanen@tut.fi
[3] Turku School of Economics, Department of Management and Entrepreneurship, University of Turku, Turku, Finland
takuus@utu.fi
[4] Innovation and Knowledge Economy, VTT Technical Research Centre of Finland, Turku, Finland
arho.suominen@vtt.fi

Abstract. The health of a software ecosystem is argued to be a key indicator of well-being, longevity and performance of a network of companies. In this paper, we address what scientific literature actually means with the concept of 'ecosystem health' by selecting relevant articles with systematic literature review. Based on the final set of 38 papers, we found that despite a common base, the term has been used to depict a wide range of hoped characteristics of a software ecosystem. However, the number of studies addressing the topic is shown to grow while empirical studies are still rare. Thus, further studies should aim to standardize the terminology and concepts in order to create a common base for future work. Further work is needed also to develop early indicators that warn and guides companies on problems with their ecosystems.

Keywords: Software ecosystem · Ecosystem health · Business ecosystem · Systematic literature study

1 Introduction

'Business ecosystem' analogy, by Moore [1,2], and its derivatives—such as 'software ecosystem'—are crucial conceptualizations for modern-day business networks. Business ecosystems, formed by firms, are seen everywhere. For example, there are several different kind *software ecosystems* (SECO) focusing on the software producing companies and their networks [3,4], *mobile ecosystems* formed by the companies producing hardware and software for new era smartphones [5], and even *mobile application ecosystems* that focus on the relationship of mobile application marketplaces and their content producers and users [6]. In this paper, we see 'software ecosystem' as a special case of more general 'business

© Springer International Publishing Switzerland 2015
J.M. Fernandes et al. (Eds.): ICSOB 2015, LNBIP 210, pp. 272–287, 2015.
DOI: 10.1007/978-3-319-19593-3_24

ecosystem' concept. That is, a software ecosystem is a-kind-of business ecosystem. While our focus in this paper is on the former, we acknowledge and use the extant knowledge of the latter.

A common approach to both the business and software ecosystem research agendas is to define a measure of *healthiness* for an ecosystem. Iansiti & Levien [7,8] state that, similarly as in a biological ecosystem, that the survival of individual actors within an ecosystem are dependant on the whole network rather than the strength of the actor itself. This creates the assumption that the health of the ecosystem is crucial for all actors joined to the ecosystem.

The concept of 'ecosystem health' is important also for software ecosystems. In this paper, we address the existing research on the concept of 'ecosystem health' in the field of software ecosystem research. We use a systematic literature review (SLR) to select papers focusing on the topic and follow Kitchenham & Charter's [9] guidelines of conducting a SLR. From the selected papers, we analyse how the term is used and defined. The research questions of the paper are:

RQ1. Is there increasing scholarly interest towards 'ecosystem health'?

RQ2. Has the scholarly debate resulted in a common understanding on the definition?

RQ3. What are the characteristics, actors and agents mentioned in literature that have an influence to ecosystem health?

RQ4. Is there empirical evidence to support definitions or characteristics found in literature?

The research questions use the systematic literature review approach to quantify the need for an discussion on ecosystem health—i.e., is this a topic of interest in the scholarly debate. The research questions also formulate the status of scholarly debate—i.e., is there a consensus on the framework and relevance of ecosystem health. Finally, this study strives to uncover sufficient empirical evidence for whatever theoretical findings has been gathered.

Previously, Manikas & Hansen [10] studied ecosystem health with a literature survey. In the article, they construct a software ecosystem framework. However, their paper relies on a few years old dataset that contains only 13 articles related to software ecosystem health. Our set contains three times more articles, and, instead of constructing an ecosystem health model, we are interested on the discussion of and the recent development in the area of software ecosystem health. This paper contributes to the field by showing a multitude of meanings associated with the term and proposing new research avenues. This paper request further work to normalize the ongoing discussion and research of software ecosystem health.

The rest of the paper is structured as follows. The following section will give a brief introduction to the ecosystem health. It is followed by the depiction of research methods in Section 3, results and analysis in Section 4. Section 5 presents discussion of the meaning of results and Section 6 concludes the study.

2   Background

In this section, we will present the software ecosystem health model by Manikas & Hansen [10], and the classical view of business ecosystem health by Iansiti & Levien [7,8]. Due to the space limitations, we do not discuss on the definition of software ecosystem or its actors but refer the interested readers to recent literature reviews [6,11].

In their work, Manikas & Hansen [10] make a categorization about ecosystem health related literature, in order to find definitions for software ecosystem health. They create four categories: software ecosystems (main category) and business ecosystems, natural ecosystems and open source software. Literature from all categories draws from the main category's definition. Nevertheless, there is one main difference between the main category and the rest: nature of the ecosystem's production. While other ecosystems see actors as products themselves, software ecosystem, according to Manikas & Hansen [10], makes a difference between the actor in ecosystem and the production of ecosystem [10].

In software ecosystem, according to Manikas & Hansen [10] health of an actor and of a product are separated, not affecting each other, whereas in natural and business ecosystems, health of an actor affects the product's health. That independence of actor's and product's health in software ecosystems can appear in form of an excellent software product or platform having positive effect on health of the ecosystem, while the actor who created that product has a negative effect on health through defects in its business model [10].

Ecosystems are also defined by the roles and awareness of roles by different actors. A differentiator between software ecosystems and other mentioned types of ecosystems is an orchestrator that creates the rules and runs the platform that is used in that specific ecosystem [10]. Also the consciousness of the existence of an ecosystem and belonging to it makes a difference between natural and artificial ecosystems [2]. Awareness of ecosystem's actors about the ecosystem affects their acts in it, and should therefore be taken into account when defining the health of an ecosystem.

Base-creating definition of measures to be used when addressing health of ecosystems, both business and biological was presented by Iansiti & Levien [7,8]. They propose that ecosystem health should be measured by *productivity, robustness* and *niche creation* [7]:

Productivity can be measured in business or software ecosystems, e.g., in return on invested capital; how much value is created turning tangible and intangible assets into production. In natural ecosystems measure, can be, e.g., biomass created using inputs like sunlight.

Robustness in its simplest form, according to Iansiti & Levien [7], is measured in survival rate of ecosystem's members, either in relation to other ecosystems or over time. Robustness means that the ecosystem can face and survive from the changes of the environment.

Niche Creation in business context refers to ability to create value by putting new functions into operation and increasing meaningful diversity in ecosystem through that. Diversity gives ecosystem potential for productive innovation and indicates its ability to absorb shocks from outside. [7]

In addition to these health measures, there are several different characteristics argued to be included into the 'ecosystem health' concept. For example, Hyrynsalmi *et al.* [12] argues that satisfaction of actors involved in an ecosystem should be considered.

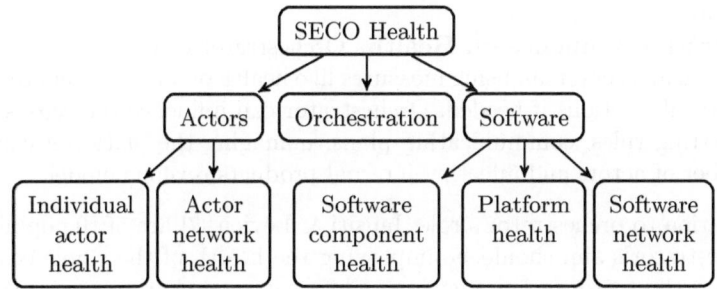

Fig. 1. A breakdown of the SECO health framework [10, adapted]

Software ecosystem health –model proposed by Manikas & Hansen [10] divides health of an ecosystem to three main components: actors, software and orchestration (Figure 1). This model, as it name specifies, is prepared taking into account earlier mentioned features that differentiate software ecosystems from other ecosystems; the separation of actor health and product health, and the existence of and orchestrator. In the model, actor component is further divided to *individual actor health* and *actor network health*. Software component in turn consists of *software component health*, *platform health* and *software network health*. Descriptions of these subcomponents according to Manikas & Hansen [10] are shortly presented below:

Individual Actor Health. Productivity and robustness mentioned by Iansiti & Levien [7] are the main building blocks of an individual actor's health in an ecosystem. Actively participating an actor probably is a robust member of an ecosystem and most likely has its place in it in the future also.

Actor Network Health. Interaction within an actor's network affects the ecosystem's health. The role of an actor in a network increases or decreases its effect on the health of an ecosystem. Key player, even with lower productivity, means more to ecosystem health than high productivity from a niche player.

Software Component Health. In case of software ecosystem, the software component is most likely a product of the ecosystem. Its health can be measured, e.g., in terms of reliability, availability, modifiability and interoperability. Software component health is affected by its relative demand and quality.

Platform Health. Platform health can be similarly analyzed as software component health, platform being a software component also. It might still have effect also on orchestration of the software ecosystem. If so, measuring platform health should include a measure for the effectiveness of orchestration actions.

Software Network Health. Interaction between software components can be measured and categorized. Connected software components form a network, which health can be measured by e.g. looking at the key players' role in it; whether they are enabling interaction or trying to dominate whole network's actions.

Orchestration Influence on Health. Orchestrator can have a role of 'caretaker' of an ecosystem; using measures like health of an ecosystem to monitor it and take actions if needed. Orchestrator can influence the ecosystem e.g. by setting rules, communicating plans, managing the platform, controlling number of actors and affecting internal products revenue model.

In relation to orchestrator's role, Iansiti & Levien [7] are of the opinion that the orchestrator's aim should be improving the health of the whole ecosystem. Effective orchestrator or key player should create and share value in ecosystem in order to tempt actors to join and keep existing actors satisfied. [7]

Orchestrator can damage the ecosystem health by being a physical dominator or value dominator, warn Iansiti & Levien [7]. An ecosystem can be suppressed by an orchestrator who aims to directly managing big part of the network or made unsustainable by an orchestrator that draws majority of value created within ecosystem to itself. [7]

In conclusion, 'ecosystem health' is defined through the network dynamics of the participating actors. Previous research emphasizes the relevance of roles, specifically that of the orchestrator, and that individual actors health is always derived from the benefit of the ecosystem. In the following, we will study how widely these definitions are used in the software ecosystem health literature and what is the strength of empirical evidence.

3   Method

We used SLR as a data collection method in this study and followed Kitchenham & Charters' [9] guidelines of conducting data collection. Due to the wide-spread popularity of the topic, we decided to use an electronic search–in contrast to a manual search where researchers read through selected journals and publication series–to large article databases. In each search engine, we used the search term `"software ecosystem" AND health`. Searches were targeted to full texts, and only research papers (i.e., peer-reviewed articles) were included when it was possible to select.

We used the following databases in this study (the number of hits is given in the brackets):

1. ACM Digital Library (43)
2. IEEE Xplore Digital Library (45)
3. ScienceDirect (33)
4. ISI Web of Science (4)

5. Proquest (9)
6. Wile Online Library (8)
7. SpringerLink (58)

The searches were done in January 15th, 2014. In total, we collected 194 unique articles in the first phase with the above-mentioned search term.

In the second phase of the review process, we went through all unique papers and kept those which dealt with a) 'software ecosystem' and b) 'ecosystem health'. Only articles written in English were included. Articles which were not published in a scientific peer-reviewed venue were excluded. Furthermore, we excluded posters, editorials, presentation notes and panel summaries. These were the only inclusion or exclusion criteria used. After the second phase, 38 articles were included into the dataset.

In the final phase, all selected articles were gone through. From each paper, we extracted how the concept 'ecosystem health' was used, were there any synonyms for it and did the paper name any sources for the ecosystem health discussion. The study is based on the quantitative analysis of the results and the qualitative discussion of the implications. The results are discussed in the following section.

4   Results and Analysis

Table 1 shortly summarizes the selected papers' view on the concept of 'ecosystem health'. The column 'Uses empirical data?' classifies if the article used empirical data. In this, we require that the empirical study of a paper is directly related to ecosystem health, and that the authors explicitly state the relationship between results and health as a whole. For example, the article by Hyrynsalmi et al. [53] is not, in this study, classified as empirical: the study is justified with the ecosystem health, but it forgot ecosystem health concept when analysing and discussing its results.

Table 1. The papers selected to this literature review with a short summary

ID	Description how a paper considers the 'ecosystem health' concept	Uses empirical data?
[13]	Uses three different views to analyze a SECO. In addition to transaction and structure analyses, the model of [14] is used to analyze the health of a SECO. Proposes simple measures for Robustness, Productivity and Niche creation; e.g., a number of downloads as a an indicator of Robustness and a number of commits as a measure of Productivity.	No
[15]	The diversity of actors (developers) supports ecosystem health. Dominators are harmful for an ecosystem as they reduce the diversity. Follows [8] in view of ecosystem health.	No
[16]	Software ecosystem modeling might help to evaluate health of an ecosystem. Follows [17,7] in a view of ecosystem health.	No
[18]	Argues that a community (of developers, experts and users) is vital for the health of a SECO and that a keystone player's mission is to promote the overall health of an ecosystem.	No
[19]*	Proposes a set metrics for ecosystem health by instantiating the software ecosystem health framework of [10]. The empirical part is based on a qualitative analysis of a case ecosystem.	No
[20]	Based on the interviews, shows that software vendors select an ecosystem based on its health, which is seen as a performance indicator of an ecosystem. Follows [7,8] in a view of ecosystem health.	No

* An article's main focus is in the concept of 'ecosystem health'

Table 1. *(Continued from previous page)*

ID	Description how a paper considers the 'ecosystem health' concept	Uses empirical data?
[21]	Notes that low socio-technical congruence might be harmful for health of a software ecosystem.	No
[22]	Argues that software ecosystem modeling might help to visualize ecosystem health and stability.	No
[23]	Discusses on health of e-learning software ecosystem. Follows [8] view of ecosystem health.	No
[24]	Uses the 'biological ecosystem' concept as a starting point and argues that healthy ecosystem requires proper feedback (from technical issues, business considerations and community participation) and management. A healthy ecosystem survives even when losing a part of its population. A healthy community (of an ecosystem) is "sustainable, livable, equitable and prosperous."	No
[25]	Health of an ecosystem describes the performance of the ecosystem. 'SECO biology' (i.e., composition), 'Lifestyle' (e.g., vision, entry barrier, openness), 'Environment' (i.e., stakeholders) and 'Health Care Organization' (banks, investors, governments etc.) can affect to ecosystem health. Follows [8] in a view of health.	Yes
[26]*	Studies how meritocracy affects to health of an ecosystem. Follows [7,27] in a view of health; measures productivity with number of commits.	Yes
[28]	Determinants of ecosystem health are productivity of and value creation by its actors. Productivity is measured with commits, LOCs, number of active partners. In a view of ecosystem health, follows [7,29].	No
[30]	Sees 'ecosystem health' as a knowledge flow (similar to a nutrient recycling process in a biological ecosystem); 'ecosystem sustainability' is defined as keystone activities to maintain the community.	No
[31]	Characteristics of ecosystem health include, at least, growth and evolution over time. The paper argues that a growth rate is a good indicator of ecosystem health.	No
[32]	Follows [7] in the view of ecosystem health.	No
[33]	Health of a project is related to health of an ecosystem; i.e., the quality of a project affects health of ecosystem and vice versa.	
[34]	Sustainability and diversity are health indicators of an ecosystem.	No
[35]	Sustainability and diversity are health indicators of an ecosystem. Furthermore, actors in an ecosystem have impacts on SECO health.	No
[36]	From technical dimension, a SECO's central platform could be analysed with productivity, robustness and niche creation. From business dimension, sustainability and diversity are health indicators of a SECO.	No
[37]	A healthy ecosystem is generating revenue (for developers).	No
[27]*	The paper focuses on the open-source software ecosystem and it notes that project health is not same than the ecosystem health. A healthy unit should be, e.g., lively, active, long-living; in the study longevity and a propensity for growth were the main characteristics. The study presents an open-source software health framework with proposed measures for different characteristics. The model has two dimensions; the scope dimension has three levels (theory, network level and project level) and the other dimension consists of productivity, robustness and niche creation.	Yes
[11]	In a large systematic literature study, the authors identified an emerging research line (13 articles) on ecosystem health. According to the article, a healthy SECO is functioning well. They also point out that while diversity is often argued to contribute ecosystem health through richer niche creation, there are no concrete studies to validate this hypothesis. Similarly, the authors note that there are few studies concretely measuring, analyzing or elaborating health of a software ecosystem.	No
[38]	Development of metrics for measuring ecosystem health is mentioned as an existing challenge.	No
[39]	'Ecosystem health' and 'ecosystem sustainability' concepts are seen capturing the same phenomenon. Commitment of actors to the ecosystem improves sustainability (i.e., health of an ecosystem). Further, authors suggest evaluating ecosystem health when analysing and designing an ecosystem.	No
[40]	Ensuring health of their ecosystems is seen as a responsibility of keystones.	No
[41]	Health of an individual actor depends heavily on health of a complete network (i.e., ecosystem). Follows [7] in a view of ecosystem health. A keystone player's actions stimulate health of the entire ecosystem. The paper proposes development of a software ecosystem health model.	No

*An article's main focus is in the concept of 'ecosystem health'

Table 1. *(Continued from previous page)*

ID	Description how a paper considers the 'ecosystem health' concept	Uses empirical data?
[42]	An ecosystem have to be healthy to be a long-living one. Follows [7] in a view of ecosystem health.	No
[43]	An ecosystem architecture can pose risks that endangers health of the entire ecosystem; an architectural analysis of the ecosystem can reveal health threats.	
[44]	Ecosystem governance leads to better ecosystem performance and health.	No
[45]*	To survive, an ecosystem should be healthy. In a healthy ecosystem, a participating firm can achieve its financial goals easier than in any other ecosystem. The study extends [7] view of ecosystem health; health of a software ecosystem is measured with robustness, productivity, interoperability, stakeholder's satisfaction and creativity. The model is empirically tested with a survey on Tunisian software ecosystem.	Yes
[46]	Motivating joined developers to work together (i.e., increase the interconnectivity) would improve ecosystem health.	No
[47]*	Ecosystem governance is argued to have an impact on ecosystem health. The paper studies Ecosystem Governance Model by [48,49] and follows [8] in the view of ecosystem health. The authors' note that the results from a case study might indicate early sign of low ecosystem health; however, the studied ecosystem is considered to be a growing one.	Yes
[50]	To be able to create value, a keystone's responsibility is to ensure a healthy and sustainable ecosystem. Follows [7] in an view of ecosystem health. Notes that 'sustainability' and 'ecosystem health' are closely linked performance objectives.	No
[51]	Health is a characteristic of an ecosystem. In a healthy SECO, there are two main roles that an actor can take: keystone or niche player.	No
[52]	Not provoking unnecessary competition between developers in a SECO improves ecosystem health. Follows [7] in a view of ecosystem health.	No
[53]	Argues that health of a marketplace is related to health of a SECO. A marketplace is seen healthy if ISVs are satisfied.	No
[54]*	Follows [29] in a view of ecosystem health; health is long-term financial well-being and long-term strength of a network. Proposes a set of metrics to evaluate ecosystem health of Platform-as-a-Service Providers. Metrics include, e.g., a number of active developers in a given time and a number of unique programming languages used.	Yes

*An article's main focus is in the concept of 'ecosystem health'

From the set of 38 papers, nine are journal and 29 are conference articles. Despite several search engines used in this study, a rather small set of publication forums are present in the final dataset. The most often used conference series are International Conference on Software Business (ICSOB, 8 articles), Management of Emergent Digital EcoSystems (MEDES, 6), European Conference on Software Architecture and its workshops (ECSA and ECSAW, 5). *Journal of Systems and Software* (4) and *Information and Software Technology* (4) have published the majority of the journal articles in the dataset.

The papers included into the dataset are written by 75 authors; however, *Slinger Jansen* (Utrecht University) has an authorship in 14 articles out of 38. Other active authors in the field of software ecosystem health are *Konstantinos Manikas* (5 articles, University of Copenhagen), *Sjaak Brinkkemper* (4, Utrecht University), *Klaus Marius Hansen* (4, University of Copenhagen) as well as *Cláudia Werner* and *Rodrigo dos Santos* (4, University of Rio de Janeiro). This shows that the field is heavily addressed by a small set of academicians.

Figure 2 illustrates the publication years of the selected articles. Oldest articles included in this study are published in 2009. The figure, furthermore, reveals

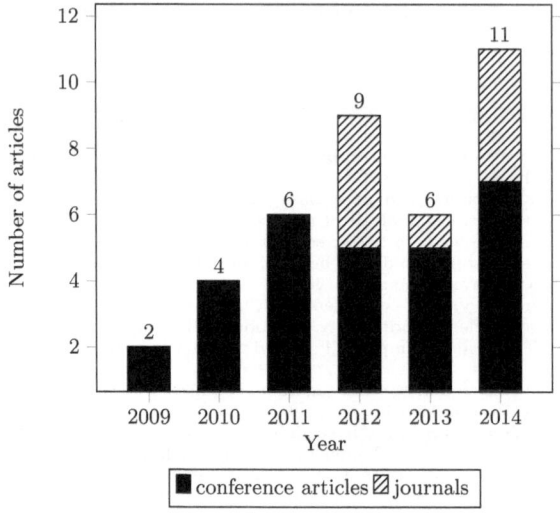

Fig. 2. Number of papers published yearly

that   activity in the field of ecosystem health is constantly growing, although the overall volume is still rather small.

The descriptives in Figure 2 yield an answer to RQ1 as it is clear that there is an increasing scholarly interest and dialogue related to software ecosystem health. This dialogue is, as seen from the conference and journal forums, related to the computer science discipline with some interdisciplinarity with business and management sciences. The discussion is based on a relatively narrow pool of authors within a narrow disciplinary setting.

Beyond the descriptive, the definitions of ecosystems are sparse. Even though the works often cite similar origins, namely Iansiti & Levien [7,8], the different works use the term 'ecosystem health' very differently. This is apparent in Table 1 where the views on 'ecosystem health' vary significantly. Where some focus on explaining ecosystem health through the diversity of actors, some look at multiple factors, such as the "biology" of the ecosystem, as a source of explanation. These differences come from the research question and the narrative of the studies which seldom focus significantly on the actual theoretical framework of ecosystem health and rather use this elusive definition to move quickly to the research question at hand. This to an extent, makes the author to pick appropriate portions of a few seminal works when making their case. Answering to RQ2, there is little support to a consensus definition of 'ecosystem health'.

Finding no support for RQ2, we look for characteristics of ecosystem health. Drawing from Table 1 factors, actors or agents that relate to 'ecosystem health' are the *internal structure of the actors* (e.g. diversity, composition and evolution), *external influences* (e.g. stakeholders, entry barrier, openness), *internal forces* (e.g. community development, feedback, joined vision) and *outputs* (e.g. productivity, value created by actors and growth). This synthesis is illustrated in Figure 3. Much of the literature emphasize the role of orchestrator and keystone

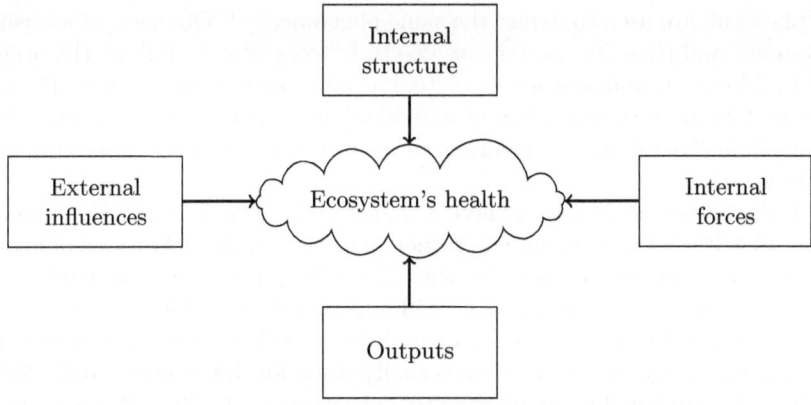

Fig. 3. Factors affecting to health of an ecosystem

actors to moderate the above mentioned factors. Answering to RQ3, there are common characteristics but these are differently referred in literature. Arguable, this is due to the absence of share theoretical frame.

Finally, finding a number of characteristics for ecosystem health, our focus turns towards empirical evidence. From the 38 studies, only a selected few focus on producing empirical evidence. From these, only one makes a strong effort to validate a theoretical frame. Furthermore, often studies propose to use of simple metrics such as a number of commits or a number of lines of code (LOC) as a measure of health (productivity). While these certainly measure some activity in an ecosystem, it is not clear how useful these are as indicators of productivity [55]. We find no or limited support for RQ4.

To summarize, our study contributes to the field of software ecosystem health by showing that there, indeed, is increasing scholarly interested towards the concept (RQ1). However, as shown in Table 1 and above analysis, there is no shared understanding on what does the concept mean (RQ2). This misunderstanding has, as discussed more in the following section, and will cause problems in the studies of ecosystem health. However, we were able to identify the common elements used and synthesize them (RQ3). It should be, however, noted that these elements differs a lot from presented two frameworks of business [7,8] and software ecosystem health [10]. Finally, we showed that despite increased interest, there is a lack of empirical studies addressing existing or extincted software ecosystem health (RQ4).

5   Discussion

Currently, there seems not to be a coherent view of what is 'software ecosystem' and several concepts are often used interchangeably to depict either the same or different objects. For example, concepts such as 'ecosystem', 'network', 'community' and 'platform' are used to depict the same phenomenon[1]. Our view of a business ecosystem—and thus, its special case, 'software ecosystem'—follows the original work by Moore [1] and sees an ecosystem as an economic community. Thus, we question does loose communities of individual developers or software firms form an ecosystem. Therefore, the scientific community would benefits from established use of the terms.

This SLR demonstrates that there is much work to do. It seems that the definition of health in the ecosystem is rather tautological; the definitions of healthy ecosystem are derived from healthy firms. A healthy firm is rarely defined, except Jansen [27] who define healthiness by willingness to grow and longevity.

We would like to raise the question on philosophical (as well as strategic) question what does a business ecosystem actually stand for. Its analogies to biological counterparts are often loosely referred to, however the actually and exact conceptual work seems to be missing here. The seminal work by Richard Dawkins, *Selfish Gene* [56], proposed how an organism is expected to maximise its inclusive fitness, the number of copies of its genes pass on globally. A firm does not have such ultimate goal but its goals are defined locally by the owner and even the survival of a particular firm is not necessary, since a firm is a tool that serves certain purpose that its owners have defined. Therefore, we should thoroughly consider the conceptual foundations of business ecosystem and deriving on this conceptual work, consider carefully again what does *healthiness* mean in this SECO context.

For instance, firstly, it is not much considered why business ecosystems do exist and under what circumstances a company should participate in the particular ecosystem [57]. Business ecosystems are considered to lead to competitive advantages for each of the partners in the business ecosystem [58]. Thus, the question remains, what are these competitive advantages and their characteristics to consider when joining to an ecosystem. Secondly, business ecosystems may provide firms resources and information "to navigate in a constantly changing competitive environment" [59]. Thus, what are such mechanisms that a firm should use to evaluate the access and availability of above "resources and information". Thirdly, it has been considered that an ecosystem should be responsible for its participants: "SECO platform ownership also brings responsibilities" [50]. This question is not clear even network literature and practice — when a network's focal company faces financial problems, its loyalty towards its suppliers has been deteriorating in many cases. In similar manner, large amount of business ecosystem literature includes rather positive expectations how firms may (or they should) behave towards their ecosystem partners.

The above ideas lead us to suggest the following questions for further research:

1. What are the philosophical foundations for business ecosystems, especially when considering the decisions to join or detach a firm to/from a business ecosystem?

---

[1] J. West (2014) "Networks, Communities, Ecosystems and Platforms". http://blog.openinnovation.net/2014/08/networks-communities-ecosystems-and.html Accessed March 24, 2015.

2. What characteristics to use for evaluating the 'healthiness' a business ecosystem? Can we define such 'early warnings' that may give a signal about "sickness of a business ecosystem"?
3. What kinds of strategic patterns do different types of business ecosystems form? For instance, further development of work by Zahra & Nambisan [59] linked with above questions may be helpful.

To summarize, we question what does, and what should, the concept 'ecosystem health' stand for. Furthermore, the different viewpoints on the ecosystem blur the overall picture even more. For example, Apple's App Store (iOS) software ecosystem can be argued to be a healthy one (for its orchestrator) due to the large numbers of application developers, customers and revenue generated. Furthermore, it has been able to absorb external shocks caused by competitors. However, the ecosystem is not 'healthy' for the majority of existing or newcomer application developers. In contrast, the ecosystem might be 'healthy' for customers (a plethora of cheap offering) and superstars (e.g., Supercell Oy and King Limited have been able to create a stable revenue flow through the ecosystem). Thus, we call for theoretical development, supported with strong empirical evidence, on the concept of 'ecosystem health' to normalize the discussion. This would help future endeavours on developing metrics and measures, early warning signal systems and government levers for software ecosystem health.

6   Limitations and Conclusions

Naturally, this study has limitations. First, we limited the data gathering only on electronic searches on article databases. This might cause a lack of articles not indexed on these databases. In a further study, a manual search of selected publication forums should be performed. Second, we focused only on SECOs' health, due to the nature of the audience. Thus, an inclusion of health of digital, mobile and business ecosystem would broaden the picture of the whole 'ecosystem health' concept.

However, this study showed that the number of articles discussing on the concept 'software ecosystem health' is constantly growing. Although the studies are often based on the seminal work by Iansiti & Levien, we could not find a consensus for what software ecosystem health stands for. The term has been used to describe, e.g., financial well-being of individual actors, performance and longevity of the whole ecosystem. Furthermore, the number of empirical studies remains low. Thus, we call for further work for defining the philosophical standpoint for business and software ecosystem as well as their healthiness.

References

1. Moore, J.F.: Predators and prey: A new ecology of competition. Harvard Business Review 71(3), 75–86 (1993)
2. Moore, J.F.: The Death of Competition: Leadership and Strategy in the Age of Business Ecosystems. Harper Business, New York (1996)

3. Jansen, S., Finkelstein, A., Brinkkemper, S.: A sense of community: A research agenda for software ecosystems. In: 31st International Conference on Software Engineering — Companion Volume, ICSE-Companion 2009, pp. 187–190. IEEE (2009)
4. Jansen, S., Brinkkemper, S., Cusumano, M.A. (eds.): Software Ecosystems: Analyzing and Managing Business Networks in the Software Industry. Edward Elgar Publisher Inc., Northampton (2013)
5. Basole, R.C.: Visualization of interfirm relations in a converging mobile ecosystem. Journal of Information Technology 24(2), 144–159 (2009)
6. Hyrynsalmi, S.: Letters from the War of Ecosystems — An Analysis of Independent Software Vendors in Mobile Application Marketplaces. Doctoral dissertation, University of Turku, Turku, Finland, TUCS Dissertations No 188 (2014)
7. Iansiti, M., Levien, R.: Strategy as ecology. Harvard Business Review 82(3), 68–78 (2004)
8. Iansiti, M., Levien, R.: The Keystone Advantage: What the New Dynamics of Business Ecosystems Mean for Strategy, Innovation, and Sustainability. Harvard Business School Press, Boston (2004)
9. Kitchenham, B.A., Charters, S.: Guidelines for performing systematic literature reviews in software engineering. version 2.3. EBSE Technical Report EBSE-2007-01, Keele University, Keele, Staffs, United Kingdom (2007)
10. Manikas, K., Hansen, K.M.: Reviewing the health of software ecosystems — a conceptual framework proposal. In: Alves, C.F., Hanssen, G.K., Bosch, J., Jansen, S. (eds.) Proceedings of the 5th International Workshop on Software Ecosystems, Potsdam, Germany. CEUR Workshop Proceedings, vol. 987, pp. 33–44. CEUR-WS (2013)
11. Manikas, K., Hansen, K.M.: Software ecosystems — A systematic literature review. Journal of Systems and Software 86(5), 1294–1306 (2013)
12. Hyrynsalmi, S., Suominen, A., Mäkilä, T., Knuutila, T.: The emerging application ecosystems: An introductory analysis of Android ecosystem. International Journal of E-Business Research 10(2), 61–81 (2014)
13. McGregor, J.D.: A method for analyzing software product line ecosystems. In: Proceedings of the Fourth European Conference on Software Architecture: Companion Volume, ECSA 2010, pp. 73–80. ACM, New York (2010)
14. Iansiti, M., Richards, G.L.: The information technology ecosystem: Structure, health, and performance. The Antitrust Bulletin 51(1), 77–110 (2006)
15. Manikas, K., Hansen, K.M.: Characterizing the danish telemedicine ecosystem: Making sense of actor relationships. In: Proceedings of the Fifth International Conference on Management of Emergent Digital EcoSystems, MEDES 2013, pp. 211–218. ACM, New York (2013)
16. Boucharas, V., Jansen, S., Brinkkemper, S.: Formalizing software ecosystem modeling. In: Proceedings of the 1st International Workshop on Open Component Ecosystems, IWOCE 2009, pp. 41–50. ACM, New York (2009)
17. Iyer, B., Lee, C.H., Venkatraman, N.: Managing in a "small world ecosystem": Some lessons from the software sector. California Management Review 48(3), 28–47 (2006)
18. van Ingen, K., van Ommen, J., Jansen, S.: Improving activity in communities of practice through software release management. In: Proceedings of the International Conference on Management of Emergent Digital EcoSystems, MEDES 2011, pp. 94–98. ACM, New York (2011)
19. Monteith, J.Y., McGregor, J.D., Ingram, J.E.: Proposed metrics on ecosystem health. In: Proceedings of the 2014 ACM International Workshop on Software-defined Ecosystems, BigSystem 2014, pp. 33–36. ACM, New York (2014)

20. van Angeren, J., Blijleven, V., Jansen, S.: Relationship intimacy in software ecosystems: A survey of the Dutch software industry. In: Grosky, W.I., Badr, Y., Chbeir, R. (eds.) Proceedings of the International Conference on Management of Emergent Digital EcoSystems, MEDES 2011, pp. 68–75. ACM, New York (2011)
21. Syeed, M.M.M., Hansen, K.M., Hammouda, I., Manikas, K.: Socio-technical congruence in the ruby ecosystem. In: Proceedings of The International Symposium on Open Collaboration, OpenSym, pp. 2:1–2:9. ACM, New York (2014)
22. Handoyo, E., Jansen, S., Brinkkemper, S.: Software ecosystem modeling: The value chains. In: Proceedings of the Fifth International Conference on Management of Emergent Digital EcoSystems, MEDES 2013, pp. 17–24. ACM, New York (2013)
23. Pettersson, O.: Software ecosystems and e-learning: Recent developments and future prospects. In: Proceedings of the International Conference on Management of Emergent Digital EcoSystems, MEDES 2009, pp. 64:427–64:464. ACM, New York (2009)
24. Dhungana, D., Groher, I., Schludermann, E., Biffl, S.: Software ecosystems vs. natural ecosystems: Learning from the ingenious mind of nature. In: Proceedings of the Fourth European Conference on Software Architecture: Companion Volume, ECSA 2010, pp. 96–102. ACM, New York (2010)
25. van den Berk, I., Jansen, S., Luinenburg, L.: Software ecosystems: A software ecosystem strategy assessment model. In: Proceedings of the Fourth European Conference on Software Architecture: Companion Volume, ECSA 2010, pp. 127–134. ACM, New York (2010)
26. Eckhardt, E., Kaats, E., Jansen, S., Alves, C.: The merits of a meritocracy in open source software ecosystems. In: Proceedings of the 2014 European Conference on Software Architecture Workshops, ECSAW 2014, pp. 7:1–7:7. ACM, New York (2014)
27. Jansen, S.: Measuring the health of open source software ecosystems: Moving beyond the project scope. Information and Software Technology 56(11), 1508–1519 (2014)
28. Aarnoutse, F., Renes, C., Snijders, R., Jansen, S.: The reality of an associate model: Comparing partner activity in the eclipse ecosystem. In: Proceedings of the 2014 European Conference on Software Architecture Workshops. ECSAW 2014, pp. 8:1–8:6. ACM, New York (2014)
29. den Hartigh, E., Tol, M., Visscher, W.: The health measurement of a business ecosystem. In: van Eijnatten, F.M. (ed.) Proceedings of the ECCON 2006 Annual Meeting: "Organisations as Chaordic Panarchies" — Towards Self-Transcending Work Holarchies, Bergen aan Zee, The Netherlands, European Network on Chaos and Complexity Research and Management Practice, pp. 1–39 (2006)
30. dos Santos, R.P., Werner, C.: Treating business dimension in software ecosystems. In: Proceedings of the International Conference on Management of Emergent Digital EcoSystems, MEDES 2011, pp. 197–201. ACM, New York (2011)
31. Hoving, R., Slot, G., Jansen, S.: Python: Characteristics identification of a free open source software ecosystem. In: 7th IEEE International Conference on Digital Ecosystems and Technologies (DEST), pp. 13–18. IEEE Computer Society (2013)
32. Mizushima, K., Ikawa, Y.: A structure of co-creation in an open source software ecosystem: A case study of the eclipse community. In: Proceedings of PICMET 2011: Technology Management in the Energy Smart World, pp. 1–8. IEEE (2011)
33. Pérez, J., Deshayes, R., Goeminne, M., Mens, T.: Seconda: Software ecosystem analysis dashboard. In: 16th European Conference on Software Maintenance and Reengineering (CSMR), pp. 527–530. IEEE (2012)

34. dos Santos, R.P., Werner, C.M.L.: ReuseECOS: An approach to support global software development through software ecosystems. In: IEEE Seventh International Conference on Global Software Engineering Workshops (ICGSEW), pp. 60–65. IEEE (2012)
35. dos Santos, R.P., Werner, C.M.L.: Treating social dimension in software ecosystems through ReuseECOS approach. In: 6th IEEE International Conference on Digital Ecosystems Technologies (DEST), pp. 1–6. IEEE (2012)
36. Santos, R., Werner, C., Barbosa, O., Alves, C.: Software ecosystems: Trends and impacts on software engineering. In: 26th Brazilian Symposium on Software Engineering (SBES), pp. 206–2010. IEEE (2012)
37. Yamakami, T.: Stage models of middleware platforms and applications: Transitions in the mobile application landscape. In: 4th IEEE International Conference on Digital Ecosystems and Technologies (DEST), pp. 165–170. IEEE (2010)
38. Axelsson, J., Papatheocharous, E., Andersson, J.: Characteristics of software ecosystems for federated embedded systems: A case study. Information and Software Technology 56(11), 1457–1475 (2014)
39. Christensen, H.B., Hansen, K.M., Kyng, M., Manikas, K.: Analysis and design of software ecosystem architectures — towards the 4s telemedicine ecosystem. Information and Software Technology 56(11), 1476–1492 (2014)
40. Wnuk, K., Runeson, P., Lantz, M., Weijden, O.: Bridges and barriers to hardware-dependent software ecosystem participation — a case study. Information and Software Technology 56(11), 1493–1507 (2014)
41. Jansen, S., Brinkkemper, S., Souer, J., Luinenburg, L.: Shades of gray: Opening up a software producing organization with the open software enterprise model. Journal of Systems and Software 85(7), 1495–1510 (2012)
42. Kilamo, T., Hammouda, I., Mikkonen, T., Aaltonen, T.: From proprietary to open source—growing an open source ecosystem. Journal of Systems and Software 85(7), 1467–1478 (2012)
43. Kazman, R., Gagliardi, M., Wood, W.: Scaling up software architecture analysis. Journal of Systems and Software 85(7), 1511–1519 (2012)
44. Baars, A., Jansen, S.: A framework for software ecosystem governance. In: Cusumano, M.A., Iyer, B., Venkatraman, N. (eds.) ICSOB 2012. LNBIP, vol. 114, pp. 168–180. Springer, Heidelberg (2012)
45. Ben Hadj Salem Mhamdia, A.: Performance measurement practices in software ecosystem. International Journal of Productivity and Performance Management 62(5), 514–533 (2013)
46. Kabbedijk, J., Jansen, S.: Steering insight: An exploration of the ruby software ecosystem. In: Regnell, B., van de Weerd, I., De Troyer, O. (eds.) ICSOB 2011. LNBIP, vol. 80, pp. 44–55. Springer, Heidelberg (2011)
47. Wnuk, K., Manikas, K., Runeson, P., Lantz, M., Weijden, O., Munir, H.: Evaluating the governance model of hardware-dependent software ecosystems – A case study of the axis ecosystem. In: Lassenius, C., Smolander, K. (eds.) ICSOB 2014. LNBIP, vol. 182, pp. 212–226. Springer, Heidelberg (2014)
48. Jansen, S., Cusumano, M.A.: Defining software ecosystems: A survey of software platforms and business network governance. In: Jansen, S., Bosch, J., Alves, C.F. (eds.) Proceedings of the Fourth International Workshop on Software Ecosystems, Cambridge, MA, USA. CEUR Workshop Proceedings, vol. 879, pp. 41–58. IWSECO, CEUR-WS (2012)

49. Jansen, S., Cusumano, M.A.: Defining software ecosystems: a survey of software platforms and business network governance. In: Jansen, S., Brinkkemper, S., Cusumano, M.A. (eds.) Software Ecosystems: Analyzing and Managing Business Networks in the Software Industry, pp. 13–28. Edward Elgar Publisher Inc., Northampton (2013)

50. Fotrousi, F., Fricker, S.A., Fiedler, M., Le-Gall, F.: KPIs for software ecosystems: A systematic mapping study. In: Lassenius, C., Smolander, K. (eds.) ICSOB 2014. LNBIP, vol. 182, pp. 194–211. Springer, Heidelberg (2014)

51. Viljainen, M., Kauppinen, M.: Software ecosystems: A set of management practices for platform integrators in the telecom industry. In: Regnell, B., van de Weerd, I., De Troyer, O. (eds.) ICSOB 2011. LNBIP, vol. 80, pp. 32–43. Springer, Heidelberg (2011)

52. van Angeren, J., Jansen, S., Brinkkemper, S.: Exploring the relationship between partnership model participation and interfirm network structure: An analysis of the office365 ecosystem. In: Lassenius, C., Smolander, K. (eds.) ICSOB 2014. LNBIP, vol. 182, pp. 1–15. Springer, Heidelberg (2014)

53. Hyrynsalmi, S., Suominen, A., Mäkilä, T., Järvi, A., Knuutila, T.: Revenue models of application developers in android market ecosystem. In: Cusumano, M.A., Iyer, B., Venkatraman, N. (eds.) ICSOB 2012. LNBIP, vol. 114, pp. 209–222. Springer, Heidelberg (2012)

54. Lucassen, G., van Rooij, K., Jansen, S.: Ecosystem health of cloud paaS providers. In: Herzwurm, G., Margaria, T. (eds.) ICSOB 2013. LNBIP, vol. 150, pp. 183–194. Springer, Heidelberg (2013)

55. Jones, C.: Software Assessments, Benchmarks, and Best Practices. Addison-Wesley Information Technology Series. Addison-Wesley Longman Publishing Co., Inc., Boston (2000)

56. Dawkins, R.: The Selfish Gene, 1st edn. Oxford University Press, Oxford (1976)

57. Hyrynsalmi, S., Seppänen, M., Suominen, A.: Sources of value in application ecosystems. The Journal of Systems and Software 96, 61–72 (2014)

58. Clarysse, B., Wright, M., Bruneel, J., Mahajan, A.: Creating value in ecosystems: Crossing the chasm between knowledge and business ecosystems. Research Policy 43(7), 1164–1176 (2014)

59. Zahra, S.A., Nambisan, S.: Entrepreneurship and strategic thinking in business ecosystems. Business Horizons 55(3), 219–229 (2012)

Author Index